Praise for
To the Limit

"*To the Limit* is a first-person journey into the grit, grimness, and chaos of war, told by a helicopter hero in a way that nails the feel, the mood, and the talk of air cavalrymen in battle."
  —Robert F Dorr, author of *Chopper: A History of American Military Helicopter Operations from WWII to the War on Terror*

"This is the real thing: helicopter combat at its birth. No wonder Army helo drivers were among the most-decorated aviators of the Vietnam War. Tom Johnson truly shows us what the rank-and-file Huey crews experienced."
  —Peter B. Mersky, author of *From the Flight Deck: An Anthology of the Best Writing on Carrier Warfare* and *U.S. Marine Corps Aviation: 1912 to the Present*

"Always leery of superlatives in book reviews, I feel compelled to use them in describing Tom Johnson's *To the Limit*. It is an intense, compelling, gut-wrenching narrative—by far the best account of helicopter warfare I have read."
  —William L. Smallwood, author of *Strike Eagle: Flying the F-15E in the Gulf War* and *Warthog: Flying the A-10 in the Gulf War*

TO THE LIMIT

An Air Cav Huey Pilot in Vietnam

TOM A. JOHNSON

NAL
CALIBER

NAL Caliber
Published by New American Library, a division of
Penguin Group (USA) Inc., 375 Hudson Street,
New York, New York 10014, USA
Penguin Group (Canada), 90 Eglinton Avenue East, Suite 700, Toronto,
Ontario M4P 2Y3, Canada (a division of Pearson Penguin Canada Inc.)
Penguin Books Ltd., 80 Strand, London WC2R 0RL, England
Penguin Ireland, 25 St. Stephen's Green, Dublin 2,
Ireland (a division of Penguin Books Ltd.)
Penguin Group (Australia), 250 Camberwell Road, Camberwell, Victoria 3124,
Australia (a division of Pearson Australia Group Pty. Ltd.)
Penguin Books India Pvt. Ltd., 11 Community Centre, Panchsheel Park,
New Delhi – 110 017, India
Penguin Group (NZ), 67 Apollo Drive, Rosedale, North Shore 0632,
New Zealand (a division of Pearson New Zealand Ltd.)
Penguin Books (South Africa) (Pty.) Ltd., 24 Sturdee Avenue,
Rosebank, Johannesburg 2196, South Africa

Penguin Books Ltd., Registered Offices:
80 Strand, London WC2R 0RL, England

Published by NAL Caliber, an imprint of New American Library, a division of Penguin Group (USA)
Inc. This is an authorized reprint of a Potomac Books, Inc., hardcover edition. For information address
Potomac Books, Inc., 22841 Quicksilver Drive, Dulles, Virginia 20166.

First NAL Caliber Printing, October 2007
10 9 8 7 6 5 4 3 2 1

NAL Caliber Trade Paperback ISBN: 978-0-451-22218-3

The Library of Congress has cataloged the hardcover edition of this title as follows:

Johnson, Tom A.
  To the limit: an Air Cav Huey pilot in Vietnam/Tom A. Johnson. 1st ed.
    p. cm.
  Includes index.
  ISBN 978-1-59797-001
  1. Vietnamese Conflict, 19611975 Aerial operations, American. 2. Military
helicopters Vietnam. 3. Vietnamese Conflict, 19611975 Personal narratives, American.
4. Johnson, Tom A. I. Title.
  DS558.8.J65 2006
  959.704'348092 dc22   2006004962

Printed in the United States of America

This book is dedicated to my wife, Pat McGaha Johnson.
She is one of only a few OVW (Original Vietnam Wives) that
survived the Vietnam experience.
In memory of James Arthur Johansen.

Contents

CONTENTS

Illustrations

Photos

Maps

LIST OF ILLUSTRATIONS

x

Author's Note

In this book, I have endeavored to tell the truth as accurately as possible. From the first page to the last, I have described all events as I saw and remember them and as I described them afterward in letters to my wife. If there are any inaccuracies, they are due to the passage of many years, and responsibility for them is mine alone. If in places my account differs from other accounts, it should be borne in mind many of these accounts were based on available historical documents rather than firsthand experience.

Unlike World War II bomber crews, helicopter pilots in Vietnam did not undergo post-mission debriefings; we simply went out each day and got the job done. For this reason, some of these events never made it into military records. However, less detailed but historically accurate overviews of the actions of airmobile crews in Vietnam can be found in Shelby L. Stanton's book *Anatomy of a Division* (Presidio) and *Airmobility 1961–1971,* written by George J. Tolson, Commanding General of the 1st Air Cavalry, Republic of Vietnam, and available on the World Wide Web at http://www.army.mil/cmh-pg/books/Vietnam/Airmobility/airmobility-fm.html

All names found in the index of this document refer to real people who participated directly in the events described. For those characters not listed in the index, I have used fictional names; I did not do extensive research to discover the actual names of the people whose names I never knew or did not remember.

Tom A. Johnson

TO THE LIMIT

Introduction

The 229th AHB (Assault Helicopter Battalion), 1st Air Cavalry Division, was one of the most highly decorated helicopter units in the Vietnam War and the first to test the airmobile concept. They did so in the battle of the Ia Drang valley in 1965, made famous in the book and movie *We Were Soldiers*. This battalion fought valiantly throughout the Vietnam War. Years later, in 1991, the men of the 229th AHB served with honor in the Middle East in Apache tank killers. In a somber ceremony in 2004, the colors of the 229th were folded—a casualty of the Army's reorganization plans. This abruptly ended the history of a great unit that had served the Army on both sides of the world.

The 229th Assault Helicopter Battalion, Republic of Vietnam Awards and Decorations include the following:
Presidential Unit Citation, Pleiku Province, 1967
Presidential Unit Citation, Quang Tri Province, 1968
Presidential Unit Citation, Binh Long Province, 1974
Meritorious Unit Commendation, Vietnam, 1965–66
Republic of Vietnam Cross of Gallantry with Palm, Vietnam, 1965–69
Republic of Vietnam Cross of Gallantry with Palm, Vietnam, 1971–72
Republic of Vietnam Civil Action Honor Medal, Vietnam 1969–72
Valorous Unit Award, Fish Hook, 1972

As Vietnam helicopter pilots, we held a job the Army classified as the most dangerous it had to offer. But we kidded one another about being nothing but glorified bus drivers, and, even today, no "rotor head" will take individual credit for saving thousands of lives on the battlefield, even though they often did so.

As warrant officers, our social status was somewhere between that of the commissioned officers who owned the Army and the high-ranking noncommissioned officers who ran it. We were aviation specialists who had contempt for everyone outside the aviation family. Most of us sported a strictly-against-army-regulation mustache and our don't-give-a-crap attitude kept us in hot water with other "non-rated" military officers.

The cost of the Vietnam War was very high. Out of the 2,594,000 persons who served in South Vietnam, 58,169 died. Helicopter aircrews bore a disproportionately heavy burden. For all military occupation specialties, including helicopter aircrews, the kill ratio was 1 to 45; for helicopter pilots in Vietnam the ratio was an alarming 1 to 18. By the end of the war, 2,197 helicopter pilots out of approximately 40,000 either died or were listed as missing in action. Another 2,274 crew chiefs and gunners died alongside the pilots.

At the height of the war, many individual Rotary Wing Classes suffered even heavier losses than that of the average helicopter crew. I graduated 16th of 286 men in Warrant Officer Rotary Wing Aviation Class 67-5. In the twelve months after we received our Army aviator wings at Fort Rucker, Alabama, 1 out of every 13 of us died in South Vietnam.

Of those who died, the average time in country was 165 days and the average age was 23.11 years.[1]

1. Statistical data provided by Vietnam Helicopter Pilots Association. Made possible only through the individual efforts of Gary Roush and the other members of the Data Base Committee as listed in the 2004 Membership Directory.

1

The An Lao Valley Incident

Tonight, this 19-year-old will most likely leave us. His wounds are massive. Like others before him, he thrashes about on the hard aluminum floor bathed in blood and suffering. Repeatedly, he calls for his mother, not his God. At great risk to ourselves, we will push our flying abilities and this helicopter to the brink of disaster trying to save him. Although cloaked in darkness, we must fly hard and low, cutting every corner. In spite of all my efforts, he will likely make the transition from life to death. His soul will depart, and his earthly body will finally lie in peace, without pain.

■

September 5, 1967

At 0430 hours the company night clerk awakens me and advises me that Major Eugene Beyer,[1] A Company's commanding officer, has picked me to "volunteer" for an emergency night resupply mission. Not fully awake, I plant my feet over the side of my cot and push the mosquito netting aside while attempting to comprehend the rapid briefing being given by the clerk. I "roger" as though I actually understand all he has said, then reach across the wooden pallets covering the dirt floor between my bunk and that of Warrant Officer James Arthur Johansen. Shaking him awake, I ask him to go with me. Though more asleep than awake, he agrees.

1. Eugene Beyer was later promoted to a colonel. He is now retired and lives in Texas.

The request for a night emergency resupply has come through normal channels. Although ammo and water are the only two things going in, experienced pilots know that often other things are more pressing. Infantry officers only call for night helicopter resupply in desperate situations—ammo for the living going in, the dead and badly wounded coming out.

Being quiet so as not to wake the other pilots, I put on my Army fatigues and jungle boots. Neither Johansen nor I utter a word. Grabbing my flight bag, my helmet, and my chest protector,[2] I head in the general direction of the mess tent. Once outside our GP Medium tent, home for about 20 warrant officers, I find this night to be normal for Vietnam: humid and coal black. Fumbling through my flight bag, I finally locate my red lens flashlight to light the way.

As I walk, bones and mind wracked with fatigue, I turn my thoughts to the dangers that lie ahead on this mission. The Vietnam nights are dark, with no lights of any kind marking the terrain. LZ (landing zone) English, the 1st Air Cavalry's forward outpost, out of which all military operations are based, lies on a coastal plain in II Corps area. My area of operation begins with the South China Sea and quickly graduates westerly into 4000-foot mountain peaks. Flying during the day is bad enough, but flying among mountains at night is especially treacherous.

Night emergency resupply missions are extremely dangerous and therefore generally fall into the laps of the more seasoned aircraft commanders, but I am A Company, 229th's latest and least experienced. Skill can only be attained through experience, and tonight will be my first night emergency resupply mission as aircraft commander. Though I dread it, I am honored that I have been picked to do this job. In a way, it symbolizes another step up in the "pecking order" of pilots. In calling on me for this mission, Major Beyer and other pilots are trusting me to accomplish the highly difficult task safely.

No matter what their rank or previous flight experience, all new pilots keep to the strictly maintained social order within each helicop-

2. These protective vests resembled those worn by the gladiators of ancient Rome. They were constructed of layered porcelain and covered by cloth, designed to stop a bullet of .30-caliber or less in size. We always reminded ourselves that the lowest bidder manufactured it. They were often referred to as "chicken protectors."

4

ter assault company. All new pilots, nicknamed "peter pilots," a slang term for copilots, occupy the right seat (as viewed from inside the Huey's cockpit) while the aircraft commanders sit in the left seat. To keep the pilot experience levels high, the fresh Fort Rucker graduates are put with the most experienced company aircraft commanders. After about six months, veteran aircraft commanders might begin to give their votes of confidence to a safety-conscious and levelheaded pilot. When enough of these peers have looked on a peter pilot favorably, it is possible for the company commander to recognize this judgment by promoting him to the rank of aircraft commander. The promotion does not earn any additional pay or medals, just a broad grin and the chance to learn to fly the Huey from the left seat instead of the right. By normal standards, I was promoted very quickly. Having completed Army helicopter flight school in class 67-5 (graduated in May of 1967) and having arrived in Vietnam in June of 1967, I made aircraft commander on August 24. Now, on September 5, as a 21-year-old pilot, I am getting ready to do my first night resupply. For the first time all mission decisions will fall on my shoulders alone. There will be no veteran pilot in the left seat to bail me out should I get into serious trouble. Though I feel up to the job, this thought chills me as I continue to walk sleepily in the direction of the mess hall.

I need a peter pilot who is as sharp as a razor's edge, one who can look after my blind side and make quick decisions. This is why I have chosen James Arthur Johansen Jr. Although he has never flown on a night resupply mission, he is a good pilot and one I can trust. He is affectionately nicknamed "Ingamar" after the famous "white hope" boxer of the same name, and, like the famous boxer, is a tall, blue-eyed, blond, 23-year-old Scandinavian.

In the hustle and bustle that is normal for the mess tent even at this early hour, the mess sergeant, Roy N. Beckley, sees me walk into his tent and greets me with an empty Army issue porcelain coffee cup.

"You up kinda early this morning, Mister Johnson,"[3] he utters with an exuberance that makes me sick. He obviously has been up for some time, getting breakfast ready for the troops. I am a zombie as I dodge tent poles in search of the stainless steel five-gallon pot of that life-sustaining drug, coffee.

---

3. Warrant officers are addressed as "mister" rather than by rank.

Sergeant Beckley, a black man, has been in the Army a very long time and knows all the ropes. I don't think he likes the young warrant officer pilots very much. In the old days you had to progress all the way through the enlisted ranks before you could make warrant. In the "old" Army, a warrant officer was a person well respected among the enlisted and officer ranks. Today's "new" Army takes people like me off the streets, presses them through one year's worth of boot training and flight school, and promptly pins the warrant officer bar on us. I think Sergeant Beckley perceives us as still "wet behind the ears," the unruly kids on his block. Though these defiant young warrants outrank him, they never give Beckley orders of any kind, and everyone in the company knows not to screw around with him, period. Once on his shit list, you're never off; you just move up and down on it.

I know him better than most of the other pilots, and I have found that inside the steel curtain that surrounds him is a caring, intelligent, but strictly Army person.

I like Beckley's way of making Army coffee. He brings the water to a rolling boil in one of his five-gallon stainless steel mess pots, then simply pours in the coffee grounds. After 20 minutes, he turns the fire down very low and adds the shells of two eggs. For reasons not known to me, this forces the coffee grounds to settle to the bottom of the pot. The aroma of his fresh coffee can be smelled throughout the company area.

"How's it going, Sergeant Beckley?" I ask while dipping my cup into the hot coffee. In a display of assertiveness, he does not reply. I sit alone deep in thought about home, Pat, and our future. For the moment, the mission I am about to undertake is far from my mind.

Now wide-eyed and awake from Beckley's coffee, I place the empty cup on the counter and pick up my flight gear. "Got to run. Thanks for the coffee, Sergeant Beckley."

"Anytime, Mister Johnson. Be careful out there now." The sincerity of his reply makes the conventional words sound truly like a warning.

Johansen enters the mess tent as I am leaving. He, too, has to be "kick started" in the early hours by Sergeant Beckley's coffee. Before I can tell him to meet me in the operations bunker, Beckley gets to him.

"Mister Johansen!" Beckley thunders, "What the hell you doing in my mess tent so early this morning? Somebody messing around with you pilots' beauty sleep?"

Johansen looks at me and rolls his eyes into the tops of their sockets, as if to say, "Oh shit, not again, not this early." It must be his light-hearted attitude and babyish features that naturally invite verbal abuse from almost all his friends.

I continue walking out of the mess tent, shaking my head and laughing quietly to myself. As I get closer to the operations bunker, I can still hear Beckley loudly asking questions and then answering them before Johansen can reply. This morning, Beckley and his coffee are doing an especially good job of getting two tired pilots awake enough to do their hazardous jobs.

Major Beyer is sipping coffee and scanning the large acetate-covered wall map of our operational area when I step into the tactical operations and control (TOC) bunker. He is one of the professional Army career types we call "lifers" and is, without question, the best leader of men I have ever known. His natural ability to keep cool in extremely tough situations, especially in combat formation flying, got my attention early in my tour with A/229th Company.

Even though he is a major and several years older than most of us, Eugene Beyer never raises his voice to his young pilots, no matter how angry he is. The pilots of A/229th take a very dim view of negative talk about him.

"Tom, here's what you got," Beyer begins, pointing to the wall map, and as he continues the briefing, I can tell from his tone of voice that he doesn't

Maj. Eugene Beyer, company commander of A/229th. This photo was taken when Beyer was still a lieutenant. Courtesy of Col. Gene Beyer

like sending any of his people out into the An Lao valley at night. This is especially true when the mission involves a single helicopter.

"Tom, a small reconnaissance unit has come in contact about here." He points to a spot on the map that lies on the east side of the An Lao valley. "They have been in contact for about an hour now and are running short of ammo. Their call sign is Patty and contact frequency is 47.66. Good luck.

"Tom, you got someone to fly with you?" Beyer asks, when the briefing is over.

"Yes, sir, I've asked Ingamar to fly right seat."

"OK, take Ray Thompson's ship. Ray and a gunner should already be on the hill waiting for you." After copying down the necessary map coordinates, contact names, and frequencies on paper, I embark on the uphill walk to the flight line where the "sleeping" Hueys rest between sandbag walls. Ray Thompson's 126 bird is out there somewhere, bathed in the hot and humid Vietnam darkness.

Huey 65-10126 is Specialist Fourth Class Ray Thompson's "special baby." Ray is a good aircraft mechanic and always maintains an excellent attitude. He has been with the company longer than I have and is a "short timer" due to go home in 22 days. I have been assigned to his aircraft many times, and each time I'm greeted with a big grin and a reminder of how "short" he is. As crew chief for 126, he does almost all the required maintenance on it and is therefore required to fly in it every time it leaves the ground. The same acetate board on which Ray's name appears lists Specialist Fourth Class Richard Denning as tonight's gunner. Richard, who has been in country less than two months, is likable, militarily polite, and pretty solitary.

When I get to the Huey, Ray has already untied the blades and pulled them to the startup position. Ingamar, late as usual, arrives right behind me and unceremoniously drops his chest protector and helmet into the right seat.

"Ray, is she ready to fly?" I ask, not really having the time to do a personal nighttime pre-check.

"Yes, sir, she's hot as a preacher's daughter and ready to go."

I trust Ray's work on his aircraft so much that if he says it's OK to fly, I fly it; no more questions necessary. He is one of the few crew chiefs I trust that much.

Johansen, not as confident about Ray's Huey as I am, starts his own preflight. He checks all the fluid levels in the 90-degree and 42-degree gearboxes and transmission. Using a red lens flashlight, he climbs on top of the aircraft to inspect the entire rotor blade system. After a "walk-around" inspection of the Huey, he straps himself into the right side pilot seat and awaits my next command.

I smoked my pipe as I watched Ingamar satisfy himself that Ray's Huey is OK to fly. Now that he is ready, I bump my pipe on the heel of my jungle boot to empty its now burnt-out bowl of tobacco. As I swing up into the left seat, I make a circular motion with one finger on my right, signaling for him to crank. Johansen, using standard startup procedure, holds back the linear actuator beep button located on his collective control head for ten seconds, then twists the throttle full open, then back to the flight idle detent. Pressing the red detent switch, he then further retards the throttle to a point just behind the detent, which is the start engine position.

"Clear?" he yells.

"All clear, sir," crew chief and gunner respond as one from outside the Huey.

Pulling the start trigger, tucked away under the collective pitch control head, Johansen lights the fires in the turbine. The turbine engine fuel igniters begin clicking as raw JP4 jet fuel sprays under high pressure into the combustion chamber. The electric starter motor moans loudly as it strains to spin the turbine fast enough to get startup fires going. At about 25 percent of the turbine's normal operating speed of 6600 rpm, the JP4 ignites, and the fire that will eventually deliver 1100 horsepower grows rapidly. At 40 percent N1 speed, the turbine is in full ignition and spinning on its own, so Ingamar releases the trigger. When the engine exhaust temperatures stabilize, he twists the throttle to the flight idle detent position, then continues to twist the throttle until he hits the upper limit stop. Lastly, he fine-tunes the engine governor by "beeping" the linear actuator up slowly to 6600 rpm. The main rotor blades overhead turn slowly at first, then begin to accelerate rapidly to 360 rpm. Johansen's responsibility is to do all the pre-takeoff checks and get the ship completely airworthy, then await my command to lift off.

I break open my map case and, using my flashlight, begin plotting on my map what I had seen on the big map in operations. The LZ is a coordinate identified only by intersecting lines. I look at the area where the lines cross and try to visualize what the terrain might look like during the day. It doesn't look good: a patch of uncleared land on a steeply descending mountainside. An LZ on top of the mountain or at the mountain base where the An Lao valley begins would be much easier to land on.

From what I see on the map, tonight's landing will surely be a test of my helicopter flying proficiency. Even if the LZ can be located in this misty and dark night, the ultimate test will occur when I have to take Ray's 6500-pound Huey through a vertical descent into an area not much wider than the Huey's rotor span. To do this without main rotor blade contact with a foreign object, I'll have to treat Ray's Huey like a second skin and the crew and I will have to work as one person. Any hard blade contact, especially of the fragile tail rotor, will tear the blades from their mountings and send this machine and its crew tumbling down the steep mountainside in a ball of fire.

I key the intercom, ask if everyone is ready, and turn to Ingamar. "OK, Mister Johansen, let's go."

Ingamar turns on the brilliant landing lights and slowly pulls upward on the collective pitch control to get the Huey light on its skids. (See the appendix for an overview of helicopter flight.) A helicopter pilot must "feel out" the machine, using tiny amounts of cyclic control pressures to keep it from drifting in any direction as he approaches near neutral buoyancy. The two sandbag walls that form a bunker to protect the Huey from a mortar attack also present a serious hazard during takeoffs and landings. The distance between the walls and the 126's fuselage is about 2 feet on each side, and the ground underneath tilts downhill by 15 degrees or more. There is little room for error.

Johansen continues to get the aircraft light on its skids while "feeling out" the cyclic controls. Ultimately he severs contact with the ground and the Huey rises vertically. Applying forward cyclic pressure while continuing to pull upward on the collective, we fly into the night air. At 50 feet Johansen turns off the landing lights. This combat procedural altitude allows for the clearing of antennas, yet minimizes exposure to North Vietnamese Army (NVA) sharpshooters. The heavy tropical night air now flushes the inside of 126, giving us all some relief from the heat.

Momentarily removing his left hand from the collective pitch control, Ingamar reaches to the overhead console to readjust the brightness of the glowing red instrument lights on the dash and the radio console between us. Though he is a good-looking young man, the dim glow of the instrument lights and his APH-5 flight helmet[4] make his facial features look a little grotesque. It occurs to me that I must look the same, so I stifle the urge to make a comment.

Vertical and lateral visibility are at absolute zero. During night flights, once the landing lights go out, pilots can no longer fly by sighting objects on the ground; we have to fly the aircraft solely by the array of instruments and gauges located on the dash. For me and many others, the instrument flight rules (IFR) training course at Fort Rucker, Alabama, was the toughest course of them all. We trained to take off, fly, and land the helicopter strictly by interpreting available gauges within the cockpit and were forbidden any vision outside the aircraft. An inability to believe in what the instruments are reporting eliminates more warrant officer candidates than any other deficiency. Skills learned in the IFR training have already saved my life several times.

"Patty Six, this is Python Eighty-Eight;[5] en route your location." I hope they will pick up this transmission and know that help is on the way. Less than three minutes into the flight I am already busier than a one-legged man in a butt-kicking contest.

The FM radio[6] is "up" on Patty Six's frequency, and I continue to monitor it for a reply. Using the VHF radio, I transmit required data to TOC as to our lift off time and current atmospheric conditions. During the current transmission, I continuously grind knobs on the UHF radio, trying to tune to the Red Dog GCA's frequency. This is ground-controlled approach tactical radar, which can see where mere mortals cannot.

---

4. This standard Army issue flight helmet proved to be grossly inadequate, and the high-pitched whine of the engines caused all Vietnam helicopter pilots to lose high frequency hearing. The Army had to lower their flight-physical hearing standards just to keep combat instructor pilots.
5. In radio call signs, the number was a personal call sign that usually signified the job one did in addition to flying. Eighty-eight signified company safety officer. Six always signified company commander.
6. Most Hueys maintained three different radios. FM (frequency modulation), UHF (ultra-high frequency), and VHF (very high frequency).

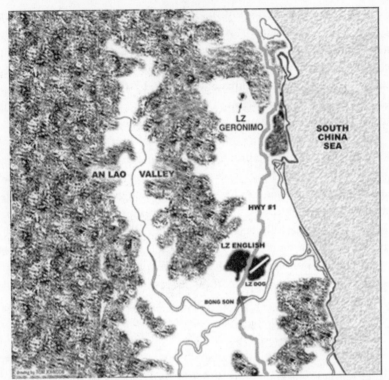

Never mind the array of maps already spread in my lap; all the little tasks necessary to ensure a reasonably safe flight seem to clutter the cockpit.

"Red Dog, Python Eighty-Eight off Python pad for Echo, Romeo, Mike. Request you stay with us." I transmit, establishing initial contact with the GCA people located beside the runway at LZ English.

"Python Eighty-Eight, this is Patty One-Six—acknowledge?" The clarity of the transmission from the ground unit to us, from this low an altitude, both startles and amazes me.

"Patty One-Six, Python Eighty-Eight is en route to your location. We have ammo and water aboard. Over."

"R-o-g-e-r," One-Six replies. He drags the word out halfheartedly in a monotone, and this concerns me greatly. It could mean that he feels his end is near and that the ammo, water, and additional firepower will be too late.

"Python Eighty-Eight, Radar Contact. I have you off Snake Pit pad heading 070 and standing by."

Snake Pit is A/229th's parking area. This transmission means he has us on his scope. This must have been an easy task, since no one else in his right mind would be out here flying in this ink at 0500 hours. I always feel more at ease when I know Red Dog is painting us on his screen. Should we have a sudden engine failure, at least the other Python people will have a general location in which to conduct the search.

"Red Dog, Python Eighty-Eight. Hold fire west. OK?"

"Eighty-Eight, stand by!"

I am asking for artillery fire from LZ English westward to pause so we will have a clear approach. At different intervals during the night, artillery fires their 105 cannons at predetermined targets just to keep the NVA and Cong off balance. They spend about one thousand dollars of taxpayers' money each session. The proper term for this practice is *harassing fire*; our question is, "Harassing whom? Them or us?"

"Eighty-Eight, Red Dog. 'Check-fire' west is approved. Over."

"Red Dog, Eighty-Eight. Thanks. Stay with us. OK?"

"Eighty-Eight, Red Dog. Have you turning through heading three-zero-zero. Say altitude. Over."

"Climbing to 1500. Over."

"Red Dog, roger. Standing by."

Instead of a verbal reply, I key the mike twice.

"Python Eighty-Eight, Patty One-Six, say location! Over."

"Eighty-Eight is about 15 out. Over."

"This is Patty One-Six. SITREP. Over," he says, which means the situation report will follow. Then he reports in a hushed, trembling monotone, "Bandit Eighty-Eight, situation bad and getting worse by the minute . . . step on it harder if you can! Have two known KIAs and six wounded. Patty One-Six Out! LZ is currently red. I say again LZ is red with incoming mortar and small arms fire!"

In radio communications, I usually talk to persons identified only by the call signs needed to establish radio communications. In this case, I feel a need to find out just who the "Patty" people are, so I grope into my jungle fatigues leg pocket for my flashlight, then retrieve my radio call sign book, called an SOI. Issued only to aircraft commanders, an SOI contains all the 1st Cavalry's radio frequencies and call signs, and it is a court-martial offense to lose one of these things. I keep mine on a lanyard around my neck and never allow it out of my sight except when taking a shower. According to my SOI, the "Patty" call sign means that this unit in trouble is an LRRP (long-range recon patrol) unit attached to the 1st Cav. The "One-Six" in the call sign means a mission leader and generally signifies a lieutenant.

"LRRPs," I transmit over the intercom.

"Oh, hell!" Ray Thompson blurts out. He, like me, knows this is trouble. LRRPs are a breed apart from all other men. They are members of the Army's Special Forces Units, trained at Fort Bragg, North Carolina. Although they are trained "hand-to-hand" killers, their objective is to observe the enemy while avoiding contact with him at all costs. They live off freeze-dried rations and water until all supplies are expended or the mission itself is terminated. Each member of the team is tough as nails and in absolutely exquisite physical shape. Emergency extractions mean real trouble for all concerned. It generally means that their position has been compromised by the enemy. It is therefore no surprise that their men will have to be extracted "under fire."

Not more than two minutes pass before a new voice transmits, "Python Eighty-Eight, Patty One-Six. I suggest approach from valley only! Taking light arms fire from zero-one-zero degrees to one-nine-zero degrees with occasional incoming! We have hacked out the best LZ we can. Do you want flares? Over."

"One-Six, stand by!" This is my way of putting off my first major decision until I can collect my thoughts. Flares are an excellent way to locate a unit's LZ at night, but they would make us a sitting duck.

I clear my mind and divert my attention from our impending approach into the LZ to the next hazard we will face as we retrace our steps in total darkness back to the mouth of the An Lao valley and north up the valley floor between the mountains. I turn my attention back to my immediate concern, which is getting to the LZ in one piece; I will worry about the rest when the time comes.

Ingamar is doing an excellent job of processing the radio chitchat to make decisions. He correctly climbs to 4000 feet on a westbound heading. Each time he transmits to Red Dog GCA, he keys his mike and speaks with the authority and calmness of a professional pilot. Although Ingamar has been in country only two months, I have broken the cardinal rule and become accustomed to my bunkmate. Traditionally, it is not good to make friends with the new guys; they could get you killed. They must prove themselves members of the team by swiftly learning to fly combat style, just as I did.

Ingamar transmits. "Red Dog, Army 126 needs radar fix to turn up the An Lao. Call the turn. Over."

"Army 126, Red Dog GCA. Start turn now! Heading three-five-five! Say altitude. Over."

"126, four thousand."

"Roger, 126 stand by, this frequency!"

Ingamar and I know the mountain peaks, now veiled in darkness, are looming to both our left and our right. Red Dog's radar screen is now our eyes, and the success of our mission depends on its trustworthiness. With our landing only five minutes away, we do not want to lose precious time rising to clear the mountains.

"Army 126, Red Dog, suggest new heading three-five-zero! Over."

"Army 126, new heading three-five-zero, wilco."

I look at Ingamar and grin broadly at his reply to Red Dog. The radio term *wilco* went out with the B-17s. It means "understand and will comply," but, with so much on the line, why distract Ingamar with a fine point of communication?

Red Dog is correcting us for wind drift or we might have made our last turn a little too sharply. Nevertheless, I sense that we are already too close to the valley's east side mountains. Both Red Dog and I know that in about one more minute, he will lose us on his radar screen as we head up the valley.

Except for the normal sounds of a Huey flying full out, the next few minutes pass in silence. No transmissions to or from One-Six or Red Dog are necessary. My thoughts turn to the crew chief and gunner who are our "ghost riders in the sky" tonight. They can monitor all the radios just as the pilots do, but they are strictly forbidden to chitchat between themselves on intercom. They are the truly brave ones; at least I have some control over our fate, but they are passengers whose lives are in the hands of others.

Ray Thompson knows his Huey from top to bottom, but knowing the aircraft this well must be a burden, especially on night flights. Small creaks or vibrations not noticed during the day become bangs and groans on night flights. Even I notice a few unusual noises, but adrenaline is drowning out any of nocturnal engine failure.

"Python Eighty-Eight, Patty One-Six. Are you close? Over."

After the relative tranquility of the last two minutes, the transmission startles me back into reality.

"Eighty-Eight is about 3 south of your position! Give me a SITREP. Over."

His first words are about mortars. "No incoming at present time. Light arms fire coming in from three sides and close by! Suggest you approach from the valley floor. No fire presently from that direction. Advise when you start your approach. LZ is small . . . maybe too small . . . don't know for sure . . . can't get our heads up long enough to improve it. Over!"

"One-Six, I'll do a fly-by first! Will advise! Over."

"One-Six, roger."

This LRRP lieutenant's replies are concise and to the point. His radio nomenclature is perfect, but the quavering of his voice and the automatic gunfire in the background are unsettling. No amount of psychic, military, or religious conditioning can prepare you for the kind of situation these men are in. It's like deer hunting in the woods back home in Georgia, only the targets are men. I cannot begin to imagine their fear.

As we draw nearer, we see many small brushfires around the LZ. The smoke from these fires, likely started by hot grenade fragments or tracer rounds, rises, then sinks toward the valley floor in the cool night air. I must avoid this smoke on the final approach. I cannot distinguish people at this altitude, but the green and red tracer rounds streak wildly. From the air, I can see the American unit's problem. For every outgoing American red tracer, there are fifty returning enemy green tracers. Ordinarily there are three to four ordinary rounds for every tracer round seen. Patty's defensive perimeters are rapidly decaying: The distance from the origin of the green tracers to what appears to be the LZ is no more than 200 feet.

Turning my attention to the lay of the land, I see that the side of the mountain on which the LZ sits dives more steeply toward the valley floor than I had earlier imagined. The steep slope will make it extremely difficult to keep from bumping our main rotor blades into the hill before we touch down, and without any doubt, this landing would pose my greatest flying challenge to date even without the enemy fire.

"Throw the ammo and water out!" I transmit through the intercom. The purpose of the mission now changes from emergency resupply to emergency extraction. To lighten our Huey, we throw out heavy boxes of ammo and containers of water initially intended for Patty people.

"Right, sir!" come the replies in unison from Ray and Richard as they begin the task of moving from their small cubbyholes to the main cargo area of the Huey. Hurriedly they throw out the last of the heavy crates of ammo and Mermite cans of water just as Ingamar makes his turn east toward the mountain and the LZ.

The proximity of the good guys and the bad guys completely rules out artillery support. This is a tactic Charlie learned during the battle for the Ia Drang valley in 1965. Spring the trap close in, and the Americans cannot shoot you without shooting their people.

"Sir, they are getting their asses kicked bad," Thompson blurts over the intercom as we finish our west to east drag over the LZ.

With the rest of us all focused on the LZ below, Johansen alertly executes a 180-degree turn to head back west. A few more minutes' lack of attention from the rest of us on this easterly course, and we would have created our own LZ in the side of the mountain.

The LZ will now be on Johansen's side of the Huey. I can see no more than the flickering of the fires bouncing off the interior of the cockpit as we drag the LZ in the opposite direction. Without warning, brilliant flashes of white light fly up from the LZ below. Trees and other previously indistinguishable features around the battle area are abruptly illuminated. The flashes succeed each other rapidly, and in a few moments our ears confirm what our eyes have already told us: the flashes come from incoming mortar rounds! These are from NVA mortars . . . large ones. No one who has been on the business end of one of these things will ever forget it. The light, sound, concussion, and shrapnel shredding everything in their path are unforgettable.

"Patty One-Six, Python Eighty-Eight. Over," I transmit to anyone who can transmit back from the carnage below.

Seconds of silence pass with no reply.

"Patty One-Six, Python Eighty-Eight. Over," I transmit again, and then three times more without a reply.

"Tom, if there is still anyone alive down there, are we going in?" Ingamar asks.

"Mister Johnson, if it means anything . . . it's OK by me . . . I mean if you decide to go in," Richard Denning volunteers before I can reply to Ingamar's question.

"Hey! I'm the short timer here!" Ray Thompson quips.

"OK, chief, what do you say?" I ask, and several seconds of silence follow my question.

"Mister Johnson, I'm twenty-one and a wake-up. You know that."

"Chief, Mister Johnson didn't ask how many days you got left; he asked if you wanted in on this?" Ingamar interjects.

"It doesn't matter," I say. "I can't get them out of there. The Cong are too close. Without gunship support, we'll only add more bodies and a helicopter to what will eventually have to be taken out." I use a tone of voice meant to indicate that the decision is final.

During the seconds that follow, I drift into my soul, seeking answers. Up to now, I have never failed to "go in" if there was at least one chance in a hundred that all of us could survive. Two other Hueys are adorned with bullet holes in the tail boom and rotor blades as testament to my willingness to go in under fire . . . but this case is different. The chances of getting in and out again are near zero, and I have to think about Thompson. In 22 more days he turns the corner, and I could not live with myself, assuming I survive, should something happen to him.

"Python-Six, Python Eighty-Eight. Over." I need both God's and Major Beyer's help on this one, but I have only Major Beyer's call sign.

"Python-Six. Go ahead, Eighty-Eight," Major Beyer answers.

"SITREP: Patty LZ red. I repeat LZ red. LZ currently under fire with automatics and heavy mortars. Apparently they have heavy losses. I estimate four to six still alive in the LZ. Extraction impossible without Tom Cat support, and I don't think the Patty folks have enough time left for them to crank. Over."

"Eighty-Eight. Tom Cats and Blue Max departed English about ten minutes ago en route to your location. I have been monitoring Patty push. Over." Tom Cats are gunships of D/229th; Blue Max are aerial rocket artillery of 2/20th; and Patty push is Patty's radio frequency.

"Roger, Six," I acknowledge, with some relief.

"Python Eighty-Eight, Tom Cat Two-Six. Over." The voice and call sign are familiar to me, though I have never had the pleasure of meeting him face-to-face.

"Tom Cat Two-Six, say location. Over."

"Tom Cat Two-Six and a party of four are inbound up the valley floor about one out! Have probable LZ area fires in sight! SITREP. Over."

"Two-Six, Patty One-Six and unit is pinned down on the mountainside ten to fifteen meters west and south of the fires. Currently receiving heavy automatic weapons fire from the north, east, and south. Also heavy incoming mortar rounds; origin is not yet known. Contact with Patty One-Six was lost a few moments ago. Actual conditions inside LZ are unknown. Our position is north, northwest of LZ, heading two-eight-zero degrees at 3200 feet. Landing light going on for ID. Do you see us? Over."

With a flip of a switch, Ingamar extends and turns our landing light on. A landing light at night in Vietnam is a sure invitation to become the turkey in the turkey shoot if you are low enough for small arms fire to be effective. I have weighed this danger against accidentally running into the inbound aircraft; I know of no survivors of midair collisions.

"Eighty-Eight, Two-Six. I have you in sight!" Ingamar turns our landing light off immediately, but keeps it extended so that it can be instantly turned back on if needed.

" Python Eighty-Eight. Blue Max One-One. Over."

"Blue Max One-One, Python Eighty-Eight. Say position. Over."

"Blue Max flight of two is right behind the Tom Cat flight, and we have both of you in sight. Over."

What has been a gut feeling of helplessness is now replaced by exhilaration. The firepower of the Tom Cat and Blue Max flights is awesome. Each Tom Cat "gunship" wields two miniguns, each capable of firing 8000 rounds per minute of 7.62 ammo and 12 rockets. The Blue Max folks are the Cav's airborne rocket artillery (ARA). They carry 48 rockets in two pods located just outside their Huey's door.

"The Cavalry has arrived!" Thompson keys in on the intercom.

"OK, Ray. You're the short guy! The rest of us are going in, but I'll fix it so you can ride with the other guys if that's what you want!"

"Mister Johnson, I've already thought about it! You know before I did this job, I was a 'grunt' and you guys saved my ass more than once! Hell, Mister Johnson, I'm sorry this has to happen with me so short, but shit, I can't be walking away from those guys if there's any chance to pull 'em out!"

This makes me smile, and I turn in my seat to get eye-to-eye contact with Ray. "Damn, Thompson, that's the most 'Gun-Ho' thing I ever heard from a short timer! You sure about this thing, Ray?"

When Ray issues the "thumbs-up" sign, I return to the situation at hand.

"Tom Cat Two-Six and Blue Max One-One, suggest you run with 'nav' [navigation] lights on! It's going to be tight in this valley. Python Eighty-Eight will make another LZ drag at 3200 feet from west to east. Line up behind me for the drag and look for mortar tube flashes. You've got to take them out first. Last contact with Patty One-Six indicated two wounded, four KIAs, and they are almost out of ammo. We are beginning our left turn to east now. Landing light coming on! Over."

"Tom Cat Two-Six, roger."

"Blue Max One-One, roger."

Ingamar has already turned the light on as I speak. Its beam pierces the night like a sword, but except for what is lit by the fires, I can see nothing outside. It reminds me of the days back home when I scuba dived in dark water without a diving light. There is nothing the senses can key in on. Except for the gauges on the Huey's dash, we seem suspended motionless in time and space.

As we finish our turn, I can see the conspicuous red and green navigation lights of the four Tom Cat aircraft and both of the Blue Max aircraft lining up abreast. They are several hundred feet below, heading to the west side of the narrow valley. Then they begin a slow right-hand turn east to fall behind our aircraft.

"Tom Cat Two-Six, Blue Max flight will be 1500 meters behind you and following you in. Over."

"Two-Six, roger!"

The guns like to go in low when possible. Most gunship pilots joke that they get nosebleeds over 1500 feet. The ARA birds, on the other hand, need the altitude for a rocket run on the target.

As Johansen maneuvers the Huey back eastward to overfly the LZ, I can't help noticing that the eastern darkness is just beginning to give way to daylight. It's been one and a half hours since we first made contact with Red Dog.

"Patty One-Six, Python Eighty-Eight. Over!" No immediate reply; I repeat the call.

"Python Eighty-Eight, this is Patty control. Over?" a voice replies.

"Patty control. SITREP. Over!"

"Eighty-Eight, Patty One-Six is KIA and I don't know how many others! Over."

"Is the LZ currently red? Over."

"LZ is red, I repeat LZ is red. We have small arms automatic fire and incoming mortar rounds. I have one more clip of ammo left. Don't know status of others. Eighty-Eight, please get us out of here!" His accent makes him a Southerner like me. His voice trembles.

"Hold on, son, we'll get you out of there!" I say, trying to sound comforting. "I am approaching your position from the west right now! I will circle and drop into your position from the same westerly direction! Get up NOW and find the rest of your people! This will be a one-ship extraction! Be ready to get aboard! ARA and gunships are right behind me and will be spraying your perimeter! Do you copy? Over."

"I copy. Over."

I have just bet the lives of those guys on the ground and the lives of my crew. I glance at the fuel gauge, which is getting a little low for what might lie ahead. I remove the maps and other items from my lap and secure them, then watch intently as we overfly the LZ again. We are a few hundred feet lower than our last pass, and now I clearly see the carnage. I can make out about three guys inside the LZ who are still moving; the rest lay motionless. I can't see the bottoms of the craters made by incoming mortar rounds, but I figure there may be more alive in them.

Suddenly as before, all hell breaks loose. Green tracers pour into the LZ and one or two persevering little Vietnamese start shooting at us.

"Break left! Break left!" I scream into the microphone resting just off my lips. Johansen reacts instantly. From his seat on the right side of the aircraft, he cannot see the tracers that are coming up to meet us from my side of the Huey. They start slowly from a location about 30 meters east of the LZ, then ominously seem to arc toward us. As they draw nearer, they seemingly pick up fantastic velocity. The little bastard below is leading us with his fire by aiming well off the nose of the aircraft. In other words, the rounds are not curving to meet us; we are flying to meet them.

21

As Johansen breaks hard left, I hear the familiar *tic* of a round passing through the aircraft. It sounds like someone shooting a beer can with a BB gun. Jerking my body around in my seat, I check the crew. Johansen is close enough to me that I would have noticed any jerking of his body or sudden change in his abilities, had he been hit. Both Ray and Richard are looking at me with eyes wide, showing no sign of pain. Greatly relieved, I immediately check the engine instruments. Everything is in the green and the Huey is without any unusual noises.

Brilliant flashes from incoming mortar rounds hit the LZ in rapid succession. We are now low enough to hear the whooshing sounds of the explosions, and they are unnerving.

The arrival of the Tom Cat and the Blue Max is heralded by an emergency radio transmission. "Jesus Christ. Tom Cat flight, break right! Break right. The sons a bitches are right under us! Two-Two, turn it south in a hurry! Two-Three, go north!"

Bingo! The entire gunship flight has flown over the mortar tube emplacements, which are firing on the LZ, and most likely have been right in the trajectory of the rounds. Hueys begin scattering like quails; they fly all directions in an attempt to get out of the way.

"Tom Cat Two-Six, Blue Max One-One. Stay clear . . . we have 'em in sight! Rolling in hot! Repeat going hot." Blue Max flight had been high and behind the Tom Cat flight when the flashes from the mortar tubes disclosed their whereabouts. They are in perfect position, so they lower their noses dead on the target and begin their rocket run.

"Tom Cat flight, this is Tom Cat Two-Six. *Didi mau!*" Even though they are given in Vietnamese, the flight leader's instructions are clear and concise: get the hell out of there!

As Johansen completes our abrupt left turn and stabilizes on a westward heading, I can see the Blue Max birds diving in for the kill. In rapid succession, pairs of rockets ignite and fly to their target, leaving behind contrails of white, phosphorescent smoke. Two, six, then eight rockets find their mark. Even from this altitude, I can hear the shrapnel cutting paths through the underbrush. I can see secondary explosions of NVA ammo, which proves beyond any doubt that they have the right place.

With the timing that can only be gained from experience and

working together, the first ARA bird breaks off the run to the south when the second ARA bird is already 25 percent into his aiming run. Just as his first wingman breaks from his rocket run, the second bird unleashes his rockets by pairs and in rapid succession. This maneuver, called "daisy chaining," protects the breaking birds' exposed undersides. It's hard to stand up and shoot at a Huey when his wingman is firing rockets at you.

"Tom Cat Two-Six, this is Python Eighty-Eight! Get into position! We're going into the LZ! Do you copy? Over."

"Python Eighty-Eight, Tom Cat Two-Six copies! Tom Cat Two-Two, fall in on me for lead! Tom Cat Two-Three and Tom Cat Two-Four, make your setup! Do you copy?" All three Tom Cats roger their boss's instructions.

"Python Eighty-Eight, Tom Cat Two-Six, are you ready to make your run? Over."

"Two-Six, stand by!" I switch the radio selector back to position 2, which is the FM radio.

"Patty Control . . . Patty Control, this is Python Eighty-Eight. Over!" No reply.

I repeat the call twice more. The radio comes alive with "Eighty-Eight, Patty Control. Over."

"Control, SITREP. Over."

"Eighty-Eight. We are still in heavy contact from the east. No incoming in the past minute. Over."

"How many of you for pickup? Over." I ask.

After a pause, the voice on the other end of the airway replies, "Eighty-Eight, by head count, four known passengers! All the rest are KIA . . . I think. We have one seriously wounded . . . bleeding bad! Over!"

"Patty, I will approach from the valley floor on an easterly heading. We have gunships and ARA on station. The gunships will lay down fire on approach! Assemble your people on the north side of the LZ and keep your heads down! Over!"

Patty rogers the transmission.

"Blue Max One-One, Python Eighty-Eight. Can you make them keep their heads down for our approach? Over!" With this command, I'm asking the Blue Max folks to break off their attack on the mortar installation and join up for the attack on the LZ.

"No worry, Eighty-Eight!" is the reply. From the sound of his voice and the slight moaning of his master pilot, it is apparent to me that Blue Max One-One must have been in at least a turn of at least 2G when the reply was made, turning back into position before his wingman completes his rocket run.

"Python Eighty-Eight, Tom Cat Two-Six. Are you ready to run? Over."

"Eighty-Eight is westbound and will be making a left turn eastbound in one. Over."

"Two-Six, this is Tom Cat Two-Three. We have Eighty-Eight in sight. Over." This is Tom Cat Two-Six's other lead pilot. As soon as Two-Six starts his run with his wingman, Three and his wingman must carefully count down to be in position to fire when Two-Six makes his break. Now it is a matter of timing the approach.

"Python Eighty-Eight, Python Six. Over." The call catches me off guard. The number six always indicates the company commander. It suddenly dawns on me that others, including Major Beyer and the entire TOC, are monitoring this frequency back at LZ English.

"Six, go ahead!" I reply, reserving room in my already crowded brain for additional conversation.

"The RRF [Ready Reaction Force] is cranking. Over."

The short, sweet communication from Major Beyer is filled with innuendoes that send my personal fear skyrocketing. I take a quick glance around the crew. No one else has caught what I have caught, and I can't see telling them the importance of the transmission. It seems that "Black Horse," 1st Air Cavalry division[7] headquarters, is also monitoring our push. They have launched the RRF—an infantry unit and an air assualt helicopter company—because they are unsure whether the hostiles are part of a much larger NVA force. I wonder if we are all flying into a trap. If so, it will not be a first for me. A favorite tactic of the NVA is to lure their prey into a battle using a small skirmish as bait.

I reply that I understand his transmission.

"Tom Cat Two-Six, Python Eighty-Eight. Making our turn. Over."

"Eighty-Eight, Two-Six, roger. Starting our run!" His voice is calm.

---

7. A division comprises approximately 20,000 soldiers.

Reflexes take over as I unknowingly slip hands and feet onto 126's controls and say into the intercom, "I have it." Without any hesitation, Johansen relinquishes control of the Huey to me.

The Huey and I again become as one. Johansen has already initiated a turn to our left when I take over. We are maintaining an altitude of 2500 feet. I tighten the turn dramatically and lower the collective pitch to begin our slow descent toward the LZ, which now lies dead ahead.

While in this steep turn, I look out "greenhouse," the green window over the Huey's cockpit, and can see the fires still burning at the LZ. I roll level for the approach. My eyes strain to pick up Two-Six and his wingman, who have already begun their assault.

"Patty Control, Patty Control, Python Eighty-Eight and company beginning final approach. Get your heads down. Do you copy? Over."

After a short delay Patty Control gives an urgent "Roger," over the firing of small arms audible in the background.

Tom Cat Two-Six "throws the switches" about 1000 yards out from the LZ, and the total destruction of everything around the LZ begins. Leaves, small trees, foliage of all types, and—we hope—the bad guys begin to fall. The rockets kick clumps of earth 40 feet in the air. The first rockets test the accuracy of Two-Six's "grease pencil mark crosshair."[8] Almost before each pair of rockets explodes, Two-Six and his wingman begin punching off another pair of rockets . . . then another. With each pair, Two-Six and his gunship moves closer to the LZ's perimeter by adjusting the alignment of his aircraft.

As the Tom Cat twosome break off their attack, we continue our descent about 50 yards out from the LZ. I know that at any moment Two-Six's other two birds will be cutting loose with their rockets to continue the daisy chain, but those few seconds between Two-Six's breakaway and the two other Tom Cats' cutting loose can kill me. Two-Three must be on the run and in place before Two-Six's break. A failure of timing would put us at great risk.

The roar of a solid propellant motor and the sight of its vapor trail interrupts my deep concentration on landing. The second set of

8. Because helicopters had no sophisticated device to aid in aiming guns or rockets, pilots would watch the course of their rockets and put a mark on their windshields to serve as a crosshair.

Tom Cats are in place. The timing is perfect, but I jump nervously as they pass very near us en route to the LZ. We are already lower and closer than Two-Six had gotten on his run, and my tribulation is about to begin. Multiple rockets bullet past my aircraft at Mach 1 speed, and I can only hope the Tom Cats continue to be accurate enough not to run a rocket up my own Huey's tailpipe.

At close range, the explosions of the rockets have a blinding effect, and my eyes are continually readjusting. Depth perception is critical; target surveillance for stumps and degree of slope is critical; gauging the size of the LZ for rotor clearance is critical; and positioning the aircraft close to the troops for extraction is critical. This mission will give new meaning to the term "combat seasoned" for me.

At 30 yards, I can make out the floor of the LZ itself. The fires flicker. The bottom of the mortar craters are black and seem endless. As the fires dance, so does the floor of the LZ, making accurate depth perception impossible.

"Johansen, get ready!" I break the silence over the intercom. The command is not really necessary. He has already slipped his hands closer to the cyclic and collective pitch controls, and his heels are buried in the floor just off the anti-torque pedals.

"Clear to fire, Chief!" I yell, and both the crew chief and the gunner open up with their M60 machine guns, mounted from the roof of the Huey on a bungie cord. Before I've completed the word "Fire," swarms of bullets are hitting the jungle left and right of the aircraft. The gunners fire quickly, first sweeping forward and below, then sweeping back to fire straight ahead of them, then forward again.

I turn the aircraft's nose up to decelerate. Experience and sound, more than any gauges, tell me that our forward airspeed has slowed to about 20 knots, and we are about to leave translational lift.

Looking between my feet and the pedals now instead of through the windscreen to see the LZ below me, I approach the edge of the LZ. The Huey is moving forward at 15 or 20 knots. As we continue to slow our forward motion, we fall right on cue through translational lift, a mode of flight in which a helicopter transitions from hovering to actually flying, or vice versa.

I pull up on the collective for more pitch in the rotor system, and the Huey responds. The enormous 48-foot rotor system begins to load up. Biting for more air to stay aloft, the entire power system, including the turbine engine, the transmission, the main rotor blades, and the tail rotor, takes on a new, higher-pitched whine.

Tall trees, silhouetted by the fires, pass only a few feet underneath the aircraft, dancing violently from the hurricane force winds generated by the Huey's blade system. I remind myself that we are in a tail low attitude—the tail rotor must clear the trees before I descend any lower.

"Tail rotor clear, sir," Thompson yells over the intercom. He is leaning out of his cubicle and has a plain view of both the tree line we have just crossed and the tail rotor itself.

At near zero forward speed, 30 feet up in the air, I smoothly push the collective pitch control down, and we begin to settle vertically into the small clearing.

Alternately looking straight ahead and through the chin bubble while descending, I size up the conditions in the LZ. It slopes alarmingly downward underneath the aircraft toward the valley floor and is filled with stumps and mortar craters. If we maintain our current direction, the hover will be so high that it will be impossible to take the "Patty" people aboard.

"Stop fire—left turn!" I call over the intercom.

"Tail rotor clear, sir," is the reply as the guns go silent.

Both Thompson and Denning are leaning dangerously outside their cubicle for a clearer view of the main and tail rotors. Striking any object with either will mean certain death. On this much of an incline, we would fall to the bottom of the LZ and roll downhill in a fiery ball.

As I press the left pedal to rotate the fuselage to the left on its vertical axis, I repeatedly cross check the engine and rotor system tachometer for any sign that we are running out of power. This would be a disaster of the highest magnitude, since we are now inside the LZ's walls, with nowhere to go except up or down. If we run out of power, the aircraft will begin a slow settling toward the ground, and with the degree of incline of the LZ floor, the first part of the helicopter to touch the ground will be the tips of the main rotor blades. If this happens, the rotor system will separate from the helicopter.

I am oblivious to the carnage within the LZ and the gunfire around me. My fear level has increased dramatically. At the moment, I am far more afraid of dying from some slight miscalculation in my flying than I am of dying at the hands of my enemy. As the aircraft finishes its rotation to a point 90 degrees left of our approach heading, I concentrate on the trees directly ahead, with occasional glimpses downward through the chin bubble. We continue our descent.

"CALL THE ROTOR TIPS!" I yell. We all depend for our lives on one another.

"Come on down—about eight feet off, six feet off—tail rotor clear, sir," Ray calls.

"HOLD IT! HOLD IT!" Johansen and Denning, who are on the "uphill" side of the aircraft, yell as we reach the lowest point to which we can safely go. We are at a 4- or 5-foot hover above the ground. This means the rotor tips must be no more than 3 feet above the ground to compensate for the incline. My mouth goes dry with panic. In their haste to get aboard, will one of the Patty people run headlong into the spinning rotor blades? The blades would be about waist high to anyone running downhill.

"KEEP 'EM OUT OF THE ROTOR! KEEP 'EM OUT OF THE ROTOR!" I yell over the intercom.

I cannot look anywhere except dead ahead, where I have fixed my hover target to keep the Huey still. At the thought of someone running downhill into our rotor blades, every muscle in my body tightens. I will not be able to see it coming, so I brace myself for the big thump of one body meeting one blade.

There is a good bit of movement and scuffling on the part of the two crewmembers in the rear, causing the center of gravity of the Huey to change quickly and requiring me to adjust rapidly. I can tell that Thompson is leaving his post on the downhill side of the aircraft and racing to the open cargo door on the uphill side to carry out my orders. To do this, he has to unplug his helmet from the intercom system. He is yelling at the top of his voice. I can hear him shouting but can't make out what he is saying.

The Huey lurches abruptly to the right in a rocking motion. Since the chief is unplugged, there is no prior warning. Someone has just gotten on the skids outside. From the yelling and melee in the back, I guess we have our first passenger.

The desperate scuffling and clawing continues. The Huey begins to settle with the extra weight. I pull up on the collective pitch control to increase horsepower and maintain a uniform altitude above the floor of the LZ. As I pull in, I tap Johansen's hands and feet, which are near the controls; we are hovering the aircraft as one pilot. Out of the corner of my eye, I can see that he, too, is staring dead ahead at some invisible hover target of his own.

How many survivors are there? Will there be more than I can get out? Who will be left behind?

Helicopter lifting capacities are strictly limited by density altitude, an equation that adjusts current altitude for factors of temperature, humidity, and barometric pressure. All helicopters can lift more when the air is colder and drier and thus denser. In the States, the Huey could easily transport a crew of four plus as many as ten soldiers, depending on how heavily loaded they were with packs. In Vietnam, the tropical heat and humidity reduces the maximum safe capacity to six troops with packs. Any more than six or seven can be a real problem. It's to our advantage that these survivors will have nothing but their shirts and trousers, and that it is the coolest period of the tropical day . . . just before daylight.

The scuffling continues, and I continue adding more power and fearfully glance at the main rotor rpm gauge on the dash: The needle is steady at 6600 rpm.

For the first time I think of the possibility of being shot. I am less than one-third of the way through my one-year tour. At first, I felt invincible. It only happens to the other guy. Now—reality. We have been a sitting target for over 60 seconds of my life. It seems more like an eternity.

The sound of exploding rockets nearby drives home the fear. I had completely forgotten about the Tom Cat and Blue Max aircraft, which are doing their jobs with surgical precision. Two-Six himself must now be on his second run. The firing and the exploding of the rockets make different sounds. The explosions of the rockets have a cracking sound, much like some enormously heavy object being dropped on a cardboard box full of paper or like some giant's footsteps through a dried forest. The trees that encircle me prevent me from seeing the white flash of the rocket explosions, but I can see their occasional bright orange balls of light curl upward and die in the darkness.

A blow to the shoulder with a fist jars me. The fist, belonging to Thompson, has its thumb pointed straight up. He moves it rapidly up and down: We are fully loaded. It is time to depart.

I have no idea how many passengers we have aboard. All that matters is having enough power for vertical ascent. At about 20 feet above the ground, we will lose "ground effect" and experience a few moments of serious danger.

For a second, I take my eyes off the dead-ahead hover target and glance through the green Plexiglas overhead. The tops of those trees that seem so far away are now a far more formidable obstruction to my living another day than they were before. Leaves, twigs, dirt, and small limbs are being propelled off the LZ floor and into the night sky by the force of the Huey's rotor blades. I lose sight of their trajectories when they move out of the reflective light of the burning fires.

I pull on the collective pitch to start our ascent. The Huey responds sluggishly, but the hover target ahead moves steadily downward. The whine of the turbine announces to our trained ears that Thompson's Huey is straining. The faltering of this whine, more than any gauge, will herald our destruction. The intercom is quiet as the crew listens intently. I look up again.

Now, near the end of our vertical ascent, the thing I've been dreading happens: The whine of the turbine makes a distinct change in pitch! I am asking for more power than the Lycoming turbine engine can deliver. We are 30 feet above the floor of the LZ, very near the tops of trees on the downhill side, but we are in serious trouble. Johansen and I lock our eyes on the rpm gauge mounted on the dash of the Huey's instrument panel. It confirms what our ears have already told us.

I arrive at the limit of travel for the left pedal: yet the Huey begins a slow turn to the right . . . out of control.

My mouth goes dry, and my eardrums throb with each heartbeat. Trying not to panic, I force my mind through all the possibilities. The answer jumps out at me.

The anti-torque (tail rotor), which keeps the aircraft steady against an overhead rotating blade system, consumes enormous amounts of energy. My usual strategy of pressing the left pedal to compensate for a right yaw now has to be overcome with uncertain results. I ease up on the left pedal and the aircraft begins to spin more rapidly to the right on its vertical axis. My natural tendency to apply the left pedal is so powerful that I cannot "lift" my left foot; I force my left foot free of the pedal limit by pressing hard on the opposite pedal with my right foot, causing the left pedal to rise.

Johansen mutters without keying his mike. I can't tell if he is giving me words of encouragement or praying. At the moment, either would be suitable.

Halfway through our rotation, the low rpm warning light on the dash comes on, illuminating the whole. The audible alarm shrills in the intercom—the third time I have heard it in flight.

I lower the collective slightly, then instinctively pull it back up a fraction, then lower it again as an afterthought. My mind is in total conflict over the best course of action, and now it takes two routes simultaneously. Up a little . . . down a little . . . up a little . . . down a little. Bobbing and milking. This is certainly what has to be. As I relax a little pressure on the collective, the low rpm alarm silences, only to start on again as I again pull up on the collective.

As I release more left pedal and allow the aircraft to spin slightly faster to the right, I can milk a little more on the collective. I cannot tell if we are in fact climbing until the nose sweeps through its fourth or fifth revolution and I can see over the tops of the downhill trees.

Another turn will do it. We are already above the tree line, but when I nose the Huey to fly forward, I will lose lift. Some of the energy that is being consumed for vertical flight now has to be used for forward flight. It is a natural tendency for the aircraft to settle, and this phenomenon would normally be compensated for with additional power; but we are already maxed out, and I choose to let the Huey make another complete turn, rising, before lowering our nose toward the valley floor.

In the final turn, I begin to apply forward pressure on the cyclic control between my legs.

We begin a slow corkscrew spiral up from the LZ below. As the valley floor appears in Johansen's window to my right, I make a desperate move—I push the cyclic straight forward toward the dash. The momentum of our spin continues to turn the fuselage of the aircraft, even though new control pressure has been applied to the rotor system. I feel my cyclic movement taking effect. Slowly, the stumbling

Huey begins to move forward. As the nose of the aircraft comes around, we are definitely trading off hover power for forward motion and thus are starting to settle toward the tops of the trees below us. But I have committed our lives now and there is no turning back. The sound of the Low RPM alert is the Huey's awesome cry of pain; I am pulling her guts out.

As we sink rapidly toward the first tree, I must fight the impulse to pull in more power. This would further slow down the blade system and cause a more rapid descent. I let fate take its course.

The skids drag the top of the tree; then we clear it. I push forward on the cyclic hard, and we plummet down the side of the mountain, picking up airspeed and lost rpm quickly. The Huey lurches as we pass through translational speed. We are flying again. Though the altimeter on the dash unwinds wildly, indicating rapid descent, the angle of the mountain toward the valley floor is far greater than our rate of descent.

We've made it—our apocalypse will have to wait. Ingamar slaps me on the shoulder, and the intercom goes wild with noises of deliverance and joy. I can clearly feel Ray and Richard stomping the aluminum floor and hear the clapping of their hands. They are happy just to be alive.

"Python Eighty-Eight is out of the LZ," I transmit to the other aircraft.

The flight leader of the ARA flights had a comment about our circus act at the top of the trees. "Eighty-Eight, Blue Max One-One. Looked like you were having a little fun at the top of that one. Over."

Too busy to formally reply, I key the mike twice to "break squelch."

"Python Eighty-Eight, Tom Cat Two-Six. Anyone left in the LZ? Over."

I do not know and instruct Two-Six to stand by. I pull the trigger switch halfway for intercom. "How about it, Chief? Anyone left?"

"Only bodies, sir, far as I could tell."

I pull the trigger all the way back and radio the information to Two-Six. He rogers the transmission with disappointment in his voice. He would like to blast the entire area to hell, including the LZ, but this will have to wait with KIAs still there. Both his flight and the ARA boys are out for blood, though, and will continue firing into the perimeter of the cleared area until help arrives or they run out of ammo.

"Python Eighty-Eight, Tom Cat Two-Four. Python Six is trying to reach you. Over."

We have now descended to an altitude too low for clear reception over the mountain.

"Tom Cat Two-Four. Relay the message. Over."

Major Beyer wants an immediate SITREP. Tom Cat Two-Four relays that we are out and headed to the medevac pad with the injured, but many KIAs are still in the LZ. I know that Beyer will coordinate the RRF's mission for the extraction of those I left behind.

I turn control of the Huey over to Johansen and look over my right shoulder to get my first glimpse of our new passengers. My eyes meet theirs, one by one, as I scan their faces. Their stares are blue steel, cold and empty. Their bodies are here with me, but their minds are elsewhere. There are six or seven survivors on board. Two individuals are lying crosswise on the floor. From my vantage point, I can see that their feet stick out the right door. I turn further in my seat to get a better look. The brown eyes of the guy in back drill through me, his stare cold and without emotion. His left arm is elbowed under the neck of his friend whose head hangs sideways toward the cargo floor at an awkward angle. His right arm, which is badly burned and bleeding, is tightly wrapped over and under the stomach of his buddy. I am horrified when I see that he is actually holding the intestines of his buddy to prevent them from falling on the cargo floor.

I quickly glance back into his eyes, feeling ashamed for even looking. His buddy, not yet dead, repeatedly calls, "Oh, Momma . . . oh . . . Momma." I turn my head away, but I cannot disconnect my mind from this moment. In my few short months in Vietnam, I have hauled many seriously injured people. I have found that when faced with the transition from life to death, most of these young men call out for their mothers. Some, in their agony, call for their God, but most simply call for Momma.

"Dear God!" I say into the intercom, startling the crew, who are very edgy.

Johansen's eyes meet mine; his face is a big question mark: What imminent disaster am I about to reveal?

"Look behind you! The guy on the floor. His guts are hanging out."

A quick glance is all it takes, and Johansen shakes his head from side to side in utter disbelief.

Without another word between us, Johansen pulls more collective and "bends the nose over," calling for more speed. We have been descending slowly, maintaining about 90 knots forward airspeed. Now Ingamar will trade altitude for airspeed and push 126 to its red line. We have all seen mere minutes make the difference between living and dying. We must get this soldier to medevac as rapidly as Thompson's Huey can fly.

I glance at the torque meter on the dash and fumble with the SOI around my neck.

As I reach to change the UHF radio in the center console, I glance outside. Johansen has the Huey "hell-bent for leather." Having run out of vertical airspace and thus no longer able to trade altitude for airspeed, we are now skimming across the floor of the valley at breakneck speed. The airspeed indicator is stabilized at 90 knots and our low nose attitude is dramatic. We are asking this Huey one more time to give us everything she has.

The range of most small arms fire is 1500 feet straight up. If we cannot fly above that altitude, then we must contour fly, which means to get very low and run very fast. The idea is to get past any prospective shooter before he has time to raise the rifle and fire. Such flying is dangerous, but the alternative is more so.

Johansen has the tips of the skids some 3 feet above the ground; we will rise higher only to clear a tree and then descend again. We overtake the Bong Son River, which flows south through the length of the valley and eventually to LZ English, where the medevac pad is located. The buffeting of the air through the rotor at high speed causes a very noticeable vertical vibration inside the aircraft. The crew and the passengers bounce up and down at a frequency jokingly referred to as a "one to one."

"Mercy Control. Mercy Control. This is Python Eighty-Eight. Over." Mercy is the call sign of the 15th Medical Detachment, located on LZ English. I alert them we have seriously injured on board and are inbound to their location. Once they roger my transmission, I switch to the tower frequency used by LZ English and receive a priority clearance to nosedive through their area of operation to land at the medevac pad.

As we arrive at the western edge of LZ English's perimeter, the barbed-wire passes under our skids in a blur.

Johansen now places the collective control all the way to the bottom and applies aft movement of the cyclic. This maneuver, if properly executed, will bleed off forward airspeed. Too much rearward pressure on the cyclic will cause the Huey to rise and too little will cause the aircraft to settle into the ground. In fact, we are in a fast decaying power-off glide.

Letting the Huey rise just a little to clear the multitudes of antennas that protrude above the sandbag bunker city, Johansen continues his reduction of forward airspeed. We brush by the wooden control tower, still at a blazing speed.

Now we approach the runway designated for fixed-wing aircraft. The runway is constructed of perforated steel planking rather than the typical wood. Johansen has planned his approach for the medevac pad to be on his right, but his forward speed is way too fast for the approach. With the collective still on the bottom, he tries to correct this error by pulling back hard on the cyclic, putting the Huey in such a nose-high attitude that all I can see ahead are puffy white and gold clouds drifting quietly in the dawn sky.

Johansen is not looking forward; he is looking out his right window at the large red cross and white background painted on the PSP (perforated steel planking) below.

The needle on the forward airspeed gauge quickly drops to near zero; as it does, Johansen presses heavily on the right pedal to make the aircraft turn right on its vertical axis.

"Ingamar, don't forget you're loaded," I quietly remind him over the intercom.

We are very heavy by Huey "D" model standards, and to make the kind of aerobatic maneuver Ingamar is attempting with a Huey loaded to near maximum capacity demands much skill. Inexperienced pilots who find themselves at zero forward airspeed tend to find themselves in an unusual attitude, the nose too high for ground effect and plummeting toward the earth at an alarming rate. When this happens, there is not enough inertia in the blade system or power in the turbine motor to stop a very hard arrival. Such landings will scare the passengers and send ground personnel scurrying for cover. The skids and body also usually incur significant damage when the skids spread level with the cargo bay floor. The proper terminology for this in helicopter circles is "out of luck and rpm—all at the same time."

Johansen avoids this disaster. As the helicopter rotates right, still in an extremely nose-high attitude, he begins pulling upward on the collective pitch, loading up the blade system. In completing the right pedal turn, he has applied enough power to make a controlled descent into the landing pad.

Without his knowledge, he has made this aircraft an extension of himself. Though this maneuver is not yet complete, he has already demonstrated the proficiency it takes to become an aircraft commander. He sets our Huey down in the dead center of the red cross on the PSP. Normally our mission would be completed with the delivery of our passengers to qualified medical help, but looking back into the aircraft, I see that only one passenger has disembarked on his own; the rest just sit there. They stare at me as I look back at them. I make a motion with my hands for them to exit now. Most obey, but their obedience is ghastly and robotic. These men have truly lost their sense of time.

A peculiar amount of verbal activity is going on immediately behind my seat. The voices are loud but unclear through my helmet.

"What's going on, Chief?" I ask Thompson over the intercom.

"This guy won't let his buddy go! Sir. He's still holding on to him . . . won't let nobody else touch him."

Both Ingamar and I turn to look. His buddy is dead. His lips and fingernails are already blue. We did not make it in time.

"Shut her down, Ingamar!"

As I begin to unbuckle from the safety straps in the seat, Ray exits his cubicle, and as is customary, opens my door and slides rearward the armored protection plate attached to my seat. I almost step on Ray in my hurry to exit the aircraft. I remove my helmet, and my hair is drenched in sweat. As I run my hand through my hair to push it into some kind of order, I receive the full impact of the situation.

I have hardened my heart to many things, but this scene causes me great anguish. The injured soldier is still holding his buddy tightly as before, still stretched on the floor of the aircraft. His hollow brown eyes meet mine again. His cries send chills down my spine. "Oh God . . . don't let him die, Lord. . . . Oh God, don't let him die." Breaking eye contact with me, he looks beseechingly at the medics who are dressed not in Army olive drab, but in white. They, in turn, look to me for some decision.

"I'll take care of him. Please let us alone," he wails with tears flooding his eyes.

As one of the medics for the second time reaches in to take his buddy away, the injured man's facial expression changes abruptly. He ceases his wailing and growls like a cornered animal. I notice something that the others may not have—an M16 rifle tucked away under the bloody remains. This could get more serious before it's over.

"His name is Richards, sir," Denning, standing beside me, says softly in my ear.

"How do you know that?"

"I saw his name on his jacket."

I step forward toward Richards and ask him to let go so the doctors can help his buddy. His face relaxes; I dare not reveal to him that his buddy is already gone.

I continue to plead, as the rotor blades overhead finally coast to a stop. Stillness replaces the loud grinding noises of the Huey's transmission. For now, there is only a sobering quietness; no war, no loss of a friend, just Richards and me.

The medics take a chance and again slowly move in with the stretcher. Richards relaxes his hold this time. One medic produces a "body bag." When Richards catches sight of this, he grabs his buddy tightly again as the medics are sliding it off the cargo floor.

"No body bags . . . Man! . . . No body bags!!" he screams at the top of his lungs; he leaps into a squat as near to upright as he can inside the Huey. He grimaces insanely as he grabs the loose M16 rifle and points it at the medic personnel.

In a flash, the medic drops the body bag and retreats, first walking backward, then turning and running full speed toward the sandbag–protected tent that serves as operations facility for the "Mercy" detachment.

Time and movement freeze for ten seconds. Finally Richards relaxes a little, then looks directly at me. Maybe now he is returning to the real world around him. So far in this war, I have been able to avoid this kind of thing. Two small tears begin to trickle down the contours of my face. At first only one or two, then, as the emotion of the incident gradually makes itself felt, I retrieve a handkerchief from my trouser pocket and wipe both eyes.

Looking straight at Richards I whisper, "Man . . . I did my best."

Pondering what I have just said, Richards seems moved by someone else's compassion for his buddy. He leaps from the aircraft and lands in a half-crouching position with his M16 in his right hand, the barrel pointed toward the ground. He rises slowly to a completely upright posture and throws his arms around my shoulders. Embracing me tightly, he says softly, "I know you did all you could, man. You did all you could." Now the situation reverses itself: He is in control of his emotions and I lose mine.

We both shed more tears and do so without shame. I listen as he talks about his friend for the next 20 minutes. Then we say our goodbyes to each other. He follows his buddy's body into the tent, and I strap back into the Huey and crank. It is a low circling flight to the POL (petroleum, oil, and lubrication station), where we take on fuel and, eventually, enter the Python landing area in a low hover. No one utters a word throughout the brief flight. The entire crew is heartbroken, not just for the young dead soldier we did not know, but also for his friend and his family who will learn, in a matter of hours, of their loss.

Not until 126's blades come to a complete stop do the four of us discover how mentally and physically exhausted we are.

During the walk down from the "'hill" toward the company area, I finally have a moment for my own thoughts. Today I cheated death again, but how many more trials like this will there be? Today I successfully accomplished a glorious aviation feat of helicopter pilotage and I felt good about it. Back in the States, completion of such a heroic task would have brought great credit upon myself and the crew, but in Vietnam this is just another day. Avoiding conversations, I retire to my open-air sleeping quarters. My flying is over for today. I smoke a bowl full of tobacco in my pipe, drink two cans of semi-cold beer, and then lapse into sleep.

I try to dream of Pat and of a tranquil September day in Carrollton, Georgia, but I cannot. So many things have happened to me in such a short period of time that my dreams won't obey. Tonight, deep sleep brings images of leaving the California coast behind as I begin my journey into manhood.

2

1st Air Cavalry Division: My New Home

June 10, 1967

The Standard Airways Boeing 707 jet is slicing through crystal-clear air at a speed of nearly 500 mph somewhere off the coast of California. I have never been this high above the earth, yet this combat-loaded airplane struggles for even more altitude on its long journey to Vietnam.

Peering out the small porthole window, I am awed by the beauty of a sky that seems to go forever in all directions. Far below I can see the pale blue ocean; but except for the sandpaper texture made by the tiny waves, it lacks detail. Far to the east I see the coastline, but I dread the moment it will move from my view. Once it is gone, I will not see it again for another year. I—or my body—will return sooner only if I'm unlucky, God forbid.

It's 0700 hours. Less than an hour ago, I boarded this plane in San Francisco and was glad to escape the Army's late night stockyard in-processing environment. But at least there I had no time to think; now in the quiet and solitude, I am again in touch with my soul. I find it hollow with loneliness yet filled with the uncertainties that lie ahead. Never before have I been so mixed-up emotionally—so far from home and surrounded by so many strangers. I could use a friend.

"Excuse me, sir." An apologetic voice and an elbow disturb my self-pity. Contorting himself, a soldier in the seat to my left is attempting to retrieve a magazine that has slipped from his lap onto the floor.

"Let me get it for you." I, too, have to scrunch up a bit, but finally I am able to retrieve what turns out to be this month's issue of *Playboy*.

As I return it to its rightful owner, the centerfold accidentally extends itself, partially exposing Miss June 1967. Positioning the book vertically and not quite ready to let go, I complete the task of fully exposing her. Gaping intently, only gradually do I become aware of the hot breath emanating not only from the soldier to my left but from the three guys immediately behind me.

"My God!" the three men groan almost in unison.

"All right, you guys, don't look. This is my sister!" the magazine's owner wisecracks as he again takes possession of it. "Not bad, sir . . . don't you think?"

"Nope, not bad at all." Turning slightly I address the three hanging on the back of my chair. "You guys best get a long look-see 'cause there are no round-eyed ladies like this in Vietnam."

"That's OK, sir. I heard the Vietnamese women aren't dogs."

I turn further left to address the speaker. "That's what I've heard, too. My instructor pilots at Rucker told me the Vietnamese women are pleasing to look at."

"Rucker? Are you a pilot, sir?"

"Dumb ass," my acquaintance to my immediate left answers for me. "Where did you think he got those silver wings pinned on his chest, at the PX? Sir, glad to meet you. I'm Private Gary Rowlings, and these other three guys are Larry, Curly, and Moe." It is clear that the foursome know each other very well.

"Don't pay him any attention, sir. He's been bucking for a bruising since Fort Polk," says one.

"We're going to bleed him when we get to Nam!" adds another.

"Fort Polk, Louisiana? That's where I took basic training. Leesville . . . I guess it's still there?"

"Yes, sir, it's still there."

"Mister Johnson will do just fine, guys." I tell them. "Let's drop the "Sir" stuff. I'm Tom Johnson from Carrollton, Georgia." Having graduated from Fort Rucker, Alabama, only 30 days ago, I still feel a little uncomfortable being an officer.

Before graduation, warrant officer candidates are reminded every waking hour that they are the lowest-ranking persons in the Army. Although this is untrue, generous amounts of West Point–style hazing have humbled all of us to the point where we salute anything wearing a uniform regardless of rank. Then suddenly, in one graduation cere-mony, we went "above the best."

"How did you get into helicopter flight school, Mister Johnson?" Gary Rowlings asks, bringing me back to the present.

"I really didn't have a choice. I've flown since I was fourteen years old. One day I met the Army recruiter in my mother-in-law's office. She's head of the Veterans' Service at home. Recruiters drive to Car-rollton from Atlanta once a week and use her office to fill their quotas. It happened that one day the Army recruiter visited me at home on a Saturday. He convinced me that I was about to be drafted. He said, 'You can get drafted and walk for two years or join up and fly for four, but you're going to Vietnam one way or the other.' I was convinced he was telling the truth, so I joined."

"Flight school as tough as I've heard?" the one identified as Moe inquires.

"You bet! A lot tougher than I ever imagined. Counting basic train-ing at Polk, primary in Mineral Wells, Texas, and advanced training at Rucker, my hell-on-earth lasted a year. Rotary Wing Class 67-5 started at Wolters with about 320 prospective pilots. Forty-two got the ax dur-ing preflight without ever laying a hand on a helicopter. I think an-other thirty-five got 'pink-slipped' out of the course during primary 'cause they couldn't learn to fly. Another thirty or so got the ax at Rucker. In the end, 67-5 became a mixture of those of us who started with it plus candidates from previous classes who had been recycled. On graduation day, the total was 283."

"You married, Mister Johnson?" Gary asks.

"Oh, yeah. Pat was my high school sweetheart. We got married when she was fifteen and I was sixteen."

"Oh, yeah! Me too. I married in February. I really didn't want to till I got back from Nam, but I found out Karen was three months pregnant." Gary Rowlings smiles a little bit. "Hey, we dated for two years and I really love her. I just wish I could have waited until after Nam." He daydreams in the silence for a moment. "I'll be a father in August if everything goes OK."

"Gentlemen, this is your captain speaking." The intercom blares throughout the aircraft. "Our route will take us to Anchorage, Alaska, then to Yokohama, Japan, then to our destination, Bien Hoa, Republic of South Vietnam. We will be cruising at an altitude of 45,000 feet. With current forecast winds, we should arrive in Bien Hoa about 22 hours from now." Loud moaning fills the Boeing 707. "Because we are racing around the globe with the sun, it will be nineteen hours from now before you see a sunset. On behalf of Standard Airways and your crew, we want to make your journey as pleasant as possible."

It is a very dark night when the airplane finally passes over the coast of Vietnam. What has been a reasonably noisy flight grows quiet when the captain reports that we are in country and wishes us the best of luck.

I make a hasty trip to the lavatory, and as I push my way down the dimly lit aisle, I wonder how many of these mostly adolescent Americans will return home in the same condition in which they have arrived. Perhaps they also are wondering if they might go home in a body bag.

After landing we are all processed at Bien Hoa. Gary Rowlings and the other three are also headed for the 1st Air Cavalry, and they promise to look me up someday. In jest, I offer them a helicopter ride if they do. We say our good-byes and walk in different directions.

I fly by a C-130 Military Assistance Command, Vietnam (MACV), Air Force cargo plane 250 miles north to the city of An Khe, home of the 1st Air Cavalry Division. An Khe's official name is Camp Radcliff, named after a Major Radcliff, killed in an advance party trying to set up the area prior to the Cav's arrival from Columbus, Georgia.

Vietnam is divided into four tactical areas of operations, with Camp Radcliff in what the Army calls the II Corps area. I Corps is at the far north of the country bordering on the DMZ (demilitarized zone) that separates North Vietnam from South Vietnam. South of I Corps is II Corps, the largest of the four areas. An Khe is located in the upper portion of II Corps, midway between the South China Sea to the east and Cambodia to the west. Next is III Corps, then IV Corps, which is located in the extreme southern part of the country and is made up of river deltas. To me, the rolling hills and scrub bushes of the Central Highlands that surround An Khe are reminiscent of Fort Wolters, Texas.

Radcliff is the world's largest heliport, a sprawling 300-acre complex on uneven, treeless ground. Near its western perimeter is a small (by Georgia standards) hill named Hong Kong Mountain, better known as

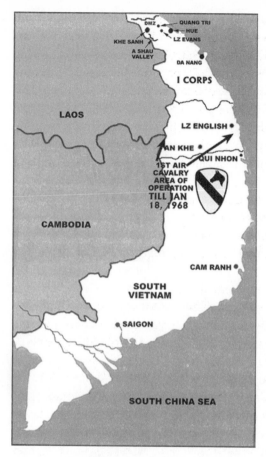

Signal Mountain. On its top is a collection of communications antennas and Signal personnel. To the east, just outside the perimeter, is the Song Ba River, which flows lazily southward toward the town of An Khe.

Signal Mountain is one of God's little mistakes in this country, for Radcliff rests on a plateau. Other than the mountain range some 20 miles to the east, there are no other hills anywhere in any direction. This makes Hong Kong Mountain look mystically out of place.

An Khe is the logistical operations hub of the Cav, but the forward tactical base is LZ English, which is east of An Khe and some 40 miles north of Qui Nhon on the coast of the South China Sea. Only 2 miles northwest of LZ English, the southern end of the An Lao valley opens into the coastal plains.

Within 2 miles southwest of LZ English is the town of Bong Son, which stretches along the banks of the Bong Son River. It is here that the Cav sets up its forward tactical operations and control center, known simply as "Black Horse." It is comprised of the division-grade officers and staff who oversee the entire 1st Cavalry deployment.

When I arrive at the Cav in June 1967, the mission is to clear and secure a 1600-square-mile area that stretches from the South China Sea coast to the Cambodian border. The mission is dubbed Operation

Pershing. At the Cav's helm is a street-brawling major general named John "Jack" Norton. General Norton took over from General Kinnard on May 6, 1966.

The 1st Cavalry Division consists of many specialized elements. Forces that fly troops and their supplies into battle are known as assault helicopter battalions (AHB). First Cav has two of these battalions: the 227th and the 229th. Each consists of three companies of troop-carrying helicopters, called slicks, and one company of gunship helicopters, called guns. Companies A, B, and C are the slicks, and D is the gunship company.

During initial processing, I am assigned to A Company of the 229th AHB. When I arrive at the company rear area, I find it empty except for a very small cadre needed to do the paperwork. I soon learn that I will not be staying in An Khe very long; I will be with most of the Cav at LZ English. I will catch the next Huey for English in the morning.

It is only 1400 hours, Vietnam time, but the trip over and the extensive processing into the unit have taken their toll on my body. My body clock is totally out of whack, so I lie down for some badly needed rest.

"Sir . . . sir, excuse us, but can you tell me how far it is to Carrollton, Georgia?" Wiping sleep from my eyes as I rise from my bunk, I see two figures standing in the doorway of my officer quarters billet.

"Carrollton, Georgia, is a long way from Vietnam!" the other voice says.

Much to my disbelief, standing in my room halfway around the world, are two guys I have known for years—Doyal Shirey and Joe Wayne Mashburn. They are stationed at An Khe and have read in the hometown paper that I am headed to the 1st Cavalry.

"Hey, what are the poor people doing today?" I ask.

"They're all in Vietnam!" they reply in unison.

This is the uplift that I dearly need. Having arrived many months before, these old friends from my other life begin filling me in on the current situation. Doyal's job is working on helicopters that cannot be fixed at the forward bases. He vividly describes damage done to the Hueys by AK-47s and other hostile weapons. His conversation unsettles me somewhat.

The three of us spend a very good afternoon together, and I listen intently to all they have to say about living in Vietnam. When they depart, I light up my pipe and rest. I have been issued a Smith & Wesson .38 pistol with holster, standard issue for a pilot. My recent conversation makes me decide to keep it nearer to my person than I originally intended. Earlier, I felt out of place wearing the sidearm, but now I feel it to be necessary to my survival. I just cannot yet imagine being shot by another person; but even less can I imagine shooting another person with intent to kill.

As the sunlight fades on my first night in Vietnam, I feel alone and desperate. I have the billet in which I am currently housed to myself, and it is getting spooky. A wire ventilation screen runs around the top of the thin plywood sides of the structure. The exposed roof support beams are made of pine 2-by-4s. Upper and lower bunks jut from each long side of the building, which is much longer than it is wide. It could sleep about 30 officers; and there are no privacy partitions, so I can see from one end to the other. On closer inspection, I see planks laid at irregular intervals across the A-frame roof supports, and on these planks I see various types of baggage including tote bags and suitcases. I've been told that occasionally A/229th is given a little R&R here in An Khe. I can imagine myself here someday, swapping flying stories with the other one-day-old pilots and drinking lots of beer.

The lighting in the billet—five clear 60-watt bulbs strung haphazardly on a wire over the center aisle of the building—makes stark, ghostly shadows appear everywhere. Occasionally I hear large bugs hitting the tin partitions or screens in their futile attempts to reach the lightbulbs. Doyal and Joe Wayne have already told me about large indigenous spiders that like to crawl into boots. With this on my mind I stuff my socks into the tops of my boots immediately after removing them. I decide that the safest place might be in a top bunk. Very tired, I begin removing my jungle fatigues in preparation for bed. After seeing that the only light switch lies at the opposite end of the billet, I move all my belongings to that end. It's time for lights-out; I walk barefoot to the light switch and turn it off.

Pausing to look through the screen door, I see bright lights in the distance. I remember hearing that An Khe's perimeter is ringed with high-intensity lighting. In a flashback, I recall that one of my last instructors in Rucker had been in the Cav. He told me that the perimeter of this, the world's largest heliport, is a cleared area containing multiple barbed-wire fences. This no-man's-land is also mined, and after sundown it is so brightly lit that on a clear night pilots can use it as a navigation reference from 50 miles away.

The temperature outside has cooled somewhat, making the air very humid. As I lie on my bunk, the night noises seem to become louder and louder. Uneven footsteps outside sound sneaky to me. I have heard tales of sappers who slip into camps at night with satchels of explosives. I slide my hand under the pillow where the pistol lies and listen more intently, relaxing only when the sound dies away.

After about two hours of light dozing, a sound overhead startles me awake. Motionless in the dark, I strain all my senses, trying to picture what is causing the sounds. It is no bug, for sure. It moves unevenly, pausing for a few seconds at a time. It is also very heavy, for I can hear the 2-by-4s creaking under the weight. Crack! A rifle is fired right above my head!

Grabbing the .38 revolver, I fall headlong from the top bunk, hitting the concrete floor in a squat. The noises don't make sense yet. It sounds more like something or someone crawling among the rafters rather than on the roof. In escape and survival training, one is taught to look away slightly from an object one is trying to identify at night. This works well enough for me to see something very large directly overhead.

I am so scared I find the next breath hard to take. I methodically ease nearer to the light switch, keeping aim on the object. My heart pounds in my ears. Half-afraid of what the lights might reveal, but afraid not to look, I flip up the toggle switch.

I start, stumbling backward, knocking over two bunk beds and yelling obscenities at the top of my lungs. Suddenly two specialist fourth class soldiers, summoned from the next building by all the ruckus, race through the doorway to my right with M16 rifles in the firing position. Both look at me with blank, frightened stares.

"Look in the damned rafters!" I shriek, motioning above my bunk.

They look, then look back at me with faces unchanged. "Sir . . . that's George . . . you know . . . our mascot."

"Mascot?" My fear does not diminish. "Mascot, my ass! That's the biggest snake I have ever seen in my entire blessed life, and you guys are telling me it's your frigging mascot!"

"No, sir, he's not *our* mascot—he's the company's mascot, sir!" they say apologetically, noticing that I still have a violently shaking finger curled around the trigger of the .38 revolver I am gesturing with. Apparently I am the most pissed-off warrant officer they have ever seen. "Sir, A/229th is known as the Python flight, and ol' George is a python snake!"

"What the devil is this thing doing in my quarters?!"

"Sir, we let George out of his cage all the time in these empty buildings. He eats the rats and other snakes! Someone just forgot that old George is in this building tonight! He's really harmless."

George is at least 25 feet long and maybe 9 or 10 inches in diameter. I would guess his weight at approximately 300 pounds. He is the largest snake I have ever seen anywhere.

As I calm down and my shaking diminishes, the two specialist fours invite me to spend the night with them in the next building. The invitation is accepted when I find out that they have in their possession an illegal bottle of my favorite drink—Jack Daniel's.

Sleep is out of the question for all concerned, so the three of us just drink away what is left of the night. As "Jack" relaxes me and my tongue, I tell them about another snake in my life.

■

I arrived for boot camp at Fort Polk, Louisiana, on May 6, 1966, and without my authorization, was immediately appointed squad leader for the barracks. This position of responsibility taught me something new: Not only did I have to get along with others in very confined quarters, but I had to depend on them. When a member of my squad screwed up, we all paid for it.

There was a guy from New Jersey in the squad. He was intelligent by all standards, but had been raised in a tough neighborhood and then drafted into this man's Army. His name was Jeremy Crowder, and he was a purposeful screwup during every waking hour. Everything that could be done to disrupt authority, Jeremy would do in an efficient manner. He did not fit in with the rest of us and went out of his way to remind us of this. The squad was punished on a regular and repeated basis for his attitude and behavior.

47

*One hot June night the entire squad had to pay for one of Jeremy's viola-
tions by carrying their heavy footlockers as they fell out and ran around the
entire company area three times. It was the last straw. Upon our return from
this 2 1/2 mile run, I advised Jeremy to get his act together or face the consequences.*

*That same June night, after my warning to Jeremy, I slithered into my
top bunk—slithered so as not to disturb the hospital folds at the corners of the
blankets. Every smart recruit entered his bed in this manner to reduce the
amount of time it would take to make the bed for inspection the following
morning. However, this night when my feet reached the bottom of my bed,
something else was slithering there! It was cold and clammy, and traveled
very quickly up between my legs.*

*In my haste to resolve the crisis, I managed to turn over not only my own
bunk, but also several others down the row, thanks to the domino effect. I
landed on the hardwood barrack floor with a resounding thud, much to the
surprise of other recruits around me who were watching in total amazement.*

*Out of the debris—torn covers and metal bunk supports—crawled one
non–military-issue snake that was immediately pounced upon by a dozen
shoe-wielding troops. The critter was hardy; it was not until the eighth person
and the 144th attempted shoe bashing that it finally succumbed in a blaze of
guts and no glory.*

"Where the devil is Jeremy!" I demanded aloud.

*"He's in the shower, I think," answered several different recruits, almost
at once.*

*I proceeded to upright my footlocker, collect my scattered personal be-
longings, and place them neatly inside. I picked up a large can of Right Guard
deodorant. I reached inside my olive drab Army issue fatigue pants to recover a Zippo lighter, which I had carried for years. I found Jeremy in the
shower, and much to my good luck, the opportunity of the year presented
itself: Jeremy had just dropped his washcloth on the floor and bent over to
retrieve it. Jeremy's back was to me, and two circular components of his male
anatomy were swinging freely between his skinny thighs. With the precision
of a surgeon burning off a wart, I held the deodorant can 6 inches away from
the target area and pressed down firmly on the aerosol nozzle. At the same
time I flicked the flame from the Zippo into the path of the mist emanating
from the Right Guard canister.*

The shower erupted into a storm of foul and violent language mixed with the smell of burning hair and flesh. Jeremy did what anyone would have done in the same predicament; he ran, dancing from side to side to evade his assailant while continuing to put out the fire. I did my best to stay behind him and light up his skinny round ass as fast as the Zippo would strike.

Naked as a jaybird, Jeremy bolted out of the barracks at full throttle with me right behind. The following day witnesses reported that every time I struck the torch, Jeremy took a different stride.

I gave up the pursuit in the middle of the parade field and returned amidst a round of applause and laughter from the entire barracks.

Jeremy did not return for the morning assembly, and this did not go unnoticed by the company executive officer, who had apparently heard scuttle-butt about the previous night. I was immediately pulled from formation and called on the carpet for a question-and-answer session. Never having been around officers before, I feared them more than the snake. Instead of telling a tactical lie, I told the truth. When the company commander, Captain Francis Cummings, and the executive officer, 2nd Lieutenant Robert Sanchez, got through with my butt, there was not enough of it left to sit on a commode. They used sharp language to refer to my character and leadership as a warrant officer candidate and viciously declared that I was not officer material and would never make it in flight school.

When finally dismissed, I was certain I had just made the mistake that would cost me my dream of flight school. They were sure to shoot my mother, rape my dog, and court-martial me all in the same day. That notion was shattered when, upon leaving, I overheard Cummings trying to stifle a laugh. Sanchez whispered something about how it was a good thing they didn't allow recruits to keep their rifles.

Anyway, old Jeremy never came back. He went AWOL and was hardly missed by anyone at Company D 1st Battalion 1st Brigade.

■

With tears of laughter in our eyes, all three of us lapse into sleep in the early hours of the morning.

"Mister Johnson, you have a bird en route to take you to English!" A voice awakens me from sleep.

Pushing up on one elbow in the bunk, I nod that I understand, and the stranger disappears through the screen door. I have a Jack

Daniel's headache, aggravated no doubt by the lack of food and sleep. I am now, for the first time in several days, actually hungry. I rub my hands through my hair and look at my watch. It is nearly 1000 hours Vietnam time and long past morning chow call. I look around, but the specialist fours from last night are nowhere to be seen. I guess they've gotten up right on time and are already performing their regular jobs.

As I struggle to pack up all my belongings, sweat beads on my forehead and runs into my eyes. My jungle fatigues become drenched in sweat, changing from Army drab to a deeper green. I can't tell if this is the Jack Daniel's or the tropical heat. I estimate that the temperature is already over 90 degrees. The humidity is exceptionally high, making it seem much hotter than it really is.

My head says "ouch" as I step outside into the bright Vietnam sunshine, lugging two duffel bags. As the pain increases, I know it is the Jack Daniel's, not the heat.

"Heard about your meeting up with George last night, sir!" A sergeant who processed me yesterday chirps with a grin on his face as he grabs for the heavy duffel bags. "Let me help you. The jeep's right over there." He gestures toward the rear of the headquarters building. "Ol' George is certainly a big one, ain't he?"

I simply do not feel sociable enough to carry on a conversation with anyone right now, so I just nod my head, climb into the jeep, and head toward the "Golf Course," the world's largest heliport.

I have not seen so many helicopters parked in one place since I departed Rucker. Hueys are parked side by side, pointing either east or west in lines running north and south. Each Huey is protected on each side by a sandbag wall. Each line of Hueys is about one-half mile in length.

"That's just a fraction of all the Hueys, sir," the sergeant volunteers. I guess he noticed my amazement. "None of the Cav's units are back here at An Khe right now. It's a sight to see when they are."

I notice a Huey that has just landed, its blades still coasting to a stop as we pull alongside. The aircraft doesn't shine like those at Fort Rucker. Instead, the top of its tail boom is covered with smut from the turbine exhaust outlet. The crew shows even more wear-and-tear than the Huey. Their fatigues look unwashed and disheveled. Their baseball caps, put on after removing their flight helmets, have nasty dark sweat rings. The sergeant and I look out of place.

"How's it going?" I address the entire crew as I carefully approach the Huey on foot, crouching low to avoid the large rotor blades still coasting overhead.

At first they are too busy to care about my presence. The gunner is grabbing for a rotor blade, now stationary. The crew chief is busy peeking into the various confines of the engine and transmission compartments, doing a postflight on the aircraft. One pilot is busy removing his chest protector and securing the loose items in the cockpit. The aircraft commander is finishing his write-up of the trip just completed in the aircraft's logbook—the Dash Five. I continue to stand by the aircraft on the commander's side, still waiting for some reply, until the crew chief says, "Excuse me, sir," as he brushes me aside on his way to the open pilot's door. He steps onto the skid tip, unshackles the armor plate, and places it behind the commander's seat. When the seat is in the forward position this appendage will stop a bullet of up to 30 calibers. But it limits the pilot's visibility considerably. And it is nearly impossible to exit the aircraft unless the armor plate has been slid into the rearmost position. As the crew chief finishes moving the plate and brushes by me again to continue the postflight, the aircraft commander unceremoniously exits the Huey, ass first.

"You must be the replacement?" he quizzes, first removing his flight gloves, then offering his hand.

"Yes, sir!" I reply, shaking his hand and feeling a little uncomfortable, seeing the captain's insignia on his fatigues. "Sir, I've been told not to salute over here. Is that true?"

"That's true! Don't!" is his reply as his eyes search my fatigue shirt for the name label. "Mister Johnson, I presume?"

"Yes, sir!"

"I'm Captain LuRay, executive officer for A/229th, and this is Mister Leggett!" he says, introducing the pilot still sitting in the other cockpit. With a broad smile, he points a finger in the direction of Leggett. "This ugly bastard will be leaving us day after tomorrow! He's headed back to the States, and you'll be taking his place!"

An emptiness penetrates my soul. Here both ends of the tour of duty in Nam meet: I have three days behind me, he has two to go. God, how I envy this man, and I don't even know him.

LuRay looks about 35 or so, which means he's probably a senior captain about to make major. He's about my height, but a good deal heavier. From his accent, I guess he's a Midwesterner.

"We won't be going right out, Mister Johnson! I've got some very necessary paperwork to do here, and Mister Leggett has just one more flight duty to perform as a member of A/229th. Occasionally we have to fly 'ash-and-trash' for the perimeter guys, and today is 229th day."

"Ash-and-trash, sir?"

"Yeah. It's a milk run—resupply of the perimeter people pulling guard duty. Mister Leggett will be in charge and has graciously agreed to take you with him while I finish my other duties. We'll leave for English sometime late this afternoon." LuRay walks past me toward the jeep where the sergeant is waiting. He motions for the sergeant to place my bags back into the jeep.

With LuRay's departure, Leggett exits from the Huey and introduces himself. "Want to go with me?" he asks.

"Sure . . ."

"Better grab your helmet from your bags, then!"

Shocked at my forgetfulness, I run to the rear of the Huey just in time to flag down LuRay's jeep and rummage around through my two duffel bags until I find my helmet.

When I return, Leggett is leaning against the sandbag wall looking over his map. I guess he's about the same age as me. He is very skinny, also like me, maybe 120 pounds soaking wet. His skin is tanned dark by the Vietnam sun, and his dark hair is slightly longer than the stateside Army would allow. Although he's a warrant officer like me, Leggett immediately gives the impression of someone superior in ability and aptitude. I have to resist calling him "sir."

When the crew chief is satisfied that his Huey can fly, the gunner unties the rotor blades, swings them 90 degrees from the helicopter's axis, and climbs back on board.

As Leggett helps me get reacquainted with Huey design and controls, he maintains a patter of small talk, not about the war, but about the excitement he feels at going home: all those girls to do, all those fast cars to buy. He is very interested when I mention my 1967 Camaro; he has only seen Camaros in pictures. For a moment, I see him as Robinson Crusoe. Home has changed a great deal while he's been gone.

Once we get everything up to speed and are ready to hover, Leggett looks at me and speaks words that I will never forget.

"Johnson, look . . . this is my last flight of my last day in Vietnam! *You* are the only thing between *me* and that Boeing 707 out of Cam Ranh Bay! I want you to keep your mouth shut and your hands in your lap, and don't touch anything in this helicopter unless I tell you to. OK?"

This is unexpected, to say the least, and a 180-degree reversal from his attitude of just a few seconds ago. But I have been out of touch with a Huey for over a month now and really do not care to fly. I just nod my head, since the proper intercom reply would violate his instructions by requiring me to touch the intercom button on the cyclic stick.

Leggett pulls us into a smooth hover, then requests permission to "high hover" to some infantry unit's pad. We do so and are met by several people who proceed to load the Huey's cargo area with canisters of hot food and ammo. We high hover to different points around the perimeter, unloading stuff and taking on stuff. I keep silent, as requested, simply taking in the sights while Leggett does his last job in Vietnam. After about five or six sorties from the supply pad, he gets softhearted and asks if I would like to fly the next run.

I am not feeling left out because I am simply enjoying being airborne again in the Huey, but at his request, I take my position on the controls. He releases them with a "You got it."

When the Huey is loaded, Leggett gets permission to take off and gives me the thumbs-up sign—*go to hover*. I pull up on the collective control feeling a little cocky and wanting to strut my stuff as an aviator. Only thing is, the Huey simply gets light on the skids, and the low rpm warning light and buzzer go off. I have never experienced this before. I reduce the collective slightly, making the helicopter heavy again and allowing the rpm of the engine to pick back up to 6600 rpm. Again, I pull up on the collective, with the same results.

"Having a little trouble, Johnson?" Leggett asks sadistically. I can almost hear the crew chief and gunner giggling in the back.

"Seems like we're overgrossed! She doesn't want to fly—she's too heavy!"

"Here, let me try. I've got it!"

"You have it!" I reply.

53

Leggett pulls up slowly just as I did, and the Huey rises to a 2-foot hover without even a whimper.

"No, we're OK, Johnson. Try it again. You have it!" Leggett says after putting the Huey back on the ground.

Again, I try, with the same results: rpm warnings go off all over the place, and the dang thing just will not clear the pad below us.

"Let me show you something, Johnson; you're overcontrolling. Just relax. When you start to wipe out the cockpit with the cyclic, you lose lift!" Leggett demonstrates using an exaggerated roundhouse motion with the cyclic control. "This is a D model UH-1 Huey with an 1100 horsepower turbine engine, which does just fine at Fort Rucker, Alabama, but over here, due to the density altitude, it's like having a 900 horsepower engine and trying to do the same job. You'll have to learn all over what you thought you knew about flying this machine. Now, get on the controls with me as I hover. OK."

I do as I'm told, but I cannot feel the difference between what he's doing and what I was doing. Nevertheless, he has my undivided attention.

As he talks, the Huey rises to a hover. "All right, you have it now. Just nose it over a little—I mean a little—and start your forward motion."

Ever so slowly, I start applying forward pressure on the cyclic, endeavoring to coax the UH-1 into some type of forward motion, but knowing that any time you move off the cushion of air that forms under a helicopter while it is in a hover, you lose lift. Normally, to compensate for this loss of lift, you must pull up more on the collective for more power. The engine on this bird is already maxed out. That means only one thing is possible: settling back to the ground with forward motion. The thought of this begins to unnerve me somewhat because once we've left the safety of this pad, there will be nothing but ditches and barbed-wire beneath us.

"Come on, Johnson . . . you're rushing it . . . you're rushing it . . . back off just slightly; baby it . . . baby it . . . that's right . . . that's right, now . . . a little more forward pressure . . . she'll fly!"

The Huey clears the pad, and about the same time, the low rpm alerts begin blaring and red lights flashing. Again, like last night, my adrenaline rises. At Rucker, the Army attempts to duplicate heavily loaded Hueys by putting very large drums of water in the cargo compartments. Although this works to some degree, the fear doesn't reach the same level, because one of those gods, the instructor pilots, is always in the other seat. As the instructor is with you, you feel that you will never get hurt. Today there is no instructor with me; there is only Leggett, just another pilot like myself, albeit one who has already pushed the aircraft past any limits I have seen before.

"Milk it . . . Milk it . . . let off the power just a little . . . trade it for airspeed . . . that's it . . . that's it!"

I respond to Leggett's commands without hesitation. Things are already out of control as far as I'm concerned. As the Huey begins to settle for a certain crash into the second row of barbed-wire, she suddenly lurches through translational speed and begins to fly almost at the point of wire contact.

"OK, Johnson, we're flying. Take a little power out and let the engine catch up a little!" The jolt of entering translational speed has taken me so unawares that I have already begun to take out power instinctively. Now the aircraft does begin to respond to my control movements—just like the last one I flew at Fort Rucker.

"That's all right, Johnson. All you need is a little practice, and you'll get plenty of that in Vietnam. Do you want to take her in?" When Leggett looks over at me with this question, he breaks out in a big grin. I am drenched in sweat, and this time it isn't Jack Daniel's or the heat, either.

Like an accident looking for some place to happen, I reply, "Sure, why not!"

Leggett immediately begins to direct me to the place where we are to land; unlike the others, it is outside the perimeter. As we approach, the camouflage-clad group of soldiers below pops a smoke grenade to better identify their exact position, and the drifting smoke gives us wind direction. A pilot should always land his aircraft into the wind, especially if it's a loaded aircraft. Throughout the landing pattern, and during final approach, Leggett talks his head off, and I do the best I can to listen and control the Huey at the same time.

On short final, some 100 feet in the air and 1/4 mile or so from touchdown, Leggett gives me a good one.

"Johnson . . . if you overcontrol at the bottom of this approach, this baby will run out of power." There is a new seriousness to his tone of voice. "Don't try to hover because she can't do it! Shoot your approach all the way to the ground . . . don't stop . . . OK?"

Crap, I have only done two or three landings to the ground without a hover at Rucker, and they were in ideal conditions on a smooth asphalt runway. The dangers here are many. First, I need exceptional depth perception to judge the rate of closure to the ground I am about to land on, else I might get a very hard impact. Second, timing—I have to keep up my forward speed until the last moment, just above the touchdown area to remain in translational speed. This is the main purpose of a "running landing." Since it requires far less power to fly than to hover, if I time it right, I might be running out of power only at the touchdown point. Third, this type of approach offers little time to judge the condition of the landing area for stumps, vines, and other obstructions. Should I hit one of these just right, the aircraft could flip over before I have time to stop it. At Rucker I felt reasonably comfortable with my approaches of this type, not only because of the instructor pilot, but because the Huey at Rucker seemed to have an unlimited amount of power available. This extra power was my ace in the hole to save my butt should I foul up that bad. Now Leggett is calmly telling me that the Huey doesn't have enough power to stop down there at the end of this thing.

"Keep up your speed, Johnson . . . don't stop out here . . . you're looking good . . . keep your approach going . . . looking good!" His words of encouragement help, but I am already way outside my comfort zone.

As we pass over the threshold of the LZ at 15 knots forward speed and a 100-feet-per-minute rate of descent, dirt and debris begin flying in all directions in the 100 mph winds produced by the loaded Huey. The 48-foot blade system overhead is now churning the air all around us as we fall through translational lift right on cue. The rate of descent accelerates dramatically. In an unpremeditated move, I pull up farther and farther on the collective to slow it. Just before impact, I push abruptly forward on the cyclic to change the Huey's tail low landing posture into a level one for impact.

In a jumping flash it is all over. Just as I level, the skids of the Huey touch down so softly they would not have broken an egg. I relax pressure on the collective and push it all the way to the downward stop so that we will stay right where the best approach I have ever made has placed me.

"Johnson . . . there is hope for you yet! That was an excellent approach . . . excellent . . . couldn't have done it better myself! Let's give this new guy a round of applause, guys!" Leggett turns around in his seat clapping, and I can hear the muffled sounds of the two crewmembers in the rear putting their flight-gloved hands together repeatedly.

Little do they know how far over my head I was! Right now, though, I am doing all I can to remain nonchalant about the whole thing, when what I really want to do is exit the aircraft and clean out the seat of my jungle fatigues.

The Huey is empty now, and Leggett insists that I fly us home. This is the last sortie for Leggett, and he is now a very happy man— happy that I didn't crash him, and happy that he is going home.

The approach to the Golf Course is a piece of cake considering what I have just been through. I shoot the approach to a hover in a very wide corridor between the parked Hueys. Leggett then points out the bunker assigned to us, and once again puts his life into my hands by allowing me to hover the aircraft into the narrow space between the two sandbag walls. I do so with some consternation, but without fault.

With the flight over, I say my good-byes to Leggett and tell him from deep within my heart how brave a person he must be to have let me fly him today. Leggett just grins and heads toward the waiting 229th jeep that has arrived to pick him up and to drop off Captain LuRay. Leggett waves and wishes me the best of luck, then drives away.

Suddenly my soul stills again. God, if that were only me, I'd be headed home to Pat, and this nightmare would all be behind me.

My next thoughts take me from Warrant Officer Leggett back to my very first helicopter instructor pilot at Fort Wolters, Texas.

■

None of us could wait for our first day of flight training. At reveille, most were already awake and getting dressed. After breakfast and the usual stringent morning inspection of our appearance by our hard-driving 2nd

WOC *(warrant officer candidate) Company—Flight Group A4—tactical officer, George Marcotte, we were bused to the flight line a mile and a half west of the barracks. There, we saw our first military instructor pilots dressed in fluorescent-orange flight suits that made a sharp contrast to our Army-issue dull gray suits. Horror stories about their bad dispositions had us in awe and fear of these Vietnam combat veteran pilots, who would soon be our instructors. For now, however, we would receive eight weeks of basic flight training from more easygoing civilians who were under contract from Southern Airways.*

My first helicopter flight instructor was another Johnson—Richard Johnson—from somewhere on the West Coast. About all any of us knew about him was his name. There was nothing military about Richard; he let you know not to call him "sir" in private, although when in the company of others, everyone had to play the game by military rules. Richard had black hair, which, though neat, was definitely too long by military standards. He was a bachelor who struck one as the party animal type. Slightly taller than me by a couple of inches, he had an athletic build and a deep tan. I guessed his age at 28 or 29.

All the instructors were assigned two candidates for eight weeks of training. Candidate Tom Huhn (pronounced Hewn) and I would be assigned to Richard. On the first day there would be only an orientation flight around the Texas countryside.

After being seated by the candidate in charge of Flight Group A4, Richard introduced himself to Huhn and me, then looked over our personal records, which had been handed to him previously.

"Candidate Huhn, I see you have a college education, you're not married, and you have no previous flying experience. Is that correct?" Richard asked in a normal tone of voice.

"Sir, Candidate Huhn, that is correct, sir," Tom replied almost loud enough for the entire room to hear.

Looking first at Huhn, then at me, Richard smiled. I relaxed considerably, imagining that this might be the first compassionate person I had met since driving on post.

Richard continued with Huhn's background, politely asking how he got into the flight program and what his goals in life were. After this small talk, which was in fact designed to calm us down a little, he opened my dossier.

As he was reading my background data with interest, he looked pleas-

antly surprised. "Johnson, looks like you do not have any college and are already married. I also see that you have a great deal of previous flying time—nearly 200 hours according to this. Is that correct?"

"Yes, sir, but all small plane and very little pilot-in-command time."

"Why is that?" he inquired.

"I started flying when I was fourteen. You had to be sixteen to solo. So most of my flying has been with an instructor or some other pilot. I got married when I was sixteen and did not have the money to pursue it any longer."

"Think you know how to fly a helicopter?"

"I've heard that they are a lot different, but I think I can do it," I replied. Somehow the casual environment Richard had created generated in me a cocky attitude.

"Well, Candidate Johnson, I'll see about that real soon, but first, I have to teach you that there are only two ways to fly: a) the Army way, b) the wrong way! Is that clearly understood?"

"Yes, sir."

I felt slightly relieved when Richard stood up, grabbing his helmet and other flight gear. "OK, Candidate Huhn, you can fly with me first. Johnson, you remain here until 1030 hours, then walk out to the refueling area right over there," pointing out the window behind him. "Our tail number will be 102. Look for me. If you cannot find me, then return here, and I will find you. Is that understood?"

"Yes, sir," I replied. I felt a bit let down that I wouldn't get to try my wings first, but I consoled myself with the thought that when I had my turn, it would be a snap.

Finally 10:29 arrived and I did as I had been instructed. Richard refueled the Hiller OH-23 and I climbed aboard. Exhilaration overtook me as the blades overhead began to whirl and the Lycoming engine roared to operational speed. I was truly excited.

Richard did all the right things, then pulled upward on the collective pitch control, and the Hiller vaulted airborne. I intently watched his every move, hoping to learn something. I should have suspected that this flight was going to be different from Huhn's flight when Richard requested a special takeoff direction from the tower.

Ordering that he remain at an altitude less than 100 feet, they cleared him for an abnormal east departure.

Soon we were sailing like birds just above the treetops. I had never flown like this before. Low-level flying was a definite no-no in fixed-wing flying. I had an adrenaline rush as Richard eased back on the cyclic to clear a small hill, then pushed it forward again, returning the helicopter to its 50-foot altitude.

We soon reached a wide-open field where Richard pulled the Hiller to a stop. We hovered about 4 feet above the grass. Richard began his instruction. Speaking over the intercom, he demonstrated each of the helicopter's controls—cyclic, collective, pedals, and the throttle—and the Hiller responded obediently to each of his motions.

"Candidate Johnson," Richard said, when he had finished his demonstration, "place your right hand on the cyclic stick between your legs." Without hesitation, I shifted my body forward slightly and gripped the constantly moving flight control. "This is your lateral movement control. If you want to go left, you move the cyclic left. If you want to go forward, you move the cyclic forward. Now you try it!"

Using only minuscule movements, called control pressures, not visible movements, I nudged the cyclic stick forward, and sure enough, the helicopter began to move forward. Releasing forward pressure and applying backward pressure on the cyclic to stop the forward motion, I bumped into Richard's hand. This was unexpected, but it was comforting to know his experienced hand was very near the cyclic on this dual control machine. When the OH-23 finally stopped its forward motion, I began to experiment by applying right pressure to the cyclic control—the helicopter began drifting right. Taking out the right pressure and inducing left cyclic, I induced the machine to end its right drift and begin a drift to the left. "This is easy," I mused to myself.

"OK, Candidate Johnson, I have the cyclic!" At this command, I relinquished control back to the boss. "Next is the collective pitch control, which is on the left side of your body. Its function is to change the pitch in the blades collectively, or all at one time. Put your left hand on the collective and feel what I do." I obeyed his request by gingerly cupping my left hand around the collective pitch control. "At a hover, the lift of the blades is equal to the weight of the helicopter. If I decrease the pitch of the blades, then we upset this balance and the helicopter will descend—like this." Ever so gently, Richard pushed down on the collective pitch control and the helicopter stopped hovering and gently impacted the ground beneath us. "Now I will pull up on the collective pitch control, and when the lift generated by the rotor blades exceeds the weight of our helicopter, we will take off—like this." I felt Richard's upward movement of the collective pitch control, and at some point in his *upward pull, the helicopter broke free from the ground and began a vertical rise. The more he pulled, the higher we rose above the ground. At about 12 feet, Richard stopped pulling and with a slight downward movement brought us back to a 3-foot hover again. "Now you try it!"*

I pulled upward on the collective, and we ballooned upward more rapidly than I had intended. With nerves of steel, Richard simply put his hand on the control to stop its movement before we got near heaven. Now for the landing. I felt pretty cocky until the first impact with the ground occurred at about 15 feet per second. The Hiller hit hard and bounced skyward, reminding me that for every candidate's action there will be an equal and opposite reaction. Attempting to stop the upward climb, I overcorrected by putting the collective down rapidly—that's where the second hard landing occurred, only this one was much harder than the first. I wanted to yell, "TAKE IT!" but restrained myself. My pride at this moment was greater than my fear. Determined not to let this happen again, I regained control at about 15 feet in the air, and spent nearly 15 minutes nudging this helicopter beast closer until I finally had it on the ground. "Good job, Candidate Johnson," Richard finally said. "Any landing I can walk away from is a good landing!" He was actually grinning at my collective pitch control episode.

"All right—I have it now!" Richard said, and I released control again. He pulled up on the collective, and the helicopter again soared upward to a 3-foot hover. "Now for the pedals and the throttle. You may have noticed that when you were applying and taking away collective pitch on the blades, I had to roll on and roll off power by twisting on the throttle control located on the collective pitch control. If I had failed to do this, the rpm of the engine would have either decreased with pulling up on collective or increased when you pushed down. We have a 300 rpm envelope on the rpm for this engine!" Richard temporarily removed his right hand from the cyclic and pointed to the tachometer on the console in front of us. "The engine must remain at 3200 rpm at all times! If you get 150 rpm low, you start bending the main rotor blades. If you get over 150 too high, you are overspeeding the engine!" Again Richard pointed to the tachometer, and this time I noticed the rpm envelope he had described was marked in green paint. The rest of the arc was painted red.

"When you apply power, the helicopter will attempt to rotate right on its vertical axis. The opposite is true when you reduce power. The cause of this effect is engine torque. The main rotor system is rotating in a counterclockwise

direction. When you apply power, the torque produced by the engine will at-tempt to rotate the fuselage of the helicopter in the opposite direction to the blades. To offset this effect, you have a small variable pitch anti-torque tail rotor on the tail boom of the helicopter that is controlled by the pedals.

"Watch this, Johnson!" Richard pushed on the left pedal and the heli-copter turned left on its vertical axis. He continued his turn left until we ar-rived back at our initial direction. He then pushed on the right pedal and the Hiller rotated right. Again we did a 360 turn.

"OK, Candidate Johnson, I have the cyclic and the collective! You have the throttle and the pedals—OK?"

I replied, "I have it!" and Richard pulled up abruptly on the collective. The rpm took a nosedive and I rolled on throttle to compensate. With the sud-den application of power, the helicopter turned right on its vertical axis before I could push left pedal.

"3200 rpm!" Richard yelled. A quick glance at the tachometer revealed an engine rpm well below the green arc. Just as I twisted in more throttle, Richard pushed the collective down. Now it all went to hell in a handbasket! The rpm went from 300 rpm below to I don't know how high above the red line, and the helicopter yawed violently from a 30-degree right heading to 40 degrees left of our original heading.

"I HAVE IT!" Richard yelled. I was glad he had taken back the controls, but he did not let me off the hook. Again and again we repeated the exercise until I got it close to right.

Finally the dreaded moment came.

"Now, Johnson, you take over all the controls and hover this helicopter!" Richard spoke this time with laughter in his voice. "Keep us at a 4-foot hover and pointed directly at that scrub bush in front of us!"

Intimidated but still cocky as a barnyard rooster, I graciously accepted his challenge.

Trying to outsmart Richard and the Hiller, I eased my hands around the controls and braced every muscle in my body. I thought that if I held the controls in the exact positions in which Richard handed them over to me, the Hiller would do for me exactly what it had done for him. Boy, this strategy could not have been more wrong. When he gave me total control of the Hiller, the helicopter was motionless at a perfect hover exactly 4 feet from the ground. That lasted exactly two seconds.

First we started drifting right, so I put in a little left cyclic. We contin-

ued going right, only faster, so I put in more left cyclic. I suddenly realized that not only were we drifting to the right at an ever-increasing rate, but our altitude had slipped to where we now felt a major bump as the aircraft's skids gently touched the ground. I pulled up on the collective. The pull caused Richard to tap on the glass of the tachometer. Whereas a second or two ago the gauge was sitting steadily at 3200 rpm, now it was down to 2800 rpm and falling. I had to roll in more throttle to increase the horsepower output of the engine to compensate for the demand of the collective and get me back to 3200. I did this, but I forgot what I had just learned. When you pull in power, the helicopter's fuselage will tend to rotate in the opposite direction of the blades spinning overhead, because of the torque of the motor. For every action, there is an equal and opposite reaction. To compensate for this rotation to the right, one must press the left pedal. "Where is that bush anyway?" I said under my breath, making a vain attempt to return to the original area where this horror had begun.

The Hiller went up, the Hiller went down, the Hiller went round and round. Again and again, just at the time I was about to kill us both, Richard would say, "I've got it!" In his hands this noisy, vibrating, unforgiving piece of junk would calm down like a dog stroked by its master and obediently move back to its original position in front of the small bush. Then Richard would again say, "You've got it!"

Again and again this machine would take me off to a nightmare land of uncontrollable movements. My cockiness was replaced by muffled whimpers. This was not the smooth-flying J-3 Piper Cub I was used to, but a repulsive, disobedient monster of aluminum and motor that was destined to throw my butt right out of flight school in the first week. "There is no way I can learn to fly this thing!" I thought. I would have said it aloud to Richard, except my jaws were glued together by desperation and fear.

After 15 minutes of this, I simply grew weak. My knuckles were white from gripping the controls, and beads of sweat were racing down my nose. What had recently been the exhilaration of wanting to fly a helicopter had transformed into anguish and the fear of failure. My dream of being the first candidate in our class to solo had vaporized.

In the end, I was begging Richard to take the controls rather than begging to try it one more time. We departed the area and headed back to Wolters. Richard's job was to teach and mine was to learn, but first he had made me humble. From that day on, I listened intently to every word he said. I pre-

ferred that my previous background in flying never be brought up again. The ONLY thing helicopters and fixed-wing aircraft have in common is that both are flying machines.

The ride back to Wolters was very quiet and I did not speak unless requested to do so. Richard tried to console me by saying repeatedly that I had done pretty well at hovering for my first try.

3

LZ English

With LuRay at the controls, we depart An Khe at 1600 hours. Turning east, we begin a steady climb to 3000 feet. This is the first time I have really seen the country and it is beautiful.

It is a notably fine summer afternoon. Today's visibility is unlimited, and the pale blue sky is dotted with puffy white clouds drifting at the 5000-foot level. To the north, I can see a mountain range that is lightly cloaked in gray smoke. I estimate the tallest peaks at somewhere around 6000 feet. There is a strong resemblance to the Smoky Mountain range in northern Georgia.

Below us is the Central Highlands. Almost treeless and very flat, it soon gives way to thick elephant grass, then to jungle the farther east we fly. The grass below surges in the gentle breezes and looks very much like ocean waves. The clouds overhead cast their shadows on the grass and move across the plateau unmolested by obstacles or the war. It is a memorably fine summer afternoon. LuRay makes the grass seem slightly less attractive when he warns that at places it is probably 5 or 6 feet deep. His warning is well taken—a pilot who is attempting to land or, in an emergency, autorotate his helicopter, will not be able to tell exactly where the grass stops and the ground begins. Therefore, he will have difficulty knowing exactly when to pull the last bit of pitch to cushion the landing. LuRay mentions several recent crashes that resulted in casualties because the pilot had a hard landing.

Ahead of us the grassland seems to stop at a small mountain range whose peaks average about 1500 feet. LuRay points dead ahead to a gap that extends nearly to the floor of the plateau. This is called the An Khe pass, and through it Highway 19 snakes its way westward to An Khe. This dirt road is the only path linking the seaport of Qui Nhon to the upper Central Highlands.

"Mister Johnson, at times—in fact more often than not—the An Khe pass will be the only open-air area that you can fly through when traveling from An Khe to LZ English," LuRay announces unexpectedly. "Throughout most of the winter and spring months, the clouds will remain low enough to cover those peaks on both sides of the pass. There are two basic problems with trying to navigate the pass in bad weather. One: ol' Charlie knows you're coming, and since your altitude is usually eight hundred feet, you are well within their range to blow your butt to 'kingdom come.' Two: you must bear in mind that since this is the only path for east or west traffic from An Khe, it will be very busy with other aircraft of all types. We've had a few midair collisions here and near misses by the dozens. So keep your head out of your ass and on a swivel. Look out for the other guy at all times. In order to get to English, you have to fly through the pass, then turn north up Highway 1. Once clear of the pass, the ground below will drop off rapidly to sea level and it's pretty safe territory to fly in."

"Captain LuRay, why can't you go direct to English on a clear day like today?" I ask, drawing a straight line on the map in my lap from An Khe to the town of Bong Son, on the outskirts of LZ English.

"All this territory here"—he places his finger on the deep green colored area—"is triple-canopy tropical jungle. Some of it will go as high as three hundred feet from the floor below it. If you happened to have an engine failure over there, there is a high probability that you'd never be found even if some other guy saw exactly where you went in. That's also Charlie country! If the fall through the jungle canopy doesn't kill you, Charlie will!"

As we reach our 3000-foot altitude, we go through the An Khe pass. Just as LuRay said, the earth below drops rapidly out from underneath us. It is like leaping over a cliff. There are sharp curves on Highway 1, which snakes down the backside of the pass and repeatedly disappears out of sight into the jungle, only to reappear a few hundred yards later from the overhanging foliage.

One of the most breathtaking views I have ever seen lies just off the nose of the Huey. Down and forward, the jungle gives way to an expanse of cleared coastal land dotted with hamlets and rice paddies. A few miles farther on are sandy white beaches and the South China Sea. I am simply flabbergasted by the radiance of the lush green fields and the sharply contrasting deep blue ocean.

We turn north over the coastal plains that parallel the seacoast. The first checkpoint on my map is Phu Cat air base, near the base of the Phu Cat Mountains. This is home for the high performance Air Force jet jockeys. From here they will fly, some for the last time, into North Vietnam.

Our route takes us up Highway 1, the only road running north and south. This dirt road goes the entire length of the country. About 10 miles farther, my next checkpoint, the Dam Tra-O Lake, comes into view. This inland saltwater lake is about 1½ miles long and 1 mile wide. Just north of the entrance to Dam Tra-O Lake, the Cay Giep Mountains rise from the floor of the coastal plains, right out of the South China Sea, to an altitude of about 1500 feet. As the range progresses westward, it suddenly stops long enough to allow Highway 1 to pass through it, then rises again on the other side. This area where the mountain range drops to sea level is labeled on my map as the Bong Son pass. It is not as deep as the An Khe pass, because all the land around it remains at sea level. LuRay begins his descent. As we navigate through the pass, we can see the Bong Son River and the town of Bong Son, right at the river's edge. I strain my eyes for the first glimpse of my destination, LZ English.

When my new home is distinguishable, the only surprise is that it's a lot uglier than I had envisioned. Varying shades of beautiful green vegetation surround LZ English, but the landing zone itself is a rape of nature. It has been created by grading the only high ground left between the Cay Giep mountain range to the south and the mountains to the north. It is a plateau of dry red dirt rising only a few feet above the lush green rice paddies surrounding it. Scattered within the barbed-wire perimeter are tents, helicopter pads, wooden fixtures, and other objects that I am unable to identify from this distance. The LZ itself is probably about a mile wide and is interlaced with small roads just wide enough for jeeps.

At long last the 1st Cav lies before me in all its glory: men in a helicopter war living with their helicopters. All the reports I have heard and read indicate that the Cavalry troops exist on the barest of personal essentials, even by Vietnam standards. During the last week of training at Fort Rucker, I had to live with my helicopter in the field; but the Army aviation course failed to prepare me for the massiveness of the First Air Cavalry Division.

There are helicopters flying all about the LZ like mad hornets looking for a kill. On the south side of the LZ is the fixed-wing operations area, consisting of a 3500-foot runway and parking ramps. All types of airplanes will be landing there at all times of the day and night. At the core of English will be elements of the 229th and 227th Assault Helicopter Battalions, each with its own living quarters and aircraft-parking areas.

LuRay makes the radio calls and receives clearance to cross the approach end of the main, east-west, runway to get to the Python parking area. After slightly more than 45 minutes flying time from An Khe, we touch down at LZ English, 1st Air Cavalry's main forward firebase, Republic of Vietnam.

Stepping to the ground and gathering my two duffel bags, I notice a sergeant approaching the Huey. Upon his arrival, he summons both the crew chief and the gunner with a simple wiggle of his forefinger. He looks very unhappy about something, inciting both enlisted men to say "Oh, crap!" as they make the 10-foot walk to the rear of the aircraft where the sergeant is standing. The insignia on his jungle jacket consists of three *v*'s on top and two rockers below, which identifies him as an E-7, a sergeant first class. He is probably the platoon sergeant of the crewmen being summoned. He is thin and about 5 feet 10, but he must seem 10 feet tall to the guys doing the walking. His dress is as untidy as that of the other Cav people I have met today. When the crew chief and gunner get within earshot, the sergeant lets go with a barrage of four-, five-, six-, and maybe even some ten-letter words that I've never heard before. I hear him say something about their mothers two or three times—perhaps even their sisters. They had walked into his presence with heads down, but as the sergeant discusses their futures in the Army, their spines go straight and their necks go stiff.

Boot camp and flight school have planted in a fear of anyone
wearing a rank higher than our own. Being chewed out from stem to
stern on a recurring basis is simply part of every aviator's life, but I
still cringe. I do not attempt to lift the two heavy duffel bags off the
cargo floor, fearing this might make noises displeasing to the sergeant.
The only available exit would take me through between the aircraft
and the sandbag wall in the direction of the confrontation. I choose just
to wait until it is over, then go quietly, avoiding the sergeant. I take no
joy in watching the two young enlisted men get chewed out. Just a
short few months ago, it was me on the receiving end of such abuse. I
turn around when I hear LuRay chuckling. He glances up, then turns
away smiling, saying nothing.

"What's going on, sir?" I ask, walking to the front of the Huey
where LuRay finishes packing up his remaining flight gear.

"McCrary!" he replies. "That's Sergeant Eugene McCrary. He's
Second Platoon's sergeant and acting top sergeant, head honcho by
enlisted rank! These two guys are from Second Platoon and they must
have screwed up somewhere along the way!"

SERGEANT EUGENE MCCRARY INSPECTING A HUEY ENGINE IN 1968.

McCrary's voice continues to rise and fall like wind through a canebreak, but I can tell he loves using sarcasm. When he is finally through, McCrary invites the two young men to leave his immediate company, which they do in such quick order that they nearly slip down on the loose rocks.

Sergeant McCrary wastes no time in walking to the front of the Huey where LuRay and I stand.

"Really pissed you off today, huh, Mac?" LuRay asks.

"Nothing that I can't handle, sir," he replies. Then he glances at me. "You must be Mister Johnson, the new guy," he says in a hazing tone of voice.

My old flight school habits nearly make me reply "Yes, sir," which might piss him off even more since he is a sergeant, not an officer. "That's me—Sergeant McCrary!" I extend my hand for a handshake and he accepts it with a firm grip.

"Where you from, Mister Johnson?"

"The South!"

"Where in the South?"

"Georgia."

"Where in Georgia?"

"West Georgia!" I think he's the nosiest person I've run into lately.

"Where in west Georgia?"

"Sergeant McCrary . . . I'm from a small town about 50 miles west of Atlanta named Carrollton." I'm sure that the tone of this last statement gives away my intention of not pursuing this twenty-questions game any longer.

"Well, hell's bells!" McCrary grabs my hand again and begins to shake it violently. "Welcome to Vietnam, Mister Johnson, I'm from Douglasville, Georgia!"

"Are you kidding? Douglasville!" I am overcome with delight. Douglasville is only 25 miles from Carrollton.

I have found my first new friend in Vietnam, and unforeseen by

1. Sergeant Eugene "Gene" McCrary—"Mean Gene," as he was known in 1st Cav— would survive Vietnam for two tours of duty and would eventually retire out of the Army and return to Douglasville, Georgia. Gene and I remain the best of friends and spend much time together remembering the past and contemplating how lucky we are to have survived.

me, the friendship will last a lifetime.[1] We are both excited to find out that we have hunted rabbits over the same woods and know quite a few of the same people. Sergeant Mac helps me with my bags and moves unnecessary people out of the way in an attempt to make sure I get settled in quickly so we can talk some more. He has his troops racing here and there, gathering up supplies in the form of poncho liners, cots, and other field-issued essentials.

Mac introduces me to all the warrants in the tent when we arrive, and they direct me to the far end of the GP Medium, where there is an unoccupied 7-by-4-foot space on the dirt floor. This is to be my new home. Mac asks one of the specialist fours who has carried my bags to go to the supply tent and check out a cot, air mattress, poncho liner, and mosquito net.

We then depart the tent to find the company commander, Major Beyer.

When we find Major Beyer, he is relaxing in his single-occupancy tent, which is one of the few privileges of rank. He is writing a letter home and sipping a glass of Kool-Aid. I will soon find this to be the standard Army drink throughout the entire Southeast Asian combat theater. It takes Kool-Aid to camouflage the bad taste of the local water even after it has been purified. Soft drinks and ice are very rare, and real milk is nonexistent.

"Welcome aboard, Mister Johnson." Beyer rises from his director's chair and offers his hand, which I take, fighting the urge to leap to attention and salute.

Sergeant Mac informs Major Beyer of our common bond, then leaves to attend to his other duties. Beyer offers me a seat on a wooden ammo box, the only other thing he has that's suitable to sit on.

As the moments pass, Beyer makes me more comfortable, telling me about the 229th and how things work. He mentions names and places and who's who within the company, as well as the daily routines.

A Company's basic flight line structure is divided into two flight platoons. Each platoon consists of 20 pilots and 20 enlisted crewmen, who will man ten Huey helicopters. Major Beyer is the boss, followed by Captain LuRay, who is the executive officer. Next come the platoon leaders who are lieutenant grade. First platoon's immediate overseer is First Lieutenant Gary Runyan,[2] who will become my boss. Second platoon's leader is First Lieutenant Stephen MacWillie.[3] For the enlisted crew chiefs and gunners, Sergeant Mac is the platoon sergeant of 1st Platoon, and Sergeant Evans is platoon sergeant for 2nd Platoon.

Besides the flight line structure, many other people are involved with tactical operations and communications, where the missions are received from the 229th Assault Helicopter Battalion headquarters. Their job is to assess missions and assign the pilots and crews accordingly. There are also supply personnel—mess stewards who feed us, mail clerks who sort things out, and an entire platoon of aircraft repair people to keep the Hueys flying. The total strength of the company is around 150 persons.

Major Beyer is fair-complexioned, about 5 feet 10 inches in height, and has an average build. From his mannerisms, I can tell right away he has been in the Army for quite some time. I guess his age at somewhere around 35, which is old compared to the 20-year-old warrants in his charge. One of the things about him that stands out is his dress. The humidity is so high that the average person's fatigue clothing is untidy and soiled from blown dirt that has stuck to the sweaty areas. Beyer's uniform is neat and clean right down to his boots. He must change uniforms three times a day to keep his appearance up to this standard. I don't know if this is his personal preference or some standard laid down by his bosses. Anyway, I am impressed with his easygoing attitude and hospitable nature.

We leave Major Beyer's tent and walk around the company areas, where he introduces me to everyone we meet as if I'm a long lost friend.

With the walk-around complete, Major Beyer excuses himself to take care of company business, and I head for the 1st Platoon's tent. It is now into late afternoon, and on my arrival, I find several pilots had been out flying various missions when I dropped off my belongings. With some exceptions, each stops what he is doing, introduces himself, and makes me feel as much a part of the group as possible. I figure that the less friendly people are perhaps the older, more experienced guys—maybe guys, like Leggett, who are getting short.

2. Lieutenant Gary Runyan left the Army and lives in Texas, where he owns his own business.
3. Stephen MacWillie made full bird colonel (meaning the emblem of his rank is an eagle) and retired at Fort Rucker, Alabama.

There is some type of social structure within the tent, which is evident from the number of belongings each man has in his small living space. Besides the basic Army issue living devices, these guys have each used wood from empty artillery ammo boxes to construct other objects, like small bookcases and flooring to keep their bare feet off the dirt.

The most lavishly decorated cubicle is that of Warrant Officer William P. Charbonnier. Bill has made himself a home within this tent. He has constructed a mini-apartment complete with a solid wooden bed, including headboard, a wooden floor, several bookshelves filled with assorted reading materials, a clock radio, mirrors, and a wide variety of pinup posters from *Playboy* magazine. He has done a very good job of creating a homey environment within the small space allotted to him.

I make my way to the end of the tent and start setting up my cot, but I can't figure out how to organize the mosquito net since there is nothing to attach it to on either end of the cot.

"Need some help, new guy?" I turn to find Charbonnier standing in the aisle with a hammer in one hand and some nails in the other. Under his arms he holds two wooden boards.

"Sure do!" I reply, stepping back a little.

Charbonnier takes charge, and when he is done, I am a little more settled in than before he arrived. He drives one end of each board into the dirt floor, and nails each to an end of the cot. Next he fastens a string by each end to the boards. Then he untangles the mosquito net and proceeds to attach it to the tops of the boards. Now I have a mini-tent draped from the string down to the ground all around the cot.

"Now tuck in the netting on three sides under your poncho liner like you did your blankets in basic training," Charbonnier says confidently after he steps back to assess his handiwork. Then he disappears without another word. I will not learn until later how scarce wood, hammer, and nails are in this pioneer habitat.

As the subsequent days turn into weeks, Charbonnier and I become such good friends that he begins to take up for me in times of trouble. One evening, another aircraft commander dresses me down in the tent about something I did that was not exactly according to the standards of the day. Charbonnier, rocking back and forth in his Bong

Son–bought rocking chair, simply listens to the lecture. When the other guy completes his speech, Charbonnier lights into him as Mc-Crary had done to the crew chief and gunner on my first day. Although he never uses vile words, his command of the English language is superb. His vocabulary is endless, and his ability to make his adversary feel inferior is a trait that sets him above all the rest—not to mention he's been here longer than any other pilot in the tent. He is my mother hen and my friend at a time when I can really use one.

Soon I am accepted into the group. Admittedly, some older pilots never accept younger ones, seeing no reason for making a friend of someone simply because he is a comrade. Every day is a new day on the edge of the envelope; no one wants to get hurt by losing a friend. This thick shell can crack unpredictably, however. One day out of ten, the "short timers" are as friendly as they can be, while the other days each is the sole owner of an ice castle. I have understood this from the beginning and have no problem with it. This behavior is limited to a few and is not the norm. Some of the older pilots even talk to the younger ones about it and try to explain the reasoning behind it.

4

My First Engine Failure

June 30, 1967

The time I spend reading Pat's letters is special for me. As I read her words, she and home seem close and I can block out, for a few moments at least, my loneliness.

"You'll be on stand down tomorrow, Johnson." A voice abruptly cuts into my thoughts.

"Oh, yeah?" I reply sharply, before looking up from my seat on the edge of my cot. Rick Peterson, one of the older aircraft commanders, is looking at me.

"Got to give you a checkride! You'll have to do some autorotations and demonstrate some basic piloting skills. Meet me in operations at 0800 hours . . . OK?"

"Sure," I answer meekly. Rick leaves the tent and disappears into the darkness. A sense of apprehension fills me, and I wonder why I'm getting a checkride.

I stand up so I can see Charbonnier, who is reading a novel in his living area. "Hey, Charbonnier, what does Rick want me for?"

Charbonnier looks up from his book, squinting his eyes over his reading light. "What is it?" he asks. Obviously he has been so deep into the novel that he hasn't registered my question.

"Rick Peterson just came by to tell me I won't be flying tomorrow. He wants me to go with him to do some autorotations."

"Oh. That's mandatory. Rick is the company instructor pilot, and all new guys have to have a refresher course with the IP. Don't worry about it; it's a good day off from the rest of this hysteria. Anyway, what're they going to do if you fail the test? Send you to Vietnam?" Nonchalant, Charbonnier goes immediately back to his novel.

The more I think about it, the better it sounds. It's been a very long time since I've shot an autorotation. The practice will do me good, not to mention the late wake-up call. I relax and attempt to read Pat's letter again, but instead, I find myself daydreaming about my first autorotation. It occurred at Fort Wolters during primary helicopter training, and I can remember Richard Johnson, my civilian IP, talking me through it just like it was yesterday.

■

"Candidate Johnson, I am about to demonstrate an autorotation. If you lose an engine in a helicopter, you must immediately push the collective all the way to the bottom. If properly rigged, the main rotor blade pitch, even if the collective is all the way down, is preset to a positive 3 degrees pitch. As you fall toward earth, this positive pitch angle will cause the main rotor system to continue rotating at normal rpm even though the engine has quit. Essentially, you can maneuver the helicopter just as you did in powered flight, with one main exception: you are going down and going down fast. This OH-23D Hiller will fall at a rate of about 1500 feet per minute, but a Huey in Vietnam, depending on how you are loaded, will fall even faster."

Richard had the Hiller lined up on one of the six runways at a remote stage field in the Texas countryside. He rolled off power in one very rapid motion, and the helicopter yawed slightly to the right. On the tachometer, the engine rpm needle went to zero while the rotor rpm stayed right where it was—this is referred to as splitting the needles. The bottom dropped out and the helicopter went heart-thumpingly quiet. We were hurtling out of the air. I glanced at the IVSI (instant vertical speed indicator) gauge that showed rate of climb and decent, and it verified what Richard had previously said—we were actually falling to earth at 1500 feet per minute. And I thought I had been scared before.

The paved runway was coming up fast, and Richard made slight adjustments to compensate for a crosswind. At the last moment, Richard pulled rearward on the cyclic to bleed off airspeed and at the same time, to stop our forward motion, he pulled upward on the collective. He was using the inertia in the blade system in lieu of engine power to cushion our landing—there would be no hovering here! With only a slight thump, the helicopter arrived on the ground just as the main rotor system ran out of lift and rpm.

"Think you can do that?" Richard asked me.

"I'll try, sir!" I replied. In fact I was gut wrenched in fear of the maneuver. I had said "OH, JESUS!" seven times in that one autorotation and they all came in the last twenty seconds before ground impact. It was that day that I learned that helicopters, unlike fixed-wing aircraft, don't glide very well.

Four warrant officer candidates opted to quit flight school after their first autorotation. They found themselves in Infantry Training within one week of departing Fort Wolters.

■

After chow the next morning, I meet Rick at the operations bunker, and we walk to the flight line. Preflight inspection reveals no significant mechanical flaws, but I notice that the Huey we are about to fly was written up in its Dash 12 two days ago as having an unusual turbine noise. It is noted that the maintenance people checked it out and signed off on it as "flight tested and found OK."

"Hey, Chief!" I call to Specialist Fourth Class Earl Fuller, crew chief for this bird. "What kind of unusual turbine noise is the Dash 12 talking about?"

"High-pitched whine. We picked it up on the way back from An Khe day before yesterday. It went away before we landed. I couldn't find anything on the outside to cause it. After we shut down, I reported it to maintenance, but when Mister Stewart, maintenance officer of 229th, started it up, it was gone. He took it out for a flight check; it didn't whine so he wrote it off." Earl seems concerned, so I call it to Peterson's attention. Rick shrugs and says, "We'll check it."

The Army Huey unceremoniously cranks and comes to full rpm without any turbine whine. We take off from LZ English, then head south through the Bong Son pass.

"Where're we going?" I ask.

"Black Mountain," Rick pauses. "It's down Highway 1, maybe 5 miles below the Phu Cat Air Force Base. It's an abandoned Special

Forces camp with an airstrip. The South Vietnamese have a base camp there so it's reasonably secure territory, but mostly there's no traffic in and out of there. The airstrip is used by almost everyone for training."

We fly south for about 25 minutes before I spot the small mountain ahead; it is truly black. It is treeless, with little or no vegetation. This makes me feel a little better about snipers.

"Let me shoot the first ones, then I'll let you try a few." Rick's statement makes me feel more at ease. At least this isn't going to be a Rucker type of checkride.

Rick lines up on the pedaprime (pronounced "pinta prime") runway and splits the needles. We fall from the sky at an alarming 2000 feet per minute, but at the last possible moment, he executes an engineless landing so smooth that there is hardly a bump as we touch down. I am slightly intimidated by his excellent piloting. Rick brings the Huey back to full rpm, takes off again, and executes one more autorotation with the same precision as before. He is happy with his landings and now it is my turn.

"OK. Johnson, don't scare me!"

I take off, circle, then enter autorotation. As I bottom the collective pitch, I notice an unusual change in the sound of the turbine, but I am so intent on making a safe landing, I shrug it off as nerves. The Huey touches down on the pedaprime runway with too much forward airspeed, which causes a slight forward rocking motion. Although it is a survivable emergency landing, the tension has produced a noticeable amount of sweat, which drips from my forehead into my lap.

"That's fair, Johnson. Let's do another!"

I take off again. There is no mistaking the turbine whine that begins as I turn downwind.

"Chief, is that the whine?" I inquire over the intercom.

"Yes, sir," Earl replies.

"That's nothing to worry about, Johnson!" Rick breaks in, but somehow his reassurance doesn't make me any more comfortable.

I cut my pattern in a little closer to the airstrip just in case this baby decides to die. The autorotation goes just fine this time, and I set the Huey down without any forward motion.

There is yet another noticeable change in the whine as we touch down, but I am hesitant to bring up the change; I don't want Rick to think I am overreacting.

"I have it!" Rick says over the intercom as he takes over the controls. "Think I'll shoot another, and then we'll go home."

As he pulls in the collective the whine turns, for a few brief seconds, into a squeal, then goes back to a whine.

"Mister Peterson," Fuller keys his mike, "I think we had better go home now."

"OK, Chief," Rick understands that Fuller knows his aircraft better than anyone else, and when he says go home he means something is wrong.

The squeal does not intensify as we climb for altitude, but both Rick and I notice how low on fuel we are. This is very abnormal for the short time we have been out. Normally we would have enough to reach English, but now we are down to 400 pounds, according to the notoriously unreliable gauges.

"We'll stop for fuel at LZ Sandra," Rick decides.

LZ Sandra is a small helicopter refueling depot about 2 miles east of Highway 1 at the base of the Phu Cat mountain range. It was established as an emergency landing site by the Cav as it moved from An

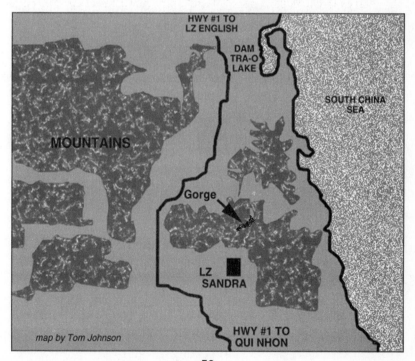

map by Tom Johnson

Khe to the coastal plains. It serves the Cav traffic flying from both LZ English and the port city of Qui Nhon. I have heard the older pilots talk of getting caught out in bad weather and having to *logger out*, meaning lay over in the aircraft, at LZ Sandra.

We land at Sandra without incident. Fuller begins the refueling process from the round rubber fuel bladders and a gasoline-driven pump. Although the engine is still whining, this is only a remote LZ with no maintenance facilities, so Rick doesn't shut down. Both he and I remain in our seats.

Suddenly in my right window a face appears. Apparently this is a Cav soldier from some unit.

"Hey, man, me and my buddies need a ride to English! Where you guys going?"

"We're going to English, but I don't think you want to ride with us today!" I reply, moving my boom mike away from my lips and shouting over the Huey's normal at-flight-idle blade and transmission noises.

"Hey, man, we been in this place since early this morning! Come on, man, we need a ride! You guys are the only people landed here all day!"

I understand their plight. As a rule, to get anywhere in Vietnam, you have to beg to ride on any bird headed in that direction. Sometimes you're lucky enough to catch a ride on an Air Force Caribou fixed-wing plane, but, more often than not, you catch a Huey.

"Look, I don't mind taking you with us, but we have an engine problem. It might quit on us any minute. We're just trying to get this sick old bird home!"

"Sounds like it's OK to me, man!"

This catches me a little off guard and also pisses me off. Who the hell is this guy? Some kind of Bell Helicopter technical representative? How does he know whether or not the engine sounds OK?

"What's he want, Johnson?" Rick can't hear the conversation over the noises and through his helmet.

"They want a ride to English," I shout to him. "I told them we could have trouble, but this dickhead informs me that our engine is running just fine."

"Tell them again we have a problem, and if they still want to go, let them get aboard," Rick says, looking past me at the guy standing outside the skids.

"Look, fellow. We have an engine noise that is not supposed to be there. It may quit any minute, but the aircraft commander says to tell you if you still want a ride, then get on board."

The guy smiles and jumps off the skids. He tells his two traveling companions something, then all three grab their duffel bags and run back to the aircraft. As soon as they board, they begin talking loudly and slapping each other's hands. Their duffel bags and jubilant mood seem to indicate that they are coming back from R&R.

Finished with refueling us, Fuller boards the Huey. Rick pulls pitch, clears behind and overhead, and takes off. We will not be able to continue our journey due north right away. For some unknown reason, Sandra has been built near the base of a small mountain chain that juts out from the much larger Phu Cat range to the east. The peaks are not high, but they lie directly in our path to English. We could fly a couple of miles to the west and avoid the mountains, but that conflicts with our desire to get to English as soon as possible with a sick bird. Rick flies us in an ever-widening circle flight path right above Sandra in order to gain altitude. The whine is neither more nor less intense, but I still feel a little uncomfortable with it. Rick, on the other hand, behaves as if he is driving a truck down the road with the engine knocking—cool and unconcerned.

As we make the final 360-degree turn, Rick points the nose north again. Although we are still below the peaks that lie ahead, our rate of climb will put us over the top before we actually reach the peaks. I'll feel much better once we're past the mountain range, since there is nothing but flat land filled with rice paddies all the way to LZ English.

We have just reached an altitude of 1500 feet and are about to cross the backbone of the mountain chain. A high-pitched squeal rips through the Huey. It is followed by the tearing of metal and an explosion. Terror squeezes my heart. The engine fails and goes silent. When I look to my left at Rick, he is looking at me with a "What did you do?" expression. Quickly he realizes that I have nothing to do with the sudden change in our condition and slams the collective down hard. We enter autorotation. For the first time in my life, I am caught in a life-or-death situation. What happens in the next few seconds will determine whether I go home in a box.

My head is already on a swivel. I'm looking forward, right, down, and behind almost at once, searching for a flat landing area.

"What do you see?" Rick yells over the intercom.

"Nothing over here! Straight ahead, I guess!" I realize that my voice is higher than normal. There is no place to go on my side of the aircraft. I can see nothing to the right but mountain slopes tapering off in the direction from which we have come. I tune the UHF radio to 243.0 megahertz, which is the international distress frequency, and begin calling "Mayday, Mayday" and giving our present position. I repeat the call four times before I think about our passengers. I twist my body to the left slightly and look back. It is clear that none of them has any idea how much trouble we are in.

"Buckle up! We're going down!" I yell. They begin scrambling for the seat belts that are rarely worn in a combat aircraft.

The Huey is falling fast. My attention turns to the instrument panel to check on how Rick has set up the autorotation. I am astonished at how fast my Fort Rucker training comes back. The Huey's best glide speed is 60 knots and Rick has already nailed it down. He has bled down from the normal cruise speed of 80 knots and traded the 20 knots difference for more distance across the ground.

We both know we are in serious trouble. The Huey is falling out of the sky at a rate of 2000 feet per minute. As we soar over the spine of the mountain range with barely a hundred feet to spare, we see that the north side of the mountain is sloping below us, but at only half the rate at which we are falling. This surely means that the flat rice paddies ahead are outside our autorotational distance, and we will hit the ground somewhere about midway down the slope. The steep angle of the ground below will ensure that we roll into a fiery ball on impact.

"Ravine on right!" I yell to Rick. He has already seen the minivalley, which twists first right then left down the side of the mountain. He heads for it. The mountainside is coming up fast beneath us. We float quietly past the cliff that is the beginning of the ravine, and I feel the tail stinger touch a tree. Beyond the cliff, the ravine descends sharply 200 to 300 feet before disappearing into the jungle. The top of the ravine is about 1/8 mile wide, but its sides form a *v* shape, the bottom of which is narrower than our rotor system width.

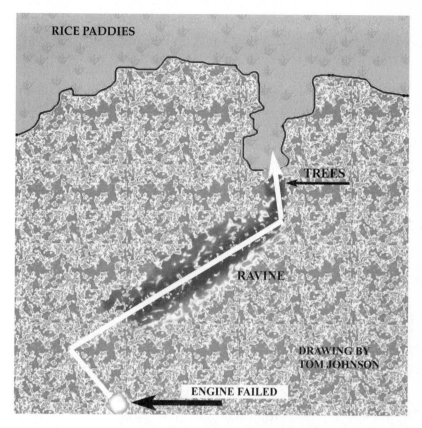

RICE PADDIES

TREES

RAVINE

DRAWING BY
TOM JOHNSON

ENGINE FAILED

Army UH-1 helicopter tail number 71555 with its crew of four and three hitchhikers silently glides into the ravine, whose sheer walls now tower above us. Directly ahead, the ravine makes a 45-degree turn to the north; we cannot see around this bend. The ravine narrows to a couple hundred yards wide. Rick pilots the engineless craft dead center of the gully. Smoothly, he makes a gentle left turn and, much to our delight, dead ahead we can see flat rice paddies. Our ravine terminates in a cul-de-sac that penetrates 200 yards into the mountain. Without this anomaly, our Huey's glide ratio would not have been enough to reach the rice paddies that lie outside the normal contour of the mountain. Although this gives us our first real hope of survival, it ain't over yet! Just before the ravine ends, it narrows considerably. Located on both sides and just before the rice paddies begin, the branches of two large trees nearly close off our approach to the cul-de-sac exit. The distance between their limbs appears to be about 40 feet or so. I doubt any pilot, even in the best of circumstances, could take the Huey's 48-foot-diameter rotor blades between the trees without making blade contact.

Rick sets up his final approach by shifting our glide path to the left side of the ravine. Then, at the last moment, he banks the Huey hard, first to the right, then to a steep left. This maneuver is timed perfectly. By banking hard left at the last possible moment, he dips the left side of the rotor system nearly vertical to the ground below us so we sail between the last two trees in the blink of an eye. He has about five seconds before impact to level the Huey and go nose-high in a flare to stop our forward motion.

As the rice paddies fly by under our skids, Rick stops our fall by pulling back on the cyclic. He gradually reduces forward airspeed to slow our descent, until we have nearly zero forward motion. Pulling up on the collective, he begins to cushion our controlled crash into the wet rice paddy.

Our terror is not yet over. Rice paddies rest on marshy mud and are surrounded by dry mud dikes protruding approximately 1 to 2 feet above the waterline. If we touch down with any forward airspeed into the marshy paddy, or if we strike a dike, we will certainly flip the helicopter end over end.

Again with the precision of a surgeon, Rick holds us up over the dike, then rears back hard on the cyclic to zero out the last bit of forward motion. He cushions our final fall into the marsh with all the collective remaining. As the skids hit water and sink beneath the rice plants, Rick hits the stop on the collective pitch control. So smooth is the landing, I wait for a final jolt of impact that never comes.

"WE GOT A FIRE!" Fuller breaks the silence that had fallen on us at the top of the mountain. He grabs the fire extinguisher and jumps from the Huey into the muddy rice paddy.

I quickly remove my helmet and am jerking loose the seat belts and shoulder harness when my door opens wide. Turning my head, I expect to see the gunner sliding the armor plate back, but instead it is the guy who hitched a ride with us back at Sandra. Before I can think, he plants a big kiss right on my lips. I'm sure my eyes are now as wild and wide as his.

"Jesus Christ! . . . Oh! . . . Jesus Christ, we made it! Aw, God . . .

bless America . . . you guys did it!" This man has my face squashed between his two strong hands and is hysterical. Releasing his grip on my jaws, he jumps onto the nearest dry dike, then jumps back to my door again. Jumping up and down in the sticky mud, he looks like a child who has found a mud puddle after a rainstorm. He is praising his Lord and yelling various obscenities all in the same breath. This man is truly happy to have survived his brush with death this sunny day in Vietnam.

Rick is busy shutting off electrical switches and fuel flow switches in an effort to contain the fire in the engine compartment.

I hear the euphoric former passenger talking to himself. It is "ol' Vernon" this and "ol' Vernon" that.

"Vernon, grab the sixties! Help the gunner grab the sixties!" I yell. "This is Charlie country. Get the sixties and get down!" I know that we are not safe yet. We are deep into Viet Cong territory with no protection but our personal weapons and the two M60 Browning automatic machine guns mounted on the Huey. The gunner is already in the process of extracting his sixty from its mount and grabbing spare boxes of ammo.

Vernon stops dancing and dives into the cargo compartment. In a flash, he dismounts the crew chief's sixty, ammo belt and all. He leaps out of the dry cargo compartment, sloshes his way to the nearest dike, and falls facedown with the dike as cover. The sixty doesn't get a drop of water on it even though Vernon created a tidal wave during his trek from the aircraft to his cover. All this has happened so fast, I suddenly realize I am the only guy still left out in the open. So, like Vernon, I dash to the nearest dike and dive facedown into its smelly mud-bottom.

Now things get really quiet except for the last few swishes of the rotor blades. When the blades finally stop, I hear my heart pounding in my ears. It is not from fear of contact with Charlie, but from the sudden realization of what has just happened. At the time, I was not scared; now, however, I am terrified. My hand is shaking the .38 Smith & Wesson revolver uncontrollably.

In response to my Mayday calls, a 1/9th[1] Cavalry gunship comes

1. 1/9 signifies "First Squadron Ninth Cavalry." Notations such as this are pronounced "[n]th of the [n]th."

abruptly over the nearest tree line, hell-bent for leather. He is as wide open as the B model Huey will go with its nose tucked down hard. He makes a high-speed pass right overhead and disappears over the next tree line on the other side of our Huey. Suddenly, another gunship makes a low high-speed pass. This is standard procedure because we lack radio contact to tell them we are not taking ground fire.

Rick, still thinking, gets up from his prone posture and returns to the Huey. He extracts a green smoke grenade from the crew chief's tool box, pulls the safety pin, and throws the grenade out some 20 feet. The grenade begins belching deep green smoke even though it is submerged in the water. This is the signal to our rescuers that this is not a "hot" LZ; had he thrown red smoke, it would have meant we were receiving fire from the direction in which he had thrown the grenade.

The gunships begin to circle low around our position. A D-model Huey like ours flies under the gunships and enters the protective circle they have formed. The UH-1 is from C Company 227th Assault Helicopter Battalion. The pilot hovers as close as he can, then puts the Huey down gently on a narrow dike. Still hovering with only his skids touching the ground about midway of the empty cargo compartment, he waits for us. This is our signal to go, and go we do. That is, except for Vernon.

We all yell repeatedly at Vernon to come on. Vernon will not move. Rick and I walk back, wondering what his problem is.

"I'm telling you guys I ain't gonna fly in one of them things again. God told me in a dream last night not to get on that damn airplane at Cam Ranh Bay; but Vernon didn't believe him! God told Vernon not to get on that helicopter at An Khe; and Vernon didn't believe him! God told Vernon not to get on this thang a little bit ago; but Vernon didn't believe him! *NOW VERNON BELIEVES WHAT THE MAN SAYS!* Vernon is just gonna have to walk out of here cause he ain't gonna fly no more!"

"Come on, Vernon," I plead. "It's three or four miles from here to Highway 1, and it's all Charlie country! You can't walk out of here! You've got to get on board now before you get all of us killed!"

"Dang it, Vernon, get on that Huey . . . NOW!" Rick, as concerned for our safety as I am, is in no mood to argue his case. "GET ON THAT AIRCRAFT OR I'LL SHOOT YOU RIGHT HERE!" Rick yells at the top of his lungs and draws his revolver partway from his shoulder holster. Both Vernon and I believe that Rick will indeed shoot. Vernon decides that flying one more time is the lesser of the two evils. He leaps out of the rice paddy and into the waiting Huey.

As the 227th pilot pulls out, we meet the RRF coming in with a squad of troops to secure the aircraft. Taking a second to glance around me, I find that both the crew chief and gunner have done their job of removing from the downed Huey the precious M60 Brownings that now lie across their laps. Now, we are all passengers.

Tonight, there is plenty of beer for the entire group. Rick's piloting saved our lives and I am thankful. I try to write Pat a letter, but my hands are still shaking. I put away the pen and join the celebration.

5

The Bong Son River Crash

August 7, 1967

I turned 21 on February 14 of this year and have been in Nam since June 11. So far, I've been lucky enough to avoid the gory sights talked about by the older pilots, but this is about to change.

Charbonnier and I have been working ash-and-trash missions all day for the 2/8 of the Cav, transporting ammo, food, and water into, and refuse out, of the An Lao valley, when we receive a call to extract casualties from the extreme north end of the valley. Charbonnier accepts the mission and we break off from our normal ash-and-trash routine. A major engagement took place at the designated location that afternoon, and it looks like a flying circus when we arrive: helicopters going everywhere. Amid the confusion, Charbonnier finds the right spot to land and puts us down.

I look to my right out the window as soon as the Huey stabilizes on the soft ground. Time seems to shift into slow motion as I watch ten battle-worn soldiers rise to their feet. First one, then the next, walks slowly toward the five young men whose bodies lie faceup on the sandy soil. One falls to his knees alongside his friend and gently strokes the corpse's hair; others simply touch their comrades' faces for the last time and retreat. Three of these guys are encased in body bags, but there must have been a shortage of bags, because two of the dead men are uncovered. They will have to be loaded just as they are. As gently as possible, the living lift the dead from the ground and place them on the cargo floor of our Huey. The three in body bags seem almost as impersonal as any other cargo, but the other two make things different.

Reports of snipers spur Charbonnier to execute an unconventional rapid departure from the area. During one of his abrupt maneuvers, a bloody arm flops unexpectedly across the radio console. Charbonnier is as startled as I am, but he moves the arm gently aside, all the time maintaining his attention on his dangerous job—dodging obstructions that lie in the way of our high-speed escape.

There was not enough room to place all the soldiers on the cargo floor, so two have been placed on top of others right behind our seats. My eyes follow the lifeless arm to its body. I find myself looking right into his open eyes. They are fixed on me. His color is already a deep blue and his body is contorted as a result of his wounds. His face does not show the signs of peace I expected to see in death.

Though uncomfortable about it, I continue to stare because for some strange reason I feel I have seen this person before. Awkwardly I move about to get a better look at the camouflaged name tag sewn on his jungle fatigue jacket. "Rowlings," I read to myself.

"Aw, Jesus! Not him!"

"What's the matter, Tom?" Charbonnier asks, having heard me say something without registering just what it was.

"Gary Rowlings. This guy's name is Gary Rowlings."

"You know him?"

"Yeah. He and I sat next to each other on the plane all the way from the States." I cannot talk for another minute. "This guy, me, and three of his buddies made the trip together. Last time I saw him was after we landed in Bien Hoa." I pause again. "If I remember correctly, he's got a kid due this month."

Blood and other body fluids ooze freely from Gary's body, creating an odor of death I have never before smelled. Breaking away from this grisly view, I follow the arm back to the radio console where I see something I had missed earlier: Gary Rowlings's wedding band.

"Right this minute, I don't feel as sorry for Gary as I do for his wife and family. How long do you think it'll be before they'll know?" I ask aloud.

"Three or four days, they say."

Once again I look back. The crew chief and gunner are looking at our cargo; they look at me. The crew chief gives me the "stink" sign by grabbing his nose and shaking his head. I realize that they are behind the bodies and, therefore, downwind.

As Charbonnier approaches English, I am forced to move Gary's arm to change the radio's frequency. It is cold and clammy. I am now touching my first dead person and, unfortunately for me, I know him.

Charbonnier lands at the medical detachment pad and our cargo is removed. He requests clearance from English tower to fly to the Bong Son River bridge to our west. I do not know why we are flying to the bridge and do not bother to ask.

We pass north of the Bong Son bridge right at the village of Bong Son itself. Charbonnier makes an unexpected left turn and begins a descent into the river. His target is a high and dry sandbar located in the river some 100 yards below the bridge.

"Ever landed on a sandbar before, Johnson?" he asks me.

"Yeah. Back in Wolters my instructor pilot let me land on one in the Brazos River. That was a trip!"

"OK, buddy . . . it's all yours . . . put me down on the one closest to the bridge!"

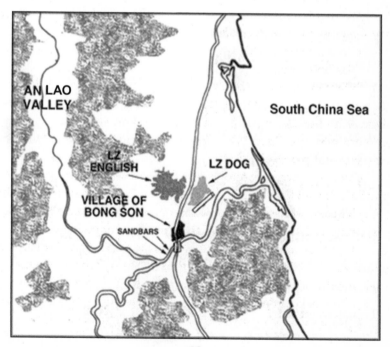

I execute a reasonably safe landing on Charbonnier's chosen sandbar and shut the aircraft down upon his commands.

"Hey, Chief, you still got those air mattresses?" Charbonnier inquires.

The crew chief responds by producing two Army-issue drab air mattresses and two plastic pails. It is then that I realize the purpose of this trip. The blood and body parts left in the cargo compartment have to be washed out. There is no efficient method of doing this on a helicopter pad, so it is standard procedure to utilize this sandbar.

Charbonnier and I strip down to our shorts and hit the muddy river with our freshly blown up rubber mattresses while the other crewmembers wash out the cargo area of the Huey. The water is especially soothing both to my hot, sweaty body and to my mind, still full of thoughts of events just past. The river is very shallow, and the current is mild. Charbonnier reminisces about our days spent on the beaches back in the States and how pretty round-eyed women are. He is very short now, having been in country over 11 months, and he is having great fun kidding me about how many days I have to go.

"I'm twenty days and counting . . . kid . . . how short are you??? . . . My *God*, two hundred and *how* many?!" he jests, answering his own question before I have a chance to respond.

We have floated out about midway in a football field–wide river when we both notice a 1/9th Huey setting up an approach for the river in our general area.

"What the hell do those guys think they're doing?" Charbonnier asks aloud, using his hand to shield his eyes from the bright Vietnamese sunshine. "Oh, crap. Head for the sandbar!" he suddenly bursts out and starts paddling through the water as fast as he can.

The Huey executes an approach to a point not 10 feet upriver from us and comes to a hover. The hurricane force winds generated by the Huey's rotor system blast Charbonnier and me downriver with great power. Holding on to the rubber air mattresses for dear life, we scoot across the surface of the Bong Son River as over a flat rock. As the visitor continues to hover down the river, we are blown nearly 100 yards away from our Huey. Our visitors finally break off their devilish little prank and land on the sandbar some 20 yards downstream from our helicopter.

Charbonnier and I are forced to paddle and occasionally walk—when it is shallow enough, upstream. As we pass the 1/9th bird, one of the pilots is gesturing that he is sorry, he didn't see us, but he says so amid outbursts of taunting laughter.

This pisses Charbonnier off to no end. He yells obscenities drawn from the furthest limits of his vocabulary. I have never heard some of the names he calls these guys; I don't know if the words even exist. He tells them things about their mothers, discusses their anatomies, and calls them something that sounds like "nerds." I am cracking up, along with the other guys, at Charbonnier's reaction to the whole thing. The 1/9th guy, who is trying to smooth things over, is built like a heavyweight wrestler, and Charbonnier is smart enough not to attempt to actually kick his butt. In fact it might take our whole crew to do such a thing.

Charbonnier continues yelling things about their human worth and family heritage as he furiously paddles upstream toward our Huey. I just smile and quietly follow.

Upon reaching the Huey, he is still talking a mile a minute. He hurriedly deflates his air mattress and begins changing into dry clothes. It is very apparent that he is about to crank up and take off with or without his crew on board, so the gunner and the crew chief terminate the washing process and start getting the ship ready for takeoff.

I have hardly buckled in when we get light on the skids.

"Clear behind us?" Charbonnier asks the two crewmembers. There is a devilish tone to his voice. The gunner is already seated in his place and replies quickly that all is clear on the right. The crew chief, on the other hand, is midway in the cargo compartment attempting to secure his tool box and has to race to Charbonnier's side of the helicopter and lean out to issue the "all clear on the left" call.

We come to a hover. Then Charbonnier unexpectedly takes the Huey off backward instead of forward. Now I realize what he is about to do. There is going to be hell to pay for the crew of the 1/9th. He is going to execute a rearward takeoff right over their position, and given his frame of mind, it probably will be a very slow transition from hover to translational lift.

When executed properly, a rear takeoff is beautiful. It can save your life when you must enter and exit a hot LZ from a single approach path. First you get light on the skids. Then, just as you reach a 2-foot hover, you apply rearward pressure to the cyclic stick to start the helicopter traveling backward. It takes a very experienced pilot to orchestrate the cyclic, pedals, and collective pitch controls and keep the nose pointed in its original direction while making it fly backward. At some point, the pilot must slam all the right pedals he can to make the Huey rotate on the vertical axis. Once this 180-degree rotation of the fuselage is accomplished, he dumps the nose over hard to make the thing fly the way it's designed to fly.

Charbonnier lifts off but forgets that the Huey's tail is exceptionally low at a normal hover. When he applies rear control pressure to start the backward movement, he keys the mike and shouts, "Watch this, Johnson!"

The Huey's tail dips lower, and neither the crew chief nor the gunner is prepared for the backward takeoff. In fact, they do not have any idea what is going on until the tail rotor hits the water. The contact of the fast-spinning tail rotor with the flat surface of the Bong Son River immediately causes the tail rotor and tail rotor gearbox to detach from the tail boom. Charbonnier has the engine running at maximum power when this happens. Since there is no longer an anti-torque rotor to counteract the torque produced to rotate the blades overhead, the fuselage begins to rotate violently in the opposite direction from the blade system overhead. This spin to the right is so violent that the crew chief's unsecured 75-pound tool box leaves the floor of the Huey's cargo compartment and sails right between Charbonnier and myself and exits the aircraft, taking out the windscreen and most of the upper part of the instrument panel with it.

We have repeatedly trained for a tail rotor failure, and the proper thing to do is shut off the engine, which stops it from producing torque. It should then be possible to achieve a hovering autorotation.

Charbonnier's problem is that the loss of the tail rotor and the gearbox has radically altered our center of gravity. The gearbox normally sits at the extreme end of the Huey's tail boom, and the gearbox and tail rotor together weigh about 65 pounds. The Huey is balanced on its vertical axis at a point near the mast connecting the fuselage to the main rotor system. Without the usual weight on the tail, the helicopter becomes severely nose-low. As we spin, Charbonnier fights to raise the nose, and we go to an extreme nose-high position. We need to be reasonably level before power to the engine is cut.

Our unusual plight ends as abruptly as it begins when the retreating rotor blade on the left-hand side of the helicopter makes contact with the Bong Son River: The Huey ceases to fly, and we crash hard into the shallow water. The transmission breaks loose from its bonds and sends the mast crashing forward into the pilot's compartment with such force that the overhead circuit breaker panel collapses onto the radio console between Charbonnier and me.

My brain is having a hard time following events. When I finally realize I am still in this world, I feel pain in my left shoulder. It is caused by the pressure of the twisted metal of the overhead electrical panel. The panel blocks my view of Charbonnier. I work my shoulder free, tearing my fatigue shirt in the process, only to discover that I am up to my lap in water. The river water is so muddy that I cannot see any of my body under the surface. Nor can I feel anything.

Just a few moments ago there was a great commotion and excitement; now there is dead calm. There are no voices or other sounds to jerk me fully alert. Half by instinct, I begin to unbuckle my seat belt. I don't know whether anyone else has survived the crash until the gunner begins jerking on my door in an attempt to open it, which is his job every time we land.

Realizing that the crash has jammed the door, I pull the emergency door release, and the door comes loose at the hinges. The gunner's tugging, along with the current of the river pushing the inside of the closed door, ultimately breaks it free, and it disappears out of sight. The gunner pulls back the armor plate on the seat. He is wild-eyed and confused about what has happened to us. My somewhat casual attitude evaporates when I realize that I am submerged not only in river water but in JP4 jet fuel that is leaking from our Huey's fuel tank.

The first words spoken after the crash are mine to the gunner: "JP4 . . . JP4 . . . Let's get the hell out of here!" These words pierce the silence. Before I can turn around to check for Charbonnier again, the gunner disappears from the doorway with a headlong splash. I follow suit, only to have my heavy chest protector pull me to the shallow bottom like a brick. Once I have my head above surface in chest-deep water, I remove the chest protector and race as hard as I can downstream and away from the Huey.

"Hey, asshole, *upstream . . . go upstream, not downstream!*" It is Charbonnier, ankle-deep in water upstream from the aircraft. I am currently too scared to be glad to see him alive. Beside him stands the crew chief.

The gunner and I reverse our direction, but we go wide out into the river to avoid the flow of JP4 downstream.

"How'd you like that little takeoff, Johnson?" Charbonnier asks when we get within a reasonable talking distance. His demeanor is as cool as if nothing had happened.

"Charbonnier," I reply, "you eccentric bastard!! You just busted my cherry! Not to mention the crew chief's pride and joy! You damn near killed us all—and you act just like nothing happened!" I look at the twisted wreckage, then back at him as we slosh our way into shallow water.

"Crap, that wasn't *that* bad, Johnson! Just a little miscalculation! That's all!" Charbonnier looks downriver and cups his hands around his mouth. "HEY, YOU ASSHOLES DOWNRIVER!" he yells in the direction of the 1/9th crew, still awestruck by what has just happened. "THAT'S JP4, YOU IDIOTS! ANYBODY GOT A MATCH?" He turns to me again. "Can you believe those fools? Just standing there on their little sandbar while that damn JP4 flows all around them." He calls out again downriver. "HEY, STUPID, I THINK I LEFT THE BATTERY SWITCH ON!!"

They take that last bit of information seriously and all four of them rush to their aircraft and hurriedly prepare it for takeoff. There is some hesitation before they light off the turbine engine, as both pilots calculate the chance that a spark from their engine might set the whole river around them on fire. It probably is Charbonnier's apparent insanity that makes them finally decide to start up. He did say something about lighting a match, and I think that if he had a dry one, he might have used it just to ascertain how sharp their sense of humor was.

The 1/9th boys light the fires and take off in great haste.

As we ponder our situation, Charbonnier decides that, since I am the company safety officer's assistant (Lt. Runyan is safety officer), I should write up this accident in a very special way. After saying repeatedly that I will not do such a thing, I finally cave in for the sake of saving Charbonnier's wings and keeping his butt from going to Leavenworth.

The official report states as follows:

After landing on the sandbar, both pilots found themselves and their aircraft in much deeper water than had been previously anticipated. Immediate actions were taken to get the aircraft airborne again but water had already entered the tail boom through rear compartment's access doors. The additional weight of the water at this arm and moment [distance from center of aircraft] caused an uncontrollable aft center of gravity resulting in a rearward direction of flight even though the cyclic was in the most forward position. The tail rotor and tail rotor gearbox left the aircraft after making contact with the water. Mister Charbonnier immediately found himself out of control and almost over the top of a 1/9th aircraft that was parked directly behind him. A hovering autorotation was not possible, as there was the imminent danger of coming down right on top of the 1/9th crew. Using great skill and without regard for his own life, Mister Charbonnier managed to get the aircraft away from the other crew prior to the crash. These actions reflect great credit, not only on himself, but also on the United States Army.

Nobody—I mean nobody—really believes this report, but I have written it and signed my name to it, so there it is. Charbonnier will leave for home only 12 days after the crash, but I still have hell to pay for the report. It will become the focus of my first meeting with a general.

"Mister Johnson, Major General Norton wants to see you right away in his office!" come the words of the company CQ (message runner) just as I'm waking up one day after Charbonnier has left for the States. My lips quietly repeat the CQ's words as I run my fingers through my hair.

"That's all right, guys. The general is going to give him a medal for that crash report he turned in!" jokes one of the other 1st Platoon warrants, amid a general chorus of catcalls as I depart.

I take a jeep and make the five-minute drive from LZ English to

LZ Two Bits, which is located in Bong Son. I am terrified by what is happening and curse Charbonnier with every other breath.

I find General Norton's bunker, report in to his adjutant, and sit down for a long wait. When finally ushered into his office, I salute nervously. My voice breaks high and shrill—not the commanding baritone I wanted. General Norton is the top aviation man in the division. The commanding general is his boss, but Norton is in charge of everything and everybody who flies for a living.

"Mister Johnson, I've read your report on the crash you were involved in at the bridges. Do you have anything you would like to add to this report before I give it to General Tolson?" John J. Tolson III is the commanding general of the 1st Cav.

"No, sir."

"Then you are sure this report is correct?"

"As correct as I can make it, sir."

Norton, who already knows better and also knows I had to stand straight on the report, surprises me by cracking a little smile. I am not willfully deceiving him. The report is as good as I can make it without hanging all our butts in a sling.

General Norton lets me off a large hook with a speech about the importance of not falsifying aircraft accident reports, but he does so without making a direct accusation. When he says I am excused, I exit in great haste. Again I curse Charbonnier, then laugh as I walk back to the jeep. What a guy. In spite of the accident, he is one of the best combat pilots I will ever know.

With his mannerisms, he was born 50 years too late. He should have been flying biplanes in the First World War, wearing stovetop boots and a scarf. I'm sure he would have survived that war, too.

6

The Battle of Song Re Valley

August 9, 1967

Last night was a restless one because of persistent rumors that something big is about to happen. At 0500 hours, Major Beyer gathers all the pilots and crews in the mess tent for a company briefing.

"Today A/229th will become part of a battalion-size lift deep into Charlie country. We will pick up two companies of the 2/8th battalion and airlift them into the Song Re [pronounced 'Song Ray'] valley, which is located in the extreme northwest region of the 1st Cavalry Division's operational area. Army intelligence reported a major NVA or VC headquarters located somewhere in the valley area and this is a mission to 'raid' or 'recon in force' to try to find it and destroy it. Our target is an open field that lies on a ridgeline about 100 feet above the valley floor of the Song Re. Somebody gave it the name LZ Pat." Beyer paused and looked into our faces.

"We will pick up a company of the 2/8th near the mouth of the An Lao valley." He continued his briefing by pointing to his map, "We will fly north up the An Lao valley until it ends, cross over a 2000-foot mountain range, then fly west another 10 miles and make the assault at an open field named LZ Pat. As we make the turn west, we should be able to see an abandoned Japanese airstrip named Ba To.

"Fuel is going to be a problem." He paused. "Black Horse airlifted fuel bladders into Ba To this morning. As soon as we finish the assault, we will fly back to Ba To for refueling.

"We will be flying over a triple-canopy jungle that has no clear-

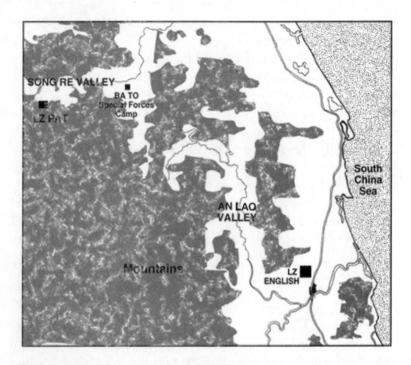

ings in it. After leaving the relatively flat An Lao valley, any engine failure will mean ditching in the trees; the likelihood of being found is remote. This entire area is controlled day and night by the Viet Cong." Beyer took a puff from his cigar and waited for questions. The tent full of young helicopter aviators remained graveyard quiet—no mumbling—no talking—no horsing around—just quiet.

Beyer ended his briefing and we new guys should have known that something was up by the silence of the older aircraft commanders. They spoke among themselves, occasionally using their fingers to draw imaginary lines on their maps. I hear one say that last month, the 1/9th went into the Song Re valley in search of the elusive 3rd NVA Division, and they found them the hard way. The enemy division consisted of regular, well-armed, and uniformed soldiers of the North Vietnamese Army, who had infiltrated via the Ho Chi Minh Trail.

It is also rumored that several squads of LRRPs from the 11th Pathfinder Company have been sent into the valley area. Those who could communicate with headquarters painted a bleak picture for anyone planning to trespass into the Song Re. They had spotted not only heavy-caliber mobile machine-gun emplacements but also 51-caliber antiaircraft batteries.

As we depart the mess tent and the crews assemble on the flight line in the morning darkness to start "preflighting" their aircraft, the air is heavy with tension. It will be an hour before the sun rises. Verbal exchanges are quiet and brief. Pilots check things on the Hueys themselves, even though the crew chiefs have just inspected the same things. Satisfied with the preflights, the pilots take positions in their seats and are strapped in to await Major Beyer's arrival. Beyer is at battalion headquarters receiving his last-minute instructions.

This thing is going to be big, even by 1st Cavalry standards. The three 229th Aviation companies, A, B, and D companies, are committed along with other aviation units consisting of the 1/9th (scouts), 228th (Chinook Helicopters [cargo carrying]), 478th (Flying Cranes [heavy lift helicopters]), 2/20th (aerial artillery), and many others from the 11th Aviation Group will be in the air all at once.

"Scared, Johnson?"

"Damn right, I'm scared."

The question has come from Warrant Officer Walley Garner, who is my aircraft commander for today. Walley is one of A/229th senior pilots and has been in country since long before I arrived; I have flown as his "peter pilot" many times. He is a professional pilot who does not take any unnecessary risks. I trust him and we work together well.

"I hear that the 1/9th has been catching hell up there." Walley is referring to the fact that since August, the 3rd Brigade of the 1st Cavalry has been slowly working its way to the valley with the 1/9th flying air cover. The standard order of battle for the 1st Cavalry is the leap-frogging of artillery support bases. Certain high terrain, which rests well inside the range of the last artillery support base, will be assaulted and secured. Chinook helicopters will then airlift 105mm artillery batteries into the LZ. Once these are operational, another piece of terrain closer to the ultimate goal will be assaulted, and the whole process will start over again. Using this technique, the helicopter units will rarely, if ever, make an assault into an area that cannot be supported with artillery.

The approach into the Song Re will be dramatically different. Customarily, these forward artillery assaults zigzag so that the last three bases established in the advance form a triangle. This means that every base is in the range of at least two more batteries. But because of the distance being covered in this operation and the speed required to cover it, all the bases will be in a roughly straight line. The lightly protected forward positions are prime targets for Charlie. If the forward-most base comes under attack, it can only depend on artillery support from the one immediately behind it. For reasons not known, the 1st Cavalry was unable to land troops into the last forward artillery base yesterday. Today will be the main thrust, culminating with air assaults right into LZ Pat; this mission will be accomplished without any artillery support. This worries me and other 229th pilots; for all we know, ol' Charlie may be sitting in the tree line as we land.

"OK, let's get the show on the road. Here comes Major Beyer," Walley calmly announces and begins putting on his helmet.

Within seconds of his comment, the starter motors on the Lycoming turbine engines jerk into motion as pilot after pilot pulls the start trigger. Slowly the main rotor blades begin to spin, and the dead quiet is replaced with the sound of 18 Hueys up to full rpm. So many Huey rotor blades are thumping the air that the Python parking area now begins to resonate. There is no other sound in the world that will make a Vietnam veteran's heart pump faster. A Company personnel who do not fly have left their tents and are standing nearby, feeling their adrenaline rush just awaiting our departure. Soon all of LZ English is awash with Hueys waiting to take off, and my blood rushes hot with excitement.

The fear of the impending battle is replaced by the more immediate fear of killing ourselves just getting to it. With this many helicopters in the air, something bad is bound to happen to someone today.

Walley and I are "tail-end Charlie" today, meaning we will be the last bird in the entire company to lift off.

Walley keys his mike, "Python Yellow One, Python Blue Six. Python flight is ready."

"Roger, Blue Six," Beyer replies.

The Pythons are split into three flights of six birds each. Beyer will lead the Yellow flight; Lieutenant MacWillie will lead the next one, labeled White; and Lieutenant Gary Runyan will lead the Blue flight.

The flights take off, one behind the other, assemble during a lazy climb east of LZ English, then execute a left turn and head west toward the An Lao valley.

The three flights land at separate PZs (pickup zones) on the valley's floor to pick up their cargo of 2/8th air troopers. Our sister company, B Company—229th—call sign "Preachers"—is already in the Song Re making a pickup of other 2/8th troops at LZ Champs. It is a 5-minute flight from Champs to LZ Pat. If all goes well, the Preacher flight will hit the LZ first, and we should be on short final for LZ Pat as their last flight pulls out.

Our pickup is uneventful. The long trip over the beautiful but treacherous landscape gives all of us too much time to think about what lies ahead. No one speaks. Beyer leads, and we follow him into the Song Re. We see Ba To airstrip and turn west toward LZ Pat.

"Python flight, that's our LZ at your eleven o'clock position about three miles," Beyer transmits. As briefed, off in the distance, I can see no evidence of any typical smoke and explosions generally associated with a preparatory artillery barrage. "Python flight, keep your heads on a swivel for the bad guys. There will not be any artillery 'prep' of the LZ."

"Damn . . . That's crazy! Probably the hottest LZ in the territory and no artillery prep!" Walley erupts over the intercom. "Some dodo is trying to get us killed. I never heard of this happening before . . . ever."

"It looks like we can get six birds into the LZ at one time. White and Blue flights, increase your separation to one minute between flights. Go to Preacher push [frequency] now and hang loose. . . ." Beyer's voice shows no signs of stress.

The commander of B/229th Air Assault Helicopter Company is Major Pearce Lane. "Rocky," as he is called by other officers, is a scrappy but disciplined leader. Word is out that Major Lane can throw a mean punch if he got mad at you. Later, I learn that he boxed in the 1956 Olympics, but to us he is better known for his 8mm porno flicks. Often he shows up in A/229th's officers club, projector and all. No time for poker when good skin flicks are to be shown.

Beyer reports to Major Lane—call sign Preacher Six—that Python flight is on their frequency and ready for the approach.

The wind direction, as reported by the command and control Huey flying high above our formations, is from the south-southwest, so Preacher Six flies north along the east side of the valley past LZ Pat, then swings left, back down the valley to land into the wind.

Preacher Six sets up his final approach path and begins the assault into LZ Pat. Beyer calls for us to go increase our flight separations a little more. The tension level rises to nine out of a possible ten.

"I'm glad it's the Preacher going in there first and not us," I mutter over the intercom, breaking the silence.

"Got that right," Walley replies.

Preacher Six and his flight of six Hueys are the first helicopters to touch down in LZ Pat, and they do so without incident. "LZ green!" Lane transmits as he departs the LZ without his cargo of troopers he just dropped off. This means no unfriendly fire and makes all of us feel a lot better. As the second flight of Preachers touch down, all hell breaks loose.

"Preacher White Four . . . taking fire . . . LZ red, LZ red! Heavy automat . . . !" His transmission abruptly ends.

Beyer is less than two football fields behind the Preacher White flight. With the Yellow and White aircraft ahead of us, Walley and I cannot see what is going on. "Jesus Christ!" Walley yells as a 1/9th gunship to our immediate left takes a solid hit and begins to trail fire and smoke.

"Mayday . . . Mayday . . . we're going in!" comes a transmission from someone in serious trouble.

The airways come alive with radio distress calls. These transmissions are nearly inaudible because of the background sounds of automatic weapons.

"*Python flight, break left, break left!*" Beyer commands as he rolls his Huey into a steep left bank and pulls in the maximum power for the escape.

Walley waits his turn, then does a three-G turn following behind the rest of the Python flight ahead of us.

"Python White Three taking fire!"

"*Tiger Two-Six! Our gunner has been hit!*" A D Company 229th gunship is hit.

"*Bandit Blue flight, taking fire! We are right on top of the bastards! Blue flight, break left. Break left!"* Runyan screams. Walley has already started his break before Runyan transmits.

Walley and I both jump as the crew chief, Mike Pulver, and the gunner open up with their M60s at the unseen enemy below. The wicked chattering of the crew chief's and gunner's M60 machine guns spitting a wall of bullets fails to give me the moral support they have in the past. We definitely are in trouble. The Yellow flight was near treetop altitude when Charlie opened fire. Beyer is pulling the guts out of his helicopter attempting to gain altitude. The remaining flights, all in a higher trail formation, have mistakenly lowered their altitudes to match Beyer's. Now all of us, loaded to the gills with troops, are trying to accelerate and gain altitude at the same time. All pilots also have their helicopters maxed out on power and are taking whatever performance they can get.

"Yellow One, Blue flight breaking north!" Runyan calls to Beyer, attempting to take us away from the melee.

"All Python flights, go loose and come up on Python Push, now!" Beyer transmits.

I switch the FM radio back to company frequency as instructed. Walley is struggling to keep from running into Blue Five, which is flying much slower than we are. His ship must be the company "dog." Every company has its strong and weak aircraft. At Runyan's command, Walley breaks trail formation and heads on his own to a more northerly course, passing Blue Five in the process.

It has grown quiet inside our aircraft, and I surmise that the crew chief and gunner have either run out of ammo or burnt the barrels of their M60s. Twisting my body around in the seat to glance at Crew Chief Pulver, I face six air troops looking at me for an explanation. Without helmets, they cannot hear radio traffic about things going on outside the aircraft. I use my finger to motion the guy nearest me to lean closer. Over the Huey's noise, I brief him and watch his face go rigid. He briefs the others, and I watch their faces as he tells them the bad news: Their buddies who survived the initial insertion are now locked in a battle.

The NVA were waiting on us. They are not as dumb as I had hoped they would be. They waited until about 120 troops were on the ground, then opened up with heavy automatic weapons, recoilless rifles, and mortars, which had been cleverly hidden on another ridgeline over-looking LZ Pat. The NVA know, and we know, there will be no rescue of those on the ground, nor will they be reinforced due to the intense firepower now aimed at the LZ.

A/229th forms up without any losses and lands at Ba To. Beyer finds the fuel bladders in the POL area, and flight after flight lands, refuels, and high-hovers over to the airstrip to shut down. The Preach-er flights do the same.

Lieutenant Mel Utley (Tiger Two-Six) has long since broken from the assault and is hell-bent for leather on his way back to Ba To airstrip with his bleeding gunner.[1]

Walley and I are the last to shut down. Removing my helmet for the first time in a long while, I notice a slight trembling in my hands. The other pilots are already assembled around Beyer, and we join them.

"Listen up," Beyer begins as Walley and I approach. "I don't know much more than you do right now, so hang loose until I get some word. I saw two aircraft bite the dust just ahead of us. I also know that two 1/9th aircraft were shot down and a 'Charlie-Charlie' got hit."

Beyer is unfazed, and his briefing is blunt. Afterward, he climbs back into his Huey and cranks on his radios to communicate with whoever is in charge of the assault now that the C&C bird has been put out of action.

Almost immediately Walley returns to our aircraft to see the crew chief about any damage he may have found since we landed.

I huddle up with Gore, Martin, and Lee, who are low-experience peter pilots like me.

"Boy, I tell you . . . that was a close one," Larry Gore[2] says as he pushes his hair back under his Army-issue baseball cap and grins nervously.

"How many rounds you guys take?" Bill Lee[3] asks Gore.

"Four or five, I think."

"Hell of a way to make a living, ain't it," Don Martin interrupts.

"Got that right!" all of us reply.

1. Gunner John M. Beyran died instantly from a head wound.
2. Larry Gore—After Vietnam, I located Larry in Tabor City, NC, where he was an air traffic controller. Larry died of cancer in May 2004. Larry and I stayed in touch and were best friends for 38 years—I miss him dearly.
3. Bill Lee—Survived Vietnam and is a helicopter pilot for a TV news station in Aus-tralia.

"Gentlemen, these guys are serious. They have at least five, maybe six, 51.51-caliber machine guns that opened up this show. I heard that two of the 1/9th aircraft bit the dust from the 51s. Those things have a 5000-foot kill range. We overflew one of them trying to get out of there. Hell, that's what you guys get your $110 a month flight pay for!" MacWillie jokes as he slaps me on the back and walks in the direction of Beyer's aircraft.

Perhaps this is when we new guys realize how lucky we are to have survived the ordeal. This enemy is a heavy hitter and armed to the teeth.

Our conversation turns to the 2/8th people who were inserted into LZ Pat before the world came apart. They are trapped and now fighting for survival against a superior force that owns the high ground all around them.

As gunship pilots return from the battle to refuel, they report that the unit inserted is A Company,[4] and most casualties are from VC in hidden, covered bunkers on or near the LZ itself. A Company has nowhere to hide and no time to dig in

Brave gunship pilots and crews from D/229th and the 1/9th companies have tried repeatedly to get suppressing fire into the LZ, only to be shot up themselves. One of those pilots, call sign Preditor 24, turns out to be a classmate of mine from 67-5: Charles Iannuzzi[5] took a .50-caliber round in the chest protector and crashed into the Song Re valley. Later today we will be told that he has bled to death from the wound. Iannuzzi was the jokester of 67-5 and was consistently the target of "Wop" jokes. His lighthearted nature made him extremely popular with the entire class. If the report is true, he will be the second of my classmates to die in Nam.

The morning wears into afternoon with rumors flying faster than Hueys. Everybody has joined the effort to save the troops in LZ Pat. High-performance F4 Phantom jets scream overhead in the direction of the LZ. Everything in the military arsenal has been brought to bear to save the lives of the young warriors. Top brass in Saigon are being

---

4. Historical data for this chapter has been supplied by A/2/8 Company's commander— Capt. Raymond K. Bluhm Jr.—and other pilots who also flew this mission.
5. Thirty-three years after Vietnam, I learned that Charles Iannuzzi survived his wounds.

informed by high-altitude Air Force communications planes of the battle's status

Our time to go back into the battle comes at 1500 hours. Beyer, who has been talking nonstop over the radios since morning, leans out of Yellow One and gives the signal to start engines.

"Oh, crap! Here we go again!" is Walley's reply.

Python flight comes alive, and the troops who have spent the day with us scurry to reboard the helicopters.

Although fearful of what may lay ahead, each feels a profound obligation to get into the battle. We, too, after watching their anguish during the long hours of stand-down at Ba To, feel compelled to do our best to aid them. These brave men will indeed kick ass or die honorably in the rescue attempt.

Anxiety again goes high as A/229th lifts off. No one other than Beyer knows where we are heading; this usually means there is no time to waste on a briefing. We again head west up the Song Re valley. The Yellow, White, and Blue flights again assemble in V formations 1500 feet above the valley floor.

As Beyer leads the Yellow flight into the small cleared area, my breathing becomes shallow and more rapid.

"Python flights go trail! Our LZ is about six miles at our twelve o'clock. According to a new Charlie-Charlie overhead, it might handle two birds at a time," Beyer transmits. "We *will* be going in cold . . . no artillery support! There will *not* be a prep of the LZ. Tell your gunners it is free fire on final."

According to my calculations, that will put us about 4 miles short of LZ Pat and more in the valley floor than on the ridgeline. This will be only the second time I have been in a combat assault without artillery prepping the LZ.

Beyer is on final approach to the LZ when he transmits, "*All Python flights, go around! Go around!*" Beyer's voice is abnormally high, and from the background sounds of the transmission, I can tell that he is having difficulty keeping his Huey from settling into the LZ with its heavy load of troops and fuel. "LZ is mined . . . repeat, LZ is mined!"

Walley and I can see the Yellow flight below us begin struggling to go around.

"White flight, break right!" MacWillie commands.

"Blue flight, break left!" Runyan commands.

As we come into visual range of the intended LZ, I can see 10- or 15-foot-high bamboo poles protruding from the LZ floor. From this distance, I cannot see the wires between the poles, but I can be certain that Beyer has. Charlie has been known to set such traps—they are called "rotor bumpers." Between the poles is a wire attached to a grenade. Any helicopter descending into the trap will certainly be blown to bits before it reaches the ground safely. Yellow flight pulls out of the assault and climbs for a safe altitude. The other flight leaders bring their covey of Hueys behind Beyer, and A/229th is again in three V formations over the valley floor.

"Charlie's got his crap together!" Walley transmits over the intercom. "Those rotor bumpers were not put in there today. He's been expecting us for a while. Hey, Chief, tell our passengers what just happened." I acknowledge Walley's comments with a nod of my head.

We again return to Ba To airstrip to refuel and await further orders.

With only two hours of daylight left, Beyer receives new orders to take our troops into a landing zone on top of a hill named simply Hill 450. We successfully land our cargo of sky troopers into this LZ without incident, although the "pucker factor" is extremely high on our short final. We refuel at Ba To again, then fly home to LZ English, arriving after the sun has disappeared. Nighttime approaches into the small sandbag revetments on Python pad requiring extreme pilotage, and their danger is multiplied when 18 helicopters try it at almost the same time. Beyer rightly decides that we should not land at POL to refuel again. Too many helicopters are flying on this night, and his pilots are very tired young men. He opts to command that the fuel trucks come to the helicopters.

By the end of the first day, the NVA has had enough and vanishes into the jungle leaving behind discarded weapons and their wounded.

The following day reinforcements from the outlying areas of LZ English and An Khe are helicoptered into Ba To airstrip using 228th Chinook heavy lift helicopters, and the original assault helicopter companies, like us, pick up those guys at Ba To and fly them into small LZs in the Song Re.

History will record that the NVA were not actually waiting for us but instead were caught totally off guard by the invading Cavalry force.

The 2/8th had mistakenly landed right in their front yard and did so with such quickness and force that the bad guys had nowhere to run. The intense battle for LZ Pat lasted four hours before the enemy could find a way to break off and slip away into the jungle. On the battlefield, the VC left behind numerous weapons and 50 of their dead comrades.

The cavalrymen remain in the Song Re until August 18 setting up ambushes and going on patrols. A/229th, along with other aviation units, continue to fly into the Song Re during this time, in support of those sky troopers who are seeking to make contact with the enemy again. We average 12 to 15 hours of flying a day, but we do it with no further losses of helicopters or crews.

7

Bill Lee Crashes Hard

August 15, 1967

"Tom, you ready for some wake-up sludge?" Bill Lee enters the 1st Platoon tent as he does most mornings to see if I am ready for coffee.

"You bet. What time do you have, Bill?"

"Official Greenwich Mean Time adjusted to Southeast Asian Combat Time is 05:45! Today is . . . [he pauses to suggest a gong] Tuesday, August 15, 1967."

"Jesus Christ, nobody fights a war this early, especially on Tuesday," I growl. It is the first time in many days that I even knew what day of the week it really is. The vagaries of war do not depend on what day it is. In fact, the only break in our hectic schedule occurred on July 4th. The Vietnamese are like termites in wood and do not pause day or night, Sundays or weekdays. This morning I am especially tired and a little ill, to say the least, but Bill always cures that with his festive attitudes. Although he also gets up a little rocky most mornings, he defies normal behavior by being in full stride within minutes of waking up.

"Aw, come on, Tom. Just think—back in the States you'd have to endure 'sleeping in,' a fresh egg and milk breakfast, and watching cartoons on TV. Join the Army and see the world . . . they just failed to acquaint you with the fact that you had to start seeing it at 4:30 every morning!" Bill laughs at his own cup full of cheer, then slaps me on the shoulder. Bill continues to talk as I continue to straighten up my living area. His attention is divided between talking to me and fending off the belligerent attacks on his early morning exuberance from the remaining 1st Platoon pilots who themselves are just waking up.

As Bill and I walk on the wooden pallet walkway toward the mess hall, we talk about old times together. We met at Fort Polk and remained good friends all the way through flight school. He was my sister-in-law's date at the graduation ball. Since I was married and Bill was unmarried, we ran in different circles throughout the Fort Rucker days. Occasionally he would pop in for a Saturday morning breakfast at our trailer. Then, as now, he always brought with him something to start the day off right. He, Pat, and I spent hours laughing over early Saturday morning cups of coffee.

Vietnam helicopter pilots tend to be lean, with an average weight of less than 150 pounds, thanks to plenty of physical training in boot camp and flight school. But even by Vietnam helicopter pilot standards, Bill Lee is skinny—about 5 feet 11 inches and around 100 pounds. He has dark brown eyes and thick brown hair. He has a noticeably receding hairline, and I often tell him that he will probably be bald by the age of 25, which never seems to bother him.

Bill and I are the same age. We arrived in A/229th the same week, along with another 67-5 classmate named Larry Gore. Both Bill and Larry are from North Carolina. Bill was assigned to the 2nd Platoon, so his living area is in the other warrant tent.

Sergeant Beckley, the mess sergeant, greets us as we move into his chow line. Beckley and Bill like each other and pick on each other all the time, with Beckley losing every confrontation. Bill is such a quick thinker and so witty, it is very hard for anyone else to get in the last word. No matter, Sergeant Beckley feels he has a daily duty to harass the young warrant officers. When Bill has finished with the chow line, Beckley simply picks on the next warrant available, but Bill is always his first choice.

Sergeant Beckley always admonishes "Be careful today, men!" as each pilot leaves the confines of his mess tent, and he is always sincere in saying it. Beckley knows that the crews live on the edge and things can and will happen. He addresses the young pilots as kids coming into the mess tent, but as men going out; thus he gives himself away. Beneath that rusty knife edge personality is a very compassionate old soldier.

Gazing around the tent in my early morning stupor, I spot what appear to be peppers neatly strung in cheesecloth and attached to the side of a tent flap.

"Sergeant Beckley, those wouldn't happen to be Christmas tree peppers, would they?" I inquire, using my coffee mug to point in the direction of the tent flap.

"Sure are," Beckley is smiling. "Hottest damn peppers I ever tried to eat. My sister grows them things in her yard. You want some?"

"Oh, no, not me! I know how hot they are! Can't cut 'em, myself." I am already involved in a serious daydream as I answer Beckley.

■

The "Wolters widows," so named because they rarely got to see their warrant officer candidate husbands, drew strength from each other. Pat made a good friend early on. Her name was Julie Hinchliffe, and her husband George was not only in 2nd WOC with me but in the same A-4 flight.

George and Julie Hinchliffe were originally from Illinois; they had been married for several years. George and I became friends long after Pat and Julie had met. Julie was blonde, pretty, and very outgoing. George, on the other hand, was laid-back and had a very unusual conversational style. He would begin a sentence very rationally and then, without pause, he would say the wildest things I ever heard of. He could tell the biggest lie in the same breath as the gospel truth and not even crack a grin. It was his simple way of checking whether you were paying attention. George was short, by my standards, but strong as an ox. After you got to know him, it was a pleasure to watch this little fireplug run his test on others, some of whom would just grin back obliviously.

"That stupid ass ought to have his hearing checked!" George would say after he had dropped one of his bombs on some unsuspecting person during a normal conversation.

One day George visited my room at Wolters and eyed an assortment of Christmas tree peppers lying on my desk. Our landlord grew these things, and the bush was beautiful. The peppers changed colors from green to red, then to purple. They owed their name to the fact that they did not all change colors at the same time and looked very much like Christmas tree lights. They were notoriously hot peppers, and I was hesitant to eat one. George, on the other hand, had a reputation as a hot pepper eater. He claimed to be able to drink Tabasco sauce right from the bottle without even grimacing. On this fateful day he was paying a visit to talk about how well our wives were getting along. He asked for a pepper.

"Hinchliffe, those damn things are very hot! Are you sure you want to eat one?"

"Heck, Johnson, I eat those Mexican cayenne things and they don't bother me at all."

"OK, George, take all you want. I'm a little afraid of them myself."

Much to my surprise, instead of waiting until dinner, he popped a purple Christmas tree pepper right into his mouth and began chewing. At the first chew, I did not see a change. However, with the second chomp, tears flooded his eyes and his face contorted in pain. He began spitting parts of the pepper all over my freshly buffed floor.

George bolted from my room gasping for breath. His bare feet made splatting sounds on the concrete floor as he ran flatfooted down the hall, then back again.

I was beside myself; I laughed so hard I had to sit on the floor. As he flew by my room for the third time, I went into convulsions. My sides were hurting and I was unable to get my breath. This was the most comical sight I had witnessed in a very long time.

George was fanning his mouth and yelling about God and Jesus Christ. Suddenly he yanked a Coke from the hands of one of the many other candidates who, by now, were all standing in their doorways observing this spectacle. The carbonated water in the Coke made the pepper burn even more, and George went into an even higher gear.

At this point, someone told George that butter would put out the fire; so, without any hesitation, he headed down the steps as fast as he could run. The entire barracks was alive now, so all of us simply followed him to see where he was going.

Out the door he flew, clad only in his jockey shorts and a T-shirt, toward the mess hall. Upon his arrival, he flung the steel doors open, leaped over the stainless steel cafeteria line, and landed right between two civilian ladies who were cleaning up.

Bewildered by this unexpected assault by a scantily clad madman, they made their escapes in opposite directions, neither taking the time to ask any questions.

George began opening and slamming large cooler locker doors one by one, looking for butter. What he finally found was a 10-pound block of the substance, with which he lathered the inside of his mouth after biting off a large chunk.

Now the spectacle of George was just too much. The creamy white butter was in stark contrast to his red face. His grunting noises as he poked handful after handful of soothing butter into his mouth took down the whole crowd. We were all in tears, but of course it was not funny to George.

The two kitchen ladies returned with reinforcements in the form of the civilian manager of the mess facility. All candidates became quiet and waited for what would happen next. The man in charge was a tall, lean, local Texan. He slowly moved over for a better view of George and stopped next to me. "What's going on here?" He inquired with a deep Southern drawl.

"Don't worry, sir!" I replied. "We have already called the MP's [military police]! These young men are under a lot of stress, and I guess this guy just broke! You ought to see what he was doing to the bushes outside the barracks!"

"Bushes?!"

"Yes, sir . . . just before he came over here, he was chewing up the bushes right outside my window and growling . . . hear how he's growling?" George was still making grunting sounds as he grabbed gobs of butter with three fingers and applied it to his mouth. "It's OK now, we have him hemmed up."

"Damn—is he crazy!!" The civilian was already beginning to lean toward the nearest exit, just in case George decided to jump over the cafeteria line again.

"You should see his roommate!"

"Roomate?"

"Yes, sir, this guy damn near bit off his ear!" I said as calmly as I could.

"Bit his ear . . . Really?"

"If I were you, I would go for some extra help!"

Those last words went unheard by the Texan, however, because he was no longer around to hear me but was en route to the nearest exit at full speed. Never seen a man that tall and skinny run that fast.

The jig was now up; the manager would be returning with either a gun or the cops. We all grabbed George and exited.

George still calls me very nasty names when we talk about this incident.

After about a week, George's mouth healed and our relationship was none the worse for wear.

■

"What the hell you thinking about, Johnson?"

"Do you remember George Hinchliffe?"

"Yeah. Oh, yeah! Thinking about the day he ate those Christmas tree peppers?"

When the tale has been told all over again, Bill and I wipe the tears from our eyes and walk to our tents. The shared laughter lightens our spirits as we prepare for the day. We gather our gear just as dawn is breaking over the South China Sea; then, together and still laughing, we walk to the TOC bunker to get our morning assignments.

Today's assignment involves the entire A/229th company. Last night, Major Beyer only alluded to today's mission by saying it might be a combat assault. Such missions require far greater pilot skills than single-ship resupply missions into relatively secure landing areas. The tension generally runs very high, not only because each approach could be your last if Charlie has his way, but because tight formation flying is relatively unsafe. Pilots with little experience, like myself, will not have gotten much chance to fly this way because the aircraft commanders prefer to rely on their own finely honed flying skills in these stressful flights. Resupply missions provide a better setting in which to teach basic flying skills to the new guys because instruction can be one-on-one and because the margin for error is wider, so that a slight miscalculation will not likely take out the crew of another Huey.

"Hey, Tom, you're going to be flying Yellow One today!" Bill says with glee as he gets first look at the acetate and grease pencil schedule just completed by Captain LuRay.

By this point, I have been well indoctrinated in the responsibilities of "peter pilots" during combat assaults, but even though it is quite an honor for Major Beyer to pick me as his pilot, I do not feel ready for "lead ship." The peter pilot in Yellow One is expected to do all the flying while Major Beyer orchestrates the attack. This requires the skills to fly in absolute harmony with every other pilot in the flight, as they will be tucked in tight formation on both sides.

I have been told horror stories by all the older pilots. New guys flying in the Yellow One position have damn near killed everybody with an abrupt maneuver or even mistakenly taken the entire flight into the wrong LZ. I suddenly feel a little sick to my stomach.

During the assault, there will be less than 12 feet separating the tips of the rotor blades between helicopters. This is dangerous but tactically required. Most of the jungle LZs in Vietnam are small; and because Charlie is well disciplined and will generally wait until all the helicopters are in the LZ to open up, it is imperative to bring in as many troops as possible on the first landing so that they can ward off an initial attack. Because the average number of combat troops a Huey can carry into battle on a good day is six, the most dangerous time for both us and the troops is just before the actual touchdown.

Major Beyer, like all the other 1st Cavalry commanders, requires that his pilots fly tight almost all the time, even when there is nothing but wide-open sky. He does this so that the old guys stay sharp and the new guys learn new skills.

Major Beyer arrives at the Huey assigned to us today. I have already preflighted and strapped into my seat; I'm ready to go, as are the others in the flight. Beyer has gotten his last-minute instructions from battalion. As he walks up the flight line he makes a circle over his head with an outstretched finger, which means to light the fires and start the blades turning.

All at once the air is filled with the sounds of the igniters clicking and the high pitch of the starter motors arduously spinning the Lycoming turbine shafts. Slowly at first, the Huey's main rotor blades begin to rotate. The smell of burning JP4 jet fuel and the beating of the air from so many helicopters would make anyone's blood start to pump. Within three minutes, all 16 birds have come to life at full rotor speed.

The noise generated by a flight of this size naturally attracts much attention all over the LZ. Those who are not crewmembers stop what they are doing, look up, and wait for the moment of takeoff.

"Python flight, this is Six!" Major Beyer says, keying his radio. "We'll depart to the east and form up north of English as soon as I can get English tower to clear us! Yellow Eight, are we ready to go?"

"Six, that's a roger!" The last bird in the formation makes the call, since he can see all the other birds ahead of him. He can tell if everyone is loaded up and at full rpm.

"White flight, are you ready?" Beyer inquires, directing his question to Captain LuRay, who will be leading the 2nd Platoon formation as White One, just as Beyer and I will be leading the 1st Platoon.

"Python Six, White flight is ready!" comes the reply from White Eight.

"Tom, get us clearance!"

I have done at least one thing right so far by tuning the UHF radio to the English air traffic control frequency. On Beyer's command, all I have to do is key the mike switch located on the cyclic control to ask for takeoff clearance.

"English tower, this is Python Yellow One with a flight of sixteen ready for takeoff Snake Pit . . . over!"

"Python Yellow One, English tower . . . flight of sixteen cleared to depart Snake Pit. Remain north of active runway; we have fixed-wing traffic inbound . . . over!"

"Yellow One copies!" I acknowledge.

Major Beyer gives me a thumbs-up, and I begin to load up the Huey's rotor system by pulling in pitch using the collective. As we get light on the skids, the crew chief and gunner make a routine call over the intercom that all is clear behind and overhead for takeoff. I pull in more pitch, and we become airborne out of the sandbag bunker with forward movement.

Beyer, already busy communicating on his other two radios, glances up only occasionally to see what I am doing. Remembering both my flight school training and Major Beyer's initial instructions, I slow to 60 knots after takeoff and set in a climb of a nominal 500 feet per minute, thus allowing all the other aircraft to catch up. As they successively form up on my left and right, the noise around me grows. I do not have to look to know that they are there.

"Yellow One, Yellow Eight. Python Yellow flight is formed up!"

"Roger, Yellow Eight!" I reply, then slowly begin to push the cyclic forward and pull in power to advance to our normal cruise speed of 80 knots. I also overhear White Eight call to White One that the White flight is also formed up.

I begin a slow turn from east to north just as Major Beyer has instructed. This will put us on a course parallel to the coastline.

Beyer has not said a word to me since the command to take off, and I feel way out of my comfort zone.

"Python flight, we are going to be picking up some folks who are off to your immediate right on the beach and carrying them up north." Beyer transmits, in total control of himself and our situation. "Stay loose!" He is Mister Cool and I, his peter pilot, am terrified.

"Tom, turn right. Give me a right turn to a heading of about 170 degrees!"

I am relieved to be given something immediate to do—I can handle a compass heading.

I complete a slow right turn to the south on a heading of 170 degrees.

"Can you see the purple smoke on the beach?" Beyer inquires, pointing out his left window at about my ten o'clock.

"Yes, sir . . . I see it."

"Set up your approach accordingly!" Damn, that leaves me on my own again. Why not give me headings and altitudes?

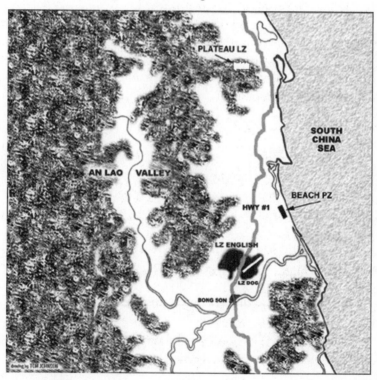

I set the Python flight up on a left downwind leg for the approach. I lose perspective as the target PZ passes from view behind the left cargo compartment's open door. Still I continue south for another 30 seconds before lowering the collective and making a wide sweeping left turn back north. "Don't rush it!" I keep repeating to myself, as the Huey responds to my control pressures.

Near the last part of the U-turn, I can see I am overshooting the desired ground track northward over the beach. We are still descending as we turn. To adjust for my mistake in judgment will require a tightening of the turn itself, which I execute, hoping that Yellow Three and Yellow Five, who are on the inside of the formation, can slow down enough to remain in position. Yellow Two, Yellow Four, and Yellow Six will have to accelerate forward airspeed to remain in position.

Bill Lee is also getting broken in; he is flying Yellow Two on my immediate right. I dare not look away to see how he is doing for fear of screwing up the entire turn.

The Python flight completes the required turn to final approach, and now the most immediate problem for me is to maintain a constant rate of descent that will carry the entire formation right to the touchdown like a ball suspended on a tether string. As with turns, any dramatic change would cause an "accordion effect" that would ripple throughout the entire flight. I now realize how good Major Beyer is. When I am flying his wing, we move as one solid unit through the air. I have never realized what skill this required on the part of Yellow One's pilot.

I am now high and fast, which requires very definite and abrupt changes in my approach posture. I push the collective pitch down to reduce power and simultaneously pull back on the cyclic to slow our forward airspeed. These actions must be accomplished as smoothly and slowly as is practical. If I am unable to make them I will have to issue a "go around" command, which will tell the flight I have screwed up so badly it is no longer possible to make a safe approach into the PZ. "Go-arounds" can kill you in hot LZs.

I manage to make the adequate adjustments, and the complete Python flight touches down on the brilliant sandy beach of the South China Sea, where a platoon of the 2/7th Cavalry waits to be carried into combat.

As I sit on the beautiful South China beach waiting for the 2/7th passengers to board, I look hard over my right shoulder at the waves breaking. As I continue to scan right, I am suddenly aware that I am looking into the cockpit of Yellow Two. Sitting in the right seat waving back like a kid with a new toy is Bill Lee. His grin, as always, will simply bust you up. Caught off guard, I belatedly wave back. I can see Warrant Officer Bill Woolen, his aircraft commander, first look over at me, then turn his head toward Bill, and, if the look on Bill Lee's face was any indication, say something funny. It must be a comment about this schoolboy interaction—two new guys waving back and forth. Bill would normally be flying in the White flight since he is a member of the 2nd Platoon, but more often than not, new guys are shuffled from platoon to platoon to fill needs. This is especially so when the oldest aircraft commander and the newest peter pilot are in different platoons.

"Yellow One, Yellow Eight. Python flight is ready!" This means that all the assigned troops are now loaded inside all the Python birds and the flight is ready for departure.

"Python flight, this is Python Six. Watch your takeoffs. The sand is very loose—be careful! Yellow One departing!" This is a way of alerting those not paying attention to detail that the now-very-heavy Hueys have their skids buried into the loose sand and can very well suffer much grief if one skid breaks loose before the other. This is especially true when the rotor blade separations between aircraft are so narrow—less than 20 feet. Any pilot who even temporarily loses control of his helicopter during liftoff will certainly drift directly into the rotor system of the helicopter adjacent to him.

At Beyer's command, I again pull pitch to lift off. This time we are a lot heavier. I did not count the troops getting on, but from the amount of power being required just to get the helicopter light on the skids, I suspect that there are at least five and maybe even six.

"How many we got, Chief?" I ask over the intercom.

"Five, sir," the crew chief replies.

"Tom, continue up the beach for a while and climb for altitude. Here's where we're going." Beyer points to a spot on the map. The general area where his finger is located is "hard core"—Charlie's territory; if I read the general topographical lines correctly, our LZ will be a 2500-foot plateau.

Beyer takes a lot of the pressure off by telling me what headings and altitudes to take. From the sea level PZ, we have to make lazy S turns in order to gain the altitude of 3000 feet: We don't want to cover a lot of lateral distance, because the LZ is barely 5 miles from the beach. The temperature drops as we climb, and this is a relief for my sweaty body. On Beyer's instructions, I start the flight into a slow standard rate left 360-degree turn, and as we do this, I get a very good look at our target. It is something out of a prehistoric monster movie. From sea level, the ground suddenly pushes straight up over 2000 feet. With its surrounding jungle and sheer rock walls this geographic enigma looks like a natural fortress. The plateau, located on the top of this flat-topped mountain, is barely larger than five or six football fields and has only one small cleared landing area. From this distance I guess that it will be a single-ship, or at most a two-ship, LZ. The rest, from this distance, appears to be dense foliage. Artillery starts up as we swing south. I can see great explosions and the resulting devastation of the forest around the LZ.

Beyer is talking to a lot of people on many radios and still continuing to give me directions. The atmosphere in the cockpit begins to get heavy, but Beyer isn't fazed. To me, this is leadership of the highest quality.

I complete the 360-degree turn, then, following to Beyer's instructions, head due north on what would be called a base leg for the approach if I were a civilian flying at the Carrollton airport. On Python Six's command, I turn west to final approach. I have been on quite a few combat assaults, but flying lead ship is totally different. We will be the first to touch down in a single-ship LZ. That sucks, by anyone's standards, because if Charlie is there, we will be the ones calling out to the other Python aircraft that the LZ is hot!

"Python flight, go trail!" This is Python Six's command for the V formation to break up. Yellow Two will slide in at my six o'clock, followed by Yellow Three and all the rest. There will be approximately 40 seconds' separation between aircraft—that is how long it takes for the bird directly in front to touch down, unload, and take off again. When the sequence is properly executed, just as the first bird clears the LZ, the next bird will be setting his skids on the ground.

We are now on final approach, and without waiting for Major

Beyer's order, I start the flight down. Looking dead into the artillery barrage is slightly unnerving even for me, and I'm not there yet. I can also imagine ol' Charlie's state of mind if he is, in fact, down there waiting on us to arrive.

"MAYDAY, MAYDAY, YELLOW TWO GOING DOWN!!"

I realize instantly that this is Lee and Woolen.

"Yellow Three, Tom Cat Two-Two, follow them down!" Beyer calls out over the Python frequency so quickly I cannot fathom his attentiveness. Tom Cat Two-Two is one of the four D/229th gunships that are escorting us on this mission. I want to break off the approach and go after Bill, but that would be reckless. "Rest of Python flight continue the approach! Yellow Three, do you have them in sight?"

"Three, roger . . . !"

"Yellow Four, tighten up . . . !" Beyer commands it to speed up and close the gap in the trail formation vacated by birds two and three.

Without any further delay, Major Beyer changes radios to continue coordinating the combat assault. I continue the approach, still watching HE (high explosive) rounds going off directly in front of me. At slightly less than 60 seconds, the "wooly peter" round goes off in a blaze of radiance. The brilliant white smoke and thousands of Roman candlelike fireballs shoot 50 to 100 feet in the air. With that, the three remaining gunships flying just outside the formation dive in for the kill.

We are now on very short final and I am scared! The Tom Cat flight lets loose with a barrage of rockets and 7.62 miniguns, which fire a blistering total of 4000 rounds a minute. I can see trees and other foliage plummeting to the ground under their onslaught.

"Python Six, Yellow Three. Two has crashed hard! They are on their side now and on fire . . . over!" The voice of Tom Galiger, Yellow Three's pilot, trails off in despair.

"Three, roger," Beyer replies simply. "Tom, you're a little hot!"

"Yes, sir!" I reply, realizing that Yellow Two's plight has caused me to lose concentration on the most critical stage of the mission.

As I clear the last tree line and drop the Huey into the small grassy area, the 2/7th troops are already on the skids ready to leap off for the relative safety of terra firma. At least there they can fall flat on their faces in the prone position. This will feel far better to them than being part of a slow-flying target.

"Yellow One is in . . . Yellow One is out! LZ is green!" Beyer calls to the other Python birds as we momentarily touch down, unload our cargo of troops, and pull pitch immediately to get the hell out of there.

"Yellow Four is short final . . . Four is in . . . Four is out!" Four bird is eating up our ass end as I pull out of the LZ.

"Tom, break left and let's get to Yellow Two!" Beyer calmly says over the intercom. "Python flight, this is Six! Return to Python pad!" The major does not want a flying circus over the crash site, so he sends the rest of his covey to home base. This is family, and everyone wants to do something to help, but he makes the right decision.

"Python Six, this is Red Rider Six. LZ is green! I repeat, LZ is green!" This is the grunt commander of the 2/7th we have just put into the LZ reporting that he does not have any enemy fire at the current time, the LZ is cold. Typically the gunships are committed to continue close in support of the troops they have just landed and must stay on station until the green or red call comes in. This particular communication, therefore, releases the Tom Cat flight to follow us to Bill's crash site.

"Tom Cat flight, support the crash site!" Beyer orders.

"Tom Cat Two-Six, roger!"

With that, the remaining three gunships dump their noses just as I have done, and now all four of us are racing to the wreckage we are sure to find.

Without gaining much altitude, I have the Huey bent over forward very hard, trying to gain airspeed. We pass the edge of the sheer wall down from the plateau, and the sensation reminds me of a nightmare of falling off a cliff.

As I bottom the collective for descent and break hard left, the perpendicular rocky walls quickly rise higher than we are flying.

"It can't be that bad," I think to myself, but the details of Yellow Three's earlier call—the severity of impact and the ensuing fire—evoke a very bleak mental picture.

As I round the east wall and plummet toward sea level, the smoke and fire emanating from the jungle floor come into view. The bird's fuel bladder has ruptured—the result of a very hard landing—and has caught fire. The orange flames are leaping higher than the trees around the crash area and producing a thick black smoke. Both Beyer and I can see Tom Cat Two-Two and Yellow Three helplessly circling the area at some distance.

"Yellow Three, Python Six. What do you see? Over."

"Six, . . . they hit hard and rolled over! No sign of survivors since the crash! Suggest you remain well clear of the site. Ammo is going off everywhere!"

"Oh, Jesus!" I blurt out as the burning Huey comes into sight. No survivors! Both Bill and Woolen are gone. I break off the approach and pull back on the cyclic both to reduce the high airspeed and to avoid the .30-caliber rounds going off as a result of the fire.

Again Beyer changes radios, this time to report to 1st Cav Division headquarters concerning the loss of one of his flock. The division officer at LZ Two Bits wants to know if Python Six wants the Ready Reaction Force to crank for support.

"That's a negative, Black Horse! Fire is too hot! Alert Tom Cat Six that we will need air cover over the crash site until we can get in!" Beyer replies.

"Roger, Python Six. Black Horse will advise other Tom Cat flights to crank!"

"Black Horse, this is Tom Cat Six. Monitoring frequency, and have already cranked. ETA [estimated time of arrival] will be zero five. Over!" This is the company commander of D/229th gunships reporting that he has been listening in to the Python frequency and already knows about the crash. Any aircraft that crashes within the 1st Cavalry Division becomes a family affair. All the assets of the entire Black Horse Division will immediately be diverted.

"Python 6, Blue Max Two-Six. Flight of four en route." As the news quickly spreads, the Python company frequency comes alive with other units reporting they are en route to help.

I fly left in a wide arc that will put the crash site on Beyer's side of the Huey.

"Tom, nothing we can do here till this thing cools down. Take me back to Python pad!" I bank sharply right and pull back on the cyclic control to pull the turn in tight so I can get a close look at the crash site prior to departing. What I see makes me want to puke: where they hit is the only bare spot in the jungle for any reasonable distance. I surmise that Woolen was slightly out of autorotation range of the grassy area.

Rather than commit to the jungle trees, he had bled off rotor rpm at the last moment in an attempt to make the bare spot. He did make it, but he didn't have enough inertia in the blade system to soften the landing. When he pulled up on the collective pitch control, the blades must have nearly stopped turning altogether.

They hit very hard and with considerable forward airspeed. In fixed-wing aircraft, you must maintain forward motion at all times for the aircraft to continue to fly; in helicopters, which can hover, the safest emergency landing is accomplished by zeroing out all forward airspeed just before touchdown. I can see the initial impact area and then the skid marks that lead to the aircraft. It is upside down and burning furiously. Parts of the helicopter are scattered along the trail made by the skid marks, but I cannot see any bodies. On board at the time of the crash were Bill, Woolen, the crew chief, the gunner and at least five of the 2/7th people. In a crash this hard, at least a few bodies would certainly have been pitched clear of the wreckage on the first wallop with the ground.

As the wreckage fades out of my field of vision, a small glimmer of hope remains. The Yellow Three and the Tom Cat gunship were not on the crash site for at least one to two minutes after they hit. Maybe . . . just maybe . . . they all got out and are hiding from the barrage of bullets being cooked off by the fire.

The ride back to Python is quiet; we are all deep in our thoughts and prayers for the crew. The silence is broken only when Beyer changes radios to the English tower and requests permission for us to land.

The flight line is already buzzing with A/229th Company people interviewing the pilots who landed earlier. I shoot an uneventful approach into an empty sandbag aircraft bunker and Beyer departs immediately. I go through the standard shutdown procedure from memory without missing a step. The Huey's engine, being a jet turbine, has to run at an idle speed (*flight idle*) for at least one minute. This allows all its components to cool down slowly before I turn it off.

I look up and see Sergeant McCrary standing just clear of the rotor blades with a very grim expression on his face. As the one minute at flight idle lapses, I turn off the fuel control and the turbine shuts down. The only sounds are the slow whooshing of the blades overhead and the normal sound of the transmission.

Mac approaches my open door and steps onto the skids. "Who were the chief and gunner?" I ask him before he has time to speak.

"Miranda and Young . . . " his voice trails off. "Any chance they survived?" Mac is watching my facial expression carefully, looking for a glimmer of hope to replace his despair.

"Mac, I just don't know. " I pause. "Galiger was flying in the Yellow Three slot when they called mayday. He and one of the gunships broke off to follow them down. When they got there, which could easily have been one or two minutes after the crash, they both reported not seeing anyone get out. They hit very hard, rolled upside down, and then started to burn. Ammo is going off all over the place, so I don't believe they could get very close. If anyone is left, then they're inside the aircraft or hiding in the jungle till things cool off."

"What did Mister Johnson say, Sergeant Mac?" This comes from one of the men who have gathered in the tight area behind Mac, between the Huey and the sandbag wall.

Mac turns around and repeats what I said. Faces turn grimmer and heads go down as they listen intently to Mac's every word.

"Are you going back there?" Mac turns and asks me.

"Don't know! Major Beyer said there was nothing anyone could do right now until the thing cools off. There is barely enough room for another ship to get into the LZ with the wreckage. The way that thing is burning, it will be several hours before all the loose ammo quits cooking off." I can see the anguish in Mac's eyes. His thoughts are the same as mine: If anyone there is still alive, he could be bleeding to death even as we speak. Major Beyer, I'm sure, is right now fending off other pilots who are volunteering to go in, no matter how hot it is. Sanity has to prevail here, and Beyer knows this more than any other person.

I exit the Huey, grab my helmet and other flight gear, and walk to the warrant officer tent, stopping often along the way to answer questions from the other enlisted men about what happened. I walk through the tent Bill is assigned to and briefly glance at his empty cubicle. It wrenches my gut, but I have not given up hope. "Where are the bodies?" I ask myself.

I enter my tent, drop my gear in my cubicle, and find the prone position on my cot. The wait will be a long one. When I can stand my own thoughts no longer, I get up and walk to the TOC bunker. The room is already full of other guys who are listening intently to the radios blaring the conversations among the aircraft still circling over the wreck site.

"Tom, one of the 1/9th Blue Team birds made a high-speed low pass a moment ago right over the site and thought he saw people lying down at the north side of the LZ right at the tree line!" It is Captain LuRay.

"You're kidding!!"

"Don't get your hopes up," LuRay cautions. "He didn't see any movement."

"Yes, sir, I understand, but, sir, I don't think they could have been thrown that far . . . they would've had to have walked or crawled." I say softly but with authority; I have been there and LuRay has not.

"Python control, this is Python Six. I'll be departing for the accident site. Over."

Captain LuRay picks up the FM radio tuned to the Python company frequency and rogers Major Beyer's transmission. I didn't notice a Huey cranking up on the hill above the TOC. "Mister Cool" himself can wait no longer.

"Tom Cat Six, this is Python Six. Are you still on station? Over." A different radio in the TOC cracks.

"That's a roger!" The gunship company commander replies.

"I have departed English en route to your location. Can you give me a SITREP? Over."

"Six, this is Tom Cat Six. Tom Cat Two-Six is making his approach now for a high-speed run look-see. It's a little cooler in the LZ now, but ammo is still going off sporadically. Stand by. He's just about to cross over the area now." Breathless seconds pass. All the radios are quiet.

"OK, OK, OK. Tom Cat Six this is Two-Six; I have seen at least *four*. . . I say again . . . *four* individuals at the north edge of the LZ! I have seen movement! I say again: someone has waved back at me!" There is a touch of fear and excitement in Two-Six's voice when he makes the transmission. From the noise of the rotor blades beating the air in the background, he must be pulling some god-awful Gs as he recovers from the high-speed run. His voice is strained.

"All right! All right!" The voices in the TOC bunker are excited but restrained. Everyone knows that there are still at least five more to be accounted for, and no one knows if the individuals that Two-Six spotted are our people or 2/7th.

"Tom Cat Six, this is Python Six. . . . Has there been any enemy activity down there?"

"That's a negative far as we can tell, Six, but with these rounds going off like they have been, it would be hard to tell if any of them are Charlie's rounds coming out of there. Over!"

"I'm about three more minutes out and will be going into the LZ to extract. Cover me! Over!"

"OK, Python Six, the Tom Cat flight will cover you all the way! Tom Cat flight, you heard what the man just said. Get ready to cover Python Six's extraction!"

"Tom Cat Two-Six, you and your wingman break off west and be ready. Tom Cat One-Six and I will fly Python Six's wing going in! You guys be ready when we break off!"

The other Tom Cat birds acknowledge their leader's instructions, and we hear Major Beyer call short final to the LZ. The radios are as silent as death again and long moments pass. Beyer's aircraft will be out of radio range to the TOC as he drops below the jungle line into the LZ. Then we hear him transmitting again.

The words sound garbled at first, but we understand that he is lifting out of the LZ.

Tom Cat Six transmits, "Coming out of LZ . . . roger!"

Python Six keys his mike, and the squelch breaks with his excited voice, "OK . . . Tom Cat Six we have five . . . I say again five . . . survivors on board. There are more individuals alive and still in the LZ. Do not fire for any reason. Python Yellow Three, are you still on station? Over!"

"Yellow Three, that's a roger!"

"Ok, Yellow Three, it's pretty cool down there now. How about going in and extracting what you can of the others!"

"Six, that's a roger . . . on the way in now!"

"Python control, if you copy, we have both Lee and Young on board! Lee says he knows that Woolen and Miranda are OK and are still in the LZ. Do you copy? Over."

LuRay has to transmit twice that he has understood Beyer's transmission, as the TOC is awash in outbursts of joy.

Filled with relief, I say, "I'm going to choke the life out of Lee when I get my damn hands on his throat! He scared the hell out of me with this crap!"

The entire crew of the downed eagle is welcomed home with a beer bash in their honor and already under way. Woolen reports that when the Huey rolled upside down, he looked over and saw that Lee was missing from his seat. Woolen assumed that he had been thrown out of the aircraft during the rollover. Lee's own account is that he had unbuckled his seat and shoulder belts and exited out the window. This meant that he had taken his slender frame out his window with the armor plate still forward on the seat. Now that is damn near impossible. There is a lateral distance of only 6 inches between the outside of the armor plate and the inside of the Huey's door, not to mention that someone would have to contort his body into a severe U shape to negotiate this type of exit. Not one of us believes Bill on this issue, and just to prove he could not have done it, 14 drunk warrant officers and 4 highly tipsy commissioned officers call Bill's bet that he can do it again. Lee is taken up the "hill" that night to a Huey. The door is closed and the armor plate is pulled forward.

One hour and seven cases of beer later, in spite of the taunting, pushing, shoving, and dousing with beer, Bill Lee finally gives up. He cannot get out of the Huey the same way he must have exited it after the crash. Of course, anything is possible when the adrenaline is really pumping. Perhaps the door sprung wider from the crash. Still, whether the armor plate was pulled forward or not, Bill Lee set the world's speed record for exiting a Huey out the window on his own. According to Woolen,[1] he did it so fast no one saw him leave.

---

1. Woolen became a hero after the crash. After unbuckling his seat and shoulder belts, he fell to the roof of the Huey. In an attempt to evacuate the wreckage through the open cargo doors, he found the 2/7th's black hat (radioman) trapped within the maze of strewn cargo and nylon webbing. With the aircraft already on fire, Woolen used his pocketknife to cut loose those bindings detaining the black hat. Endangering his own life, Woolen removed the severely wounded man from the wreckage and dragged him to the relative safety of the jungle some 50 feet away. For his courage, Warrant Officer Bill Woolen was later awarded the Bronze Star with V for valor.

8

Changing Seats

August 17, 1967

Pat writes me every day; I write her an average of one letter every other day. I miss her and home more each day as familiarity with the daily Air Cavalry routines gives me more time to think. I do not yet realize that these will be the most exciting times of my life.

This morning we are issued a new SOI; our call sign changes from Python to Bandit, and Tom Cat changes to Smiling Tiger. Recently, Lieutenant Gary Runyan finished his tour of duty in Vietnam and DEROS'd, or saw his last day in country; I became the safety officer for A/229th. After being in country for one month and eleven days, I no longer had to use the "MIKE"[1] in my transmissions. Now I am A Company's newest safety officer, and my call sign is Bandit 88.

Safety officer is a powerful position in an aviation company. At the top of the chain of command is the division safety officer; then comes the battalion safety officer, and then, the company safety officer. The job entails keeping our pilots abreast of things that can affect their flying safety, but it also gives me absolute authority when it comes to the safety conditions at every LZ where an A Company helicopter will land. Recently, I landed in a secure LZ named Bird. Poncho liners and other loose objects went airborne from the helicopter's rotor wash. A wooden box lid nearly went through my rotor blades during the

---

1. In radio call sign terminology, mike means assistant. 88mike means safety officer assistant.

landing. In addition, the barbed-wire that formed the perimeter was dangerously close to the landing pad. If an unsuspecting pilot accidentally put his tail rotor into this wire, he would lose control and likely kill not only himself and his crew, but also many soldiers on the ground. I discussed this with the captain in charge of the LZ, but he blew me off by saying, "War is hell," and simply walked away. On my return to LZ English, I spoke with my battalion safety officer, who in turn called division. Four hours later, the division safety officer, a brigadier general, landed on LZ Bird to "blow off" a captain. Changes were implemented as the general watched. For a lowly warrant officer like me, this is a chain of command I could really learn to like.

A few hours ago, a rifle company of the 2/8th Cavalry was pinned down with heavy automatic and mortar fire just east of LZ English near the coast. A call has come in that a platoon was separated from the rest of the company in the skirmish. They need artillery support badly, but the company commander cannot call in support of any type until he knows the exact whereabouts of his lost platoon.

Radio contact is being maintained; but the platoon leader cannot get his bearings accurately enough in the dark to tell anyone where he is. A/229th is on RRF duty tonight, and two birds launch.

In one ship, the aircraft commander is Charles Boyd and the pilot is Larry Gore. In the other are Captain Stephen MacWillie and myself. Our job is to locate the lost platoon by any means possible and do as the situation dictates. MacWillie, formerly Lieutenant MacWillie, has been promoted to the rank of captain and moved up to A/229th executive officer. Beyer has also christened him our newest flight leader. After leading several combat assaults, he has proved he knows how to get the job done and is a good leader of men. As senior aircraft commander, he leads the mission. Both ships launch into the darkness from what used to be called the former "snake pit," now called the Bandits' Hideaway.

As my eyes adjust to the dark, I see a three-quarter moon reflecting from the rice paddies below. The visibility is better than fair, but the high humidity could change this into night fog almost before I would know it.

Immediately after climbing away from LZ English on an east heading, we see the telltale signs of the battle near the coast. There are small fires blazing, overhead flares drifting back to earth, and the rico-cheting of spent tracer rounds flying all over the battle area. These sights always strike fear deep into my heart in spite of their paradoxical beauty.

MacWillie is already in contact with the ground commander as I fly the Huey in the direction of the battle. He also has contact with the lost platoon. The guy on the other end of the radio speaks very quietly when he replies to MacWillie's questions. Such a small unit could easily be wiped out if it is found separated from its main unit. There are two Smiling Tiger gunships already on station just waiting for us to do our jobs so they can get into the action. Unlike the gunships, our Hueys have a homing device built into the FM radio . . . the antennas look very much like two cat whiskers protruding vertically off the nose of the aircraft. MacWillie orders the radio operator to key for five seconds, and I adjust our route of flight until the squeal in my FM grows loudest. MacWillie then looks at the compass and draws a straight line on his map starting at our location and pointing in the direction the compass reads. I then change our route of flight to approach the same general area from a different direction. Using the same procedure as before, we draw another line. Where the lines intersect is our target. Since they do not want to be discovered as sitting ducks by Charlie, MacWillie tells them to give us a blinking flashlight and not to use any flares. We overfly the imaginary intersection and strain our eyes to see their light. On the third pass overhead at 1500 feet, the crew chief spots a blinking light, but there is no way of being sure this isn't Charlie.

Much to everyone's astonishment, the lost platoon is more than half a mile east of the rest of its company; there is no way for them to get back. MacWillie advises the company commander on the ground that the best thing we can do is to extract them. We transmit a compass heading that will guide the platoon to the beach. MacWillie instructs Boyd to return to refuel with us. While taking on fuel at the POL in English, Boyd and MacWillie exit their aircraft for a strategy session, leaving Gore and me in our seats with the blades still turning. We complete refueling and, when the commanders return, take off again toward the beach as fast as we can. In our absence, things have gotten worse for the 2/8th company on the ground and they are in desperate need of support. Charlie is probing the perimeter in force and knows very well that the closer he stays to the American company, the less likely he is to get hit by artillery.

The Smiling Tiger gunships have also rotated back to English for more fuel, but have left two more of their members on station. A Smiling Tiger reports to MacWillie that he has maintained visual contact with the lost platoon by requesting an occasional flicker of the flashlight. They have made their way to the edge of the trees on the west side of the sandy beach and have lain down in cover awaiting our return.

"Bushwhacker Two-Six, Bandit Yellow One. Over," MacWillie calls to the radio operator on the ground, whose call sign indicates a lieutenant-grade platoon leader.

"Bandit Yellow One, . . . go ahead."

"OK, Two-Six, have your people run for the beach—we are turning final!"

"Two-Six, roger!"

With that transmission, MacWillie makes a hard left turn from a heading of south to north and bottoms the pitch.

"Yellow Two, go trail!" The command is for Boyd to fall behind us in a trail formation. "Hang loose, Yellow Two!"

"Yellow Two, roger!"

"Tom, stay on the controls with me . . . this thing could get real hairy down here," warns MacWillie, with a degree of urgency in his voice.

The white beach glimmers under the moon. The tree line is easily visible to the west, as are the waves breaking against the shore to the east. However, it is still too dark to make out people from this height. There is real danger here.

First, there is no way to confirm that the flashlight signals are coming from the Bushwhacker troops. Charlie is not stupid: He monitors our radio frequencies and sometimes employs people who can speak perfect English. This could be an ambush. Second, when we land here in the night we produce a target that can be seen up and down the beach for miles. Last and most important is the danger we face in simply landing on a beach at night. It is very difficult to maintain depth perception and, therefore, very easy to fly right into the sand.

"Bushwhacker, give me a signal!" MacWillie keys his mike and transmits.

Sure enough, dead ahead, a tiny glow appears, goes out, then reappears.

"Tiger flight, Yellow One and Two are on final approach to Bushwhacker's location; can you guys cover the tree line? Over."

"Smiling Tiger, One-Six, that's a roger!"

As I glance through the "greenhouse" glass overhead, I can faintly see the navigation lights and rotating anticollision lights of the two gunships as they break to get into position to cover us.

"Tom, kill the lights!" I reach to the overhead panel and place two switches to the *off* position. "Yellow Two, Yellow One going lights out . . . keep your distance and stay alert!"

Now there is the additional danger of Yellow Two colliding with us. We continue our descent, maintaining a steady rate. The beach below spreads wider and wider as we come in for the landing. MacWillie focuses on the altimeter to determine how high above the ground he is, but it is a poor instrument to rely on. Because it functions by barometric pressure, it does not give a reading in absolute altitude. As we go through 200 feet on the altimeter, MacWillie is unable to figure out his height above the beach. There is nothing for the senses to grasp.

"Yellow Two, it's too hairy down here! I'm going to have to turn on a landing light! Bushwhacker, give me a signal!"

I push forward two toggle switches located on my collective pitch console to extend the landing light and the searchlight; now they will be ready for use when MacWillie calls for them. The landing light extends from the belly of the Huey, and the searchlight extends from the underside of the nose. I can adjust the searchlight with an umbrella-shaped switch located on my collective pitch.

"Landing light on!" MacWillie orders.

I push the same two toggle switches all the way forward, and both lights shoot through the darkness. Using the umbrella switch, I try to aim the searchlight. We are still higher than either MacWillie or I thought. MacWillie is also moving more quickly than he realized and begins flaring the Huey to slow down. This change in the attitude of the aircraft requires me to keep adjusting the landing light. The intensity of the landing light blots out any further signaling by the Bushwhacker people, so MacWillie targets their last signal location as our LZ.

"Smiling Tiger flight, *do not* fire until we know that we have all of them on board!" MacWillie transmits.

The danger of killing ourselves on the approach momentarily dulls the fear of a waiting ambush. The latter resurfaces as the landing light silhouettes 10 to 15 armed soldiers in the kneeling position some 30 feet ahead of us. MacWillie sees them, too, and starts making rapid last-minute adjustments to land just short of their position. The fear that these guys might be Viet Cong makes blood rush to my head. But it's too late now for us to avoid what might be certain death. MacWillie makes a last-minute flare before the skids touch down and the rotor wash kicks up a sandstorm, obscuring the people who were visible just moments ago.

In the blink of an eye, they charge straight for the nose of the Huey. As they run, they hold their heads down against the wind from the blades, making it impossible for us to identify them as friend or foe.

"Yellow One, you are taking fire from the tree line! I say again . . . Yellow One, fire from the tree line!" One of the Smiling Tiger birds has seen muzzle flashes.

Instinctively, I tighten my grip on the controls. Glancing out MacWillie's window, I see five or six flashes of light in the darkness. It looks as though someone in the tree line is taking our picture using a flash camera. The older pilots have told me that most weapons have flash suppressors on the ends of their barrels that prevent you from seeing the muzzle burst unless you are looking right down the barrel of the weapon as it fires. Within less than a second of the first flash, I hear the *tic, tic* of two bullets passing through the aluminum skin of the Huey—the very first time I hear this ominous sound. It amazes me how fear can dim one's sense of reality. A moment ago I was terrified at the thought that we had fallen headlong into a trap, but that was a "maybe" . . . now there are no "maybes" to the new danger and it feels like a dream. It seems that rounds are coming at us from every direction. I flinch as the first soldier passes by my window. But he is definitely a GI and is running to board his ride to safety.

"Richardson, find out if all of them are here. *Hurry!*" MacWillie calls to the crew chief.

I look over my left shoulder long enough to see Richardson push a couple of guys off the aircraft. We are loaded beyond our capacity to take off, and he is trying to tell those remaining that another bird is coming in right behind us.

"THUMP, THUMP, THUMP!" Suddenly, we see blinding flashes of light and loud thumps fill the air!

"MORTARS!" MacWillie yells so loudly that I do not need the intercom to hear what he says.

"All the troops are on the beach, sir!" Richardson screams.

"Smiling Tiger flight, take out the tree line, all the troops are on the beach! We are taking incoming!" MacWillie begins pulling pitch.

"Yellow Two on short final!" Boyd calls.

"Yellow One is out of here!" MacWillie replies, having a little trouble pulling us out of the sand.

Again looking back into the cargo area, I see Richardson using his foot to kick loose the grip of one GI who is determined to get aboard our overloaded Huey. As we get to an unstable 2-foot hover and begin a tail turn toward the South China Sea, Richardson gives up on the guy and is now helping him inside the aircraft. I do not have to tell MacWillie how full the cargo is as we stagger toward the sea. He nudges the Huey into forward motion, and we hit translational speed at almost the same time the low rpm warning light comes on . . . MacWillie milks the collective until the red light goes out. We now begin to fly.

Our attention turns to Boyd and Gore, who must be on the ground by now. MacWillie makes a gentle right turn so he parallels the beach. Out my window I hear and see the incoming mortar rounds hitting the beach. The VC are firing and adjusting their aim with each round, so that each successive explosion gets nearer to Yellow Two, sitting on the beach with landing lights glaring. The sand that is airborne all around glistens from their Huey's high-intensity white landing lights. In the center of these sparkles are their blinking red and green navigation lights. Combined with these sights, the flashbulb-effect of exploding mortars produces an image of festive beauty.

"Yellow Two is outta here!" Gore yells.

I see them lift to a hover, then disappear within their own blinding sandstorm. Boyd makes a right pedal turn, lowers the nose and punches out into clean air just as a round goes off right where they were just moments ago.

"Yellow One, Bushwhacker Six, did you get them all?"

"That's affirmative!" MacWillie replies.

"Good Job! Remain on your southerly heading until crossing the Bong Son River before you turn back in! Artillery rounds on the way out of English! Do you copy?"

"Yellow One copies. Yellow Two, do you copy?" MacWillie asks.

"Yellow Two copies!"

Bushwhacker Six is the battalion commander for the 2/8th, and the people on the ground are his. We do not know exactly where he is, but he is "up on our push," and it is obvious that he is somewhere overhead in another Huey watching our rescue take place. Within seconds after he ends his transmission, all hell breaks loose: The First Air Cavalry Division Artillery has decided it's time to flex a few of its muscles. The sky around LZ English lights up with muzzle flashes of 105mm and 155mm cannons that have been poised to strike. Within four seconds of the flashes, the rounds begin to impact in and around the battle zone. The Smiling Tigers expend their ammo into the tree line and are content to get out of artillery's way by falling behind us for the ride home. We pass south of the Bong Son River and turn inland. No fireworks display I have ever seen comes close to what we and our passengers are witnessing. Every tube in range of the battle is firing. I did not know those guys could reload so quickly. LZ English glows in the light of artillery tube explosions that forewarn that an angel of death is airborne.

MacWillie tells me to request a landing to the airstrip. Since it is night and we are so heavy, he makes a running landing on the metal runway in the same manner as you would land a fixed-wing airplane.

Yellow Two is right behind us. We deplane our passengers on the English hard surface runway and fly very low to POL to refuel, then back to Bandits' Hideaway to park.

As the Huey's blades make their last rotation, I find myself still strapped into my seat, helmet off, with sweat running off the end of my nose. I cannot move. I am exhausted.

"Come on, Tom . . . let's get some breakfast!" Gore has walked over.

Although it is several more hours till daybreak, that idea sounds wonderful.

"How many holes have you found, Richardson?" MacWillie, who is already outside the Huey, asks.

"Seven, sir, as far as I can tell right now!" Richardson replies as he walks around his Huey counting bullet holes.

MacWillie laughs aloud and continues packing up his flight gear. "Good job, Johnson! You really know what's going on out there! I think you're ready for the aircraft commander seat."

I am both taken aback and delighted by his comment, especially since it has been made while my classmate is standing outside.

"You got to be kidding, Mac; I don't want the job, but thank you anyway."

As Gore and I leave the parking area and head toward the mess tent, I notice that everyone is already awake and outside their living areas. Bushwhacker's artillery is firing, and occasionally in unison. The earth under our feet is vibrating with the concussions. I feel a little pride as those who have just awakened ask what is going on.

As Gore and I recount the events of the mission, I realize that we both added to our experience tonight with three firsts: seeing the muzzle flashes, taking hits, and being the target of incoming mortar rounds. The next stop after my breakfast and coffee is my cot. In spite of the noises around me, I simply lie down and go to sleep without even undressing.

Too soon the company CO awakens me. I am startled and pissed-off—I was dreaming of Pat and home.

"Major Beyer wants to see you, Mr. Johnson."

Since I am already dressed, in the finest Cav style I simply brush my teeth to remove the foul aftertaste of breakfast, rinse my face, and proceed to the operations bunker.

Upon entering the bunker, I find that MacWillie, Boyd, and Gore are already there with Beyer and some "light" colonel, whom I do not know. Introducing me to the senior officer, Beyer tells him I am "Mister Johnson, our newest aircraft commander." This is news to me. The senior officer is Colonel Roland, known as Bushwhacker Six, the battalion commander for the 2/8th. It was he with whom we talked last night. He has taken time to drive over to our company area to look up the guys who executed the rescue last night.

The battle raged all night, but as a result of the Cav's support, Colonel Roland's people went on the offensive at daybreak and destroyed Charlie. When the meeting breaks up, I corner Major Beyer.

"What's this crap about being the company's newest A/C, Major?"

Beyer looks at me with a hard face, then takes another deep draw on his cigar. "That's right, Johnson; I cut the orders this morning."

"Sir, I've been in country two months and seven days! Do you think I'm ready for that?"

"Don't necessarily matter what I think. The other A/Cs say you're ready, so I think you're ready, too." He nods and walks away, leaving a trail of cigar smoke.

"Congratulations, Johnson!" Gore offers his hand. "Newbie aircraft commander!"

"Thanks, Larry, but I don't know about this. It's quite an honor, but I really don't know if I can handle the left seat."

The four of us are grounded for the rest of the day. After chow we get together to tell others of last night's exploits. Much of the conversation involves making fun of Larry and me for finally getting our cherries busted.

"Gore, if ol' George Marcotte could only see me now!" I croak.

"Marcotte!" Gore shoots to attention, backbone straight and feet together. "Present Arms!" he yells, pulling his right hand above his right eye in perfect military style and spilling a glass of green Kool- Aid in the process.

I do likewise, then make a very sincere Kool-Aid toast to a man whose name will forever live in my memory.

■

Following preflight training at Fort Wolters, Texas, I was assigned to flight A-4 of the 2nd WOC Company. The "den mother" for flight A-4 was a chief warrant officer 2nd class named George I. Marcotte. When I first saw him, I almost laughed out loud. At 5 feet 5 inches Marcotte was barely chest high to the candidates he was in charge of. What Marcotte lacked in stature he made up for in décor. On his head he always wore his green Army combat helmet, polished to a shine, and around his neck was a brilliant yellow scarf, neatly tucked into his shirt. He also carried a black swagger stick reminiscent of the old horse soldier days. It didn't take us very long to verify the old adage that dynamite comes in small packages. Marcotte surpassed all standards previously set for TAC officers. He was a man to be feared by all, a "shaker."

When you least expected to see him, he would surface right at the nape of your neck, breathing fire and brimstone.

Now that I had finished preflight, I felt like we were about to really get the show on the road. The first four weeks had been miserable ones for every-body, but at least now I was going to get to fly. Actual flight training would begin on Monday, and we were excited about it. But first, our new TAC officer, Mr. Marcotte, had all weekend to make sure there was no doubt that he was the boss.

Preflight housing had been in old World War II Army barracks, but now we were on the hill, in freshly constructed two-story brick and mortar dormitories. Each building could house about 180 candidates. The interior of our dormitory had many rooms, each designed to billet four candidates. Each WOC had his bunk, closet, and study desk with lamp. The floors were unbelievable. They were concrete, which was typical, but the concrete was polished—and I do mean polished. I thought I had learned the meaning of "spotless" at preflight, but here I gained an entirely new understanding of the word.

My first run-in with Marcotte came quickly. It took ten candidates work-ing one hour a night to keep the floors up to his standards. We all took turns based on quickly established work schedules. Some of us would be on hands and knees applying the Johnson's wax; others would follow with buffers.

It was our first Sunday night in 2nd WOC. While I was running the buffer, Marcotte suddenly appeared without warning. The first WOC to see a TAC officer must yell at the top of his voice so that all on the floor will hear the command for "attention." Without any delays, you must stop whatever you're doing, find the cinder-block wall immediately in front of your cubicle, and straighten your back and shoulders with your eyes straight ahead.

I did not hear the command over the noise of the buffer. I was daydream-ing about finally getting to fly the next morning. I knew I was in trouble when it suddenly dawned on me that I was the only candidate still in the hallway. A quick look over my shoulder confirmed my worst nightmare: some 20 feet down the hall stood Marcotte, and he was zeroing in on me. In a flash, I let go of the buffer and found the wall—it didn't have to be my wall, just any wall. The buffer motor began to wind down slowly, and since no one was holding on to the handle, it began to make 360-degree turns, thus winding the power cord all around it. I saw my life passing before me as I heard the unmistakable cadence of Marcotte, the mad scientist, approaching. The buffer came to an abrupt stop when it finally jerked the power cord from its outlet. At the same moment Mr. Marcotte appeared in front of me.

"OK, clown!" he growled, snapping his black leather swagger stick against his pants leg. "What's your name?"

At this point, all I could see was the top of his brilliantly polished helmet, because he was so short and I was nearly 6 feet tall. So, trying to be polite, I looked down at him, only to realize as I moved my head that I had screwed up big-time. Immediately, I snapped it backward and bumped the cinder-block wall with a resounding thud while also attempting to reply to the question. My reply went unheard as Marcotte took my mistake personally.

"Just who do you think you are, candidate!!" He yelled at the top of his voice. He moved in closer for the kill.

"Who told you that you could look at me? Are you rubbernecking me, candidate? Did your daddy lose his rubber when he was screwing your mother, candidate! Is that the same rubber that's connecting your ugly face to your miserable body, candidate?" Marcotte moved in even closer, and I felt his hot breath up under my chin. "Are you a rubbernecker, candidate, or are you just trying to piss me off?"

How could I begin to answer those questions without inviting more abuse?

More footsteps from up the hall signaled that Marcotte was not alone and that additional suffering was imminent.

Marcotte gritted his teeth and spoke calmly, almost civilly. "I asked you for your name, candidate."

"Sir, Candidate Johnson, sir" I said, glad that my vocal cords still worked.

The instant the sound waves escaped my lips, Marcotte turned and yelled it up and down the hall.

"Candidate Johnson! Candidate Johnson! Mister Parker, have you ever heard such a redneck speak the English language so clearly?" Marcotte addressed his question to one of two additional tac officers who had arrived on the scene.

"Mr. Marcotte, I think this candidate must be from the South, don't you?" TAC Officer Parker replied loudly while moving in for the kill.

Marcotte again turned his attention to me. "Where are you from, Candidate Johnson?"

"Sir, Candidate Johnson, Georgia, sir!" The vocal cords worked but with a distinct quiver.

"Georgia! Oh, well, Candidate Johnson, you can just go on and pack

your bags 'cause nobody from Georgia has ever passed this course. If you're from Georgia, then you're like all the rest—stupid rednecks. I don't allow Georgia crackers to fly my helicopters!" Marcotte shrieked.

"You are stupid, aren't you, Candidate Johnson?" Parker added.

"Sir, Candidate Johnson, no, sir! I'm not stupid, sir!" I replied, fearing a hesitation in answering the question would be worse than the reply itself.

"Candidate, explain to me then how it is that you come from Georgia and are not stupid, because everyone from that cotton-picking state is stupid!" Parker barked even louder. "Johnson, you've been in this school four weeks and I'll bet you can't even tell me the difference between a 23 and a 55!"

This last statement was drawn from standard hazing practice, and was designed to expose my lack of knowledge about the two helicopters used as flight trainers at Wolters. They were the OH-23 Hillers and the TH-55 Hughes aircraft; we had spent untold hours of classroom time studying every minute detail of the physical and flight characteristics of each. A candidate was expected to answer this question by talking as long as possible about the mechanical and aerodynamic differences between the two helicopters, but my answer just slipped out before I could help myself.

"Sir, Candidate Johnson, the difference between 23 and 55 is 32, sir!" God, why did I just say that?

Both Marcotte and Parker were clearly caught off guard by my reply. They simply said nothing. I don't think either of them could instantaneously comprehend that I had just said what I said.

The silence didn't last as long as I thought it might. First there came a crack, in the form of a stifled laugh, from some candidate to my left, then another from my right. I saw Marcotte and Parker quickly look to their right in the direction of the stifle, then to their left. In only a fraction of a second came outbursts of wind from between other lips, as candidates within the range of my voice, tried in absolute desperation to hold back laughter that was certain to lead them directly into the infantry.

"Well, Mister Parker," Marcotte said patiently. "It seems we have a smart-ass on our hands!"

But they had totally lost total control of the situation. They were not laughing at all.

"Get down and give me fifty, Candidate Smart-Ass!" Parker yelled. "All of you get down and give me fifty! RIGHT NOW! I want fifty push-ups! HIT IT!" Parker began yelling up and down the hall as he marched off,

rapping on the metal doorframes with his clipboard along the way. "It seems you candidates have a real smart-ass in this flight named Candidate Johnson! He has now ordered you to do some push-ups for Mr. Marcotte!" His voice trailed off slightly as he walked away down the hall. That left just Marcotte and me confronting each other, and neither of us thought the other was funny. I spotted an indentation of mortar between the cinder blocks of the opposite wall, and glued my eyes to it. I could see the top of Marcotte's helmet with my peripheral vision, but I didn't dare move either my body or eyes to get a better look. I simply waited until he moved slightly out of my way so that I could fall to the floor and begin my punishment like the rest. At the earliest possible moment, I hit the floor and began counting off push-ups. Marcotte stayed nearby, and I guess he was trying either to size me up as a candidate or to measure me for a coffin. I was sure I would get my walking papers by Monday and have to be satisfied with having at least gotten this close to being an Army aviator.

The entire floor was alive with candidates bobbing up and down and counting. Marcotte and Parker began walking up and down the hall, stepping over candidates in the process and occasionally stopping to heap their abuse on various men.

After the last man finished counting and we again braced against the wall, the hallway fell dead quiet. I fully expected a return visit from one or both of the TACs, but instead they simply left the floor. The at-ease command was given by a candidate, and I nearly fainted in relief. Laughter broke out from our section again, and as my comment began to pass down the hall in both directions, an attitude of merriment took over.

I finished buffing the floor and hit the sack, trying to figure out why I had said what I had. It had seemed like the right thing at the time.

In all the time I knew Marcotte, I saw him smile only once, and that was when he gave two candidates their walking papers for the infantry. But as I studied him (from as great a distance as possible) and as I thought about him later, I recognized him as one of the finest officers I had met in the Army. Every time you saw him, he was doing his job well. He was "spit and shine" from head to toe and so military that I believe his teeth shone in the dark. He was dedicated to his job of turning boys into men and men into officers and pilots. His philosophy on punishment and reward was based on clear principles. No one ever was rewarded, but when someone in the flight messed up, everyone got punished.

9

The LZ Geronimo Incident

October 1967

I can easily envision the leaves falling from the oak trees back home. Carrollton, Georgia, is near the base of the "Great Smoky Mountain" chain. You have only to drive a few miles north to enter the most breathtaking mountain scenery imaginable. Near the end of September, the leaves begin to lose their greenish complexions. In mid-October, the maples and red oaks that line Bankhead Highway are dressed out in hues of gold and red. Near Halloween, leaves—one by one—will say good-bye to their hosts. I long for the aromatic smell of burning piles of leaves that often fills the air on cool Saturday afternoons.

I miss Pat and home very much. She writes every day and occasionally sends photographs. I look long and hard at the images of her, and my heart breaks from the loneliness. Often I worry about our relationship and wonder whether I will arrive home in one piece. She has depended on me to make most of the decisions . . . now she is on her own. How will Vietnam change me? Will we ever pick up our lives together with the same harmony we had before?

Sometimes there are problems with the mail and I receive no letters. Then four or five letters come all at once. I receive the *Times Georgian*, our local paper, regularly. I feel angry at the war protests going on at home. I don't especially want to be here, but I didn't run from my responsibilities when my country called.

The Vietnam War is a first in several ways:

It is the first war my country has ever fought in which higher education provides a deferment to mandatory military service. If you get into college and maintain a *B* average, you won't go to Vietnam.

It is the first war my country has ever fought in which the Reserves have yet to be called up. Back in the States, it is well known that if you want to avoid Vietnam, you need only to join the Army or Marine Reserves. In all other wars, the Reserve Units were put on active duty prior to the drafting of civilians into military service.

It is the first war my country has ever fought in which if you can survive 12 months you will go home. In previous wars, you were there until it was over. The way I have it figured is that if everybody who had been here before me had stayed here, then they wouldn't have needed me and I might have stayed home with Pat.

Now it seems to me there are only the war-protesting hippies at home and us folks over here just trying to stay alive for 12 months. The gut-wrenching conflict between these two camps reflects the differences of philosophy that will split the United States of America for many years to come. At this moment, I feel like I'm shooting the wrong Communist—like I need to be at home hiding in the bushes along the antiwar march routes of the students of West Georgia College.

A recent letter informed me that a very close friend has died in Vietnam. Jimmy Taylor and I grew up in the same neighborhood and walked to grammar school side by side for many years. In high school, Jimmy was forced to stay out and help his dad a lot. As a result he failed a couple of grades and got drafted into the Army. He lasted barely three weeks in Vietnam. I found it chilling that when Jimmy Taylor's flag-draped casket arrived home in Carrollton, Georgia, a West Georgia College professor was flying the Viet Cong battle flag in his classroom.

The fall of 1967 brings more intense tropical weather to Vietnam; temperatures run in the 90s with the humidity about the same. I continue learning how to be a good pilot. The responsibilities of the left seat bear heavily on me. Most of the helicopter pilots easily attain the maximum flying time of 140 hours before the end of each month. Once this happens, we get a couple of days off. We spend this time getting haircuts and periodically catching a jeep ride to "downtown" Bong Son. We catch up on our writing or just sit around and drink with friends. Too much of this time is dangerous: homesickness is an enemy that sneaks up after a little idle time and a couple of beers. The sounds of the latest music blast over radios scattered around the tents— courtesy of "A-Farts," the Air Force Radio and Television Station (AFRTS) broadcasting from An Khe.

Today is my day off and I am enjoying the solitude. I have just finished writing a letter to Pat and have begun washing out some socks when the company CQ, Specialist Four Rett Morrison, runs inside the tent yelling my name. Morrison is the company operations errand boy. Generally, if he is looking for me, it means someone in operations needs something. I choose to ignore his calls and quietly continue to rinse out my last few socks.

Morrison checks every cubicle in the tent to no avail, then starts to exit out the west end and finds me.

"Mister Johnson, Major Beyer needs you right now! We just lost three birds on LZ Geronimo!" Morrison sounds as though he is expending his last breath; sweat is pouring over his face.

I retreat into the tent to recover my flight gear, and Morrison follows. "Anybody hurt?" I ask.

"Don't know yet, sir. It just came in over the radio and we called Major Beyer. He was south of the Bong Son pass headed to An Khe. He instructed me to find you and have you meet him on the flight line. He's inbound now . . . maybe two minutes out."

Assuming that Beyer wants me with him not as an aviator but as safety officer for A/229th, I race into operations, where Lieutenant Lonnie Rogers, our operations officer, stands, clad only in his olive drab underwear and jungle boots. Lonnie stays up most of each night scheduling the next day's missions and aircraft, and apparently he has been awakened from his sleep.

"Geronimo Four-Eight, Bandit Three-Six. Can you give me a SITREP? Over." The 2/12th Cavalry has occupied LZ Geronimo since it was first assaulted, and Lonnie is trying to get a situation report from the black hat on the LZ.

"Bandit Three-Six, Geronimo Four-Eight. Three of your aircraft have crashed during landing at the south end of the LZ. Don't know if your people are OK or not. We have one KIA here and several others hurt. Medevac is on the way. Over."

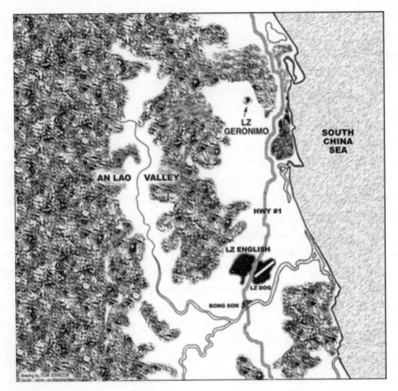

Lonnie turns to me, pauses just a moment, then picks up a micro-phone connected to another radio. Deep concern has clouded his whole face.

"Bandit Six, this is Bandit Three-Six. SITREP, over."

"Three-Six, go ahead," Beyer replies.

"Injuries and casualties to Bandit people unknown. One Geronimo person KIA and apparently many injured. Geronimo Four-Eight says crash occurred during landing on south side of LZ. Do you want me to call in some of our people to go up there? Over."

"That's a negative. Eighty-Eight and I will give you a call when we are able to look things over. Tell Eighty-Eight that I am on short final to Bandit's pad. Over!"

With that I scoot out of the operations bunker and rush uphill to meet Beyer.

LZ Geronimo lies some 6 or 7 miles northeast of LZ English and is near the coast. I can almost tell Beyer what has happened before I climb into the cockpit of the Huey. Geronimo is constructed on a hilltop that rises some 80 to 100 feet above the rice paddies. The southern side of the LZ is a ridgeline barely wide enough for a Huey. Approach must be perpendicular to the ridgeline. Some smart-ass figured out real quick that due to the helicopter traffic in and out of Geronimo, they needed more than one landing pad. The ridgeline has a low spot in its backbone, so in went the bulldozers to grade three flat spots. On both sides of the low spot, two LZs are created. They are 10 feet higher than the low spot and therefore form a saddle when viewed from the side. There is not enough blade clearance in this architecture. Any Huey that lands in the bottom of the saddle has to wait until those above on each side take off, else there is a very good chance of intermixing rotor blades. As long as the first helicopter in lands in the base of the saddle and takes off last, after those to the left or right, everything will be okay—at least this was so in the minds of those who constructed the LZ. In the real world, pilots flying well over a hundred hours a month will make critical mistakes. Most of the time the error is not terminal and the only harm done is a scare. Any mistake of this nature during takeoff or landing at Geronimo will be disastrous. Many pilots have complained loudly, including myself, about this unsafe landing area. Major Beyer has already warned the 2/12th commander that unless the architecture of the LZs is changed, he will no longer send any of the A/229th helicopters into LZ Geronimo.

Neither Beyer nor I am ready for the scene at the crash site. One bird on the North Slope looks intact, but as we near, it becomes evident that a rotor strike between two or more of the helicopters has indeed occurred. Its blades are twisted like pretzels. The transmission has been jerked out of its mountings and lies a short distance uphill

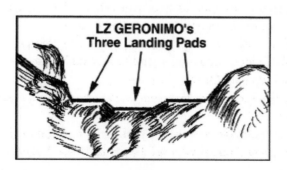

LZ GERONIMO's Three Landing Pads

from the rest of the aircraft. The Huey that had landed on the southern side of the slope is now lying on its side midway down the slope of the ridgeline. The third bird is not on the LZ at all.

Beyer, who is flying, makes a low west-to-east pass. Then we see it. The rest of the accident took place at the base of Geronimo, down in the rice paddies. The main section of the fuselage is almost flat, the skids spraddled level with the base of the cargo compartment. Blades, transmission, and other bits of wreckage are strewn down the slope.

There are 10 or 12 persons around the wreckage. Beyer makes a hard 270-degree turn left, from east to south, and gently puts our Huey down into the rice paddies as near the wreckage as possible. He bails out, leaving me to shut our Huey down. As I sit here waiting for the turbine engine to cool down, I begin to recognize our people one by one. Three wounded can walk, but one is lying on his back across a dry rice paddy dike.

From out of nowhere come two more Hueys, which proceed to land on the opposite side of the wreckage. One is a medevac bird and the other contains Lance Stewart, A/229th maintenance officer. Lance slogs his way across the ankle-deep rice paddy as fast as his legs can carry him. In his haste, he occasionally falls down, only to recover and slosh even faster.

His first stop is the injured crewman on the dike; then he moves on to the others without even noticing Major Beyer. I feel impotent—before I can rush to the side of my comrades I have to wait out the one-minute cooling-off period of the Lycoming turbine. Impatiently I sit until the second hand passes 12 and I shut down. When I jump out of the aircraft, I sink in wet muck above the ankles, but I go as fast as I can toward the downed Huey.

"How bad are our people, Stew?"

"I think they'll be OK, Tom. Richards, the crew chief, is worse than any of the rest. Probably a back and neck injury." As Stew speaks, the medevac bird lifts off for English with Richards and the gunner on board. Both pilots are alert and talking to Beyer. One of the pilots finally plops down on the dike. His actions cause Stew and me to look in that direction, thinking he is fainting.

"Have you heard about the rest of the guys on the hill?" I ask.

"Yeah. The black hat told me that our people are OK, but a rotor blade caught one of their people in the back."

"How bad is he?"

Stew pauses. "In two parts," he replies grimly.

Turning to look uphill, I can see several helicopters hovering precariously on the tiny ridgeline, attempting to take aboard the injured. They cannot land. Others fly overhead in a pattern, waiting their turn into LZ Geronimo's south side.

Beyer and I take the two pilots back to our aircraft. We depart and drop them off at the medevac pad near the runway at English.

All our people recover without serious injuries, including Richards. In light of the severity of the crashes, I cannot understand how any of them survived. Back at the A/229th Company, the mood is somber. Depression has set in on the pilots who made a mistake and took a life needlessly. There are no words of comfort—only time will ease the burden of this accident.

I fill out the required accident report. It happened as I had thought, with the center helicopter lifting off into the blades of the adjoining helicopters. Division will now send in engineers with heavy equipment to level the ridgeline to accommodate three helicopters. The sad thing is that so much grief has been caused by a worthless piece of ground.

As safety officer, I feel partly responsible for this accident. LZ Geronimo was there long before I arrived in Vietnam and it has been accepted landing and takeoff practice for the two outer helicopters to land last and take off first, but today, someone had a "brain fart."

10

Battle of Tam Quan

November 28, 1967

For two weeks now the 1st Cav high command has been aware of an increasing incidence of Viet Cong probes of perimeters all over the Bong Son plain and around LZ English. In fact, LZ Laramie, which is high on a ridgeline along the mountains that form the eastern side of the An Lao valley, has come under a night attack in which four Americans were killed and several wounded. A sizable enemy force has been probing LZ Geronimo's perimeter. Even LZ English's defenses have been tried two nights in a row; when the flares and claymores went off, the enemy retreated in great haste. Everyone knows something is going on, but we have no idea what. The 1/9th[1] scout pilots are working overtime sniffing around in every hamlet and village with their Bell H-13 helicopters in an attempt to find out the strength and location of the enemy. The pilots and crews of the 1/9th are members of an elite family of either the craziest or the bravest people I have ever known. They are the only unit in Vietnam consistently programmed at 100 percent strength. Due to the high attrition rate in the war, rarely does the programmed strength of a unit equal the authorized strength. Except for the 1/9th, most units generally function with 80 percent of the troops authorized for them.

It is a normal occurrence for scout pilots to hover up and down

---

1. The movie *Apocalypse Now* was based on some of their exploits and is highly accurate in its detail of how the 1/9th conducted its own private war.

trails looking for footprints or other signs of Charlie. Once, I witnessed a pilot put the bubble nose of his H-13 helicopter right into the doorway of a village hooch just so he could get a better look. All the 1/9th aircraft have the old Cavalry "cross sabers" insignia painted on them in bright 1st Cav yellow. I think all those guys get nosebleeds if they ever fly above 50 feet.

Debonair does not come close to describing these guys. Membership on this team is open to volunteers only. They are the only folks in the Army who wear western-style black hats with gold braid tassels as a part of their official uniform. The hats are often worn in "Aussie" style, with one side held up with a crossed sabers pin. They wear these with great pride. They play just as hard as they work—rough and tumble leisure time is the only thing that can distance them from the savage Russian roulette they play in their daily routines. In 1967, there is a greater than 50 percent chance that any given member of the 1/9th will depart Vietnam in a casket. There is a 70 percent chance that if he survives, he will return with at least one Purple Heart. The 1/9th is in fact a "Mini Cav" that includes its own support personnel, scout helicopters, and air assault troops. Almost every battle the 1st Air Cavalry gets into is a result of the 1/9th getting into some type of brawl. When it is too big for them to handle on their own, the rest of us get a call to assist.[2]

The 1/9th Cavalry helicopter crews maintain the highest one-on-one kill ratio of any units in the war. This is not "push button warfare." They repeatedly meet their enemy eyeball to eyeball on his terms—in his backyard—and terminate him with a vengeance. The organization of the 1/9th consists of three troops, labeled Alpha, Bravo, and Charlie. Each troop consists of ten Huey gunships (Red Platoon), Ten OH-13 Bell "Bubble Job" Scout helicopters (White Platoon), and four troop-carrying Huey helicopters (Blue Platoon).

When Charlie is finally found, it will be the 1/9th Cavalry that finds them.

My long awaited R&R has arrived—December 1, 1967. I have been in country for six months and have managed to schedule it during the

---

2. Two good sources of information on the 1/9th are Matthew Brennan's *Headhunters* (Novato, CA: Presidio Press, 1987) and *Brennan's War* (Novato, CA: Presidio Press, 1985).

week of Pat's and my fifth wedding anniversary. In our letters to each other, we have counted down the days until we meet in Hawaii. I process through Armed Forces Recreation Center at Fort DeRussy as fast as the idiots in charge allow. I just can't believe my ears when the officer of the day announces that all officers will attend a conference on "how to conduct oneself on R&R" and "what sights to see in Hawaii." It takes nearly 30 minutes to assemble the group and then 30 minutes more for them to say what they have to say. They command the same level of attention as a flight steward demonstrating emergency procedures of the Boeing 707.

This is my time now; I have earned it the hard way, and the Army is encroaching upon it. As soon as I am released, I jog from the discussion to the hotel where Pat is waiting.

The closer to the door I get, the more apprehensive I become. I realize how far apart our worlds have grown in a few short months. Vietnam has changed me, and I know that Pat's world has somehow made her different, too. Our letters to each other have probably burned the postman's hands with their passion, but they are written to the persons we once were.

She has slimmed down considerably, changed her hairstyle, and streaked it. It is the current fashion, but it is not the girl I left back home. I have dropped to less than 120 pounds. The tropical environment has turned my skin to a golden brown, and I have grown a mustache, the trademark of young warrant officer pilots in defiance of the old military establishment's rules.

Instead of making passionate love immediately, we sit on the beds and chairs of our room at the "Reef" hotel on Waikiki Beach and talk. I find myself repeatedly opening fresh beers and using foul language, things the "other Tom Johnson" never did. I have been sexually faithful to Pat, but the environment has played a dramatic roll in keeping me on the "straight and narrow" path. When you fly for the 1st Cavalry, the days are very long and our base areas are far from the civilized places that might pose temptations. And there is the other factor—certain chemicals that normally circulate in a man's body go into remission when he goes without for a long time. I guess this and many other more complicated things in my head make me want to avoid lovemaking for nearly three hours. When it does finally occur, Vietnam temporarily washes down the sink with body sweat and bath-water.

"Hinchliffe speaking." I have called an old friend, George Hinchliffe, and this is George's usual style of answering the phone. Julie and Pat made sure that all four of us put in for our R&R at the same time and hotel.

"Listen, George, if you can tear yourself out of that bed for a few hours, let's go out on the town to get something to eat. OK?"

"Gee, Tom . . . I don't know. I've got a lot of catching up to do." In the background I hear a loud slap issued to George by Julie. "On the other hand, sounds like a good idea. We'll meet you up in your room in a few minutes."

"We're in room 4614."

"4614—no problem. By the way, have you been listening to the news?"

"Are you kidding! We haven't turned on the TV since I arrived. Why?"

"Cav is kicking ass again. This time it's right outside your tent."

"Outside my tent?"

"Yeah, the biggest battle in Nam is going on right now without us. Ain't that a pisser?" George is using his dry humor again. "1st Cav has committed everything to an area two miles outside the perimeter of LZ English. It's on national news right now."

"Thanks, George, we'll be looking for you and Julie. Let me see if I can catch it. See you later." Abruptly, I hang up the phone and tune in the news. Chet Huntley and David Brinkley are reporting, and as they speak, the film footage shows Hueys with blue triangles on the doors making assaults.

Chet Huntley reports:

1st Cavalry Division became embroiled in battle on the Bong Son plains this morning when a scout helicopter from the 1st Squadron Ninth Cavalry observed a communication antenna sitting in the top of a palm tree near the village of Dia Dong. The H-13 helicopter, along with his wingman, were immediately shot down. Other elements of the 1/9th were air-assaulted into the area and were immediately destroyed. Other elements of the 1st

Cavalry Division in battalion strength have been flown into the area only to be pinned down by deadly cross fire. The enemy is believed to be forces of the Twenty-Second North Vietnamese Regiment who infiltrated around the 1st Cavalry's forward base LZ English. The fighting is at such close range, GIs are reported to be in hand-to-hand combat with their adversary, and the NVA are looting the bodies of the dead Americans. The enemy is firmly entrenched in spider holes and hedge-groves. Using B40 rockets, the NVA have destroyed three personnel carriers, killing six American soldiers.

Flying through virtual walls of bullets, helicopters of the 1st Cavalry continue to pour in reinforcements to the battle area. Some of the units are coming from as far away as Dak To, which is 70 miles to the west.

Vietnam has crept into Hawaii.

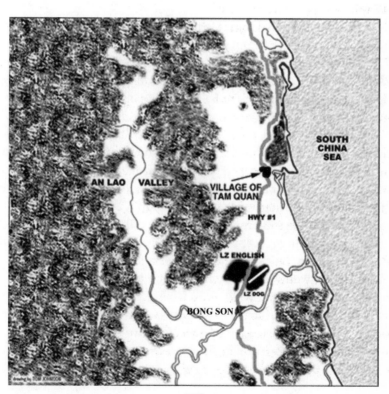

Pat rubs my arm softly and speaks not a word. Her touch diverts my attention for a moment. She presses her bare breasts against my back as we sit on the end of the bed.

Huntley/Brinkley World Report finally breaks into a commercial and I turn off the TV. A rush of sadness goes through me. I open another beer and move to the veranda outside. I remain deep in thought, once again remote to Pat's world, until the door to our room opens. It is George and Julie.

"Did you see our guys kicking ass?" George flies for the 2/20th ARA, 1st Cavalry Division.

Although we both are in the Cav, it is the first time I have seen him since we met in San Francisco just before shipping over. We embrace like brothers.

For the next hour, George and I drink and talk about things in Nam. Julie and Pat catch up on one another's worlds. Somehow talking to George brings me back to Hawaii. I put the newscast behind me and the four of us depart for dinner.

The highlights of our visit to the Aloha state turn out to be getting onstage with Don Ho at Duke Kahanamoku's club, renting a Triumph TR6 Bonneville motorcycle and getting a speeding ticket within the first city block of the rental store, and "bulldogging" the bike in a pineapple field. The owner of the field does not appreciate it one bit and gives chase.

Throughout R&R, I never turn on the TV again. Days fly by like hours; true love clogs our veins; we laugh and play. Vietnam seems so far away, yet it is always near. A backfiring motorcycle once sends me hurtling from our bed to the floor. Pat looks down in astonishment, concludes it is the start of some kind of kinky sex, and immediately joins me. I find myself checking under the pillow for my .38 revolver and doing a lot of nighttime bed sweating. At sunset, with the ocean door wide open, we lie on the carpeted floor, caressing each other's bare skin . . . wet from the tropical heat. For the moment, the entire world consists of just the two of us. During our first night together, Pat said that I have changed. I asked in what way, but she could not describe it. She has changed, too, and this is of some concern to me. It is already well known that only the very strongest marriages will survive Vietnam.[3] The suspicions provoked by separation and broad swings in the personal habits of a mate are only a few of the snakes that will rise to poison a relationship.

The dreaded day arrives. I ask Pat not to cry. At the airport, I kiss her tenderly and hold her close. A strong premonition tells me this will be the last time I see her. My emotions are screaming to get out, but I keep them in check as much as possible. I kiss her for the last time, turn to walk to the airplane and never look back.

Already I miss her so much that I hurt inside. The return flight from Hawaii to Vietnam seems to last twice as long as the one we had only a week ago. Silence reigns for the first hour—all the men are deep in thought. Returning to Vietnam entails a difficult change in state of mind.

For A/229th, the battle around Dai Dong and Tam Quan is still raging. So far, we have lost two helicopters, but all our people have survived without a scratch. All the crews are bone-tired from endless hours of flying. The continuous adrenaline rush also is taking its toll, in the form of fatigue. I arrive in LZ English at 7 in the morning of December 10 and have strapped myself back into a Huey by 1000 hours. Within hours, Hawaii is only a dream.

The weather is miserable, with low ceilings and scattered heavy rain showers. There are at least 100 aircraft in the sky at all times trying to service the battle area, which is the size of Fort Rucker's main post. The danger of midair collisions is so prevalent that all formation flying is done in trail formation.

When not flying combat assaults, each A/229th aircraft commander is assigned by Lonnie Rogers to support a particular unit. We land at the helicopter pad associated with that unit. There we receive cargo, coordinates, call signs, and radio frequencies for their units in the field. Today I am flying ash-and-trash sorties for the 1/8th Cavalry whose call sign is Shotgun. We have been running ammo, water, and C rations all morning. The Bandit Huey and its crew are at the disposal of the battalion commander until released.

"Bandit Eighty-Eight, Shotgun Six. Over."

"Six, go ahead."

3. It has been written that Vietnam veterans who were married prior to entering service have exceeded an all-time military record for divorces. An astonishing 62.3 percent of their marriages would fail within five years of their return from Vietnam.

"Say location, over."

"Outbound to Shotgun Four-Six's location. Over."

"Return to Shotgun pad immediately and pick me up, over."

I roger his orders and we turn back from the coast toward English. It is out of the ordinary for a battalion commander to call his ash-and-trash bird. His personnel aviation needs are generally taken care of via a command and control Huey. In this case, if the AC were airborne in the "Charlie-Charlie," the aircraft's call sign would be Shotgun Charlie-Charlie and would immediately alert all who were listening that this particular Huey is the airborne control center for the 1/8th. A Charlie-Charlie Huey is loaded with all the radios needed by a field commander to talk with his troops on the ground or his immediate commanders back at 1st Air Cavalry Division headquarters.

"Ingamar" Johansen, my copilot for today, shoots the approach into the Shotgun pad where Lieutenant Colonel Christian Dubia, commander of the 1st Battalion Eight Cavalry, waits. Before the winds and dust subside, Dubia is standing on the skids of my Huey. I remove my sweat-soaked helmet.

"Beyer tells me you're a good pilot!"

"Sir?" I inquire, wondering what he could be getting at.

"I've got to go out near the coast and pick up one of my men. It's an emergency. We just found him and he may be the only survivor! It's a very tight LZ. Beyer said you could get me in and out of it."

I give the thumbs-up sign without replying. Dubia, a major, and a medic scramble aboard. The major hands me a map and points to a grease-pencil mark. The mark represents a point south and east of English near where the Bong Son River flows into the South China Sea. I know the area well—well enough to know that a bloody battle took place there last night and the area is still hot. The NVA are trying to break free of the Cav's grasp.

"What the hell does he mean only survivor?" I ask the crew over the intercom.

"A platoon from Delta Company got wiped out last night, sir." Jerry Tiggs, the gunner, is apparently better informed than the rest of us.

"The entire platoon?" Johansen echoes.

"Yeah, that's what the supply people on the pad told me this morning while I was loading ammo."

We stay low and head first due south to the Bong Son River, then east to the coast to avoid artillery that is still firing into the area just north of our destination. We make a call to the black hat on the frequency given by Shotgun Six.

The LZ is reported green and is not as small as I had first envisioned, so I let Johansen shoot the approach. It has been hacked out of the underbrush, which lies loosely strewn all about its floor. There are several very large craters partially filled with water. When an artillery shell explodes in the soft sand, it frequently will create a crater 20 yards wide at the top and narrowing to a point at the bottom. These particular craters I judge to be about 12 feet deep.

Dubia and his people exit the helicopter instantly. I watch as he powwows with six or seven of his people and then returns to my side of the Huey. Instead of removing my helmet (never do that in a hot LZ), I extend the tiny boom mike toward him and press the mike key switch in the floor. Whatever he is about to say will now be heard over the intercom throughout the entire aircraft.

"We got a situation here. We need to transport one of our people who may be dangerous."

Instinctively, I look to the right and see the major, the medic, and two other guys wrestling to the ground some poor filthy slob of a human being. All four are taking a beating in a fight with fists and teeth. The individual clubs himself free of their grasp twice, only to be attacked and wrestled down again. "The medic is giving him morphine . . . What do you think?" Dubia asks me.

"Sir, I'll take him only if you tie him down! I'm afraid he might kill us all if he got into the cockpit."

Dubia nods his head.

"Chief, take the pole out of the seat and give it to them."

Jerry Glase, the crew chief, leaves his cubicle and slides the 7-foot aluminum pole out of the canvas seat that forms the customary seating area for personnel in the Huey's cargo compartment.

Using web belting and the aluminum pole, the Shotgun people subdue this guy. Eventually, they load him aboard.

"Jerry, listen up. Get your M16 ready. If this poor bastard gets loose, take him out—understand me?"

"Yes, sir, Mister Johnson. I understand."

161

Glase unfastens his M16 and locks and loads the first round. This does not escape the attention of Shotgun Six, but he says nothing.

Johansen lifts us out of the LZ and flies as fast as he can toward English. Throughout the flight, the dangerous passenger alternately yells obscenities and calls for mercy from his God.

He stinks of the excrement and dried blood that cover his jungle fatigues. His cries and curses are so loud they can be understood even over the noises of the Huey. Often he beats his head against the metal floor and spits saliva across the radio console.

Dubia instructs me to land at the Shotgun pad. We do and shut down. Later that day, we learn that this soldier survived the ambush that took the lives of 12 others. All died except for him. During the night in a pelting rainstorm, he accidentally fell into one of the bomb craters. One by one, NVA soldiers, themselves walking in a dark night of terror, accidentally fell into the crater.

Like flies in a Venus flytrap, they slid to the bottom of the crater and into its shallow waters. This guy, one by one, killed each with his jungle knife. He would then lie just below the surface of the bloody water, alongside the bodies of those who had fallen his prey, and wait for the next. When he was finally found this morning, there were nine NVA bodies in the bottom of the crater.

This is the type of thing that happens to the heroes of many novels, but today there will not be a hero. The thing we extracted out of the crater is not human, only an animal. This war will never be over for him. I prophesy that later in his life he will wish he had died along with the rest of his platoon last night.

As the sun rises, Air Force C-130s and C-141s continue to make sorties out of LZ English, hauling the caskets home and the wounded to Japan. It is a difficult scene to watch.

11

The LZ Tom Incident

December 1967

Nearly a month before my R&R, I inherited a very special mission, called a lightning bug. Lieutenant Runyan, who had originally been the A/229th representative for this mission, somehow convinced me that I needed to take his place just before he DEROS'd.

The customs and practices of war in Vietnam can sometimes seem strange. During daylight hours, when helicopter crews find VC or NVA out in the open, they have to get permission from headquarters to fire on the targets. This is not an unreasonable order since South Vietnamese troops in uniform look identical to North Vietnamese regulars. Before any engagement, Black Horse must be sure that the people you are about to kill are not the "friendlies."

These rules change at night. Leaflets have been dropped and distributed throughout the coastal fishing villages and inner Bong Son plain hamlets clearly stating that any person or boat found on any waterway at night will be considered an enemy. At night anything on the water is subject to destruction.

Lightning bug is a night mission. It consists of four Hueys and other support. One Huey, outfitted externally with seven C-130 landing lights in a cluster, flies the waterways and coastline looking for targets. Two gunships, whose assignment is to destroy the targets illuminated by the "lightning bug" ship, follow 500 yards behind the lightning bug Huey. The fourth ship is the "target ship"—an innovation developed prior to my arrival on the scene.

The gunships generally used to go "lights out" to prevent Charlie from seeing them, but this greatly increased the risk of midair collisions between gunships in the dark. So one gunship would turn on its rotating beacon (Grimes light) so that the other could see him. This helped a lot in avoiding midair collisions, but it created a new problem: rarely did the VC shoot at the lightning bug Huey; instead, they fired on the target indicated by the rotating beacon of a following gunship Huey.

Two weeks before my taking on the responsibility of Lightning Bug, the powers that be got a really good idea. They added a Huey to run right behind the lightning bug. Now both gunships would go lights out. The ploy works very well—ol' Charlie falls into the trap. He fires on the target bird, thinking it is a gunship, but to his surprise, the actual gunships are following the target ship by 500 yards. They are obviously in the perfect position to see muzzle flashes and then roll in hot right on the target. Once contact is established, the lightning bug Huey screams for altitude and punches out two million–candlepower flares. These flares illuminate a one square mile area in a sundown amber-colored daylight. The gunships destroy the target, while the "target ship" stays out of the way. The entire Lightning Bug mission is an especially dangerous one because you're still more likely to be killed by your friends or yourself than you are to be killed by Charlie. The target ship is flown only by a volunteer crew.

Four Hueys take off from LZ English and fly up and down the waterways at an altitude of 50 feet. Depth perception over water during daytime is nearly impossible; it is absolutely impossible at night. The aircraft commander concentrates on flying the Huey in a certain direction. The peter pilot takes total control of the collective pitch and glues himself on the barometric altimeter. No matter what the A/C does, it is the responsibility of the other guy to maintain 50 feet by adjusting the collective as necessary. Fifty feet above water, at night, at 120 miles per hour, is only a breath from disaster. We run these missions three times a night at varying times. Sometimes we change areas and sometimes we repeat an area. The whole idea is to keep Charlie wondering where we'll hit next and catch him unprepared.

A variation of the mission involves Army snipers who ride aboard the aircraft armed with high-powered rifles with top secret Starlight rifle scopes. Starlight scopes magnify by many times any available light source; in this case it's starlight, hence the name. What appears to the naked eye to be the blackest Vietnam night becomes daylight with a green tint when seen through these special devices. I fly these sharpshooters around the Bong Son plains while they look for targets of opportunity. Often Charlie will think he is cloaked in darkness, only to be terminated by a 30-06 round from a source in the night sky. The snipers achieve a high kill ratio almost every night we go out. Normally, we are accompanied by two gunships just itching for a target. In such cases, the snipers fire tracer rounds to mark the target, then gunships roll in hot where the tracer round disappears or ricochets. It takes ol' Charlie a very long time to figure out what is going on.

The cockpit of the Huey is aglow in red. I have a habit of turning down the instrument lights till they are only a glimmer. This aids night vision outside the aircraft. Tonight Ed Almazol has them turned exceptionally high. This is his first lightning bug mission. Fresh from Fort Rucker, he is now the new guy on the block.

"Ed, let's turn down the lights just a little, OK?"

"Sure, Mister Johnson."

He reaches up in an attempt to twist the instrument knobs on the overhead breaker console, only to find that his short stature won't allow this.

"I have it, Ed. Raise your seat a little."

"OK." Ed's voice is smooth and polite.

New guys should be polite, I think confidently. I have never flown with Ed before tonight. I saw him arrive, duffel bags and all, only a few days ago. He is of Filipino descent—dark skinned, shiny black hair, on the short side. Back at the company area, he has always offered a smile and a pleasant hello. Very few new arrivals come across that friendly. A few guys who were sent in a couple of months ago are already earning some very big black marks from the aircraft commanders—including myself. I personally feel intimidated by their "John Wayne" flying and "better than thou" attitudes. All the ACs "peel their oranges" on every mistake, knowing that their road to being aircraft commanders for A/229th will be precarious and long. Ed, on the other hand, is eager to learn, just as I was back in June.

The learning experiences are simple exposures to the elements.

New pilots can only hope that their young aircraft commanders are experienced enough not to let them get in too deep—to the point of endangering persons, things, or property. Flight school is the kindergarten and flying in Vietnam is the graduate school. Fort Rucker just grants the license to go out and kill yourself. To survive, each new pilot must learn from the experiences passed down by those who went before. Ed Almazol will do well in this school if he continues to listen more than speak.

"Mister Johnson, I can take it now if you want me to."

"OK, Ed, you have it. We're passing through the Bong Son pass now. Can't see the mountains tonight but they are there. Just keep this heading and you'll be all right." We are racing south to make a run on the Dam Tra-O Lake.

Our four aircraft are flying at 100 feet, cloaked in darkness. Trailing somewhere behind us is Bug Three, another A/229th bird, crewed by AC Don Martin[1] and one of the new guys as copilot. Don and I came into A/229th almost on the same day. Behind Don are two of the D/229th gunships. The night air is rushing through the cockpit and cooling my sweat-soaked body.

There is no radio traffic, all the instruments look OK, and Ed is doing a good job. I daydream of Pat and home. . . . It is daylight in Carrollton, Georgia. Pat has a job at the biology department of the local college. I look at my watch. It is 0230 hours; that means it's 1430 hours at home.

"Lightning Bug Six, Night Hawk leader. Over." This radio transmission suddenly grabs my attention. Night Hawk, an Army Mohawk twin engine fixed-wing aircraft flying up and down the coast of the South China Sea, is transmitting a call to action. We have worked together many times in the past, and together we form a hunter-killer team. This mission is about to be productive.

"Night Hawk leader, this is Bug Six. Go ahead."

"Six, I have a target for you. Are you ready to copy?"

"Stand by." I grope in the darkness of the cockpit for my map and kneepad. "Six is ready, go ahead," I transmit, reaching overhead to the tiny map light and turning its narrow red beam all the way up.

---

1. Don Martin survived Vietnam only to die of cancer two years after his return to Fort Rucker, Alabama. I have not been able to find his family.

"Ninety degrees, ten minutes north, ten minutes east in Tam Quan waters, looks like a 30-footer. He's under power and making for the channel at about eight knots. Say your ETA to the target. Over."

"Damn." I say loudly without transmitting. "Stand by, Hawk Leader." I know the area well because I worked all those inland waterways just two hours ago, but exactly where the target is has to be determined quickly. I open up my map by unfolding it three times in three directions, then locate the map coordinates. "Hawk Leader, we can be there in six minutes."

"Roger, Bug Six. These guys are really making steam now. You'll have to hurry if you want them inside your area of operation. I'll alert the Swift boats to hurry. Three of their boats are just south of the channel now."

"Roger, Hawk Leader, we're on our way. Bug Three and Tiger aircraft, did you monitor Night Hawk's transmission?"

"Three, roger."

"Tiger Two-Six, roger."

"Tiger One-Six, roger."

"Tiger aircraft break for the target now. Don, go with them and stay clear. We may need you for help later."

"Bug Three, roger."

"Bug Six is already through the pass at this time. We are going to climb for altitude and attempt to go over the mountains. This will be a flare mission. Over."

"Tiger Two-Six, roger. Tiger One-Six, roger."

"I have it, Ed." Grasping the controls firmly, I pull pitch and nose over. We need to fly fast and gain altitude quickly. The Cay Giep Mountains form the east side of the Bong Son pass between the Dam Tra-O Lake and LZ English; they top out at 1896 feet. Flying over mountains at night should be avoided whenever possible. On this night, we will not see them until we clear their peaks and pick up whatever light might be escaping from the tents at LZ English. When I can see English, I will be sure there is no hard earth rising up in my flight path.

We head due east until we reach 1500 feet, then I turn north, betting that we are far enough south of the mountains to clear them before reaching the peaks.

"Ed, take over and keep us climbing. Keep your eye glued on the

VSI. You have to keep us climbing at 700 feet per minute until you reach 3000 feet—understand?"

"Yes, sir," Ed replies with a quiver of excitement.

"Red Dog GCA, Lightning Bug Six. Need a 'hold fire' east immediately. Over."

"Red Dog GCA, stand by, Bug Six."

Things happen now at a hectic pace. I have asked the radar approach controller to shut down all artillery that might be firing in our flight path.

"Lighting Bug Six, Red Dog GCA. Hold fire east approved. Over."

I roger the hold fire east and then think about Ed Almazol. He has no idea what is going on but has sensed correctly that this is no time to be asking. All of us breathe a sigh of relief as the altimeter passes through 2000 feet and we continue to climb without running into anything. Puffs of clouds, illuminated by our navigation lights, suddenly consume us, then just as quickly disappear as Ed takes us through the bottom of a broken layer. The beauty that awaits us as we break out above the night clouds is just awesome. The moon is in its last stage tonight and is emitting enough light for us to see the cloud layer below. The tops of the puffy clouds are charcoal gray, but their bodies are ink black.

We are now level at 3000 feet and going in and out of cloud tops. This is a unique sensation. Flying through clouds won't hurt as long as nothing else is in them, but it's very hard to quell the avoidance instinct when approaching one of these monsters. At first it just looms ahead. As it gets nearer, it becomes awesome in its size, like some entity waiting to swallow the entire aircraft. Night clouds appear even more ominous because the entire outline cannot be distinguished. Sometimes the cloud towers thousands of feet overhead just before you enter it. You feel meek and defenseless against it. At the time of penetration, there is usually rough air that bounces the Huey about a little, then quiet. You must rely on the aircraft's gauges to keep it flying straight and level. It really gets dark inside the night clouds. It reminds me of underwater cave diving back home. Most guys, including me, hold our breath a little until we exit out the other side. No crew chief or gunner I have yet to fly with likes IFR flying—even just a little bit—and they are quick to let you know it.

"Ed, Night Hawk Leader is a Mohawk fixed-wing aircraft out of Fan Rang. They cruise up and down the coast all night. Do you know what SLAR is?" I ask as we exit our first large cloud.

"No, sir."

"SLAR stands for Side-Looking Area Radar. As they fly up the coast, the SLAR unit produces a continuous negative. Land appears white and the water is black. Anything that's on water will produce an image that these guys can see. Whenever they see something suspicious, they turn around and approach from the opposite direction. By overlaying the two negatives, they can tell whether the target is moving or not, and if so, how fast and in what direction. They monitor our frequency all the time they are in our AO. They have found me some targets in the past but nothing near this size. Night Hawk indicates this one may be a thirty-footer. That's a very large boat by anyone's standards.

"They're making for the channel right here." I hold the map under my red lens flashlight and point my finger at the Tam Quan inland waterway. "If the target gets out into the open sea, we are no longer allowed to engage it. It then becomes the property of the Navy swift boats. That's why we have to hurry. This is my baby." I fold up the map and store it between my seat and the console. The excitement of the hunt is beginning to flood me with adrenaline.

"Red Dog, Lightning Bug Six. Are we clear of the mountains? Over."

"Red Dog has you almost due east of LZ English heading zero-three-zero degrees. You are well clear of the mountains and clear to let down."

"Roger, Red Dog." Ed descends to 1500 feet. "Do it in a hurry—make at least a 1500 feet-per-minute descent. We've got to get below these clouds quickly."

Both Tiger birds and Bug Three are hell-bent for leather trying to get into position. Right this minute they are less than 2 miles south of the target area.

"Night Hawk Leader, Bug Six. Say target's coordinates."

"Target is now 92 minutes north longitude, 12 minutes east latitude and has increased speed to fourteen knots. That will put them just about ¾ of a mile south of the channel. Over."

"Hawk, call the swift boats and tell them to stay well clear of the entrance to Tam Quan. We are in pursuit of the target and ETA is two minutes. I don't want to mistake them for the target. Do you roger?"

"Night Hawk rogers and will inform."

"OK, Chief, let's get the flares ready."

We carry 22 flares inside the Huey. Each flare contains candlepower of two million and will turn the darkest night into a gold-colored day in a flash. I never like carrying these things for two reasons: If we take a round just right, we will look like a meteor plummeting to the earth. And these flares date back to the Korean War and World War II and are subject to misfiring.

Each flare is contained in a 6-foot-long tube. Each has two timers that must be set. One timer will ignite a small explosive charge in the head of the flare and deploy the parachute, and the second will cause flare ignition. Timer settings are based largely on the weather, which determines how high we can be before deployment. Attached to these timers is an 8-foot steel wire lanyard. When told to do so, the crew chief will take one of these tubes and attach the lanyard to a D ring on the Huey's cargo floor. On the next command, he will throw the flare out the cargo door, being sure that it goes out on a path parallel to the aircraft. This last requirement was a hard-learned lesson for some poor souls who came before me. During their days, it was thought that the safest way to deploy the flares was to throw them straight down outside the skids. One night, a flare misfired. When the lanyard pulled tight to start the timers and the parachute explosive went off, the aluminum tube container shot upward into the Huey's main rotor blades. The Huey crash-landed with a small chunk out of one main blade, but the crew survived the ordeal. I have already had two misfires, in which the tube made very large dents in the Huey's tail boom. I dread the day that one of the lanyards that are designed to break free of the flare fails to do so. We will have a nasty situation on our hands with a two million–candlepower flare burning holes in the tail boom.

Richard Rieson is the crew chief tonight and has handled these flares many times. Though he is a "short timer," I remind him not to get careless—just for the sake of my peace of mind.

"Richard, are you ready?"

"Ready, sir."

"Tiger flight, Bug Six will be over the target in thirty seconds. Are you guys ready?"

"Six, by the time you get your first flare out, we'll be in position. Over."

"I roger that. I want one of you guys to make a low pass across the target. I repeat . . . give me a low pass for positive ID. Do you copy?"

"Tiger Two-Six will make the pass. Over."

Although anything on water at night is a free fire target, we have often in the past found some old fisherman disobeying the 1st Cavalry's decree against night boat traffic. In such cases, the gunships will make a few passes with their miniguns shooting well clear of the local and his boat. This is always enough incentive to get them back to shore. Tonight we won't be engaged with some old fisherman; this is a major contact. Yet I still feel compelled to make a visual sighting before engagement.

"Tiger Two-Six, first flare is out!" I transmit and, simultaneously, Richard throws it.

The timers are set to four and eight seconds, respectively. After a very short delay, the world below goes from night into golden day, and for the first time we all can get our bearings.

There it is, much larger than I had envisioned! Night Hawk is right; this is at least a 30-footer, and she is churning the Tam Quan waterway under full power. The target is leaving behind it a long trail of white foam on the black water. From our vantage point, we see Tiger Two-Six as he acquires the target, adjusts his direction of flight, and lowers his altitude to treetop level. He flies right over the top of the boat at 120 miles an hour and makes a hard left to pull behind some trees for cover.

"OK, Bug Six, I have a visual sighting of many—I say again many—uniformed soldiers on the deck. Stand by for another pass!" Two-Six's voice is high with exhilaration.

"Tiger One-Six, you had better call home and get us some help up here quick. This is going to be a big one."

One-Six rogers and calls back to Tiger TOC for more gunships. I call Bandit TOC and request they alert Black Horse immediately.

Two-Six makes several evasive maneuvers at low level, then comes in for the second pass, this time from east to west.

"Bug Six, I confirm again: many uniformed individuals on the deck. Our crew chief saw weapons and one possible recoilless rifle."

I pause only a moment before making the call. "Tiger flight, engage and destroy the target. Do you copy?"

"Tiger flight copies."

These are most likely NVA who have escaped detection during the many sweeps of Tam Quan after the main battle. They are now trying to escape with all their heavy weapons.

We punch out another flare and the two Tiger gunships go to work. The water boils all around the boat. Tiger's miniguns are literally taking both men and the boat apart in a fury of gunfire. The ship's single mast, about 1 foot in diameter at the bottom, is cut down in a single pass. Two-Six continues to work on the boat, and One-Six makes his passes up and down the waterway taking out those who have jumped overboard. I continue to punch out the flares, lighting up the mayhem below. The target remains under way at full speed, but One-Six takes care of that when he sends his rockets right up the stern, causing a secondary explosion that raises the boat partway out of the water. When both Tiger birds have expended everything they have, Don Martin comes on station, and using his M60s, lets his gunner and crew chief get in on the kills. Two-Six and One-Six depart the area to refuel and rearm. Four other "Tiger" gunships arrive on station and, in short order, send what's left of the boat to the bottom.

We are getting low on both fuel and flares when another Bandit Huey arrives on the scene to take our place. On the last pass down the Tam Quan waterway, I make a high-speed run just above the gunships. Bodies and wreckage from the boat are strewn for 2000 yards along our route.

Still reeling from the surprise of the Battle of Tam Quan, Black Horse troops are in high gear and have already launched a Charlie-Charlie Huey to synchronize what might be another major engagement right at our back door. Taking no chances, they have directed that the RRF be on standby for a dawn combat assault.

Our services are no longer needed, so after briefing Major Beyer, two very tired pilots find their bunks and go to sleep.

"Mister Johnson, Mister Johnson, please wake up." The words

seem to come from far in the distance but fit perfectly into the dream I am enjoying. "Mister Johnson, please wake up." My brain finally comprehends that this is no dream and brings the rest of my body to full alert.

"Mister Johnson. General Norton wants to see you and Mister Almazol right away down at Black Horse headquarters." The voice is that of Specialist 4th Class Justin, the company CQ for today.

"General Norton, what for?" I ask, in some degree of shock.

"Don't know, sir. He called about ten minutes ago on the land line."

"Go wake up Mister Almazol."

"I already have, sir. I woke him a few moments ago."

Just then Ed appears at the end of my cot. "Who is General Norton?" he asks, a little shaken by the rank.

"Division aviation officer."

"What does he want with us?"

"Don't know. Maybe something to do with last night. Maybe he wants to pin a medal on you or something." I continue dressing in three-day-old jungle fatigues.

After procuring a company jeep, Ed and I drive the 2 miles from LZ English to LZ Two Bits, division headquarters.

"Ever been here before?" Ed asks nervously.

"Yeah. So far I've been to see General Norton twice. Once because of a crash in the Bong Son River and again a month later, when his aircraft nearly had a midair with some idiot in the Bong Son pass. His pilot got the last three digits of a tail number that happened to match the bird I was flying that day. It wasn't me, but I'm not sure he believed me. We're not on a first name basis yet, but if this keeps up, he'll likely start calling me 'son.' "

The rank of general evokes a vision of God—generals *are* the 1st Cavalry's gods. They make policy, and they own your body, mind, and soul. Ed is not alone in being uneasy about this trip. I keep saying it is going to be a pat on the back for a job well done, but deep inside I have a gut feeling it will be something not to my liking. This feeling grows stronger when Ed and I step down into the division aviation bunker. Five other people are already sitting on crude ammo box benches. One is a sulking major who does not wear any wings and is dressed in proper military fashion—definitely not a Cav pilot. Two other guys, also neatly dressed in clean starched fatigues, are sporting black Army wings on their chests. They are not part of the 1st Cavalry either. The remaining two are lieutenants, and we know they are Cav pilots because they are so grungy—or "grundy," in flight school lingo.

The latter turn to watch Ed and me. I walk down the steps from the entrance.

"You Bug Six?" one of the lieutenants asks.

"Yeah. who's asking?"

"I'm Tiger Two-Six and this is Tiger One-Six." Both stand to offer their hands.

"*All right!* What a hell of a job you guys did last night!"

"We kicked ass, didn't we!" One-Six smiles and offers his hand.

"Bug Six, we're Night Hawk and I'm Night Hawk Leader." One of the two neatly dressed pilots, a captain, stands and offers his hand. "This fine young lieutenant right here is Night Hawk One-Four."

"Glad to finally meet you guys! You do good work!" I am happy to put faces with voices.

Hawk One-Four stands up and approaches the meeting shyly.

I lean close to Tiger Two-Six. "Who is the major?" I ask in a whisper.

"Don't know. He's not too friendly. Acts like he's got a round up his ass."

"Mister Johnson, you have any idea what this meeting is all about?" Hawk Leader asks aloud.

"Not me. Oh, by the way, this is Warrant Officer Ed Almazol, my partner in crime last night." Ed blushes in the spotlight and shakes hands. "You can bet your butt it's about last night, but is it good or bad?"

The major, who is leaning back against the wall and listening to our conversation and impatiently changing feet, lets out a contemptuous snort of air.

The four of us exchange first and last names and talk of other missions we have run together. The pleasurable meeting comes to a halt when one of General Norton's aides steps out into the waiting room and announces that the general will see us now.

"Well, Mister Johnson, we do meet again, don't we." Norton is smiling as I clear the sandbag doorway.

"Yes, sir. Looks like the beginning of a long relationship, sir." I reply as politely as I know how and snap off a fine salute.

The general goes from person to person and introduces himself informally. When he gets back to me at last, his eyes draw in narrow and his forehead wrinkles in concern.

"Mister Johnson. Understand you boys bagged a big kill last night." He speaks as he makes his way to his large cluttered desk. "You other fellows seat yourself and be at ease." He motions to the rest to sit.

"Yes, sir," I reply without sitting down, "it was a good kill. Thirty-footer, I guess. Body count will be at least fifty or so."

"*FIFTY-THREE!*" The major literally jumps at my face to unleash his anger.

"*George*, sit down!" General Norton commands the major, who pauses to stare at me a little longer, then finally obeys.

"Mister Johnson, why don't you show me where the target was when you first engaged it." Norton motions me toward a large Bong Son plain map that covers his entire wall.

"Right here, sir. South of the village of Tam Quan. The target was under way, making about 15 or 20 knots headed northeast toward the channel."

"*Bullshit!* My boat was nowhere near there!" Again the major slobbers and leaps to his feet. "The boat was tied up here at LZ Tom and you people shot the hell out of it!"

The phrase "my boat" catches all our attention.

"Major, you're full of crap!" I rally as I bump him aside to point again to the spot on the map where we first saw the target. His eyes and mine lock in penetrating stares, each daring the other to look away.

"General, sir, what's going on here?" The Night Hawk captain asks, rising quickly to his feet.

"Gentlemen, this is Major George Ramsey. He is the liaison with the South Vietnamese around these parts. There has been a serious mistake here." He pauses. "You guys engaged and destroyed 53 persons in the employ of the ARVNS [South Vietnamese Army Regulars] last night. The major here claims that the boat was tied up at LZ Tom. "

The room is silent for a moment, filled with tension and disbelief. "General, that boat was under way and headed for the South China inlet," Night Hawk offers. "It was nowhere near LZ Tom when we first detected it on SLAR."

"How far would you say?" General Norton asks.

The captain, moving to the map, has to force himself between me and the major. Neither of us gives any extra ground.

The captain points to the map. "Right here, sir, about two kilometers north of LZ Tom. That's where we saw it first."

"Can you prove this, Captain?" Norton asks.

"Yes, sir, we brought the negatives with us."

More than ready to slap the pure shit out of this major should he take any combative actions, I grin broadly upon hearing the captain's reply. The major flinches first and slowly moves away to see what evidence "Night Hawk" has brought with him. I stand there a few more moments, just in case the asshole changes his mind, then sit down with the rest of the guys. Night Hawk's proof has caught the major off guard, and his face has gone blank. The Mohawk pilots lay their negatives across Norton's desk and proceed to decipher for him what he is seeing. There are several negatives showing the boat's positions relative to the Tam Quan waterway and its movement. The white, disturbed water emanating from the stern of the vessel clearly shows it was under power, not tied up.

Norton debriefs Tiger Two-Six and Tiger One-Six, who simply reiterate what has already been said. The major looks at the negatives, removes them from the desk, and holds them up to the light.

Satisfied, General Norton pauses. "OK, boys, that will be all. I don't want a word of this outside this room until I sort it all out. Do you hear me loud and clear?"

All of us acknowledge, grab our baseball caps, and exit. As we leave General Norton and ol' George the major behind, Norton's voice has already turned harsh and two octaves higher. The last words I hear on leaving: "George, what the hell is going on at your place!"

"Can you believe that?" Tiger Two-Six offers as we reach daylight above the bunker. "ARVNS. Those bastards are helping the NVA!"

"That's OK with me, Two-Six! In most people's eyes, they're all the same." I laugh and slap him on the shoulder. "We've known it for a long time. Now maybe the generals of this man's Army will get as wise as us dumb-ass helicopter pilots!" The comment brings laughter and relief to an otherwise terse situation.

"Fifty-three! Jesus, you guys worked out on overtime last night! Good shooting!"

This comment is echoed by all the rest. We say our good-byes after talking about the war for another hour or so. Ed and I are officially off for the rest of the afternoon—because I say so. No one at A/229th has knowledge of our itinerary, so we loiter in Bong Son for the rest of the afternoon. Haircuts and rice beer is the agenda. I have been in country for 6½ months, and this is only the second time I have been in the village of Bong Son. Ed drives me back in the late afternoon, as I am a happy drunk and still savoring every moment of ol' Major George's distress.

Shortly after my return, Major Beyer comes into my tent. He sits on Johansen's bunk and smiles. "Fifty-three of the little bastards. You guys did a good job." At first I am surprised that he already knows. "General Norton called earlier and instructed me to tell you and Ed that he is pleased."

"Pleased?" My eyes light up. "Pleased! Dang, Major Beyer, we kicked the asses of 53 of those SOBs single-handed and the general is just pleased! Look at all the money we saved the Cav. No Ready Reaction Force, no 1/9th, no fifty thousand dollars' worth of artillery—just us! Sir." I roar with laughter.

Beyer also laughs, and that pleases me very much. It is one of the few times I have ever seen him laugh aloud. I know he is laughing at me more than at what I just said. "Have a beer with me, sir?" I ask in earnest, hoping he will let down his hair with me.

"Believe I will!"

"I guess Lightning Bug's grounded tonight, sir." I state forcefully, after my next beer. "'Cause Bug Six is in no condition to fly. OK?"

Beyer again smiles but does not reply. No reply necessary. He and I, both slightly tipsy, proceed to wreak havoc on all the enlisted and officer tents; this night, everyone is our buddy.

The new pilots take flight in the night toward the latrine when they hear that Major Beyer and I are looking for them. We both feel the need to discuss these men's futures with A/229th if they don't straighten their little asses up.

Somewhere around 4:00AM, Major Beyer puts me to bed. It has been a long two days with very little sleep. The comedian Redd Foxx once said about his brother-in-law, "He can switch off the lights and be asleep before the room gets dark." That's what happens to me.

12

Christmas at LZ English, Republic of Vietnam

December 24, 1967

The temperature is near 100 and the humidity is over 90 percent, even though it is Christmas Eve. This day goes like any other day. The only calendar in Vietnam is the one that counts down the days until you go home. There are no Mondays or Tuesdays, no quitting time, and no overtime. I have already logged nearly 800 hours of combat flying time and another 150 hours of noncombat flying time. The average stateside private pilot will fly some 50 hours a year. Someone had to remind me about Thanksgiving, but Christmas is different.

At home in Carrollton, Christmas Eve is a big event for my family. The entire clan—brothers, sisters, brothers-in-law, sisters-in-law, and their kids—begins to show up at Mom and Dad's house around 1800 hours. The tree is piled high with gifts. Traditionally we open presents on Christmas Eve night. Now, in Vietnam, this is what I'm thinking about. I am not alone; the entire company is on a downhill slide. Some guys, including me, have already received their Christmas packages from home, and this does not help our homesickness very much. Everyone waits until his own accustomed hour to open his presents.

I have just finished a very long day of flying ash-and-trash for the 2/12th. It takes every last bit of energy to struggle to my tent and drop my flight gear.

"How's it going, Tom?" The voice belongs to Bill Lee.

"OK, I guess, Bill, except I wish this Christmas would get over."

"Me, too. I've been in the dumps now for a week. I keep thinking of back in the real world."

"You're not alone, buddy! I think the whole company is suffering."

"Hi, there, fellows." Ingamar brushes past Bill to lay his flight gear inside our dirt floor cubicle. He seems in a better state of mind than Bill and I. He picks up the mosquito netting that surrounds the cot and immediately lies flat on his back, both hands folded behind his head and ready to listen. He is never much of a talker.

"Excuse me, Lee, do you mind stepping aside?" It is Don Martin leading a procession consisting of himself and Larry Gore. They are clad only in towels, and each has a soap bar in hand. "I think there's hot water in the shower tonight, fellows, and I intend to make full use of it." Gore nods in confirmation of what Don has just said.

"Hot water? What happened, somebody screw up?" I ask.

"Screw up or not, Mister Gore and I intend to take full advantage of it before it disappears," Martin replies, and continues his trek out the west side of the tent, followed closely by Gore.

Of course there is an eruption of catcalls from everyone. Something to do with "dropping the soap."

The A/229th shower is a small 3-by-4-foot wooden structure with a metal tank mounted overhead. Some industrious individual has welded a showerhead to the bottom of the metal tank, and someone else has "borrowed" some mess sergeant's immersion heater. This submersible kerosene-powered heater is designed to bring the water to a boil to sanitize dishes. If the water truck fills the tank, and if someone lights the darn thing, you might get a hot shower sometime very late in the night.

1st Cavalry people are notorious for their lack of personal hygiene. The term used in flight school is "grundy," which somehow fails to adequately describe members of the 1st Cavalry. After flying for ten or twelve hours, it is a major undertaking to eat dinner, undress, and then stand under cold water to bathe. So most of us take showers once a week. We tend to wear fatigues for three or four days before taking time to wash them. These habits tend to attract attention to the 1st Cavalry soldier, especially at a place like the hospital-clean Qui Nhon officer's club.

CHRISTMAS AT LZ ENGLISH, REPUBLIC OF VIETNAM

On rare occasions, we will "logger out" the aircraft at Qui Nhon. To "logger out" aircraft means to move them to a safer LZ when intelligence reports to the generals that we are about to be mortared. Bless them for providing such warnings. The only problem is that we all will fly a long day, then grab a toothbrush and head 55 miles south to land. I have never landed in Qui Nhon during daylight, and I have never had the time to take a bath before going there. After landing, the first thing on the agenda is the officer's club.

This club is filled with "brass" from all branches of the military, but most of them are doctors. Occasionally we get to meet real "round-eyed" American nurses. This is a special treat—the chance to assure ourselves that they still exist. Smelly and untidy 1st Cavalry pilots entering the hygienically clean club always do cause some amount of tribulation. A common 1st Cavalry saying, "If you ain't Cav, then you ain't shit!" will start a few brawls, but the one sure remark that is guaranteed to start a big one has to do with the 1st Cavalry's patch. This emblem is the largest patch worn by any unit in the Army. On a bright yellow background are a black diagonal line and a black silhouette of a horse's head.

The worst incidents occur when some Marine officer refers to the emblem in a comment such as, "That's the horse you can't ride, the line you can't cross, and the color of the streak down your back!" I've yet to see it fail. A statement like this always starts a party for which the dress code is hard hats and baseball bats. The pilots of A/229th have been thrown out of this club a total of four times, which equals the total number of times we have set foot in it. I think we lack the proper military attitude to take a joke.

"Lee, a shower sounds like a good idea. Stand by, folks, it's time Johnson took his annual." I am already stripping down as I talk.

"Best idea all day. See you later." Lee leaves the tent to grab his soap and towel.

It seems that the entire A/229th officer corps has decided to take a bath on this Christmas Eve, 1967. Two or three at a time is all the shower can take, so a line forms on the wooden pallet walkway outside the shower. One towel-clad warrant officer eyeballs the line and departs, only to return with a case of Budweiser. *Why not?* I ask myself. The corporate Christmas party has begun. When the water gets low, another industrious pilot takes it upon himself to "borrow" somebody's "deuce-and-a-half" water truck. Not having been formally checked out in this vehicle, he has difficulty finding reverse. Imagine some 20 or so helicopter pilots giving advice to another pilot on the proper way to back up an Army truck; none of them ever having been inside one.

"Hey, grind me a few pounds!" is one comment the poor fellow makes as he is ripping through the transmission in some attempt to "cog" reverse. After ten minutes, a real truck driver is summoned and the water truck makes its 10-yard journey in reverse to replenish the now empty officers' shower. This same enlisted truck driver starts the gasoline motor–driven pump and the 2-inch water hose begins belching water all over the place at high pressure. Eventually, this same guy decides that filling the reservoir is going to be too slow a process and elects to make a command decision. Rather than pumping the water into the tank, he turns it on all of us waiting for the shower. Hey, why not? I've taken a couple baths in the tropical rain shower. Towels are thrown to the wind and we break out the soap. The beer and the water flow, accompanied by catcalls from the rest of A/229th who have gathered to cheer our fiasco.

This is just what everyone needs to pull us out of the slump.

The water finally runs out, but Sergeant McCrary has mysteriously located 19 more cases of beer. Mac and I toast one another with cold brew, and I tolerate outbursts of laughter from the other pilots as he makes jokes about my bony white ass. No matter; Mac and I are well into the Christmas spirit.

Our Christmas Eve get-together does not go unnoticed by Major Beyer, who soon joins us.

"You guys do know that we're on RRF duty tonight. If something happens, A/229th will be expected to perform. I've got a tent full of drunk pilots—how we gonna do that?" He is solemnly shaking his head from side to side, and we all realize we have made a very serious mistake; we simply forgot this fact. Our cheerful faces fall to the floor. "But, what the hell," continues Beyer, "If you guys can't fly, then I can't lead—Right!" Captain MacWillie hands him two half-gallon bottles of Jack Daniel's. "Here's a little present for you guys who really deserve it!" Beyer and MacWillie break into grins; we pick up our party faces from the dirt, and the party is on again.

"Hope ol' Charlie needs a rest as bad as we do . . . don't you, sir?" I say to Major Beyer later in the celebration.

"You're right, Tom. We do need a break!" Beyer offers the statistical data on how many hours his pilots and crews have flown over the past few months, and he notes that they have done so without so much as a single complaint.

For a sober moment, I clear my head and think to myself that if ol' Charlie wants to overrun us, tonight will be a fine night to try it. "Ah, what the hell!" I say to myself. "Ol' Charlie is probably out there in the night drinkin' some Jack Daniel's like us." It's time to blow off a little steam. The company's morale badly needs it, and Christmas Eve is an especially good time for a boost.

Before long, crew chiefs, gunners, cooks, supply people, maintenance people, pilots, and, I suspect, several folks who don't even belong to the "A" Company join us and let down their hair. What had begun in the warrant officer's 1st Platoon tent now spreads throughout the company area. All is going well until . . .

"Hey, what the hell is that?" Sergeant Mac hushes the entire 1st Platoon tent.

As the conversation dies down to quiet and our ears strain to hear, Mac rises to his feet and hustles out of the tent. We follow one by one into the darkness.

At first I cannot believe my ears . . . "Silent Night" . . . sure enough, loud and clear.

"There he is!" Mac says excitedly, pointing into the night sky.

Someone at Black Horse has decided that the 1st Cavalry troops will be more at home if they equip a Huey with loudspeakers normally used in brain control warfare and fly it around LZ English playing Christmas carols as hundreds all over LZ English gather outside their tents to see and hear what is going on.

"What the hell they trying to do? Christmas carols? Crap! That shit will depress me!" comes a voice from the dark.

Someone else must agree with his assessment of the situation. Suddenly there is gunfire . . . definitely not an AK-47, but an M16.

"Damn, somebody is shooting at the poor slob flying that thing," I yell.

Within 30 seconds, there are several others opening up on the

Huey who is now taking evasive action to keep from being shot down by his own troops. The poor pilot is trying desperately to get his Huey away from the LZ.

Sidesplitting laughter breaks out in our group. All of us can just see ourselves in his position. Any pilot would have thought this to be a very dumb idea to start with . . . like salt on an open wound.

"Hope he gets away," Mac volunteers, laughing aloud.

"Purple Heart time. How you going to explain that to the grand-kids!"

"Yeah, shot down over LZ English by friendlies while playing Christmas carols!" another cries out in hysteria.

"This action by this pilot is above and beyond the call of duty. It represents great stupidity upon the pilot and the 1st Cavalry gener-als—in general." Obviously this drunk has been at some recent awards and decorations ceremony.

The unfortunate pilot turns off all his lights in an attempt to evade being shot. His exact position can no longer be determined, but this is only a small inconvenience to those determined to blast this guy right out of the sky. Seconds after his navigation lights go out, someone fires a red pencil flare. Pencil flares are normally used only in an emergency and produce an absolutely beautiful shower of sparks that will rise hundreds of feet above the ground. Every Huey has several of these in the crew chief's tool box. The device is the size of a large pencil; all you have to do is aim it skyward, pull back the spring-loaded trigger, and release it.

The first flare is followed in rapid succession by at least six more. This unexpected fireworks display on Christmas Eve is gorgeous and very uplifting.

However, those who man the Black Horse TOC at Two Bits can also see these flares going off all over LZ English. Red pencil flares mean only one thing to them; the enemy has breached the primary perimeter of the LZ. The word *frantic* is not strong enough to convey their response. These guys hit every panic button inside their bunker. As far as they know, the perimeter around LZ English has been breached in more than six places.

They hurriedly transmit the doomsday alarm. All the perimeter guards fall back to a preplanned secondary defensive position. Shotguns are broken out of their Conex containers, generals are pulled from their Christmas Eve dinners, Air Force liaison officers get on the "horn" to their people in Phu Cat requesting immediate high performance interdiction, and guess what? The operations officer for A/229th gets the call for us to crank for immediate deployment. Size and strength of enemy unknown—get airborne immediately and await further orders.

The only person in A/229th TOC tonight is also probably the only nondrinking enlisted guy within the entire company. Upon receiving this distress call from "Black Horse," he rushes to find his boss 1st Lieutenant Lonnie Rogers, or Major Beyer. When Colonel Brown, the 229th Battalion commander gets around to calling A Company, there is not a soul to answer the phone.

Brown, fearing the worst, runs down the pedaprime road all the way to the A Company area in search of Major Beyer.

"Oh, shit! Incoming!" Gore shrieks as the sirens on both LZ English and LZ Two Bits go off.

All souls dive into their tents and hug the floor, waiting for the initial mortar explosions. This is just where Colonel Brown finds most of his A/229th pilots. Brown is less than amused when he enters our tent to find everyone on the floor. We are just as amused to see him standing there in the middle of a "mortar attack."

"Where is Major Beyer?!" Brown demands of the first drunk he encounters.

"Right behind you, sir," comes the cool and collected voice of Major Beyer, who has accidentally walked into the tent right behind Brown.

Brown turns quickly. Beyer is looking himself—he is not bobbing or weaving and his fatigues are still unwrinkled. He shows no evidence of being in the same poor condition as his pilots. Brown is in a terrible mood and it shows.

"Major Beyer, cancel Red Alert." The CQ, exploding into the tent right behind Beyer, bursts out without either seeing Colonel Brown or knowing the tenseness of the situation. "It's all a mistake. Black Horse just called on the land line."

"What do you mean a mistake!" Brown bellows at the CQ, therefore getting the specialist's attention very quickly.

"Black Horse said it was a mistake, sir. We are not under attack." he repeats in a soft voice.

"Want a beer, Colonel Brown?" offers a meek voice out of the pile of warrant officers still lying on the dirt floor.

At first Brown is offended. He looks first at us, then at Beyer, then at the CQ.

"Eugene, you still got some whiskey around here?" he finally asks, calling Major Beyer by his first name.

"All right—party time," comes the cry in unison from the floor.

"As you were, men." Brown offers as he departs—a changed man—in the direction of Beyer's tent.

Within five minutes, just as the party is getting going again, there comes a full artillery barrage from the folks on the east side of LZ English. It sounds as though all tubes are firing at once. The first volley is followed quickly by the second, then the third. We rush out of the tent to find out what is going on.

The 1st Cavalry is putting on its own fireworks display using high-altitude artillery flares. The Quad Fifties—four .50-caliber machine guns mounted on a "deuce-and-a-half" (2½-ton) truck—let loose aerial sprays of full tracer rounds from seven points across the LZ. This is breathtaking. The cannons continue to fire in salvos of five or six guns at once, and the Quad Fifties continue to spray the night sky for the next eight minutes.

Bill Lee, Don Martin, Larry Gore, Mac McCrary, and I, along with several others, have gained a vantage point up on the hill near the flight line. This gives us a wondrous view of the Bong Son plains lit up at night by the flares. In sequence, each flare descends to earth in the distance and goes out.

In the end, after a brief silence, we hear a group of men singing in the distance. Straining our ears and barely breathing, we hear "Silent Night" being sung by the guys on the other side of the main runway. The Christmas carol is emanating from LZ Dog, located on the south side of LZ English. Slowly, at first, one by one, others join in the singing from all across LZ English.

As the carol ends in a final verse, the artillery folks again let loose, using their entire arsenal. The noise, fire, and concussions from these big guns are just what the doctor ordered to keep us from slipping into a deep homesick depression again. A roar of cheers follows, then a toast among friends, and the party sets off again.

The next morning, we are missing Don Martin. He is not to be found anywhere in the company area. It is not until a gunner goes up on the flight line that this mystery is finally solved. Sitting in the left seat of a Huey, fully undressed except for his undershorts and jungle boots, yet fully strapped in ready to fly, is my friend Don Martin. Don remembers nothing about last night. How he ever found a Huey, much less how he was able to strap himself in, is a puzzle he will never solve.

We have all of Christmas day to mend our sore heads and recuperate from Christmas Eve. Some guys open presents; others simply find some shade and talk. I catch up on writing my letters home.

This is the first Christmas that I have not been with my family, and it is the first I have not spent with Pat since I met her. Our first child, Joey, was born on Christmas Eve last year, only to leave us four days later. Pat, in her letters that were mailed a week ago, mentions his name often. Had fate not taken its course, Joey would have been one year old yesterday. This Christmas night I drift off to sleep with tears in my eyes thinking about last Christmas.

Weeks at Wolters had turned into months. Pat was really showing with our first child and having some amount of difficulty.

■

The training schedules were ruthless during the week, but on Saturdays and Sundays there was only absolute boredom. Many candidates were being cut for their inability to learn to fly or for their ineptitude in academics. My first three roommates one at a time fell by the wayside, and it was simply heartbreaking to watch as each packed up his belongings and said good-bye. The fear of failing flight school drove me ever harder, especially when the possibility hit so close to home. Eventually, when many would be washed out or recycled to another class, a few like myself would have an entire living cubicle to ourselves.

TAC Officer Marcotte was still saying we could attain off-post passes if we kept our weekly demerits at fewer than ten. Being in the room by myself, I had to triple my duty to keep it clean. I tried desperately to remain free of demerits so I could get off post to see Pat.

Depression replaced desperation when one Saturday morning during billet inspection, Marcotte could not find one thing wrong. I had only one demerit for the entire week. He turned over my bunks, scattered all the clothing in my closets, and even inspected the overhead light cover. In a final display of the qualities required to be a TAC officer, he put on his white glove and opened an outside window. Wiping his hand on the outside of the glass, he was able to find dirt that nobody else could see. Pat had been sick for over two weeks, and I was in anguish from the realization that the best I could do to be by her side was not going to be good enough.

"Assess yourself ten demerits, Candidate Johnson. Dirty windows!" He belched, not even flinching. Unnoticed by him, I grimaced.

Later that day I found the courage to approach him. Pleading from my heart, I requested to leave the base for the weekend so that I could care for Pat. He went ballistic. Pouring out a stream of abuse, he even questioned whether I had a wife in the first place. "You belong to the Army, Candidate Johnson, and the Army doesn't give a simple damn about your wife!"

I survived this confrontation with Marcotte, but I resolved that he might let me off post, if he only knew how serious Pat's situation was getting. I, like the rest, did not know how far to push Marcotte. He could end my flying career with a simple document; both he and I knew that.

Somewhere about the eleventh week of training, we were again promised weekend passes. I felt that there was a one in a hundred chance that this would happen. I had quit trying so hard after the window incident, feeling that, no matter how clean the billet was, I would never be allowed off post. Suddenly Marcotte eased off. Simple inspections every morning and only haphazard billet inspections produced zero demerits.

Lying down again for a weekend with my wife washed away the hard times, even if she was as big as a barrel. At only 5 feet 2 inches tall, Pat could be rolled to the store faster than she could walk. During our private time together, nothing else in this world mattered. We rarely set foot outside the apartment, and if we did, we only took a broom handle and knocked gently on the ceiling to let Judy and Johnny Kinsey know we were coming upstairs to visit. They did the same for us.

We decided that if the baby turned out to be a boy, we would name him Joseph Franklin Johnson. Often Pat called me into the bathroom while she was taking a bath so that I could see him kick water out of the tub. She was very excited about the whole prospect of becoming a mother.

December was suddenly upon us; our tenure at Fort Wolters, Texas, was fast coming to a close. During the last week before graduation, Pat began to have pains, so we decided that she must get home right away. We packed up all our household belongings, and a civilian transfer truck picked them up for the trip to Fort Rucker, Alabama. What was left over, we put into the trunk of our Ford Fastback.

We said our good-byes to the many friends we made in Mineral Wells, Texas, and I drove Pat to Love Field in Dallas, where she boarded a plane that would take her nonstop to Atlanta. Pat was already much farther along than most airlines allow pregnant women to be when they fly; but she was able to get on board by concealing her bulging body under a large coat as cover. Gladys, her mother, would pick her up.

On the plane, a woman passenger nearly fainted when she asked Pat when the baby was due and Pat replied, "Tomorrow."

I called home every day, but there was no child tomorrow or the next day or the next. I graduated from Fort Wolters on Friday, December 17, 1966, and set out for home. Atlanta, Georgia, was the home of Johnny and Judy Kinsey, so Johnny proposed that we travel together that far. I told them it would be nonstop for me all the way home, but if they wanted to pull off for the night, I would continue on and see them in Rucker. But this was the wrong thing for me to say, and it caused me pain. Like many others, Johnny had had a rough time at Wolters. He had been recycled to the next class and would not be going to Fort Rucker. This meant that after the Christmas leave, he and Judy would be going back to Wolters to start over in another class. Pat and I were going to be "out of step" with the best friends we had known in a long time.

Another very close friend, Millard Green, was also going back to Wolters rather than on to Rucker. He had had a kidney stone and had been laid up in the hospital while 2nd WOC went on, so he and his wife, Kay, would also be going back to Wolters. Pat and I felt very sad about their misfortune.

Joseph Franklin Johnson, son of Tom and Pat Johnson, was born Christmas Eve afternoon, 1966. He was a beautiful child and I was overcome with joy at the sight of him. The first sign of trouble arose during his first feeding. A nurse brought Joey into the room, and I had to leave according to hospital policy.

When I returned, I found Pat deeply concerned—Joey was unable to suckle. The doctor told us what we dreaded to hear: our son had a cleft palate and a heart murmur.

Life ended for little Joey four days later in spite of all that everyone tried to do to save him. Pat held him close and he smiled sweetly at her many times. He lived long enough to become a part of our lives, and we knew we would miss him terribly for the rest of our lives.

I held up well until the day of the funeral, when I looked up over the casket containing my son and saw our two very dear friends—Johnny and Judy Kinsey. Unannounced, they had driven down from Atlanta for this sad occasion. Military life had put some unwanted distance between our families, and the sight of our closest friends finally caused me to break down.

Joey was buried in the cemetery at a small country church just outside the small community of Clem, Georgia. Where he is laid to rest is very hallowed ground. Many relatives from my mother's family were laid to rest there, and we found comfort in knowing that Joey would not be alone.

We made frequent visits to the grave site during our leave; then, at last, we had to say a heartbreaking good-bye, the most painful we had yet had to say. Christmas leave was coming to a close and I had orders to report to Fort Rucker in just three more days.

13

The Death of James Arthur Johansen

January 18, 1968

Throughout late December and early January, the "rumor mills" were spreading the word that the entire 1st Cavalry Division was about to pull out of the II Corps tactical area. No one really believed this until three days ago, when Major Beyer called a meeting in the mess hall.

"Today MACV Deputy Commander General Creighton Abrams ordered General Tolson to take the entire division north," he announced. "The Marines are currently 'working out' with fresh NVA divisions that are crossing over the DMZ. There has been increased activity around Khe Sanh outpost as well as the cities of Hue and Quang Tri. This will be an emergency movement in which quick combat deployment is essential. This will be the largest movement of men and materials over this great a distance in such a short time in the history of modern warfare. This movement will be code-named 'Operation Jeb Stuart.' "

"How far north?" came the question.

"Beyond the city of Hue. That is all I know right now." Everyone in the tent is stunned.

We know the Bong Son plains AO like our own backyard. Now we will have to learn a whole different territory. I Corps tactical area begins on a line east to west about 100 miles north of LZ English and extends all the way to the DMZ. In the northernmost part of I Corps are three major cities: Hue, which is the provincial capital, Quang Tri, and Dong Ha. Dong Ha is about as far as you can go without crossing over the DMZ. Quang Tri is about 15 miles south of Dong Ha. Hue is about 20 miles below Quang Tri. This northern area is currently under the command of the Third Marine Division.

As soon as the news breaks, random support units of the 1st Cavalry immediately begin pulling out of LZ English. The fighting forces will stay until relieved by the 173rd, which is expected on or before January 20, 1968.

We began packing up the day of Beyer's announcement, and we will depart as soon as daylight allows on January 20. This is what the 1st Cavalry has been bred for—emergency deployment over a large territory. This will be another test of the airmobile concept of helicopters flying great distances and inserting combat soldiers into battle.

Tonight I am mission commander of the last lightning bug mission for the II Corps. Two Hueys will fly the mission, Bug Six and Bug Three, accompanied by two gunships from D Company 229th, whose call sign will be Smiling Tigers. I am aircraft commander for Bug Six, with a relatively new guy named Larry Gold as right seat pilot and crew chief James Kessler and gunner Richard Knott completing the crew. Aircraft commander for Bug Three is Tom Burgess, and his crew includes Ingamar Johansen as right seat pilot. Their aircraft is Army Huey tail number 66-16800, which belongs to crew chief Lawrence J. Mendes. The gunner for 16800 is William Gasteno. For reasons unknown to me, Sergeant Lloyd E. Thompson has requested to be on board.

Tonight, more than ever before, I am uneasy about the mission. Only two nights ago, I awoke from a nightmare yelling at the top of my voice and flailing around on my cot. I had torn my mosquito netting completely down from its perch and had somehow managed to get it wrapped tightly around my throat, restricting my breathing in the process. This gave me the sensation of drowning, which fit into my dream.

"Tom, you OK?" Ingamar reached out in the night to grab my elbow and reassure me that I was still in the world.

I removed the netting and put both feet on the wooden pallet that separated our cots. "I'm OK," I replied and groped for my trusty pipe and tobacco. I was shaking so badly that I had trouble holding the match over the bowl. Johansen noticed.

I continued to sweat uncontrollably for the next few minutes. I could see Johansen's face emerge from the dark, spotlighted by the glow of the tobacco each time I made a long draw through the pipe's stem. The pipe has become my security blanket, and the nicotine seems to have a tranquilizing effect on my nerves in times of trouble.

"I can't speak much for the rest of you guys' nightmares, 'cause I know everyone has them. But this wasn't a nightmare; it was real. On a scale of one to ten—this was a *ten*!" I spoke in a slightly muffled voice so as not to awaken any of the other guys.

"What was it about?" Ingamar asked again, propping up his head with his right arm.

"I saw water . . . lots of water. It was rushing up to the windscreen fast. I hit the water very hard. I saw myself from above." I paused to suck long and hard on the pipe again. "The queer thing is, suddenly the wreckage is out of the water and sitting somewhere on white sand. I watched as they pulled a body from the crew chief's compartment. The others were standing over the body, and they said, 'What is he doing in there?'"

"What do you mean 'What is he doing in there?' Was it you in the crew chief's compartment?"

JAMES ARTHUR JOHANSEN HOURS BEFORE HIS DEATH.

193

"I don't know." My voice trailed off and I slumped down to stare at my feet, then looked back at Ingamar. "I couldn't see who they were talking about."

"Crap, Johnson, that's scary!"

"It's also real. It's the most realistic nightmare I've ever had. I could see and feel the wind, and right at impact, I could hear someone say 'Oh, God!' "

I finished that bowl of tobacco and quickly lit another, which was a very unusual thing for me to do. After nearly 30 minutes of calming down, I lay back in my bunk, but I could not shake the nightmare. Finally, I dozed off into a light sleep.

The following morning at breakfast I joked with some other pilots about the nightmare. It was my way of issuing what I felt was some kind of warning without being overly serious. Major accidents always come in "threes." If there is one, then another will surely follow, and then one more. I can discern no reasonable explanation for this pattern; it just happens that way. In the past four days, the division has suffered two serious crashes, one of which had a fatality. Who will be next?

The first lightning bug mission, at 2300 hours, was made without target contacts. We are preparing for the final mission at 0300 hours. At the mess hall, long since closed, I procure a cup of hot coffee and stroll to the A/229th TOC. The only guy there is the CQ, who is nodding his head in the process of falling asleep. I break the silence when I key the telephone to call the weather detachment.

"Going out again, Mister Johnson?" Specialist Fourth Class Henry Llewellyn, the CQ, stirs when he realizes I am in the TOC bunker.

"Yeah. Last mission in II Corps. We have an 0400 crank."

"How's the weather?" Llewellyn is obviously glad to have someone to talk to during his lonely all-night vigil in the operations bunker.

"The weather will be coming down later in the morning after the sun comes up. There might be some patchy fog here and there but nothing else unusual in the weather report." I manage to gulp the last drop of my hot coffee before I leave operations, toting my customary flight gear—APH-5 helmet in an olive drab cloth helmet bag, maps stuffed into the helmet, and chest protector. I have just begun to preflight my Huey when Tom Burgess walks up out of the dark. "Gasteno is sick."

"Gasteno—your gunner?" I ask.

"Yeah. He wasn't feeling too good on the first mission and now he's throwing up. Got any ideas?"

I turn off the red lens flashlight and summon Kessler.

"Hey, Kessler, what's the mail clerk's name? Isn't it Wielkopolan or something like that?"

"Donald Wielkopolan."

"Do you know where he sleeps?"

"Yes, sir, third tent on the hill, next to 2nd Platoon's tent."

"This guy has been pleading for me to let him fly for two months. He needs the whole 25 hours to get an air medal. You have any idea which cot?"

"Second on the right, I think, sir."

"Burgess, I'll go wake him up if I can find him. In the meantime get on the radio and let the Tigers know we'll be cranking about thirty minutes late, OK?"

I light up both my pipe and flashlight and amble over to the tent that Kessler has identified as Wielkopolan's tent. I wake him and ask if he still wants to fly. He leaps out of his bunk with the enthusiasm of a kid at Christmas.

Dressed in two minutes flat, he follows me up to the flight line where I introduce him to Mendes, 16800's crew chief. We give Mendes time to give Wielkopolan a quick lesson in being a gunner.

Mendes instructs him as to what is expected of him during this mission, how to key his mike properly, and when and when not to talk over the intercom. Wielkopolan is getting more excited as each minute passes.

Finally it is 0345 hours and time to crank. Liftoff out of the A/229th parking area is uneventful. I quickly establish contact with Red Dog GCA and check the direction of artillery fire, and then go back to A/229th company frequency to brief Bug Three and the Tiger flight.

"We will head due east until intersecting the coast, then turn south until reaching the Bong Son River. Turning west, we will fly up the river to the Bong Son pass, then down to the lake. Everybody copy?"

"Bug Three copies."

"Tiger Four-Eight and Tiger Three-Eight copy."

This is a routine route, and it requires no further instructions. I contact the Mohawk aircraft flying high overhead, and they report a very quiet night with no targets on their SLAR.

DONALD WIELKOPOLAN AT LZ ENGLISH IN 1968, JUST BEFORE HIS DEATH.
COURTESY OF THE WIELKOPOLAN FAMILY

Going lights out, we fly to the coast about 100 feet above the ground. There is enough moonlight to outline the white sandy areas and tree lines as we pass over them at this low altitude.

"Going feet wet," I transmit. This means that I have cleared the beach and now am over the South China Sea. "Lights on!" With this transmission, I flip a small toggle switch that has been taped to my collective control. A gear motor whines and the seven large C-130 landing lights slide to a position outside the Huey's cargo compartment and come on.

The brilliance of the lights illuminates the breaking surf as it rolls up into the shallow waters. Unlike the golden light produced by the flares, this light is similar to natural sunlight. From this altitude of 100 feet, the coverage area is a circle about one football field in diameter. I descend to 50 feet and turn south to parallel the beach.

"All right, Gold. You take the collective and keep me at 50 feet exactly. I don't mean 49 or 51! Keep your ass glued to the altimeter and adjust as necessary. I'll fly the aircraft and look ahead for obstructions. Do you have any trouble understanding what I just said?"

"No, sir. I understand," Gold replies over the intercom, a little taken back by my abrasiveness.

All our lives now depend on Gold's ability to follow instructions. The water below races by in a blur, and the sensation of height goes out the door as soon as we clear the beach. One moment I feel that we are flying right into the ocean, the next, I feel that we are at least 200 feet above it. I can only reassure myself with a quick cross-check of my altimeter against Gold's and a quick look into the illuminated area. I never trust barometric pressure altimeters, but at night, especially over water, I have no choice. The Huey is buffeting up and down as we fly through the turbulent air produced when the waves run ashore. This makes Gold's job even more difficult.

Tonight is Larry Gold's first lightning bug mission, and he is doing a very good job holding altitude. I alternately fly right down the middle of the beach, then out into the breakwater about 1000 feet from the shoreline. This keeps Charlie somewhat off guard as to my next direction of flight. We fly as fast as the Huey can take us, swerving first on the beach, then out into the water and back again. A pilot has to be damned stupid to do this mission—low and lit up like the Atlanta airport. About 500 yards behind us, Bug Three is doing his thing being the bait. His single red anticollision light rotates around and around. Somewhere behind Bug Three are two Tiger gunships. They maintain total lights-out so as not to be seen, and to lessen the chance of an accidental midair collision between them, they will not be zigzagging. One will stay over the beach at all times, and one will stay over the water.

"Bug Three, Tiger Four-Eight. You look lower than fifty feet. You might want to check that. Over."

"Three, roger," Burgess replies.

The gunships have a better idea of our height than we do ourselves. It is much easier for them, riding laterally behind both the Bug Six and Bug Three Hueys, to see the distance between where the C-130 lights emanate and where they reflect off the water's surface. Consequently, when Bug Three is silhouetted between the lights and themselves, the Tiger aircraft can also determine his approximate height as compared to mine. It is obvious to the Tiger aircraft that Bug Three is closer to the water than is the Bug Six Huey.

This is a normal call, and I do not pay much attention to it. I assume that Tom Burgess will make the necessary adjustments to the altimeter readings and have Johansen fly higher.

As we near the mouth of the Bong Son River, the beach gives way to a multitude of inland waterways that are separated by tiny peninsulas and islands. It is Charlie's favorite hiding spot since the deep brush overhanging the edges offers excellent cover to any good-sized boat.

"Larry, bring us up to 75 feet—we got palm trees up ahead."

"OK," Gold replies quickly and pulls up on the collective.

The Huey responds and the altimeter eases up by 25 feet and stabilizes. Abruptly, the tops of the tall palm trees pass beneath our skids barely 20 feet below us.

The endless narrow waterways finally widen and then become the Bong Son River.

"Bong Son River—turning right!" I transmit to the rest of the flight. "Larry, back to fifty feet. We are going up the river."

"OK," Gold makes a smooth transition back to 50 feet.

The river is especially muddy tonight. The seawater reflects in black, the river in a brownish blood red.

We are skimming just above the Bong Son River at a rate of 176 feet per second. Mendes's Huey flies especially easy and vibration free tonight.

Because of a premonition that one of these nights ol' Charlie is going to get really smart and stretch a cable between the banks of the river, I always fly in the right seat instead of the left. The copilot's collective control head houses all the controls for the nose-mounted searchlight, and I sweep this light from side to side of our route. At times, due to the extreme nose-low attitude incurred during maximum speeds, I hit the searchlight's upper limit. Flying up the river is far more dangerous and not nearly as easy as flying down the coastline. Whereas the coastline was straight, the river repeatedly changes its course. Therefore, I am constantly adjusting to keep equidistant from the trees on both sides while looking for targets at the same time. Due south of LZ English, the Bong Son River makes a horseshoe. Occasionally I reduce speed to make the U-turn in the river, but not tonight.

"Forget the horseshoe!" I transmit. The clicking of the radios tells me that Bug Three and both Tiger birds understand. We soar over the land that forms the horseshoe and reenter the river dead center.

"Six, Bug Three is flying so low he is throwing water spray onto our windscreens!" Tiger Four-Eight calls as we enter the home stretch for the Bong Son bridges.

"Burgess, you got a problem back there?" I angrily transmit.

"Six, negative."

"Then pick it up and stay up—you roger?"

"Three rogers."

Burgess is a new aircraft commander. He has not made the left seat without some opposition. Having flown with him more than once and found him a smart-ass know-it-all, I felt he was not ready to take this responsibility. Other aircraft commanders also saw him as a "hot rodder" who believed his skills were equal to those of the more experienced pilots he flew with.

When we lost three aircraft commanders to normal rotation back to the States, we found ourselves in a tight situation. Burgess was the next logical choice to make aircraft commander because he had the most in-country flight time of all the peter pilots. As company instructor pilot and company safety officer, Rick Peterson and I carry more weight in this type of decision than any of the other pilots, but it takes a consensus, including the commanding officer, to approve or disapprove the left seat. Both Peterson and I told Beyer that Burgess was not ready, but Major Beyer had more helicopters than he had aircraft commanders to crew them. After some very serious conversation with Burgess, he reluctantly convinced Peterson and me to approve him for left seat. Tonight is my forty-third lightning bug mission and Burgess's first.

"Burgess, you and Johansen roll your altimeter down by 50 feet and adjust your altitude!" This is an afterthought, but, strangely, I feel it needs to be said. This is my attempt to add a safety factor into their altimeter should it be incorrect.

"Roger," Burgess replies.

"Larry, the Bong Son bridges are coming up. I have it."

"You have it," he replies as he releases the Huey's collective.

"Lights out!" This transmission notifies the rest of the lightning bug flight that the C-130 lights are being turned off for the transition from the river to the saltwater lake named Dam Tra-O. The lake is only minutes away, and it makes no sense at all to climb to 1500 feet. Throwing caution to the wind, we all increase our separation from one another dramatically and go lights-out. For the next four minutes, the entire flight will have to navigate through the 2-mile-wide Bong Son pass in total stealth. We hope that we don't run into each other or some other idiot running out there without lights.

"Gold, stay on the gauges. If we're going to hit any fog, we'll do it in the pass. If I say 'You have it,' it will mean we've hit the soup hard. Your job is to take over and execute a climb out on instruments. You will follow my heading instructions and climb to 3000. You copy?"

"Roger. Maintain your heading and climb to three thousand."

"Gold, a lot of times Highway 1, which I use as a centerline of the pass on bright nights, has disappeared underneath me. If it disappears, you don't have to be too intelligent to know that you just hit a low-level fog layer.

"Running at night without any lights makes it impossible to accurately judge any weather conditions. If you hit the soup, the only safe thing to do is to climb as rapidly as you can to an altitude above the mountains. If you remain aware of your position at all times relative to the nearest mountain, you should be able to take a heading during the climb that will steer you clear of crashing into a mountain and going home in a body bag. You savvy?"

"Yes, sir!" Gold replies to my lesson.

Centering over Highway 1, I fly its contours on a southerly heading. Out of caution, I occasionally flip on the C-130 lights to fix our current position and allow the other aircraft to establish where we are along the route of flight. Although this risks attracting ground fire, I would prefer that to a midair collision. For their own safety the gun birds fall way behind during the transition through the pass.

"OK, folks, we'll enter the lake at the peninsula. I'll fly up the south side of the peninsula and cross the lake on a heading of 30 degrees. We'll fly the river to the coast, then call it a night."

I hear the squelch of the radio in lieu of a verbal reply. This route across the Dam Tra-O Lake is standard procedure.

I exit the Bong Son pass and continue south along the flat Bong Son plains for another 3 or 4 miles. The saltwater lake shimmers in the moonlight to the east. It is a very large body of water fed from the

South China Sea by the Song Chal Truc River. The lake is tidal, mean-ing its average depth varies from 6 to 10 feet depending on the tide. The lightning bug missions have had several kills near the center of the lake.

I bank the Huey hard to the left and take up a heading that will center the peninsula, which juts almost a mile into the center of the lake. This landmass stands out in the moonlight against the black water.

"Lights on!" I transmit. "Gold, you have the collective! Bring us down to fifty feet!"

"Bug Six is feet wet!" This notifies the rest of the lightning bug flight that we are now over the water. I'm sure they can see this when the lights come on, but I always feel it is a necessary transmission.

Gold eases off the collective and allows the Huey to descend. Upon reaching his assigned altitude, he pulls up on the collective slightly to stop the descent. We are once again racing at breakneck speed across the black water.

"Three, you'd better check your damn altimeter again!" Tiger Four- Eight calls to Bug Three.

Bug Three must really be low for the gunship to call it again, and the anxiety in his voice worries me a lot.

"Bug Three, Tiger Four-Eight!!" There is no reply.

There is a five-second pause. "Bug Three, Tiger Four-Eight!!" Again no reply.

"BUG SIX, I THINK THREE HAS BIT THE WATER!"

"Say again, Four-Eight!" I ask for confirmation of his transmission.

"I SAY AGAIN: I THINK THREE JUST BIT IT! WE DO NOT SEE HIS LIGHT! GOD, WE JUST OVERFLEW FOAM IN THE WATER!"

"Gold, I have it!" Taking control of the Huey, I make a 2G turn to the left and reverse direction.

"Tiger flight, give me your lights!"

"Roger."

Both gunships turn on their landing lights and their navigation lights so that I can see them.

"Four-Eight, where?" I call.

"Turn left a little . . . little more . . . Dead ahead!"

I reduce the airspeed to just above translational lift and allow the altitude to drop below 50 feet. My eyes follow the sweeping of the landing light left to right and back again.

"ALTITUDE!" Gold yells.

I glance at the altimeter; it shows us so low that the last graduations cannot be determined. I yank up on the collective and the Huey responds.

"Gold, take the collective. Keep me at fifty feet!"

"I have the collective, sir."

I must have been right on the water because Larry raises us up several feet.

"A little right, Six! I think you're almost over the area where I saw the foam!"

There is no wind tonight; the lake's surface has been very smooth. Then we come upon ripples. The ripples are being formed by waves coming from my hard right. I do a half-pedal turn and a half-cyclic turn hard right in the direction of the waves. I feel the Huey come out of translational lift. We are no longer flying; we are at a 50-foot hover over water at night.

We come upon a fisherman's net that gives me some sense of our height above the water. Then I see it. "Jesus!" All my muscles tighten.

Only the transmission mast and one twisted rotor blade remain out of the water, but it is definitely a Huey down there. Debris is floating all around its wreckage.

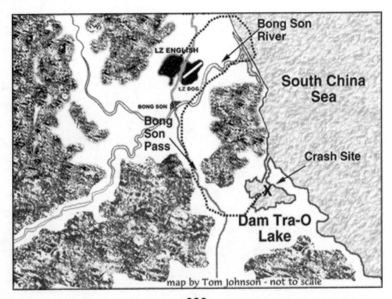

map by Tom Johnson - not to scale

"Tiger Four-Eight, you see this?" I call out.

"I see it, Six. Can you see anybody?"

"Not sure yet, Four-Eight. Stand by!"

I trigger the intercom. "Gold, I have it, but keep hands on and watch the altimeter!"

"Roger," Gold replies.

I ease the Huey forward until the C-130 light pattern centers the submerged Huey at an altitude of 50 feet.

"Somebody in the water, sir!" It is Kessler, the crew chief.

"Where, Kessler?"

"On my side, on my side about 20 feet out from the mast!"

Kessler's compartment is on the opposite side of the Huey from me. I pull the aircraft to a dead stop and do an easy pedal turn right to project the lights ahead of our extended flight path.

Sure enough, someone is in the water some 20 feet on the other side of the wreckage. His heavy flight helmet is still on and his head is bobbing, first in the water and then out, as though his neck is broken. The poor bastard's head goes forward, face-first, into the water, and remains for seconds; then somehow he jerks it backward into the water behind him. He cannot keep his face out of the water.

"Altitude!" Larry yells.

Gold, preoccupied with what is happening, has, for only an instant, taken his eyes off the altimeter; he grabs a handful of collective and the Huey balloons skyward. Even the best of barometric combat-use altimeters cannot decipher 20 feet. We must have been 6 to 8 feet above the water before Gold screamed.

I call to Kessler and Knott over the intercom. "Richard, you and James listen up! If you guys get out on the skids, can your helmet cords still reach?"

"Don't know, sir—stand by." I feel a shuffling of feet and a shifting of weight in the rear of the Huey's cargo compartment as they exit the relative safety of their cubicle and move out on the Huey's skids.

"Can do, sir!" Richard's reply comes over the rushing of wind across his boom mike. I cannot look back. My hover target is fixed on the protruding mast of the Huey in the water.

"Can you sit down on the skids and be OK?" Again I fear I am asking for the impossible.

"Can do!" Kessler responds.

"How about you, Knott? Can you do it?"

"Yes, sir . . . I'm OK."

"Get back into the aircraft and take your boots off. I want you guys to get outside and straddle the skids! Put your feet as far below the aircraft as you can, OK?"

"Stand by, sir!" Both Kessler and Knott scramble back inside the Huey and hurriedly remove their combat boots.

Pedal turning back left, I move forward and keep the Huey perfectly still right above the wreckage. I position my hover target through the clear chin bubble between my feet. I glance down and then rapidly forward at the person drowning some 20 feet over the nose of my Huey. I can feel Larry Gold occasionally overriding the collective to keep us somewhere near 50 feet above the lake. Whoever is in the water is not doing well. When I first saw him, I could see his shoulders, but now the situation has worsened—his head remains barely above the salt water, and it is continuing to fall face in, then face out, on a much slower repetition. He is drowning right before my eyes.

"How about it, guys!" I scream over the intercom.

There is a last-minute shuffling and the Huey's center of gravity again shifts.

"We are ready, sir!" comes Kessler's reply.

"Ready, sir!" from Knott.

"Larry, stay with me on the collective! OK?" I try to keep my voice calm. "OK, you guys, we are going in. The minute your toes touch water, yell like hell. Kessler, I'm going to put this guy on your side!"

I must get this Huey on the exact other side of the wreckage before this guy drowns, but I fear that losing the transmission mast as my hover target will result in vertigo. If this happens, we will become crash victims ourselves. So I choose not to hover directly to the drowning person; instead I will hover in a circle, keeping the mast in sight at all times. I back away from my hover target until I can see the transmission mast from over the nose of our Huey instead of through the chin bubble. When I feel we are the same distance from the mast as the man in the water on the other side, I release the pressure on the collective. The Huey starts to descend toward the black water below.

Neither the crew chief nor the gunner has to tell me that we are right on top of the water. I fix my altitude and position on the downed Huey's mast and watch it rise right off the nose of our Huey. As we near the surface, the Huey's great blast of wind begins blowing salt water up off the surface with hurricane force. We now are surrounded by a vortex of water spray. As we go even lower, spray begins to blow into the cockpit, covering the instruments, consoles, and the inside of the windscreen through which I am looking.

I begin a clockwise rotation around the mast and stop our descent as best I can. Continuing to aim the Huey's nose at the mast while hovering in a circle requires the continuous coordination of the pedals, cyclic, and collective. This maneuver reminds me of the exercise given to me in primary flight school in which I had to hover completely around a tree while keeping the nose of the helicopter pointed at the tree. I nurse the cyclic toward my left knee and compensate the loss of lift with the collective. As we move, I jockey the pedals.

"Water! Water!" Both Knott and Kessler scream.

Without hesitation, I pull up on the collective, hesitate for a moment, then let us down again.

I continue the sideways movement. Salt water drips off the rim of my helmet and onto my nose. It itches but I don't dare take my hands off the controls to scratch.

"Water! Water!" Again they yell in unison and again I adjust.

The C-130 lights are on Kessler's side, and they provide the light we need to make the pickup. I have long since lost visual sighting of the target in the water.

"I see two of them, sir. Go forward about ten feet!" I apply firm cyclic forward pressures.

"Forward a little more! Little more forward!" Kessler calls. His commands are terribly muffled by the wind flowing over his boom mike. "Left, left a little more!"

I ready myself for the recovery. When Kessler begins taking our passengers aboard, the added weight will make an additional draw on power. The Huey is already hovering in an extreme tail-low attitude. If the rearmost part of the skids, where Kessler's feet are hanging down, are that close to the water, then the tail rotor must be about a foot or two above the surface. Even the slightest dip in altitude will put the tail rotor into the water, and all of us will be done for.

"Take them aboard easy, Kessler. Easy now!" I scream, with this in mind.

I cannot take my eyes off the hover target, but the scuffling tells me that Kessler has a hold on something. I feel the Huey start sinking as the weight is pulled on board, and we rock heavily to the left side. I pull in power to compensate.

"Got 'em! It's Mendes and Sergeant Thompson . . . got 'em sir!" I pull in a handful of collective, and the Huey soars into the night air to a staggering 20 feet above the lake's surface.

"Kessler, I'm going to continue in your direction!"

"OK!"

Keeping the hover target, I continue in a counterclockwise circle around the wreckage. My hover target, the mast, is at the bare edge of the vortex that surrounds us—a point where the lake water turns to a heavy airborne mist and shoots skyward. If I back any further away from it, it will disappear in the mist; losing my only hover target would mean disaster for us all.

"Oh, God, sir! Go forward! Go forward! Helmet! This guy is underwater!"

I stop the movement left and ease forward on the collective. The cockpit is now totally covered with water. The flight instruments are unusable except for Gold's altimeter. He keeps wiping it with a rag to keep its glass face clear enough to read the dials. I am dripping wet.

I feel Kessler lurch again.

"Only a helmet, sir. Only a helmet!"

I hear a plastic thump as Kessler throws the helmet inside the Huey's cargo compartment.

"Water! Water!" Knott yells. I again respond and continue the trek sideways.

"Six, Tiger Four-Eight. We can't see very well through the water you are throwing up, but from my vantage point, it looks like someone is trying to climb aboard the wreckage!"

"Can you see them? Over"

"That's a negative, Four-Eight. Say location from our present position!"

"Six. Definitely a warm body! We are almost right over your head. Look left of the mast about ten meters."

"Stand-by, Four-Eight."

We are about 20 yards out from the mast. I apply forward cyclic to gently nudge the Huey toward the mast and stop the rotation around it. As I move in closer, the water curtain moves to the other side of the mast and makes it more distinguishable.

"There he is, sir!" Gold yells out. He points to a spot some 10 meters to the opposite side of the mast and to my right.

"OK, Richard, this one is yours!"

"Yes, sir!" Richard Knott replies.

I apply right cyclic to move in toward the mast and start a clock-wise rotation around it. We are in so close now that the mast is nearly bumping the nose of our Huey.

"Back sir . . . back a little!" Richard commands. "Back a little more! Down some!"

I have to try to picture in my mind what Richard's eyes are seeing in the water. Applying rear cyclic and adjusting the collective and ped-als, I gently back the Huey away from the mast. Again I remind myself we are already in a very tail-low hover. Backing up will aggravate this situation by dumping the tail boom down even more.

"Water! Water!" Kessler yells.

I let up on the cyclic a little and pull in more collective. I pause for a moment, then I put the Huey in reverse.

"Hold it!" Knott screams.

There is again a great bumping and shuffling of feet. I feel the load come on board as the Huey attempts to settle.

"Mister Burgess . . . it's Mister Burgess, sir!"

"OK, Richard. Get back out on the skids!"

"Roger."

"Six, I know you're busy, but you need to know you are taking fire from the peninsula that is to your west. Tiger Three-Six is on target and working out. Do you copy?"

"I copy, Four-Eight!" Instinctively I glance down at the electric compass, called an RMI, to see which way west is. It is totally obscured by salt water. Right now there is no west or east, only the mast sticking out of the water.

I key the intercom. "How are our people doing, Kessler?"

"Not so good, sir. Mendes is out of it. Either he's passed out or he's dead. He's not moving. Mister Burgess is holding his ribs and appears to be in a lot of pain. Sergeant Thompson is busted up real bad!"

"Damn!" I reply in disgust, without keying the intercom. Almost simultaneously one bar on a 20-bar panel lights up the entire cockpit and commands my immediate attention.

"Twenty-minute fuel light!" Gold keys as though I can't see it for myself.

"Damn!" I explode.

I very quickly remove my hand from the collective and wipe the face of the clock. The elapsed timer clearly shows that it has been over two hours since we cranked for this last mission. Twenty-minute fuel lights are not accurate. There may be more or less than this amount of flight time left. I once had a Huey out for a little over 2½ hours, and that was an emergency. As a rule, fuel starvation will cause the engine to fail after 2½ hours of flight.

"Tiger flight, Bug Six has a twenty-minute fuel light!" I transmit to the gunships. "We got to cut out right now. We have three souls on board. What is your fuel status? Over."

"Six, Tiger Four-Eight. We are out. We will be right behind you. Over."

I pull collective and hover straight up for some altitude before nosing over. Gold has removed one of his flight gloves and is busy wiping down the instruments on my side of the panel.

"Tiger flight, Bug Six. We are going direct over the mountains. Our passengers aren't doing very good."

"Tigers will follow" is the reply from Tiger Four-Eight.

I pull collective up under my armpits until the low rpm warning light comes on. I find a power setting just slightly under the light and lock it. The Huey is giving me all she has, and the high-pitched groan of the Lycoming verifies it. I keep the airspeed back to 80 knots in order to climb above the Cay Giep Mountains. After passing the crest of the mountain range, I hold the same power on and nose over hard. The airspeed indicator roars to 140 knots and the altimeter begins to unwind.

"Gold, call English and tell them to alert the medevac unit that we are inbound with three souls."

I change the UHF radio to the correct frequency as I speak. I also change my radio selector switch to FM and transmit to A/229th operations that Burgess has crashed. I inform the CQ, Specialist 4th Class Henry Llewellyn, that we are so low on fuel that I will not attempt to high-hover to POL. I ask for a fuel truck to be sent down to the runway where the medevac unit is located. During this air-to-ground briefing, I feel a bitter sting when I report to Llewellyn that Johansen and Wielkopolan are not accounted for. I switch back to the English tower frequency to monitor the instructions Gold is receiving. The main runway is very busy with many C-130s and C-141s taking off and landing. The move north is fully under way. English tower is giving Gold the runaround about his current traffic situation—they want us to enter the landing pattern in a normal fashion behind a C-141 on a 2-mile final.

"English Tower, this is Bandit Eighty-Eight! We have a medical priority! Tell the aircraft on the ground to hold their positions! Instruct the aircraft on final to go-around to the north . . . I say again: to the north. We will land centerfield at the medevac pad! *DO YOU COPY?*" My voice rises to a pissed-off roar.

"Roger Eighty-Eight. English copies!"

"Crap, that bastard knew that aircraft inbound with wounded have precedence over all other traffic!" I say through the intercom, directing my remarks to Larry Gold; Gold does not reply.

I put the collective all the way down some 2 miles out from the runway and begin the process of bleeding off forward airspeed for lift. We arrive dead center on the runway perpendicular to its axis. I see one pissed-off C-141 Air Force pilot struggling to make an emergency go-around right over LZ English. All four jet engines on this enormous aircraft are biting the air to get it up to speed. That is his problem; mine lie unconscious in the cargo compartment right behind me. I have to high-hover right over a C-130 who has stopped on the taxiway almost in front of the medevac landing area. It must be quite a sight for these guys, sitting there with all four of their turboprops running while a Huey leaps over their cockpit.

I kick hard left pedal to make the tail boom go right, and we just miss the wing of the C-130; then I set us down on the white helipad with the red cross painted on it.

"You got it, Larry. Shut it down!"

I begin to unstrap. Kessler opens my door and I exit as quickly as I can. The medics have already gotten Burgess and Thompson out and on a stretcher. Others are pulling and dragging the limp body of Lawrence Mendes off the cargo floor. I glance at both men being taken away from the Huey but feel no emotion.

Stepping a few feet outside the Huey's now slowly spinning main rotor system, I check one pocket, then the other, on my fatigues and produce my pipe. Methodically, I blow through the stem to clear water from it, then pack the bowl full with Cherry Blend tobacco that has remained reasonably dry in its foil package. I light it and draw in a lung-full of smoke; my hand is shaking nervously. As I sit down on the hard steel ASP helipad, I keep telling myself that finding "Ingamar" is only a matter of time. I am sure that he is OK, but I shake my head at the thought of him swimming around in the intense blackness of Dam Tra-O Lake. It occurs to me how distraught he must have been when we departed a few moments ago, leaving him all alone.

Donald Wielkopolan is dead—there is not a doubt in my mind of that. I lack hard evidence; I have only a gut feeling. That same gut feeling tells me that Ingamar is OK.

The fuel truck appears from out of nowhere with three or four jeeps right behind it; they all converge on us. 229th Battalion Commander Colonel Brown leaps from the first jeep and instantly rushes to where I am sitting. I gradually rise to my feet, for the first time feeling the ache in my tight muscles.

Brown grabs me under the shoulder to help me straighten my tired body fully upright. While I brief him, pilots from A/229th who have arrived in the other three jeeps listen intently.

Kessler hurriedly pulls a postflight inspection of his Huey. He is in total command and is giving both Larry Gold and Richard Knott tasks that must be accomplished while he does his thing. Two of the pilots standing around notice the flurry of activity and leave the conversation to pitch in. People are crawling all over the aircraft looking for trouble. Although the Huey is dry on the outside, water is still dripping from inside the cargo and engine compartments.

When refueling is completed, I walk away from Brown and toward the Huey in a world of my own. I bump my pipe on the heel of my jungle boots several times to clear its bowl.

"Tom, you want me to fly with you?" Colonel Brown asks in a penetrating voice. His normally smooth forehead is wrinkled.

I pause a minute. "No, sir. Gold and I make a good team. If you don't mind, I'd rather Larry fly. Anyway, sir, I don't think you want any part of this." I have not mentioned a word of the extreme conditions that we will face when we try to extract Johansen.

"I'll ride in back . . . OK?" Brown asks courteously.

I do not reply. Anyway he is my boss; he doesn't have to ask me; this Huey and its crew belong to him.

Gold, Kessler, Knott, Colonel Brown, and I strap on Kessler's Huey and depart LZ English in the darkness.

We fly over the Bong Son bridges, down Highway 1, through the Bong Son pass, then direct to the crash site. I, with my overworked brain, have completely forgotten to call for gunship support. I am elated to receive a call from Tiger Four-Eight that he and Three-Six are outbound from English. I thought they had had enough and would be sending some other D/229th birds to replace them.

Without any of the standard radio calls, I redeploy the C-130 cluster lights and ignite them. As we draw closer to the crash site, I get chills and feel goose bumps over my entire body. I am terrified that we will find Johansen or Wielkopolan floating facedown in the darkness of the lake. When I was here before, things were happening very quickly, but during the short rest, I had time to think. This trip is like coming upon a car wreck on some desolate stretch of highway; before, I was in the wreck.

My dead reckoning under the moonlight is accurate. At the time I expect, the wreckage comes into view right off the nose of the Huey. I descend to about 100 feet and leave translational lift. We are again in a night hover over water.

Colonel Brown is without a helmet and therefore not privy to any intercom communications between the rest of the crew and myself. He must be pretty surprised when Kessler and Knott exit their cubicle and straddle the skids, bare feet dangling.

Brown unbuckles and rushes forward to tap me on the shoulder. "Don't get too low!" I hear him yell at the top of his voice. He retires, to the Huey's canvas seat—he does not yet know what a bad ride he is in for tonight. His concerns are very real, and I'm sure he is terrified, being a lowly passenger whose very life now depends on the proficiency of a 21-year-old pilot. By the time Brown buckles in, we are hovering at 100 feet.

Knott thinks he sees a body floating on his side. I have already set up the mast as my hover target off the nose and proceed, by his commands, to take us down to water level and move toward the object. At 50 feet, the salt water again goes airborne. At 20 feet, we are in the middle of the vortex that shoots up the water curtain all about us. If Brown was excited before, he must be ten out of a possible ten now.

For the second time tonight, we are "dancing with the devil." Knott's "body" turns out to be floating wreckage. For the next 60 minutes, I circle the exposed wreckage of Huey tail number 16800, extending the radius of the circle with each completed turn. My optimistic gut feeling gives way to despair as each moment goes by.

Every few seconds Kessler and/or Knott yells "Water! Water!" The entire crew's personal stress level has long since been exceeded, but I feel it absolutely imperative that I find Ingamar and Donald Wielkopolan.

Less than an hour has passed when Colonel Brown unbuckles and makes his way forward. "Break this off. Now! Let's go back to English!"

This is not a request; it is an order. Brown has had enough.

I know he is right, but, God, it hurts inside as I pull collective and start the vertical ascent. Repeatedly looking down through my door window, I watch the intensity of the light cluster diminish. The circle grows larger and larger. The contours of the wreckage slowly dissipate until they are no longer clear.

For the first time, I accept that James Arthur Johansen and Donald David Wielkopolan have perished.

I high-hover, pause for one last minute, then do a pedal turn toward English and push the nose over.

We deplane an exhausted copilot, gunner, and crew chief, and one terrorized colonel. Even with all hope gone, I refuel again and get ready for another trip to Dam Tra-O Lake. Despite the presence of Major Beyer and the pleas of the other pilots to take my place, I manage to hang on as "pilot in command"—I just cannot give up my ship. Beyer and I, along with Sergeant McCrary and two others, return to the crash site just as daylight breaks.

We search again, but at Major Beyer's altitude. Two hours later and again low on fuel, we return to English empty-handed. Totally exhausted, I give in to their demands and allow myself to be driven back to the company area. Somewhere around 1100 hours, a body recovery team headed by Mac McCrary lands on the shores of Dam Tra-O Lake.

All the other infantry units have departed English in the night, leaving the men of A/229th to recover their dead. The tide is close to its lowest level at this time, leaving most of the wreckage exposed. Pilots, crew chiefs, gunners, cooks, and paper hangers are sloshing their way on foot through the soft lake bottom in chest-deep water.

Not having slept for over 24 hours, I am fully strung out. Neither coffee nor nicotine will bring me down. In desperation and without hearing any word from the search party, I go to Major Beyer's tent. He has his hands full making preparations for the company pullout.

"Sir! I've got to go down there!"

Beyer looks up from his desk and sees my pain. Without uttering a word, he reaches for his flight gear. We gather a crew and depart English for the lake with Beyer at the controls.

As Dam Tra-O comes into view, I can see a twin rotor Chinook heavy lift helicopter hovering over the wreckage site. As we near, nothing looks the same as last night. In daylight, this is a different world to me.

The 228th company Chinook is attached to the wreckage of 16800 via a nylon sling. I see McCrary and others, who are rigging the sling, leap into the water from the crumpled top of the Huey just as the Chinook starts blowing wind. One-Six-Eight-Hundred is heavy with salt water. The "Hook's" blade tips begin to "fly high," showing that it is pulling a lot of power to extract the wreckage from its grave site. After a lot of tugging, 16800 clears the lake. The Chinook does a pedal turn and high-hovers to a white sandy site at the edge of the lake. Beyer lands at the site, already cluttered with almost all the A/229th Hueys, at about the same time as the Hook sets the wreckage down.

The nightmare of a few nights ago suddenly comes alive. It has been temporarily forgotten; now it is here in living color. One-Six-Eight is a ball of twisted metal—no tail boom, no rotor blades, no distinct pilots' compartment. What used to be the crew chief's compartment is not visible because the engine cowling covers are wrapped around it.

213

WRECKAGE OF THE HUEY JOHANSEN AND WIELKOPOLAN WERE FLYING WHEN THEY CRASHED AND WERE KILLED IN DAM TRA-O LAKE. IN THIS PHOTO THE HUEY IS UPSIDE DOWN AND THE ENTIRE PILOTS' COMPARTMENT IS MISSING.

"He's in there, Major Beyer," I say, in full control of my faculties and with respect.

"Say again?"

"He's in the crew chief's compartment."

"Who is in the crew chief's compartment?" Beyer is not comprehending.

"Don't know which one, but one of them is there."

Beyer may think I have run my last race, but he slowly exits the Huey, leaving me to finish the "cool down" period and terminate the Lycoming.

He walks straight to Sergeant McCrary and speaks to him. Mac flashes orders to people standing near him using hand signals. Beyer and Mac approach the hulk that once formed the fuselage. Both peer intently into the area that once was the crew chief's compartment. Mac's people return with several long pry bars, which are most likely the canvas seat poles from the other aircraft parked nearby.

After much struggling and prizing, the engine covers and other obstructions are ripped back. I continue to sit in my Huey and observe.

I know what I know. The only question left for me is: Is it Ingamar or is it Wielkopolan?

Beyer and Mac suddenly move in close. They are immediately joined by as many as can get into the tight spot and give them a hand. The body of Donald Wielkopolan[1] emerges in their arms.

James Arthur Johansen[2] will later be found on the bottom of Dam Tra-O Lake, still strapped into his seat, which was violently ripped out of the floor of the Huey on impact.

Since Johansen's name starts with a J, like mine, for weeks after his death his incoming mail is placed into the wooden cubby hole post office box marked "J." I remove each letter and automatically call the name Wielkopolan, who was the mail clerk, so the document can be returned to its sender.

We all feel their tragic deaths and the pain that follows. I carefully pack Johansen's personal belongings in an Army olive green footlocker that will be shipped to his mother in the States.

■

Tom Burgess, Lawrence Mendes, and Lloyd Thompson were flown to Japan. I never again saw Mendes or Thompson after the night of January 18th, 1968.

Larry Gold, James Kessler, and Richard Knott were brave men.[3] They did a job well beyond the call of their duty. None whimpered or cowered over the danger. Any pilot will tell you that it's one thing to be at the controls of

1. I located Henry "Hank" Llewellyn, the company radio operator on the night of the crash and through his efforts, was able to locate Wielkopolan's family in Taylor, Michigan. It was excruciating for me to tell them what happened. Donald David Wielkopolan's name can be found on panel 34E, line 72, on the Vietnam War memorial in Washington, DC.
2. James Arthur Johansen gave his life in service to his country. He was only days away from his 24th birthday. His name is located on the Vietnam War memorial in Washington, DC, at panel 34E, line 69. Twenty years after his death, I began a long and expensive search for his last resting place. Only when I invoked the Freedom of Information Act did the Army finally give up this information. My search finally ended on July 28, 1993, when I found Ingamar buried in a crypt alongside his father in Altadena, California, near Pasadena.
3. The names of James Arthur Johansen, Donald David Wielkopolan, Lawrence Mendes, and Lloyd Thompson are factual. The names of the other crewmembers are fictional. Unfortunately, time has erased from my memory the real names of the brave men who flew with me that night.

your destiny, but it takes a lot more courage to put your faith in another pilot when riding as his passenger. To the best of my knowledge, no other helicopter crew ever accomplished what we did that night—hovering that low over water for such an extended period of time, using bare feet as our only absolute altitude reporting device. However, as on many other occasions, there were no awards or medals—only the personal fulfillment that came from a dangerous task done well.

14

Can Chickens Really Fly?

January 20, 1968

Two days after Ingamar's crash, on a sunny afternoon, I am flying what will be my last mission over the An Lao valley, another boring run in support of ARVN (do-nothing) troops. Before taking off I had the crew chief illegally requisition a white rooster in addition to the livestock that have been placed in my care for the short flight to the extreme north end of the valley. It is not unusual to carry live chickens and pigs to these courageous defenders of the "no fight" zone. One time a goat was transported.

On our return flight, this particular rooster is removed from the crew chief's olive drab helmet bag where he has been secretly placed. Climbing from my seat and taking up a station near this charming bird, I tutor the rooster now nicknamed Short Flight on the art of flying. This level of instruction would have cost Short Flight $5,000 back in the States, but I feel that he is, in his own way, a defender of Vietnam, and I am compelled to share my combat experience with him at no cost.

This cocky little Vietnamese rooster is not at all intimidated by an American helicopter pilot telling him how to fly. After all, Short Flight was flying years before the Americans invaded his country and ate his barnyard hens.

With landing gear retracted and both motors at maximum rpm,

Short Flight is unceremoniously launched out the cargo door at 1500 feet above the valley floor while our Huey is at a hover.

Diving back into the Huey's front seat, I am filled with excitement as I see my first solo student kicked out of the nest. Diving the Huey into one turn, then into another, we follow Short Flight in close formation as he soars first east, then west. I think my heart will burst with the joy of the father of a newborn as I witness Short Flight do his first aerobatic maneuver. Neck outstretched in confidence, feathers laid back in the breeze, ol' Short Flight is doing very well, I think, especially when you consider how short a time I had to train him.

The entire crew is jumping around and yelling words of encouragement as "our" rooster passes through 600 feet, barely 20 yards off the right side of our Huey.

"Did you teach him how to land?" the other pilot asks.

"Huh?"

"I said: Did you teach Short Flight how to land?" he inquires again.

"Now that you mention it, we never got that far," I reply in all honesty.

The crew gets really quiet as I hang outside the aircraft and yell at the top of my voice new instructions for landing. I can easily tell that my warnings are being heard, but this cocky little know-it-all Vietnamese aviator already knows everything there is to know about landings.

At about 10 feet altitude and with the forward velocity of an F-4 Phantom in full afterburner, Short Flight attempts to extend his landing gear and start his flare for final.

To our astonishment, all his wing feathers come out.

Out of respect, I land the Huey. I walk one way and the crew chief walks the other. We recover all of Short Flight and place him in a sandy grave alongside the An Lao River.

The gunner, using a C ration cardboard lid and a grease pencil, prepares a suitable grave marker that reads, "Here lies WO1 Tom Johnson's first solo student."

15

The 1st Cavalry
Moves North

January 23, 1968

The departure of A Company from LZ English has been delayed by three days because of Ingamar's crash. Yesterday, we broke down all the tents and burned what could not be taken on the move. LZ English, for all practical purposes, is now barren except for the thousands of sandbags that have been cut and drained of their contents. All nonessential personal belongings have been destroyed. With no tents to cover us, we spent last night out in the open gazing at the stars.

This morning, we pack all the Hueys to the gills. Each Huey will carry all the belongings of the AC, pilot, crew chief, and gunner. We have to strap things down to keep them from falling out the door.

It is barely after sunrise when Beyer gives the hand signal to start. The blades of the heavily laden Hueys begin to turn slowly with the whine of the turbine starter motors. Within two minutes, the entire A/229th ensemble is ready for liftoff.

One very important item the pilots are determined not to leave behind is the officers' latrine. It has been laboriously constructed of wooden ammo boxes and has real screen wire around it to keep out the flying critters. After much pleading, Major Beyer finally gave in to the pilots' desire, but he offered no help in transporting the latrine up north. All the trucks assigned to A/229th are already full. We have run every command gambit but to no avail.

Since there are no vehicles available to transport it, we have no choice; somebody will have to sling-load the latrine all the way. The newest aircraft commander, one of the fearless foursome, is chosen by Beyer to hook up. He does so under protest. We remind him of how much sling-load experience he lacks and point out that practice will do him good.

Beyer lifts off to the east, and his covey follows one by one. During the form-up, Beyer makes a wide 360-degree turn that takes us over the center of what had once been our home. It is sad to see LZ English so barren. Although I'm not high enough to see over the Cay Giep Mountains, I still look south for a last glimpse of Dam Tra-O Lake, thinking about Ingamar. We ride quietly over the LZ.

Beyer continues east to the coast, then turns north toward the 1st Cavalry's new home.

Two hours after leaving LZ English, I see the sprawling city of Da Nang with its large harbor. We land south of Da Nang at a place called Marble Mountain to take on fuel. Ahead of us and behind us, the sky is black with all sorts of aircraft bearing the 1st Cavalry's yellow and black emblem. This immense gaggle must be something to write home about for anyone on the ground. A/229th refuels and launches again over the Da Nang harbor, then out to sea to circumnavigate the tall mountains that are the north side of the harbor.

The only pilot with a map is Major Beyer. An hour and a half after departing Da Nang, nearing late afternoon, Beyer lowers the collective and initiates the descent toward a cemetery that is marked by a white smoke grenade. One at a time, each of the A/229th's Hueys shoots an approach, then has to jockey for position at the last moment to keep from having a grave marker damage the underside of the aircraft. We don't know it yet, but this part of the world is called LZ El Paso and is the 1st Air Cavalry's temporary I Corps home.

Lowering the collective to the bottom stop and rolling off throttle to begin the engine cool-down, I say, "You've got to be kidding me. A graveyard! We can't be setting up camp here."

"Bandit flight, *do not* shut down. Kick off your belongings right where you're sitting and attempt to remember where that spot is! We have to do a little more work before we can call it a day," Beyer transmits over the FM radio.

There is moaning and groaning. We're all physically very tired,

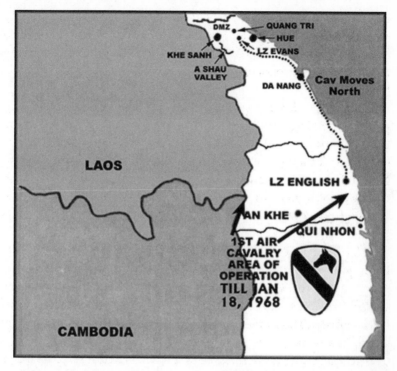

and the mental strain has taken its toll, too, but I again advance the throttle back to full rpm and wait for the crew chief and gunner to kick out all we have hauled.

White Eight calls to Beyer that the flight is up (meaning ready to take off), and Six leads the way to a small dirt airfield at Hue Phu Bai, a small city on the outskirts of the city of Hue. For the next five hours, and deep into the night, A/229th will pick up 1st Cavalry troopers who have been flown into Hue Phu Bai by Air Force C-130 Hercules aircraft and immediately deploy them into strategic defensive positions surrounding the cemetery.

When the last combat assault, that is, insertion, is finished, we refuel for the umpteenth time at the Hue Phu Bai airfield and then fly a loose trail night formation in the direction of the cemetery. Not one of us—not even Major Beyer—has any idea exactly where the darn place is; we just know the general direction. Beyer goes down to a 50-foot low hover with his landing lights on and circles this way, then that way, as all his young tired pilots duplicate his every move. Once,

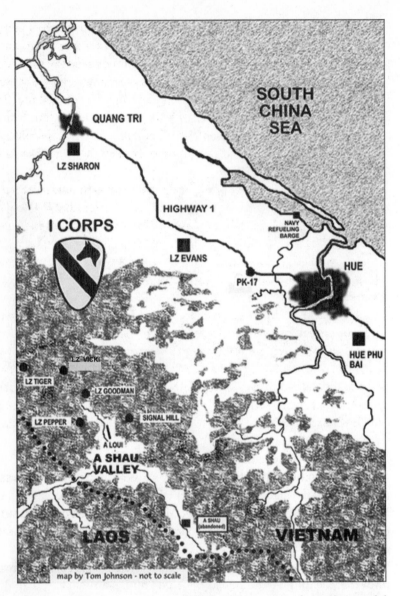

map by Tom Johnson - not to scale

Beyer does a 270-degree turn and flies under some of us who are following him. At last Six finds the graveyard and his original location. The rest of us, using his Huey as a beacon, enter a dangerous night approach, and finally, with no lack of exciting moments, we accomplish our night landing.

When the last Huey's main rotor transmission grinds to a stop, our new world becomes silent and dark. We are in a strange land and feeling naked. There are no bunkers to dive into or sandbags to hide behind—just grave markers. Not a soul strays from his Huey for fear of being shot by a comrade with a nervous trigger. I recheck my .38 Smith & Wesson, help the crew chief remove the M60 machine guns from the aircraft, crawl underneath the Huey, and quickly lapse into a deep sleep. The only thing separating me from the hard ground is a thin poncho liner.

Soon after daylight, A/229th finds itself carrying ammo, water, and C rations in support of the units we inserted yesterday. While we are working ash-and-trash, Beyer spots a baseball field inside the Hue Phu Bai compound, and to him it looks just large enough to hold us if we tighten up the formation. Late afternoon finds Bandit Six making a solo run to get his bearings on the ball field for a night formation approach.

An hour after dark, the last Bandit bird finishes the last mission. Beyer commands us to crank and follow him. This we do in quick order because anyplace will be better than the cemetery.

Six finds the ball field and A/229th fills it up, much to the surprise of the Navy Seabees who own it. Most of these Navy guys have never been near a Huey, and they run for the high ground that surrounds our new landing area. They turn out to be friendly natives and show great interest in how the 1st Cavalry fights the war.

"How long you been flying Hueys?"

"Pardon me," I reply, turning around with a mouthful of cold canned turkey.

"How long have you been flying Hueys?" The question emanates from a person standing behind me in a clean blue Navy denim casual uniform.

"Long enough," I reply, trying not to be a smart-ass and extending my hand.

The stranger introduces himself as Petty Officer Willie R. Faraday. I take Willie on the nickel tour of the Huey. He is thrilled when I ask if he would like to sit in the pilot's seat.

Watching him glow with excitement reminds me of the first time I sat in one at Fort Rucker. Willie has a passion for flying and has taken some lessons back home in a small Cessna 150, but, like so many before him, he ran out of money before getting his license. I tour Willie from nose to tail of the aircraft, but after such a busy couple of days I am soon so tired I have to sit.

"How would you guys like a hot shower and some hot chow?" Willie asks.

"Are you kidding! I'd very much appreciate it."

"Get your things, Tom. I think I can find you a bunk where you can bed down. The rest of you guys like a hot shower and some Navy food?" Yes, the crew would most definitely appreciate that.

Before he can utter another word, we grab our toilet items and fall into trail formation right behind him.

The hot shower soothes all the aches and pains of the past two days. Dressed in reasonably clean jungle fatigues, the four of us again follow Willie to the mess hall, where we are served our first hot meal in three days. We are convinced the Navy people know how to make it through this war in style. After the meal, the other three of my crew return to the Huey, and Willie shows me a bunk. This bunk has a real mattress. I have not slept on a mattress since leaving R&R in Hawaii; the last time before that was in the States. This is pure heaven.

"How would you like a beer before you turn in?"

"Fantastic. You do mean a *cold* beer, don't you?"

"Yes, cold beer. Follow me."

Willie leads me into an air-conditioned petty officers' club only a couple of buildings over from where I am to bunk down. The inside is painted a light grayish-blue navy, and the walls are adorned with various brilliantly colored emblems. The floor is inlaid with tiles, just like a stateside kitchen. Against the far wall is a dark cherrywood bar dressed out with bright red–upholstered chrome bar stools. There are about 20 tablecloth-dressed tables scattered about with chairs. I bet there isn't another drinking hole north of Da Nang that can compare with this one.

"Willie, you just wouldn't believe it if I told you how long it has been since I had a hot shower, a hot meal, and a cold beer all in the same month."

"You guys really rough it, huh?"

"There are a *lot* of guys in the Cav who have it a lot worse than the aviation companies, but living in a GP Medium, sleeping on a poncho liner, and drinking warm Kool-Aid is not my preferred style of living."

Willie grins and motions to the bartender for a couple of beers to be delivered to our table. We chat about the differences between the Army and the Navy, and as I look around, I observe that I am the only Army guy in a sea of about 25 Navy folks. Any 1st Cavalry helicopter pilot would be in hog heaven here tonight. Being the center of attention of so many nice folks who buy me beer after beer makes me forget the war for the moment.

"Where are you from, Tom?" Willie gets around to asking.

"Carrollton, Georgia."

"Is that for real?" Willie's eyes go wide open and his tone of voice startles me. "Do you know Mrs. Ivester, who lives on Cunningham Drive?"

"Sure. She's a good friend of my wife's folks. We went to visit her just before I shipped out for Nam. You know her?"

"Mrs. Ivester is my mother-in-law. We stopped by to see her a couple years ago. She's a sweet lady."

"I'll be damned! You've been in Carrollton."

"Sure have," Willie replies, eyes twinkling.

Many beers follow, and I become hoarse telling the Seabees about flying Hueys in the 1st Cavalry. They hang on every word, and I can see them trying to picture every adventure I tell them about. It is obvious that most of them have not yet been exposed to close contact with the enemy.

Without warning, a fight breaks out in the rearmost corner of the club. Three Navy guys dressed in black tiger camouflage jungle fatigues begin pummeling each other with vigor. The rest of the Navy guys move out of the way but seem otherwise unconcerned about the whole battle. The fighters are ruthless; using their fists, their feet, and occasionally their teeth, they beat each other up for the next three minutes. I cannot tell who is mad at whom; it seems there are no sides in this fracas. Whichever of the three gets off the floor first gets hit in the face by the next guy to stand up.

"SEALs," Willie says, moving his beer up over his head to avoid its being hit by a piece of a chair thrown by one of the guys.

"SEALs?"

"Yeah, SEALs. Damnedest folks you will ever meet and mean as hell." Willie leans down to grab a chair off the floor and right it. "They bunk here at Hue Phu Bai with us, but we don't know any of them. You know about SEALs?"

"I've heard about them, but that's all."

"They are tough mothers." The fight has ended with all three on the floor motionless. "They leave here and go north, and I mean real north. They kick the NVA's ass on a regular and recurring basis. They never bother us. They just like to fight amongst themselves." Willie looks over his shoulder in the direction of where they lie on the floor. "SEAL stands for Sea, Air, and Land. It's an elite group of crazy folks."

"They fight like this often?"

"You can count on at least one good one every week."

"Jesus." It is astonishing.

Willie and I drink two more beers and watch the SEALs pick themselves and their buddies up off the floor. All three are bleeding like stuck Georgia hogs, with eyes beginning to swell shut, and yet they are holding on to one another and saying things like, "I love you, man. . . . I love you, you bastard." Now they are the best of friends, just like before the fight, and they find contentment in trying to pour more beer through their swollen lips.

I retire to the bunk and lie down. I leave instructions for Richard, the crew chief, to awaken me when the rest of A/229th starts to stir. This he does, and I feel rotten.

We operate out of the ball field for a few more days and make many friends at the Hue Phu Bai Seabee base. On January 28, General Tolson, 1st Cavalry Division commander, receives permission for us to take over a Marine base named Camp Evans. Evans is some 15 miles father north than Hue Phu Bai. On our last night at the ball field, some high-ranking jokester decides to give the Cav crews a last farewell.

The Seabees' tour of duty in Vietnam consists of six months in country and six months back in the States, then six months back in Nam. On this night, the guy who owns the bunk that I have been sleeping in returns from the States. This means I'm sleeping on the ground again.

Somewhere around three o'clock in the morning, the ball field erupts in explosions so intense that dust flies up off the ground and eardrums ache. The light is as brilliant as daylight. Forgetting where I am, I rise abruptly and hit the belly of my Huey so hard the impact knocks me swimmy-headed—not to mention the dent in the aircraft.

This is the end, I am sure. The crew chief and gunner dive headlong into the dirt and slither to join me and the peter pilot underneath the Huey. To crawl under something in such a situation is human nature, I guess, but crawling under a UH-1 is actually a very bad choice. Right over our heads is 250 gallons of JP4 jet fuel that will make us french fries in a second. Right now, though, it just doesn't matter, because there is nowhere to run. I lie in the dirt facedown and cup my hands over both ears, my heart racing. As quickly as it starts, it is over. All is quiet and dark. No fires. Someone pops a small flare and lets it fall to the ground. When we crawl out from under the Huey, our ears are ringing and we are coughing from the dust.

Another flare drops on the ground on the other side of the ball field, then another. The silhouettes of the Hueys look normal. No missing aircraft; no cries of pain or suffering.

This is strange. Have the VC missed their target?

"Hey down there, you Cav boys! The SEALs thought you ought to have some type of gun salute before you airborne gladiators depart to win this war single-handed. To the First Air Cavalry—the Navy SEALs salute you!"

We turn our attention to the high ground. There stands a group of 15 or 20 Navy SEALs with their Budweisers held at port arms. Each man is offering a hand salute.

During the night, the SEALs have evidently called in some chips owed them by the Marines. A battery of 8-inch self-propelled howitzers has tracked into position up on the high ground and fired right over the top of the ball field. A man could stick his head inside the barrel of one of these babies. I count five tubes extended over the edge of the ridge.

Pissed-off but glad to be alive, the crews of A/229th don't know how to take this joke. One thing for certain, no one is stupid enough to do something about it for fear of getting their butts kicked. Best to just let it be. This is the attitude until we start checking the Hueys for damage.

Almost every barometric instrument in every Huey has had its needles wrung off by the concussion. Now this really pisses everyone off, especially Major Beyer. This will not ground the aircraft in normal conditions, but it will mean that A/229th pilots will have to fly with the hope that they do not go into IFR conditions. For sure we will not be doing any night flying for a while, which is a blessing in disguise.

The following day, Beyer logs an official protest through 1st Cavalry channels. This brings division-level folks down to the ball field to inspect the damage. Replacement instruments will be hard to find.

We have other problems too. In II Corps, the Cav depended on supply channels long since developed through Qui Nhon and An Khe. Now the 1st Cavalry is totally without its own supply chain. The hundreds of supply-laden trucks in convoys from LZ English will take nearly a week to reach our new home.

Meanwhile, MACV orders the Navy to support the Cav, and it does this by creating new, shallow-water supply depots on the coast of the South China Sea north of Hue. These seaports are not yet operational, and the supply convoys loaded with spare parts have not yet arrived as the 1st Cavalry moves into Camp Evans. All supplies are being trucked up Highway 1 into Evans from Da Nang, some 150 miles to the south.

Late January in Vietnam brings the monsoon rains. For days now, the rain-laden black clouds have been building in the west. During the night of January 30, the rain arrives in force, dumping 3 to 6 inches in about two hours. We don't know it, but we won't see the sun again for 28 days.

Beyer secures new altimeters and vertical speed indicators for us, and they are installed in the Hueys in quick order. The ceiling drops to 500 feet, and the visibility goes from occasionally obscure to 1 mile at best. Flying under these conditions becomes extremely dangerous with so many helicopters flying in the same airspace. New rules are made up as we go along. All 1st Cavalry Division aircraft will maintain the "highway rule": if flying north, find Highway 1 and get east of it; fly on the west side if traveling south. Division sets up checkpoints on the highway, manned by sky troopers, in an attempt to keep the VC from taking potshots at the low-flying aircraft.

All officers and all enlisted men are working in the sweltering Vietnam heat and rain, filling sandbags and putting up tents. The workday does not end with darkness. Electric power plants whine, and bright lights burn well into the night. The scene reminds me of the West Georgia Fair that comes to Carrollton once a year. The concessions arrive at various intervals on Sunday and start setting up under the emergency lighting system. The paper I am writing on is so damp that the ink pen will not make continuous lines when I write home to Pat. We share everything at home, but this is unlike anything we have seen together. Death and the fear of death is everywhere, and I feel no need to bring her into this world. My letters become shorter and shorter, and I lie a lot about the current environment. Lately I have ended every letter with "I'm tired" rather than "I love you." It has become an almost impossible task to sit long enough to write a letter without falling into dreamland fully clothed.

16

The Tet Offensive of 1968

January 31, 1968

Tet Nguyen Dan, the Vietnamese lunar New Year, begins on January 31, 1968. It is a national Vietnamese holiday and all MACV military commanders are instructed to stand-down. What a way to conduct a war! This has to be one of the dumbest decisions made by the stateside powers-that-be. Whoever heard of stopping a war for a holiday? General Tolson, the 1st Cavalry's top general, does not buy this bull for one minute.

The NVA and Viet Cong plan to use Tet for the uprising of Vietnamese who are disloyal to the South Vietnam government. This has been in the planning stages for a year and a half. Coordinated attacks on all the major cites of Vietnam have begun at 0230 hours on January 31. The NVA has committed all their troops and all their reserves to turning the war around, but unknown to them, American armed forces are at maximum strength when Tet breaks out.

In the 1st Cavalry's AO in Quang Tri province, the two major cities, Quang Tri to the north of LZ Evans and Hue to the south, are under attack.[1] Both battles are intense, and casualties on both sides are increasing at an alarming rate.

For Mac McCrary and me, the Tet Offensive of 1968 begins as we

---

1. Twenty years later, I would learn that the 1st Cavalry Division was sent to I Corps on such short notice because the Joint Chiefs of Staff had information that a full-scale ground invasion across the DMZ would occur during Tet in 1968. None of us was informed of this danger at the time.

sit in the outhouse. Since things are in such disorder, sergeants have been invited to use the officers' facility. We both arrive at the latrine at the same time to take a constitutional.

"Mac, I hope I never see another sandbag for the rest of my life." I make idle conversation in the dark and watch a deuce-and-a-half truck slipping and sliding in the mud that is now about jungle-boot deep in the roadway between the latrine and our tents.

Mac complains, "I wish the dang rain would let up. Everything I own is wet—and I mean wet. I pulled out a pair of clean socks a while ago and they're mildewed."

"Yeah, me, too. I'm cold and bone tired, but it's hard to even lie down. My poncho liner is so filled with moisture you can literally wring water out of it." It is so cold that we both blow fog with our breaths. "The temperature must be around sixty degrees, don't you think?" Sixty is very cold by Vietnam standards, especially when you're wearing lightweight tropical gear.

"It feels more like the forties back in Georgia," Sergeant Mac replies. The humidity in Georgia makes forty-degree weather feel much colder.

As I open my mouth to reply, a blinding light flashes about 150 yards away in the direction where the Hueys are parked. A second later the sound reaches us, just as another flash goes off.

"*MORTARS!*" Mac screams. In my tour so far, I have not been this close to an exploding mortar round; I have only heard them go off somewhere in the distance.

They possess a very unusual sound, a kind of whoomp rather than the big bang. These rounds are so close that with each explosion I can hear hot jagged metal shrapnel tearing through the nearby aircraft and tents.

Nothing else needs to be said in the latrine; the mortars are saying it all. Nobody bothers to wipe their butt as we scramble out the single door. The lead man cannot move fast enough for Mac and me, and is immediately shoved clear of the doorway. In a hunkered-down dead run, we both race toward the tent where a simple hole in the ground has been dug in the mud only hours earlier. As we encounter the boot-deep mud in the roadway, I pass Mac in a flash and make a dive for the depression. Mac arrives a few seconds later right on top of me.

The hole is so shallow, I'm sure his ass end is still extending above ground level, but it is the best hole either one of us has at the moment.

"WHOOMP! WHOOMP-WHOOMP! WHOOMP!" The mortars keep raining in. I can hear that each round is getting closer than the round before it. The VC are walking the incoming right up the flight line, two to three at a time. They lob some 25 rounds, then things go silent.

My heart is racing, and my breathing is made difficult by the weight of Sergeant Mac lying on top of me. Either some brave soul or a VC mortar has silenced the generators, and not a light shows anywhere.

"Grab your weapons!" somebody yells.

"Oh, shit—the bastards are gonna try to overrun us!" Mac yells as he rolls off of me into the mud and leaps to his feet.

"Will somebody please pass me the toilet tissue?"

"Huh?" Mac and I say in unison as I crawl out of the depression.

"I said, would somebody please pass the toilet tissue?"

To our amazement some idiot has remained in the outhouse throughout the entire flurry of incoming and is now calling from across the roadway for somebody to come over and retrieve the toilet tissue from the far side of the latrine floor so he can wipe his ass.

Mac starts toward the voice just to see who in the devil could have been so stupid when he abruptly falls facedown in the mud. Terror that he has been hit by a sniper's bullet goes through my head.

"Mac, you OK?" I ask, falling to my knees and reaching for him.

"Crap!" he says. He rises first to his knees, then awkwardly to his feet, and we both look down at his boots: surrounding his boots are his trousers. In the rush, Mac has not bothered to pull up his pants. This explains why I was able to overtake him in the mud.

This is the most amusing sight that I have seen in a long time and I howl with laughter. On close inspection of the roadway, we find that as Mac was crossing it, mud built up between his closely bound feet and rolled up and over the trousers. The trousers formed a scoop that neatly cleared a walkway from the latrine to the dugout.

Finally, when I am just getting control of myself, Mac pulls up his trousers, whereupon a mass of mud pours down into the tops of his jungle boots. This sets off another uncontrollable fit. Other pilots rush over. They can't tell if I am crying in pain or laughing. Mac faces the situation with what dignity he can muster and waddles off in the darkness to find his weapon.

An hour of calm passes, and we figure that if they were going to attack, it would have happened already; the generators are turned back on so we can assess the damage to the Hueys.

Only one Huey out of 22 has not been touched. All the rest have sustained hits, and eight are unflyable.

Lance Stewart and his maintenance crew go to work right away documenting the damage so that a full report can be given to Major Beyer.

Everything has now moved to a new level. The war up north will not be like the war in the Bong Son plains. The painful thing to me is that there are no senior aircraft commanders here to tell me what to watch out for. In this new ball game we will have to learn by our mistakes, just as the original Cav pilots did who came over to An Khe with the division.

"Beyer wants to see all pilots in the mess hall!" comes an urgent cry from the CQ, who is wandering around in the darkness, attempting to do his duty.

I look at my drenched watch with a flashlight. It is 0200 hours. The mortar attack ended two hours ago and we remain hunkered down waiting for Charlie's next move. I feel that if Charlie attacks in force, we will be unable to defend ourselves.

It is raining hard again and the clouds are now in the tops of the tents. As other pilots and I slosh our way through the mud, we wonder why this meeting has been called.

Beyer waits until almost all the pilots enter the tent before he speaks. Standing up behind the head table, lit only by a single 40-watt lightbulb, he tells us that our attack is not an isolated incident.

"Gentlemen"—he stops long enough to puff on his well-chewed cigar—"all the major cities of this country have been hit. Hue is currently being overrun. Quang Tri is under attack. Da Nang is under attack. This appears to be a major offensive launched by the North Vietnamese Army, whose size and firepower strength is not yet known. We are now on full alert for a ground invasion across the DMZ. For you folks who have yet to pick up a local area map, that's only twenty-five miles to our north."

His next comment is accompanied by a dry smile. "All pilots and NCOs will now pull guard duty as required. Additional sandbags must be filled. This you will also be required to do. Sergeant Eugene McCrary will be in charge of the detail roster."

This is the first time I have seen a senior NCO (noncommissioned officer) placed in charge of assigning officers and warrant officers to work details, but under the circumstances it just doesn't matter. Tonight, the man with the most skill-building defensive positions will be in charge—no matter what his rank. I find myself shoveling mud into sandbags as fast as I can, and lieutenants and captains stack them into defensive gun emplacements; for the moment, rank does not have its privileges.

We are all scared. The darkness, fog, and rain are so thick the enemy could walk right into our compound. The night flares fired by the artillery people will not be much help, as the fog is too thick.

Throughout the night, there are scattered outbursts of firing on the perimeter. It could be some nervous grunt shooting at shadows or it could be the NVA probing the perimeter for a weak spot—either way it tightens us up profoundly.

I lie in the darkness near the flight line with Larry Gore. There is no foxhole, no bunker, just semi-flat grassland. At times during the night, the rain beats down furiously on our ponchos. Larry and I do not talk to each other—we don't want to give Charlie something to shoot at.

The only sign of dawn breaking is the fog taking on a lighter grayish color. Little by little objects begin to take shape around us. Somewhere around 0700 hours, Larry and I are quietly relieved by two other warrant officers.

The two of us trudge through the thick mud toward the mess hall. We smelled coffee brewing there two hours ago and had to resist an awful temptation to leave our post for some of the nerve-soothing drug.

In the mess tent, we find Lee, Martin, and several other pilots sitting together fondling their heavy Army-issue porcelain coffee cups, steaming with freshly brewed coffee. Gore and I dip clean cups into the coffee vat and take our places alongside them. Serious conversation about our current predicament is already in progress as I take my first sip.

"This is the pits, Johnson," Don Martin erupts. "Hell, Beyer said something last night about a full-scale ground invasion across the DMZ." His statement goes unanswered for a moment.

"Listen, Martin, I heard the supply sergeant say that Highway

One is completely cut off. We only have enough C rations for a couple more days. There is little to no fuel and very little ammo for the aviation units. If there's a rush, I hope you're proficient in reading flying instruments 'cause the rest of us are going to crank up and get the hell out of here!" My remarks are intended to raise Martin's fear level to new heights.

"Thanks, Johnson . . . that's just the news I needed," Martin replies, not grinning. It really is no joke, though I tried to make one of it. Our supply people have not yet had time to get reoriented to the move north, so the entire division is hurting on supplies of all kinds, especially food and ammo. Gore and I finish our coffee and retire to the tent. Everything is wet. I am soaked to the bone and cold.

Before climbing into the poncho-lined cot, I attempt to find some dry clothes. Although everything is neatly folded up in the wooden ammo crate I call a footlocker, the dampness has so thoroughly invaded it that there is mildew forming around its inner edges and on my socks, which are lying on top of the damp, packed clothes. Exasperated, I simply remove my muddy boots and outer clothing, then lie back in the wet bed.

Chills run through me until I fall off to sleep. I awaken to the rattle of several M16s somewhere on the near side of the perimeter and lurch out of the bunk, almost tearing the poncho liner in the process. The intensity is now rising as many others join in the firefight. I hear our 80mm mortars start sending their rounds over our tent area in the general direction of the firing.

"*CHARLIES ON THE PERIMETER!*" someone yells.

"Shit!" I say to myself, pulling hard to get my swollen feet back into the wet, muddy jungle boots. Everyone in the tent is scurrying around, yet no one knows what is expected of a bunch of helicopter pilots in the defense of our immediate company area. My heart quickens as two enlisted guys burst into the tent with Browning automatic shotguns and ammo. The Brownings stay locked up in a metal Conex container and I have never laid eyes on them before now. They are our last-defense weapons, issued only in times of dire need. One is thrown on my cot with two boxes of shells. I don't even know how to load one of these Brownings, but in my mind it's like flying a new type of helicopter; you start the damn thing and I'll fly it.

Behind the people issuing the weapons comes Sergeant Windford Smith, who is giving a very quick class on how to load the weapon. He makes sure all the pilots know where the safety is located. Once the gun is on safety, he inserts the "double ought" 12-gauge shells into the holding chamber one by one. We all listen and repeat his every move. When we've all loaded our weapons, he rushes out to the next tent to teach others.

Two deuce-and-a-half trucks roar through A/229th company area in the direction of the perimeter firefight. Mounted in the rear of each are Quad Fifties, perimeter defense weapons consisting of four .50-caliber machine guns mounted on a rotating base. They were originally developed in World War II as antiaircraft weapons, but the Cav uses them against human targets instead of metal ones. They are capable of laying down a virtual wall of fire, and their effective kill distance is 1 mile (5280 feet).

With each passing minute, this looks more like the big one. In the past, aircraft companies were located in reasonably safe locations, well protected by sky troopers against a ground assault. Right now, the 1st Cavalry's sky troopers are scattered. The total combat perimeter force probably consists of fewer than 200 troops sprinkled around a 2-mile perimeter.

The drizzling rain turns again to a downpour as a platoon of sky troopers race through the company area, obviously being redeployed from the other side of the perimeter to the firefight. "1st Platoon follow me!" Beyer calls from the end of the tent. At these words we feel both relief from sitting around not knowing what to do and terror that we might actually end up in hand-to-hand combat with the enemy.

There are about ten of us in the tent when Beyer calls. We race behind him toward the flight line and are deployed two by two at varying locations to form a single defensive line running generally east to west on the perimeter side of the Hueys. Beyer comes back and makes adjustments, remembering that the last time we got hit the Hueys were the main target. He moves us another 50 yards toward the perimeter and farther from the Hueys. The rain subsides a little to reveal what are apparently two other firefights on the far side of the Evans perimeter. This is definitely not just a nervous grunt shooting at shadows. The NVA has returned and is probing the perimeter again.

237

I look at my watch. It is 1600 hours on February 1, 1968. I think about my birthday—a queer thought to have at a time like this. It is only 13 days away—on Saint Valentine's day. My mind wanders back to the times Mom would fix a heart-shaped cake trimmed out in red.

"Tom, you OK?" The question comes from Don Newton, lying next to me. He has noticed my blank stare.

"Yeah, Don, I'm OK. I was just daydreaming about back home." Don is fair-complexioned, with thinning brown hair. I guess him to be about 20 or 21, like the rest of us. Don seems to be more serious than the other new guys. The Vietnam sun, if we ever see it again, will soon turn his light skin to a bronze color, and the strain of combat flying will quickly manifest itself in wrinkles across his face.

Not until he spoke did I even notice who this man next to me was, and, worse yet, I do not care. In this moment of danger, as in others, I went into a shell. Self-preservation was my only concern, motivating my every movement and thought. Suddenly, for a moment now, I think I see some of Ingamar's features in Don, but this impression fades quickly. It doesn't matter. I never want to know anyone else that closely in this war.

"How are you doing?" I whisper.

"OK, I guess." He hesitates. "You guys ever got overrun before?"

"No, Don, not to my knowledge. I've been in country since last June, and this is the worst situation I've seen. How long you been in A/229th?"

"I got here last month, sir." Don forgets that I am no sir.

"Dang, Don, you got 330 days to go? Crap, I'd kill myself if I knew I had 330 days and a wake-up!" I cannot resist this opportunity to needle a new guy. "Hey, Lee," I whisper. "Don here has got 330 days and a wake-up. What you think of that?" Bill Lee is about 20 yards to my left.

"Three hundred thirty and a wake-up?! Holy Christ, Don, you're never gonna make it home," Bill whispers back, showing obvious pleasure in picking on a new pilot. "Don, you haven't been here long enough to get your cherry busted, have you?"

"No, sir, not yet, I guess," he replies sheepishly.

"Hey, Martin, Johnson has a guy with him that has 330 days and a wake-up. Can you believe that?" Lee passes the fun right on down the line.

I feel ashamed of picking on Don now that it's racing up and down the perimeter, but the teasing at least serves to deflate the current tension for all of us. As we again go silent, I occasionally notice Don trembling. I choose not to call attention to it; I don't know if it's from the cold or from fear.

At about five o'clock, the firefights end. The perimeter goes quiet and the silence is deafening. Beyer pulls us out of the rain and again we retire to our tents.

"Don, my tent is the 1st Platoon tent. I've got some Johnny Walker Red scotch, if you'd like to come over and have a snort." I still feel somewhat bad about picking on him.

"Yes, sir."

"Bring your weapons. We'd best clean them up a little. We may need one before the night is over."

Don Newton comes to the 1st Platoon tent and has to endure again all the teasing about his 330 and a wake-up. All of us have been through trials like this, but I can't help remembering how my old friend Charbonnier took me in. I guess it is my time to do the same for someone else. Don and I drink several glasses of the best scotch money can buy except for Chivas, which is very hard to find. The rest of 1st Platoon talks loudly about the experiences of the past two days as though our troubles are in the past.

I have just finished helping Newton reassemble his freshly cleaned and oiled Browning when we hear the first incoming mortar round. It is followed by five or six incoming-round explosions somewhere nearby. I shove Newton to the floor of the tent and motion toward my hastily dug hole in the ground at the base of the sandbags. It is filled to the brim with water, but this doesn't matter as Don occupies it and flushes the muddy water out with the mass of his body. I throw my back against the east sandbag wall and curl up in the fetal position as tightly as I can.

There are perhaps two more mortar rounds before the big bang. The first explosion lifts both Newton and me completely out of the bunker, and there are sounds of metal ripping through the tent. I grasp my ears and bury my face in the mud just as the world blows up around me.

Charlie hit the ammo dump that lies less than 100 yards from 1st Platoon's tent. Tons of ammo are going off all at once and each concussion from one blast sets off another. Then come great thumps against my backbone as huge chunks of shrapnel hit the outer sandbag wall at high speed. Even with my ears covered tightly, I can hear metal tearing through the GP Medium tent overhead. Two more gargantuan explosions lift my 120-pound body completely off the floor. I now accept the fact that I am about to die. Nothing that contains this much power over matter will allow anyone to survive its fury.

I dare to look up once, only to see the flickering of an explosion against the roof of the tent just before the sound and concussion actually reaches my position. In Georgia, we had some very bad thunderstorms, and I remember how Mother used to gather us children and huddle us in the center of the house. She would wrap her arms around all of us and hold us tightly until she felt it was safe. I could use Mom now, I think calmly, and in my mind I'm sending myself into her arms.

After about ten terrifying minutes, the "big boomers" subside and are replaced by thousands of smaller firecracker sounds—these are small munitions cooking off in the fires the explosions have started.

"DEAR GOD . . . SOMEBODY HELP ME!"

I hear this bloodcurdling cry loud and clear even through the ringing in my ears. I look up, and standing at the end of my cot is a sky trooper. He is silhouetted by the burning fires outside. He is bleeding from wounds to his face, and his clothes have literally been blown off his back.

"Help me, please! My buddy is down there and needs help! I can't get him out by myself. Somebody help me get him out!"

"Where is your buddy?" someone else in the tent yells back.

"In the dump—in the ammo dump. Will you help me?"

No one responds to his pleas. It is simply out of the question. It would be suicidal to run into an erupting ammo dump. We were not born to give our lives in so futile an effort.

This unknown soldier does not wait very long, but heads out the west end of the tent, still begging everyone for help. Two tents over, he finds his man. Terry Watson, one of the quietest crew chiefs in A/229th, volunteers. Terry is no hero, but tonight, for some reason, he overrules his better judgment.

Terry and the unknown guy run headlong into the exploding ammo dump and successfully extract the other sky trooper, who has one leg blown off.

Later, Terry Watson will be awarded the Purple Heart and the Silver Star with *V* device for valor. He deserves it, and I will be proud to salute him after this is all over. Like the rest of Vietnam's heroes, he was driven by compassion to help another, not by any desire to perform a brave act.

As night turns slowly to morning light and the assault subsides, I find that I can move reasonably safely around the company area as long as I am careful where I step. There are thousands of unexploded rounds everywhere, many of them embedded in the mud. The morning monsoon rains help cool down what is left and also put out the fires. The east side of LZ Evans is gone. It looks like a moonscape. I remember hearing the old-timers at LZ English talking about the ammo dump's going up just before I got there. Now I know exactly what they were talking about.

Our Hueys are the worse for wear. They have sustained much more damage, and A/229th is again down to one flyable Huey out of 20, and no spare parts. The Hueys have broken Plexiglas windscreens, chin bubbles, and greenhouses, and, once again, the barometric instruments are gone from the concussions. Shrapnel has cut some of them from one end to the other, leaving see-through holes through their fuselages, and some have broken rotor blades hanging down to the ground.

A/229th is not alone. Most of the 1st Cavalry aircraft on LZ Evans have suffered damage. The airmobile concept has been given a heavy setback at the hands of the North Vietnamese.

Lance Stewart, the maintenance officer, and his people will again work around the clock for the next two days, robbing parts off the most badly damaged Hueys in their efforts to make others flyable. They will be assisted by warrant officers who have nothing to fly.

For two days, more rain pours down from low clouds. Our only rations and ammo are coming in via parachute from C-130 aircraft at the east end of the LZ. Since there is no airfield where this giant aircraft can land in such bad weather, this is the only means of replenishing itself available to the Cav. The sorties by the C-130s are almost continuous during the semi-daylight hours. The Air Force has set up a portable TACAN radio beacon on the east side of Highway 1, which is well away from Camp Evans. Low-flying C-130s descend to 300 feet in the clouds and rain, using the TACAN beacon as a navigation device.

At the right moment, they unload their cargo on pallets pulled out of the aircraft by parachutes. Sometimes we can't even see the aircraft making its pass; we just see pallets of supplies drifting suddenly out of the bottoms of the low clouds.

Heavier items, like jeeps and artillery pieces, are rigged on pallets specially designed to absorb the impact of free-falling from 50 feet; these pallets are attached to parachutes designed only to yank them out of the aircraft. The brave C-130 pilots actually descend to well under the 300-foot ceilings, and these huge palletized items hit the sand, stop suddenly, and dismember themselves, one part from the other, over the next 100 feet.

17

The LZ Striker Incident

February 4, 1968

At this very moment, Hue is engulfed in what history will record as
the major battle of the entire Tet Offensive. Hue has been made off-
limits to the 1st Cavalry units. This battle is going to showcase the
Marines. The civilian idiots in Washington and their counterparts, the
South Vietnamese politicians, do not want the old imperial capital of
Hue destroyed. The beautiful city has survived for centuries, through
the Chinese invasion, World War II, and the French occupation. Today
it is occupied by a force of hard-core NVA troops estimated to amount
to two regiments. It is already known that these North Vietnamese
regulars have slaughtered thousands of innocent men, women, and
children, many of whom were left to rot in the streets. Secretary of Defense
McNamara orders that there will be no bombing of Hue and uses the
excuse of sparing civilians, but in truth, they do not want the city leveled
by a major military engagement. The Washington establishment has
given in to the South Vietnamese, who are content to stand by while
hundreds of young Marines are slaughtered. They are forced to fight
street to street and door to door in efforts to root out the aggressor.

Fuel was almost impossible to get here until the Navy Seabees
finished the shallow water port off the coast some 6 miles east of Camp
Evans. The pilots who have something to fly repeatedly carry supplies
to units in the field and bring in the wounded, until the fuel gauges
read somewhere around 250 pounds. They then land and shut down

243

on the ASP runway at Camp Evans to join others who are low on fuel. The control tower at Evans waits until about ten aircraft have assembled, then coordinates departures and returns on a mad low-level dash down the gauntlet to the Navy fuel supply depot. Evans tower maintains control over a single flight departing and another flight returning.

They make sure there are no more than two flights in the air at once. Since the cloud layer is so low, flights must be at treetop level, and ol' Charlie soon figures out what is going on. He moves his heaviest automatic weapons between Evans and the fuel supply. Flying in numbers makes us feel a little safer because someone who gets shot down will have a better chance of being found and rescued. We don't fly over the same ground as any of the guys ahead of us. Though we fly as a covey of ten birds, our formation is "helter-skelter." Each of us uses techniques he has developed on his own to avoid being hit. We zigzag right between trees rather than fly over them. A high-speed, low-altitude engine failure will be trouble no matter how you look at it, but better that than to be running along at 300 feet and take a round in the head.

Every trip is an exciting one, whether anything happens or not. The pucker factor chokes you from the minute you lift off till the minute you cross over the Camp Evans perimeter and report back in to the tower.

I have just made a fuel run and am about to shut down in the Bandit landing area when LT1 Peter Kretzchmar calls on the company frequency. Peter took Lonnie Rogers's job as operations officer for A/229th.

"Bandit Eighty-Eight, Bandit Two-Six. Over."

"Eighty-Eight, go ahead."

"Eighty-Eight, say your current fuel status. Over."

"Twenty-Six, we just returned from the coast and have been released for the day. Over."

"Say current location."

"Eighty-Eight is Bandit pad."

"Eighty-Eight, hover over to the base of the tower and shut down. Special mission in the making. Striker Six will arrive shortly, over."

"Eighty-Eight. Understand." I reply, then say aloud off the airways, "Oh, shit."

"What kinda special mission do you think they're talking about, Mister Johnson?" Steve Atkins, the crew chief, inquires over the intercom.

"Whatever it is, you can bet your can that it's hot," I reply as I motion for Dale Berry, the peter pilot, to hover us close to the Evans tower.

We shut down near a medevac bird, and the two pilots walk over and stand next to my door.

"How you guys?" I offer conversation as Atkins finishes his thing of opening the door and shoving the bulletproof panel back to its resting place.

"You here for some special mission?" the redheaded pilot asks.

"Oh, crap! You don't mean you guys are in on this thing too?"

"Yeah, I guess we are, but all we know is to shut down here and wait for somebody named Striker Six to brief us. You got any idea what's going on?"

"Nope." I grunt as I swing one leg out at the edge of the Huey's door and then the other, touching down on the tip of the skids. I turn to face the two pilots and simultaneously remove a handkerchief from my fatigue trousers front pocket.

"Don't know a thing." I use the cloth to wipe the sweat that is dripping from my hair into my face.

A C-model Huey gunship from the 227th lands, followed by a D-model Huey from the Charlie Troop 1/9th. I'm getting more and more edgy over the word *special*. I have already looked in my SOI for the call sign of Striker. It currently belongs to the Second of the Twelfth (2/12) Cavalry of the 1st Cavalry Division. They are not one of the units regularly supported by A/229th.

I am aware that the 2/12 and two other 1st Cavalry units have taken up positions north and west of Hue to block any NVA units who might attempt to reinforce their people already involved in the battle of Hue. Hue is a port city near the coast, and the Navy has taken up positions in the South China Sea to the east.

A jeep full of brass drives up the muddy roadway and on to the ASP runway material at the base of the tower. One guy is a "full bull" colonel and the other two are "light" colonels. As the jeep slides to a stop, the colonel exits first and walks quickly in our direction. No one dares salute.

TO THE LIMIT

"Good evening, gentlemen."

Most return his greeting while the rest just nod their heads.

"I am Lieutenant Colonel Richard Sweet." His expression is serious. He pauses to look us over, making eye contact with each one. "I am the senior officer in charge of the Second of the Twelfth. My call sign is Striker Six."

He says this so eloquently it takes me off guard. Lieutenant Colonel Sweet has been around and it shows—in his delivery, his posture, and his sternness of voice. He seems to address each one of us without actually standing in anyone's face. He has uttered only two sentences, yet I can already see Marcotte standing there before me.

"One of my units has been pinned down and has suffered heavy losses. They are currently in contact with the enemy, and, as you might imagine, are running extremely low on ammo and water." He pauses again to regain eye contact with everyone, from the most distant man on his right to the farthest man to his left. "Their defensive posture is disintegrating rapidly. Within the hour, if they have not been supplied with these necessary items"—he pauses again—"the enemy will overrun their position. It is in this light"—he pauses again—"that I have requested through Black Horse channels the finest and bravest pilots the 1st Cavalry has to offer. Your peers . . . have chosen you."

I am awestruck by this General Patton–style speech until he gets to the end, at which point I realize this: I'm going to personally shoot Lieutenant Peter Kretzchmar right in the ass if and when I get back from this mission. I know the only reason we got this call is that we are one of the only A/229th birds still flying, and Kretzchmar took it on himself to volunteer us while he sat securely back in the A/229th operations tent.

"Gentlemen, this is a volunteers-only mission. You, as pilots, represent the best that the Army has to offer. You and others like you are really 'above the best.' "

I zero in on his chest. There are no wings sewn there. He is a true sky trooper commander of the highest order. I wonder, therefore, how he knows that "Above the Best" is Fort Rucker's motto. I am awestruck all over again at this guy.

"If you want to back out, then do so now!" Striker Six goes silent and waits.

"What do you need, Colonel?" some warrant officer in our crowd asks.

That is the end of the Patton speech for Sweet. He smiles, and the other two colonels walk forward with maps.

Sweet's people spread out their maps on the cargo compartment of the medevac Huey and begin pointing to coordinates that are south and west of Hue, almost at the base of the first mountain range.

"Our people were initially inserted west of Hue as a blocking force," one colonel begins the briefing. "Instead, they ran headlong into what we think are the 7th and 9th Battalions of the 325C NVA Division trying to join the battle in Hue. These people left the Khe Sanh area on a fast march and have traveled through the A Shau valley, which empties into the coastal plains. Somewhere about here, about six miles west of Hue.

"B Company was marching to get into position when they accidentally ran headlong into a company-size NVA unit trying to reinforce their people already there. They have managed to get themselves trapped in cross fire from three sides and have been pinned down in tall bamboo all last night and today. They have taken many casualties. The ceiling is too low for gunships, and since the fighting is periodically hand to hand, it is too close in for artillery. Our other companies are rushing as fast as they can through the flooded rice paddies to reach them, but unless we get ammo in quickly, they won't make it." The colonel straightens up and checks our eyes for any reaction.

No one speaks. The mission will test our low-level navigation skills, which have not been tested like this since training at Fort Rucker. Rain and the low ceiling will reduce forward visibility to a couple of hundred yards. The unit is surrounded on three sides, meaning there will be one way in, a pedal turn in the LZ under fire, and an exit out the same direction. Any flaw in navigation that takes us past the LZ will mean body bags for everyone.

The other colonel speaks. "The black hat reports that the elephant grass is as high as ten feet around the LZ. The NVA are trying to find higher ground for their heavy weapons so that they can shoot directly down into the LZ. Every few minutes, our people are beating back attacks out of the grass."

When the briefing ends, I ask Striker Six for time for all of us to speak to our crews. I reiterate to Six that since this is a voluntary mission, our crews need to be consulted; some of them might not want to go. He agrees, and the assembled pilots disband.

As I walk away, I think to myself that if the NVA are able to set up heavy—as in .51-caliber automatic—weapons within 100 yards of the LZ, this mission will certainly be one to remember. I brief Steve Atkins and Dennis Earl Painter, our gunner, on the details and the dangers involved. Dennis is a black Southerner; he's from Georgia, like me. He entered A/229th from some sky trooper unit by volunteering to become a door gunner. He is a quiet man who keeps to himself and only grins at jokes. I have never seen him laugh out loud. In the States, he would never have made door gunner; he is too big—6 feet 4 inches, about 210 pounds. He wears a size 14 shoe and when seated in the small cubicle designed for a door gunner, he occupies every bit of it. He is so tall that he has to stoop to peek out under the top of the cargo door fuselage. He wasn't with A/229th long before we moved north. Once, at LZ El Paso, when he was gunning on the chopper I was flying, I spotted an entire pond full of ducks. There must have been 200 of the critters just sitting there in a small water hole. After checking with operations to ensure that there were no friendlies nearby, I circled the pond at 500 feet and instructed Dennis to kill us a few ducks for dinner.

Dennis opened up with his M60 machine gun to the tune of nearly a thousand rounds. Not one duck fell. At first, the surface of the pond could not be seen for the ducks. Now they all were gone. Dennis had managed to put 1000 rounds between 200 ducks without striking the first kill. That had to be something of a record. The M60's barrel was smoking white hot when Dennis finally ran out of ammo. When I looked back and frowned my displeasure with his aim, Dennis grinned a very broad, sheepish, white-toothed grin and shrugged his shoulders.

Now I say, "Dennis . . . how's your aim these days?" Dennis and his M60 may be the key to our returning from today's mission in one piece.

"I been practicing, Mister Johnson, I been doing good."

"Do you want to go?"

"Yes, sir, if y'all go, then I'll go." He grins as though he cannot take this mission seriously.

"How about you, Steve?"

"Yes, sir, count me in."

I am sure that Dale Berry has enough experience to understand the danger. Dale wants in.

All the pilots advise Striker Six that the mission is a go. As the detailed planning of the mission unfolds, Striker Six points here and there on a map. The 1/9th Huey pilots were in this area yesterday. They don't know exactly where the target LZ is located, but because of their knowledge of the terrain, they will become the flight leader.

It is already past 1500 hours. Striker Six's people have been busy loading the three Hueys with wooden boxes of ammo, C rations, and water. Under these rain clouds, it will be dark in two hours. We are given individual handshakes and heartfelt God-be-with-you's from Colonel Sweet.

The plan is simple enough. We will depart LZ Evans and head east until we reach Highway 1, then turn south. We will remain in visual contact with the roadway until we reach the PK-17 outpost. From there, we will take a heading of 195 degrees and fly as low as possible until we reach the target LZ. During the flight from Evans to a point approximately 2 miles from the LZ, we will remain in a tight trail formation with the gunship flying in the rear. The philosophy is the tighter the formation, the less chance "Charlie" will have to pick up his gun and fire should the lead bird accidentally overfly one of his positions. Trail formation is safer than the traditional *V* formation when contour flying because in *V* formation, you have to avoid meshing rotor blades with your wingman while at the same time trying not to center a tree.

At 1515 hours, the flight of four receives permission from Evans tower to take the active runway and depart on an easterly heading. This we do with the 1/9th Huey in the lead, followed by me, then the medevac Huey, and last the 227th gunship. We are heavy with our cargo, but the UH-1 performs nicely.

At Highway 1, we turn south and increase airspeed to 100 knots. The sky around us is filled with low, ragged rain clouds. We can get no higher than 300 feet without bumping their bottoms. We fly through intermittent light rain showers, and the visibility is worse than I expected. At the moment, our fear of the impending combat is secondary to our fear of killing ourselves by running into another flying machine or striking some object protruding from the ground. Our navigation lights and Grimes light are turned full on. I'm hoping that other aircraft will see the navigation lights in time to avoid a crash and that Charlie will not see them in time to pull off any rounds before I go by.

"Dale, take over and stay right on Yellow One's tail rotor. Keep us in close. OK?"

"Yes, sir. I have it."

"Steve, you and Dennis keep your eyes open. Use good judgment before you fire. I don't know what the hell is out here. South of PK-17 is virgin territory. OK?"

Both break squelch on their intercoms to indicate they understand. I break out my map. Keeping my bearings during low-level navigation is difficult in the best of conditions. I check the map in my lap while frequently looking up to see how Dale is doing. He has us tucked in so tight to the Huey ahead of us, I can see the gearbox oil level through its 2-inch glass sight-gauge. As is normal in trail formation, we are right behind and some 6 to 8 feet higher than the aircraft ahead of us.

On occasion our main rotor blades overlap his tail rotor.

"Dennis, are they tight behind us?" I ask, looking back. Dennis leans out slightly to look around the body of our Huey.

"Yes, sir, he's eating up the tail rotor. Don't slow down, Mister Berry!" Dennis requests euphorically.

"Yellow Flight, this is Yellow One. PK-17 dead ahead!" calls the lead Huey.

The PK-17 outpost passes under us in a blur, and the 1/9th bird turns immediately to a heading of 195 degrees and increases his speed to 120 knots. Following Yellow One's lead, the entire flight dives for the deck.

Everyone knows the significance of the turn west, away from the relative safety of the highway: We are now entering no-man's-land.

"Dale, back off and get down to Yellow One's altitude. This might get a little hairy." Dale allows Yellow One to advance slowly ahead, then he takes us down. We are now hurtling through the air just 4 to 6 feet above the rice paddies. Whenever he can, Yellow One dodges between the lines of 20-foot-high palm trees. Frequently he has to rise just high enough to clear them, then hastily plunge back to the "nap of the earth" cruising altitude. Always Dale stays glued to his tail.

In the excitement, I cannot concentrate on the map and have already gotten lost. Yellow One must be lost also. He climbs to an altitude of 200 feet to get his bearings, then drops back down on the deck. We do likewise, and I also find our position through this tactic. According to my navigation, we are now due west of Hue and should be arriving in the general area of the LZ in five or six more minutes.

Yellow One again rises to clear a line of trees and then executes a rapid descent. We have trees and dense vegetation on both sides at a distance of approximately 20 meters.

"YELLOW ONE TAKING FIRE ON THE RIGHT! TAKING FIRE! TREE LINE ON RIGHT!"

Almost at the same time as he keys his mike, we top the tree line and I see three or four black pajama–clad individuals step out into the clear; then I see the muzzle flashes from their weapons. I hear the first *tic* of a bullet rocketing through our Huey just before Dennis opens up with his M60. For a split second, I think that Dennis might not be quick enough to engage the target at this speed, so I turn to yell and point, but Dennis is not looking at me. He has also seen the targets and has pulled the trigger. Dennis's head is pointed ahead of the aircraft and at a 45-degree angle to our direction of flight. His gun's barrel, on the other hand, is pointed at an angle more than 90 degrees farther back toward the rear of the Huey. At this speed, shooting directly at a target is pointless, since, when the forward motion of the helicopter is factored in, all bullets will miss their mark by a great margin. One must actually fire in a direction somewhere behind the aircraft in order for the bullets to curve in and find their mark.

The flyby takes all of eight to ten seconds of my life, but it seems to occur in slow motion. Dennis has a hold on the Huey's vertical aluminum post with his left hand and is aiming the M60 freely, using only his right hand. He is firing solid tracers that make visible trajectories. He has the enemy nailed. The first and second rounds into the group of VC just miss, but the third round finds its mark on the guy closest to us and is followed by at least four more rounds in his chest and head area. The ensuing rounds find the second guy at chest level, and they cause his body to fragment in huge chunks of flesh and body parts. As we rush by, Dennis continues to lay down a wall of fire at the third guy until he can no longer fire without hitting the tail boom of our aircraft.

When he quits firing and looks forward toward me, I give him a quick thumbs-up and return to other tasks. For an instant I think back to the duck pond some weeks ago. All our lives were in Dennis's hands just now, and he came through.

We have not flown another two football fields before Yellow One again fills the airways, but it is too late.

"YELLOW FLIGHT! BREAK! BREAK!!"

He has overflown a nest of NVA soldiers who are lying flat behind a rice paddy dike. As he is transmitting, I catch a glimpse through the chin bubble as the soldiers rise quickly from lying on their backs to sitting and open fire. We overfly them in the blink of an eye but clearly hear them filling the air under us with AK-47 rounds. Yellow Three and Four will catch the brunt of this bad luck.

"Yellow Three, we are hit hard! Engine out!"

"Yellow One, Yellow Three is slowing down. I think he's going in!" comes the call from Yellow Four.

Without looking, I can imagine Yellow Three in a high-speed low-

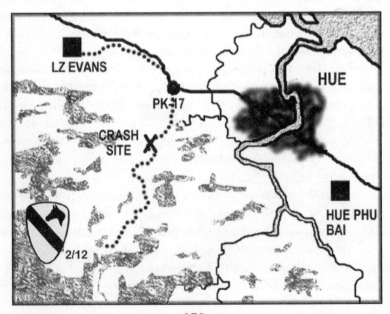

level autorotation bleeding off forward airspeed for ground contact.

Yellow One pulls into a hard left turn to reverse course and Dale follows suit at One's turning point. Just seconds after Dale swings us around, we see Yellow Three. He is extremely tail low and trailing smoke from his turbine cowlings. He has not stopped his forward motion when the Huey hits the rice paddy.

The tail stinger strikes a dike hard and nearly flips the aircraft end over end. When he finally gains control of the bumbling helicopter's flight, the pilot uses the last energy left in the main rotor system to land the Huey right side up. Yellow Four reduced his forward motion on first realizing Yellow Three's predicament and is now at almost a fast hover approaching the wreck. Yellow One sets up in a fast circling maneuver around the site, and Dale instinctively increases the separation so that we will be 180 degrees across.

To our delight, all four crewmen bolt out of the wreckage. First confused as to their whereabouts, they quickly gain their senses of direction and race toward the gunship, which is now hovering over a dry dike some 15 feet behind the downed Huey.

"Yellow Four, execute rescue. . . . Burn the Huey and return to Evans. Do you roger?" Yellow One transmits.

"Yellow Four. Roger!"

His instructions are clear. Yellow Four is to do whatever is necessary to set fire to the downed Huey and depart with the survivors solo back to Evans.

With the rescued crewmen on board, the badly overloaded gunship struggles to lift off. Then, after using the entire clear rice paddy area to gain translational lift, he executes a 180-degree turn. Yellow One and I are already in the process of departing the area when he fires his first rocket into the downed bird from more than a thousand yards out. The spilled JP4 fuel erupts into a violent explosion and the Huey burns vigorously.

The gunship makes two complete circles around the wreckage, then establishes a return heading north. Yellow One breaks out of the circle on a heading of 195 degrees with us in hot pursuit.

"Yellow Two, go to Striker frequency!" Yellow One transmits.

I change the FM radio to the frequency supplied by Striker Six.

"Yellow Two, Yellow One on Striker frequency. Are you with me?"

"Yellow Two is with you," I reply.

We monitor the radio as Yellow One contacts the Striker black hat on the radio. The SITREP is not good: Striker reports many casualties. The only ammo available is what can be stripped from the dead. They are engaged by well-armed North Vietnamese troops who have dug in on three sides of the LZ. Striker Sixteen reports heavy .51-caliber machine guns to the south and west. They have received only small arms fire from the east. Mortars are raining into the LZ as he speaks, but the platoon has dug foxholes during the night and are bravely holding the perimeter. The LZ is reportedly hacked out of a tall bamboo cane field and is 30 to 40 feet in diameter. An experienced helicopter pilot knows that if the sky troopers say 40 feet, it generally means more like 25 feet, but who could blame them when they're in such a desperate situation.

"Striker Sixteen, we have orders to resupply, not to extract. Do you copy?"

"We already have our orders, Yellow One," comes the reply. Without question, the platoon has been instructed to hold ground until reinforced.

We slow to 60 knots and climb to the maximum clear air altitude of 300 feet in an attempt to get a better vantage point.

"Yellow Two, I can see the base of the mountains just ahead. How close do you think we are to them now?"

"Close enough to pop smoke!" I reply, referring to pulling the pin on a smoke grenade. "It's my best guess that they are about two hundred meters up and to the left of your ground track right now."

"I think you're right!" Yellow One alters his course slightly to his left. "Striker Sixteen, pop smoke, over!"

"Smoke out!" comes the reply.

Things are beginning to tighten up now. Even over the noises generated by the Huey, we can hear gunfire and mortars going off. We will be in deep trouble if we miss the approach into the LZ and especially if we overshoot it.

"Yellow One, look more to your left," I transmit. "Looks like smoke."

For the past few seconds, I have zeroed in on the area, but I can't tell from this distance if what I see is smoke from combat or dense fog.

The area I see is deep within what appears to be a bamboo field. I instruct Dale to back off some more. Yellow One sees the area and alters his course to get a better look.

"Striker Sixteen, ID red smoke."

"Yellow One, red smoke is correct!" Striker Sixteen replies.

"Mister Berry, I have it." I issue the order over intercom and take over the controls. "Stay on the controls with me."

"Right," Dale replies dryly.

"Dennis, you and Steve keep a sharp eye! Looks like we'll end up doing three-sixties until Yellow One can get out."

"Striker Sixteen, Yellow One inbound. We are about forty seconds out. Over!" Yellow One breaks right out of our southeasterly heading to line up for his southwesterly approach into the LZ.

We zoom past his turn point and continue for another 100 yards in the same direction before I break hard left in a turn around some trees that form a tiny oasis in the middle of a vast rice paddy. We are going to be sitting ducks as we orbit. The visibility has decreased to a couple hundred yards. I have Dale turn off all the navigation lights.

So as not to lose the approach path into the LZ in the haze, I choose to remain very close to the island. This will also help prevent our straying into an area that might have foliage dense enough to hide the enemy. If Charlie is going to shoot at my butt, he is going to have to come out into the open rice paddies to do it.

The radio has been disconcertingly quiet since Yellow One started his approach.

"Yellow One, Yellow Two. How you guys doing in there?" I break the silence.

There is no reply. They are either very busy or have bit the dust going in. I wait a few more seconds and transmit again. "Yellow One, Yellow Two. Over."

"Yellow One is *out* of the LZ! Stand by!" comes Yellow One's reply.

There is a pause of two long minutes, then, "Yellow Two, it's all yours. It's very tight in there. You'll have to hack down some bamboo to get in. LZ is *hot*, but we did not take any hits, over."

"Yellow Two is inbound!" I break out of the orbit just west of the island and strain to see Yellow One on a reverse course.

"Mister Berry, turn on the navigation lights till One passes!"

He bolts out of the dense smoke and fog like some mad dragon defending his lair. He is coming straight at us and less than half a foot-ball field away. We both take abrupt evasive action to avoid contact. We fly by each other at a speed in excess of 175 mph. We enter the smoke and fog, and Dale again kills the lights.

"Yellow Two, there is a forty-five-degree dogleg left just before you get to the LZ. Approach narrows with trees on both sides!"

"Yellow Two, roger," I reply.

Visibility is down to 50 or 60 feet. Apprehension sets in at a level of nine on a one-to-ten scale as I bleed off forward airspeed to a high hover and cannot see the LZ. I can hear the rattle of automatic weapons out there somewhere, but where?

I arrive at the dogleg with a forward ground speed of 30 knots and make a hard left turn, being careful not to be so abrupt as to dig the main rotor blades into the ground.

"Striker Sixteen, Yellow Two is near the LZ but I can't find you! Help us out!" The tone of my voice gives me away. We could be in deep trouble if I have already missed the LZ.

"Yellow Two, I have you in sight! Just keep coming!"

Feeling great relief, I lower the nose further and continue the fast-forward hover. Without warning, Steve lets loose on the M60. He has made visual contact with the enemy and at very close range. I flinch hard, thinking we are right over the VC and are about to die. Our nerves are already stretched to their limits when Dennis lets loose without warning. Both M60s are belching bullets, not in short bursts but con-tinuously, Hollywood-style.

Finally I see what appears to be the LZ. The bright red holes in the dirt, dug either by shovels or by mortar rounds, contrast sharply with the pale-green grass and bamboo. The area is large enough only for the fuselage of the Huey. I had hoped for 20 feet, but in reality the LZ is less than that. As we go in, I can see One-Six on his back, waving his arms wildly from the cover of a diminutive foxhole.

"This is going to be a tight one! You guys watch the tail rotor!" I scream over intercom.

The M60s stop chattering as both Steve and Dennis concentrate on making sure that I do not put the fragile tail rotor into something large enough to make it come off. The Huey's main rotor system is strong enough to take down small limbs without much damage, but the tail rotor will not take that type of abuse. Most of the main rotor system will extend out into the bamboo; up to this point, I have never attempted to mow down a field of bamboo.

I glide the Huey to a stop right over the LZ and about 12 feet off its floor. As I lower the collective and begin the descent, loose dirt and debris from the LZ floor are turned into airborne missiles by the air that pushes down under the Huey's blade system. I alternately look through the chin bubble and the front of the aircraft during the descent. At 8 feet, the main rotor blades meet the bamboo on both sides. The resulting sound is that of a hundred AK-47s firing all at once. My heart stops and the Huey stands still. I know this has to be it. It is all over. When my brain starts to function again, I lower the collective. Both Dennis and Steve are yelling, "Tail rotor is clear, sir, tail rotor is clear, sir!!"

To get the tail rotor into the clearing, I must move the Huey's nose right into the bamboo canes dead ahead. The dust and debris are flying all around, even through the cockpit. At the last minute before touchdown, Steve yells, "Move to your right a little, sir, a little right. We got a KIA right under the skids."

I jockey right until Dennis calls out, "Back left a little, sir, we got another guy right under the skids!"

I cannot see what they are seeing, but it is clear that the firefight has been so intense that the corpses remain exposed. When Steve and Dennis are both satisfied, I let the weight of the Huey rest on its skids.

I look out my left window and, to my surprise, not one soul climbs out of a foxhole to unload our lifesaving cargo. There is no activity at all! Some 10 feet from the Huey's skids, three guys are lying on their backs and just staring at us.

"Dennis—Steve! . . . Throw it off!!" I command. "These guys are too scared to get up and unload us!"

The aircraft shakes as they scramble to unbuckle their seat belts, unplug their helmets, and make their way from their cubicles to the main cargo area. The situation takes us completely off guard.

Out of nowhere a sergeant first class with a black and bloody face appears with a Colt .45 in his hands and points at the three guys in the foxhole.

"Get your asses outta that hole and unload . . . *now!!*" The hammer of the Colt is all the way back! *"DO IT NOW, OR I'LL KILL YOU MYSELF!!"*

This guy is not kidding. The three soldiers leap up, rush to the aircraft, and begin grabbing the heavy ammo boxes off the floor. Dennis and Steve retreat to their cubicles and plug in.

"Crap, sir, that guy was going to shoot their asses! Did you hear that?" Dennis says excitedly over the intercom. I nod my head that I have indeed heard what was said.

The sergeant eases the hammer down on the Colt and holsters it. He rushes to my window to say something. I move my boom mike out as a form of greeting and press the intercom switch as he steps on the skids to speak.

"Will you take my wounded back with you?" he inquires sternly.

My reply is affirmative, and he barks out new orders to the three to help with the wounded. He again unholsters his Colt .45 and begins waving it recklessly, and soon the original three are joined in their task by four more troops.

I do not look back, but I hear the thumps as four half-conscious, wounded sky troopers are unceremoniously thrown onto the hard cargo floor. The dead will have to wait for a later trip.

"We are *up*, sir!" Dennis calls out.

I look left. The sergeant gives a thumbs-up, then races for the nearest hole in the ground. I assert upward pressure on the collective and the Huey starts getting light on her skids again. When I have felt out the load and controls, I pull more pitch rapidly, and the helicopter slowly lurches free of the LZ.

"Call the tail rotor clear for a turn!" I shriek.

Tic, tic, tic, tic.

"WE'RE HIT, SIR! TAKING FIRE ON THE LEFT!!" Steve yells, simultaneously laying down a barrage of fire in the direction of the muzzle flashes. Scared and hair-triggered, Dennis follows suit on the other side, although he has no actual target in sight.

There is no time to turn. Relying only on my feel for what lies behind us and how high the tail rotor is, I put the Huey in a fast reverse, cutting new cane on both sides. I say a quick prayer: that the Bell Helicopter people have built this one a little tougher than the others.

As we clear the immediate killing zone backward at about the same speed we entered it, I yell, "Call the turn! Call the turn!"

At first neither Dennis nor Steve comprehends what I have just ordered.

"Call the damn turn, Steve!" Dale screams, as he turns and motions to them what I want.

Both M60s go silent as the crewmembers grasp what is about to happen. "About fifty feet, sir . . . forty feet. Go to your right a little, sir . . . right more . . . that's good. About another ten feet, sir. Right a little. Turn now, turn now . . . straight back, straight back!"

Using Steve as our eyes, we negotiate the dogleg in rearward flight at a speed of around 30 knots. I can only look out my window at the ground zipping underneath us. We are now climbing steadily and clearing the vegetation on both sides.

"TAIL ROTOR CLEAR?" I ask.

"Tail rotor clear, sir!" comes the reply.

I apply right pedal, and the Huey begins a slow turn on its vertical axis. Near the 180-degree mark, I lower the nose, apply forward cyclic pressure, and pull hard on the collective. We are finally outward bound in normal flight.

In the excitement, I have neglected to alert Yellow One that we are out of the LZ. It is almost dark now, and he is orbiting somewhere just outside the approach path.

"Navigation lights *on* . . . heads on a swivel, guys! Yellow One is out here somewhere!" I transmit over the intercom and then pull the trigger switch all the way back to transmit over the FM radio, "Yellow Two is clear of the LZ and over the rice paddies! Where are you, Yellow One?"

Hard on my left, I catch movement just before One can reply.

"Two, we have you in sight—lead us home! We'll be right behind you!"

That is all I need. Without altering my initial heading or slowing to look for One, I pull harder on the collective, and the race for Evans is on.

"Mister Berry, you have it!" I fumble for my handkerchief.

As I wipe the sweat from my eyes, I think about the sergeant back in the LZ. I will never forget his face and the fear in it. Dried blood coated the right side of his dirty face. When he spoke, his jaw protruded awkwardly forward as though he might have been gritting his teeth. His voice, loud and clear, revealed not a hint of his fear. I'm convinced that he would have shot those other three guys in just a few more seconds had they not gotten up. They realized this, too, and at that moment were more afraid of the sergeant than of the NVA.

What separates men like the sergeant from the rest of us? Was he really that brave or had he already gone over the edge? One day America's children are playing cowboys and Indians; a twenty-four-hour plane ride later they are killing and being killed for real. An entire American generation of young people is dying at an alarming rate every day in this godforsaken country. Most have died violently. I say a silent prayer that God will have mercy on those who went to Him in this LZ today.

Dale breaks out of a rain shower directly over Highway 1, moves us east of the highway, and raises us to about 100 feet. There is not much more space now between us and the bottoms of the clouds. The ceiling is down and it is getting dark fast.

I call Evans tower and give them and everyone else in the area a good position report. Evans clears us to land on the runway. I also advise the tower that we have four souls as our cargo and request someone from medevac meet us at the base of the tower with a vehicle.

With Yellow One close on our tail, Dale flies the entire approach and hovers into the parking area to shut down. We do not have enough fuel to attempt a high hover to the A/229th parking area, so I request that Bandit operations send over a jeep to pick us up.

During the wait, I exchange polite greetings with the 1/9th pilot who is flying Yellow One. He did a very good job of leading the flight, and as we both wipe the sweat from our faces I let him know it. We laugh out loud at everything said to vent the pressure of the last few hours. I tell about the sergeant in the LZ and about how terrified I was when the rotor blades first hit the bamboo.

The medics arrive. Quietly, we watch as they remove the four men from the helicopter's cargo floor. There are no walking injured on this flight. Eyes still wide open, but minds somewhere else, they are dragged onto stretchers and loaded into a three-quarter-ton truck. One is already blue around the lips and fingernails; I don't think he survived the trip. Blood discolored by mud drips onto the ground from the cargo floor of Steve Atkins's Huey.

When I can look at this no more, I turn around to find Colonel Richard S. Sweet standing 20 feet away at the base of the tower. His head is down and his arms are folded. After a moment he raises his head and looks at me. I think he is near the point of tears for his fallen troopers, but I sense the cold desire for revenge in him. Many VC will meet violent deaths at Striker Six's command in the next days of the Tet Offensive.

Colonel Sweet gives me a thumbs-up for a mission well done. I return the sign. The noise of the arriving A/229th jeep disturbs the stillness of the moment. Steve Atkins and Dennis Painter remain behind to wash the blood from the Huey's floor. Water by the bucketful is being brought over by 2/12th people. Dale Berry and I collect our flight gear and sit our very tired asses down in the jeep for the short ride back to the company area.

18

Khe Sanh

March 31, 1968, Operation Pegasus/Lamson 207

In the early days of March, 1st Cavalry Division commander General Tolson met with the III Marine Amphibious Force commander to make the initial plans for the assault that would relieve the beleaguered Marine outpost at Khe Sanh.

Khe Sanh is in the northwestern corner of I Corps, just south of the DMZ and east of the Laotian border and some 35 miles north and west of Quang Tri. The small outpost was established there to oppose any NVA units attempting to infiltrate south from the DMZ, but it was a dynamic tactical error.

The 1st Cavalry usually builds their forward bases on mountain peaks when operating in mountainous areas. This will allow them at least to control the high country surrounding any outpost constructed near the bases of mountains. Khe Sanh, on the other hand, is on a treeless, dusty, red dirt plateau that has 1500-foot-high mountains on two of its four sides. This high ground is controlled entirely by the NVA forces and is so close to the base that NVA artillery need not arch their rounds; they simply aim the tubes dead at the base and "bore sight" them with deadly accuracy.

While the Cav was engaged in Hue, the NVA cut off all highway supply routes to Khe Sanh. The base, totally isolated by land from the rest of the war, is surrounded by triple-canopy jungle. The terrain consists of sharp falls down mountainsides to tiny obscured streams of water, then sharp slopes skyward up the next mountainside. Should you be unlucky enough to incur an engine failure in this part of I Corps, there would be virtually no chance of a fatality-free autorotation.

The fighting at Khe Sanh is so volatile that no one—not even the Joint Chiefs or the MACV commanders—can be sure if the base is still owned by the U.S. Marines. NVA sappers, under cover of darkness, have actually tunneled right up to the encircling barbed-wire. An entire 25-man Marine scout patrol was ambushed in full view of the Khe Sanh perimeter guards.[1] Every man perished, and the bodies rotted in the tropical sun for five days before their fellow Marines could fight their way out 100 yards to recover the corpses. During late March of 1968, Khe Sanh is receiving nearly 200 NVA artillery rounds a day.

President Johnson is determined that Khe Sanh will not be an American Dien Bien Phu.[2] He has instructed the entire military establishment to hold Khe Sanh at all costs. Subsequent to his order, B-52 Arc Light strikes originating in Guam have bombed the jungles surrounding Khe Sanh into stubble fields. More tons of ordnance have been dropped around this outpost than fell from the skies in all of World War II.

Khe Sanh is *the* major news headline coming out of Vietnam in late March of 1968.

It is under these circumstances that I am awakened at 0500 hours on March 31, 1968, and told to report to the mess tent immediately.

After being in Camp Evans for only three weeks A/229th has pulled up stakes again and moved—lock, stock, and helicopters—further north to the city of Quang Tri. Quang Tri lies less than 12 miles from the DMZ itself. The only town between us and the country of North Vietnam is a Marine outpost called Dong Ha. Once again, we are putting up tents and building sandbag revetments to protect the Hueys. This is in addition to our normal 12-hour workdays. Sleep is deep and days off are rare.

---

1. Historical records refer to these Marines as the "Lost Patrol."
2. Late in the Indochina War, as the French and the Vietnamese prepared for peace talks, French military commanders picked Dien Bien Phu, a village in northwestern Vietnam near the Laotian and Chinese borders, as the place to pick a fight with the Viet Minh. This was a tactical mistake, as the Viet Minh surrounded and, in the end, overran the French forces, killing 2,200 of the 13,000 French Foreign Legion troops who defended the village.

"This morning we begin Operation Pegasus/Lamson 207," Major Beyer announces to start the meeting. "At 1300 hours we will crank and join the rest of the 229th battalion for a flight to LZ Stud, which is located here." He points to a large acetate-covered map nailed to a 4 x 8-foot piece of plywood. "This will be the largest Cavalry raid in American history."

The room fills with sighs of anxiety and the shifting of asses on the wooden mess hall benches. Some change feet or adjust their baseball-style caps in response to mental images conjured by the major's words. LZ Stud lies on an almost straight path from Quang Tri to Khe Sanh. There have been rumors that we might go into Khe Sanh, but now Beyer is making it official.

"The A/229th will pick up C Troop 1st of the 7th Cav [C/1/7] at Stud at around 1300 hours and assault them into Hill 814, located here." Again Beyer uses his pointer. "Hill 814 will become LZ Peanuts. As you can see, it is about 25 clicks west of LZ Stud and about 5 clicks south and east of Khe Sanh. Our job is to assault and support C Troop as necessary until the area is secure. C Troop's call sign will be Red River and their frequency is 59.865." Beyer stops long enough to light his half-smoked Tampa Nugget cigar. In a cloud of smoke he continues the briefing.

"Intelligence reports two full NVA divisions located here." He points to the two large red grease-pencil circles north of Highway 9 leading to Khe Sanh and LZ Stud. "The 1/9th boys have been doing recon in the area south of Highway Nine. They've reported sporadic contact with the enemy but have found no evidence of a division-size force in the area around LZ Peanuts. The enemy"—he pauses to take a long cigar drag—"is reported to have heavy 31mm antiaircraft and .51-caliber stuff. Two low-flying Air Force bird dog spotter planes have been shot at with B40 rockets just south of LZ Peanuts."

We break out our notepads as Beyer gets down to the nitty gritty. What it amounts to is this: a classic "wheel and attack" deployment maneuver similar to that developed by General George Patton's crack 1st Army armor units during the battle of Bastogne in World War II.

Almost overnight, the entire 1st Cavalry will disengage from the battle lines drawn by the Tet Offensive and move all its monstrous firepower 75 miles and concentrate it on the west.

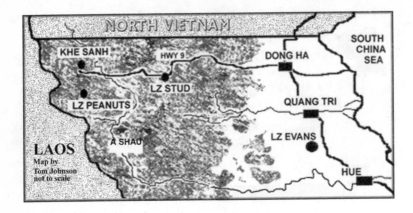

The airmobile does not depend on meeting the enemy head-on but uses "shock action" to gain the advantage. As in Patton's strategy, a fast-footed narrow force will penetrate and drive deep into enemy territory before he has time to react. But rather than using land-locked tanks to accomplish this as Patton's troops did, 1st Cavalry Division will simply fly over the enemy's fortifications and land troops by the thousands at Charlie's rear. Divide and conquer.

It's a good thing they did not tell us about this mission last night, because no one would have gotten any sleep at all. After the briefing, everyone goes about his standard duties of eating breakfast, squaring away his living quarters, and attending to flight gear. Some even take time to compose what could easily be their last letters home. As the morning sun changes the darkness to light, it reveals a company area full of jittery helicopter crews and pilots.

"Nervous?"

"Oh, hi, Bill," I say, looking up to find Bill Lee standing at the end of my cot. "I'm scared out of my mind. How about you?"

"Me, too. I don't know anybody who isn't. Do you know Beyer's route of flight on this one?" Bill inquires, noticing that I have one of the just-issued maps unfolded in my lap.

"I don't think Major Beyer has even been told that yet. He probably won't know till about takeoff time. I hope to the devil they don't send us direct to Stud. Look at this trash." I move my finger on an imaginary line between Quang Tri and the PZ, LZ Stud in this case. "This territory is NUM-BA TEN, GI! Three thousand-foot mountains on all sides, thick jungle. I have yet to find a single clearing anywhere. It's all heavy stuff."

Bill studies the map closely. "I'm too short for this crap!" is his only reply.

"I hope they head further north. West of Dong Ha we can pick up Route Nine and fly it all the way west."

"There's Rock Pile." Bill points to a small spot north of Highway 9. "I heard the Marines had a midair up there yesterday afternoon. Two Jolly Greens [large Sikorsky helicopters] ran into each other at 1000 feet. No survivors."

This is unpleasant news to get just before taking off on a division-size lift. I fold my map, grab my flight gear, and walk with Bill to the flight line.

Our new base at Quang Tri has been named LZ Sharon by the brass. On this morning Sharon is bustling. Takeoff is scheduled for 1100 hours. Like most of the aircrews, we check over the Huey, then check it again. The crew chief wisely puts on extra ammo and C rations. None of us has the remotest idea of when we might return to LZ Sharon.

Precisely on schedule, Beyer exits the battalion operations bunker and walks to his Huey. All the crew chiefs untie the blades and the pilots wait anxiously for the first sign of Yellow One's blades starting to turn.

Beyer hits the start motor and the entire company does the same. Out to my left, I see B/229th start up just as my Huey reaches full main rotor system rpm. Within two minutes after Beyer pulls the trigger, there are 40 Hueys churning the air in an area the size of a football field. As always, the excitement of a large lift makes my blood run hot.

"Bandit Yellow One, Bandit Blue Eight! Bandit flight is *up!*"

Beyer pulls pitch and his helicopter goes airborne. One by one, all the A/229th birds lift out of their sandbag revetments. We take off to the south and form up in three flights at 1500 feet as Beyer steadies up on a northerly heading.

"Bandit Yellow One, three flights formed up!" comes the call from Blue Eight. Beyer, who has been holding his airspeed back to about 60 knots, responds by gradually nosing over and taking all three flights to the new cruise speed of 100 knots. The *V* formations are tight.

The monsoon rains stop, and the low clouds recede just as suddenly as they arrived. The sky is blue and dotted only by scattered cumulus clouds whose bases are about 4000 feet around. It is a beautiful day for flying. Warm, dry air rushes through the Huey and gives us relief from the heat and sweat of sitting so long in the revetments.

Dennis Davies is my peter pilot today, and up to this point he has done all the flying. Although he has only about 100 hours of Vietnam flying under his belt, he has successfully tucked into the Yellow Two position. As I cross-check all the instruments, Davies has us flying so close to Yellow One that when I look through the window I can easily see Beyer pondering his maps while his pilot flies him into this battle.

As I hoped, Beyer leads the flight north until he intersects Highway 9, then lazily turns west. We are very close to the DMZ. As we parallel it, I can effortlessly see North Vietnam. This is the closest that any of us have ever been to it. It occurs to me that a slight screwup in navigation now could cause grave consequences.

LZ Stud has been hastily tucked into an S-curve on Highway 9. The area has been stripped of all vegetation by the engineers. The LZ features a very long pedaprime-covered runway and lots of red dust stirred up by the takeoffs and landings of a variety of helicopters. Major Beyer puts us into a trail formation, and we land along the northern edge of the runway. We then pedal-turn right and move clear of the runway by some 25 feet, then pedal-turn back to face in the original direction. Sky troopers have already been deployed en masse by Air Force C-130s and are assembled in small groups of five or six just off to our right. A/229th shuts down and refuels. Beyer instructs us to eat lunch while we have time. He then disappears in the direction of what seems to be a forward operations tent on the opposite side of the runway.

B/229th arrives in trail and lands right behind us. This is the first time I have seen so many helicopters parked in this manner. LZ Stud runway remains busy as more C-130 aircraft land one behind the other. Before the first one clears the end of the 5000-foot runway, another is touching down. Each unloads 20 rubber bladders containing JP4 fuel for the helicopters and pallets of C rations, ammo, and other essential supplies for the troops. Hundreds of supply personnel, trucks, mules, and other vehicles, all hustling, fill the PSP (perforated steel planking) parking aprons.

The Cav has arrived in force and is quickly getting ready to do battle. The sky overhead is black with flights of various 1st Cavalry helicopters going in all directions at all altitudes. I have not seen this many helicopters take part in a single mission since the day we moved north. During the flight north, we were within the mass of aircraft and could not see it. First Cavalry Division's aircraft inventory is huge, and each unit has its own special mission in the Pegasus operation.

I never played football, so I never knew what it felt like to step out on the Carrollton High School gridiron in front of hundreds of local people to "do battle." Now I find myself in that kind of situation in a real battle. There are no cheering crowds, but the eyes of the world are on us. Reporters and photographers from all the major TV networks swarm us during our wait at LZ Stud. Those interviewed behave as most helicopter pilots would; they display an aura of debonair detachment intended to mask their terror and uncertainty in the face of the upcoming battle.

Some continue to lounge on the dirt in the shade of our Hueys and consume C rations. Others, like me, walk up and down the flight line visiting the other guys.

Bill Lee, Don Martin, Larry Gore, and I end up together at Gore's Huey. With the recent departure of WO1 Charles Boyd, the four of us became A/229th's senior aircraft commanders. Major Beyer depends heavily on us.

When he returns from his forward division briefing, Beyer shares his knowledge of our assigned mission with all his pilots. We crank. The sky troopers from C/1/7th load aboard the Bandit helicopters, and we say good-bye to LZ Stud and start west. The war is on again.

The land below us is strange. None of us has ever flown in this territory, so each mile is a new adventure. Mountains bolt out of small lush green valleys. I have yet to see a single flat or jungle-free space since we took off. Engine failure here means serious trouble. Helicopters and their crews have disappeared into jungle like this and never been seen again.

Twenty minutes after departing Stud, we arrive near Khe Sanh. The jungle gives way to total devastation. Bombs from Arc Light (B-52) strikes have leveled everything that grows. The hills still roll along, not giving up a single flat spot to land, but they are treeless. Craters 50 feet wide dot this moonscape in every direction as far as the eye can see. Less than two minutes after we enter the moonscape, the infamous Marine base of Khe Sanh comes into view. This outpost has been front-page news all over the world for the past eight weeks.

Beyer flies to within about 3 miles of Khe Sanh, then turns south toward our destination—LZ Peanuts. The rest of us follow his lead. The "old guys" know how much pressure he must be under right now and feel sorry for him. Beyer has to find a single hill for hundreds to land on and has to do it right the first time. WO1 Dennis Davies has flown the entire mission so far, and I continue to feel comfortable with his flying ability. My eyes remain glued on the tactical map as I try to help Major Beyer navigate. I'm sure that Gore, Lee, and Martin are doing the same.

So far, I'm not doing very well. All these hills look just like the others. I can clearly see LZ Peanuts on the map but to relate that, by dead reckoning navigation, to the right hill on the ground is another matter entirely.

After flying some three minutes on the southerly heading, Beyer makes his commitment. High overhead is a Charlie-Charlie aircraft containing the 1/7th commanders who are supposed to help identify the LZ, but past experience has proved beyond a shadow of a doubt that aviators can read maps better than most ground commanders.

"Bandit Flight, Yellow One. I think the LZ is at my 11 o'clock position now. There will be no artillery prep."

"Oh, God," I say quietly to myself. Obviously such rapid deployment has its drawbacks. This is definitely *not* the 1st Cavalry's style. Only once before, in the Song Re valley, did we go into a hot LZ without the support of the "tubes."

"Tiger Six . . . Bandit Six, I'll make a low pass on the hilltop and drop smoke on it. Yellow Two, take the lead and give the flight a wide circle."

"Yellow Two rogers," I transmit.

"Tiger Six rogers." This is the company commander of D/229th, the gunships.

I am caught completely off guard. Beyer has terminated himself as flight leader and passed the responsibility of leading the entire company to me. And until now I was unaware of the presence of the Tiger Flight. They must have joined us after we left Stud.

Still finding no reason to remove Davies from the controls, I motion for him to race forward to fill the empty space as Beyer breaks off.

"Tiger Two and Three, cover Bandit Six as he makes his run!" Tiger Six issues emphatic orders.

Eugene Beyer is about to make a dangerous pass. In unknown territory composed of rolling hills that could hide a small army of NVA, he takes it upon himself to make a low pass to mark the LZ with a 20-dollar smoke grenade. Beyer is combat smart. He knows that everything depends on a focus point. Once that point has been identified, he can issue orders to us as well as the gunships by referring to the smoke's location.

We hold our breath as he makes his initial pass. He is to us what a minesweeper's first pass is to the Navy. If anything is going to happen, it will do so when he is very close to the ground.

I instruct Davies by hand signals to make a lazy left turn and to maintain altitude. This will give me a full view of Beyer's flyby.

The gunships, who don't know exactly which hill he is going for, fall behind and to each side. They trail his Huey by some 150 meters and are ready to react should the need arise.

Beyer makes his low pass and drops purple smoke right on target without incident. All of us breathe a sigh of relief as he does a cyclic climb for altitude with the overloaded helicopter.

Following Yellow One's instructions, the six D/229th Tiger aircraft go to work. They fire rockets and miniguns on the hill he has chosen, while A/229th forms up in trail again with Beyer in the lead.

"Bandit Yellow One, Tiger Two-Six. Over." A very excited voice fills the airways.

"Yellow One, go ahead."

"I've spotted something over here! Looks . . . looks like maybe three or four individuals on top of a hill about two hundred yards east of the LZ!!" Tiger Two-Six pauses for a moment. The rest of us sense imminent trouble.

"Tiger Two-Six, Tiger Six! *Break out of there!* Tiger flight, break off runs and let's get over there." Twenty-six's boss calls the shots.

"Six, this is Two-Six. I went by there so fast all I caught was a glimpse, but there are definitely uniformed individuals on the hilltop."

Tiger Two-Six continues his high-speed pass some 200 meters out from the hilltop, bends his Cobra helicopter around, and heads back to join the other Tiger flight. Meanwhile, he is giving Tiger Six directions to the hilltop where he has seen the soldiers.

"Bandit flight, let's take it up to twenty-five hundred feet until the Tiger people can tell us what's down there."

Beyer's orders are music to my ears.

The Tiger flight sets up an orbit at 150 meters from the hilltop. If it is the NVA, they have .51-caliber and 31mm antiaircraft weapons to defend themselves. Tiger flight is trying to be careful, but it is already in kill range of either of those weapons.

From our vantage point way over their heads, I think of shark attacks I have read about and seen in films. Sharks first circle their prey cautiously while they size up the situation and build their courage. The attack begins with a sudden rush by one shark, after which the rest make their move. In a fraction of a minute, the bloody and violent feeding frenzy begins. The thought of the sudden rush, the tearing of flesh, and the exit out the other side strikes terror into the heart of any scuba diver. I catch myself being amused by the sharklike tactics of the Tiger flight below.

"Yellow One, Tiger Six. I can see approximately three or four camouflaged individuals down here, but there doesn't seem to be any movement. I don't know what's going on. Do you have any reports of friendlies in this sector? Over."

"Tiger Six, this is Bandit Two-One. Six is on the horn now trying to find out about that. Stand by," Lieutenant Tomlinson transmits. He is Beyer's pilot and the newest officer in A/229th.

Three long minutes pass while we orbit at 2500 feet. The only radio conversation is the Tiger flight.

"Tiger Six, Bandit Yellow One. Black Horse says there are no Cav people out here and no ARVNS to their knowledge. They are attempting to contact the Marines."

"OK, Tiger flight, this is Tiger Six. I'm going to take a look-see. This could be a trap, so stay loose."

The circle breaks on all sides. The Cobras scatter away from the target, climb for altitude, then reverse course. They form up in pairs to cover their boss as he makes the high-speed run.

Tiger Six climbs high, using a cyclic climb. As his forward airspeed bleeds off to zero, he executes a pedal turn right while pulling the nose through the turn to a nose-low attitude. This classic combat maneuver is frequently used in daisy chaining, a method two gunships use to keep continuous fire on a target, but skill and experience are required to do it smoothly. As Tiger Six finishes the maneuver, he is diving toward the target from an altitude of about 1500 feet, building up speed as he goes. The Cobra can cruise straight and level at 150 mph. I have no idea what the airspeed red line is on the speedometer, but I'm sure that Six's needle will be on it when he passes over the target. Two other Tigers execute a crossing maneuver just as he pulls out so they can issue covering fire to his belly.

Tiger Six comes roaring in and executes a quick roll left as he pulls up to get a better view.

"OK, Yellow One, what I think we have here is about four dead Vietnamese." Tiger Six's voice is thin and strained from the G forces he was under in his recovery. "There could be a lot more than I originally estimated. Stand by—I'm going back in for a closer look!"

Tiger Six makes his second pass straight and level and at half the speed of the original pass. He then gets really brave, comes back in, and hovers right over the bodies.

"Yellow One, Tiger Six. I have maybe four dead Vietnamese here. They have apparently been here a very long time. No one is alive down here that I can see."

"Tiger Six, Yellow One. We're getting low on fuel. Let's put the troops into the LZ."

"Six. Roger."

The Tiger Cobras again punish the LZ with rockets and miniguns; Beyer touches down to unload his cargo of 1/7th sky troopers. It is a single ship LZ and a pinnacle landing on the hilltop, which affords barely enough room to put down the skids.

Since we departed LZ Stud, the winds have kicked up and are bouncing all of us around pretty good. I estimate the wind speed at 15 to 20 knots from the east, with much stronger gusts. I issue a warning to Davies, as we make our approach, to come in steep and be ready to compensate for downdrafts on the downwind side of the hill. Davies fights hard to keep his approach path going. When we close to about

60 feet out, Beyer lifts out of the LZ. Now it is Davies's turn. At about 50 feet out, he goes into a severe downdraft and has to rip the collective high under his armpits. Just as quickly, we come into ground effect from the hill, and he has to quickly reduce power. Our tail is wagging violently from side to side as he fights to compensate with the anti-torque pedals. Through my chin bubble I see the ground rush up alarmingly. I am way outside my comfort zone with the way this landing is going, but I fight the urge to take the controls from Davies. The only way he will learn how to be a good Vietnam helicopter pilot is through such experiences—as long as he survives them.

He does everything right, and we arrive with a sudden thud—almost, but not quite, out of control. The troops depart in a flash and Davies pulls pitch and noses over. This near miss, which has happened over a period of 30 seconds, has taken ten years off my life. I suddenly realize that Yellow One is not out in front of us where I think he should be. Quickly scanning the sky, I discover that Beyer has altered his takeoff path some 30 degrees to our left and is not climbing. It is then I realize he is dragging the hilltop where the dead guys are. I point this out to Davies, and he alters our course to fall into trail formation behind Yellow One.

"Bandit flight, when you get out of the LZ, head for LZ Stud on your own. We will not form up. I'm getting low on fuel."

Beyer's command makes me feel better. We have already been in the air for almost two hours, and it is a 30-minute ride to Stud. Those of us in the front of the formation will be cutting it close, and Blue flight, at the tail-end Charlie position will land with less fuel than the rest of us. A Huey runs out of fuel after about two and a half hours.

All the A/229th helicopters land safely at LZ Stud, and the fuel trucks are there to greet us. Beyer rushes to the operations tent to report what he has found, and a fresh load of C/1/7 troops moves up to each Huey to board.

The winds kick up higher, and dust fills the air from the freshly graded, grassless LZ. Gusts are now up to 25 to 30 knots—enough to rock the Hueys back and forth while they rest on their skids. Again Lee, Martin, Gore, and I seek out each other's company to talk about the lift we've just finished.

"Reckon those guys were North Vietnamese?" Larry Gore asks as he covers his lighter to ignite a cigarette.

"I don't know. Did anybody get a good look at them?"

"Crap, I couldn't! I was too busy chewing out Richard Adams's ass. He screwed up the approach so bad that my butt bit a hole slam through the seat cover." Bill Lee laughs and takes a long drag on his Winston. "Jesus. I'm getting too short for this crap!"

That is fast becoming his favorite saying, but we all feel the same way. We are now 58 days and counting.

"That was a tough approach, Bill." Don Martin interjects. "Skipper scared the devil out of me, too, but he did all right. In fact, I don't think I could have done it any better."

"Same here, Don. Davies scared the shit out of me. He ended up doing a good job, but I think I'll shoot this next one myself. I don't want to be the *second* pilot in the cockpit to know we're about to crash!"

Bill bursts out laughing so hard that he chokes on his cigarette smoke. Gore raises his hand for me to "give him five." All four of us are in tune with one another, and we enjoy more shop talk with the peter pilots, who have all gathered around to see what the laughter is all about. Bill Lee is unquestionably the best at this. He thoroughly enjoys giving his subordinates all the ribbing they can stand and is a master at pointing out their most subtle failings. No matter how hard they try to get something on Bill, he always turns it back onto them.

Tomlinson, who remained near the Yellow One Huey, yells down the line that Beyer is on his way.

When Davies and I climb back into the cockpit of Yellow Two, the temperature has soared to around 110 degrees. My hands are so slimy with sweat and red dust that I can barely get my Nomex flight gloves on.

Davies cranks and we depart right behind Beyer with our new load of troops. We didn't take any ground fire at all on our first mission, which makes me feel slightly better about our prospects for surviving this next assault. I look back at the six passengers. Each is sitting quietly with his M16 in a vertical position and his thoughts to himself. These men are rarely told anything. I can see the open apprehension in their faces. They don't know if the LZ was hot or cold on the first insertion. I motion the closest guy over and move my boom mike out of the way.

"Walk in the park! Nobody there but you guys. LZ is cold!"

His face lights up like I have just given him a new lease on life, and he shares this news with his buddies instantly. They all yell out loud and smile at the release of tension.

The ride this time is far rougher than it was the first time. I very nicely ask Davies for the controls. He is glad to hand them to me. We are in a *V* formation, and the turbulence makes it extremely dangerous. Flying in this weather takes monumental concentration to formation. I smoothly back off Yellow One's wing to add a safety factor, and the rest of the A/229th's pilots do likewise. We are getting kicked around pretty good by the thermals. The troops who are sitting close to the edge of the cargo compartment scramble to get hold of something to keep from falling out.

"Yellow flight, go trail," Beyer commands. "After the insertion everyone heads back to Stud on your own again and wait. This is our last mission for today. We will form up at Stud and go home."

"Bandit Yellow One, Tiger flight will cover you when you go in."

The Yellow flight goes into a loose one-behind-the-other trail and starts picking up 30 seconds separation. The flight leaders for both the Red and Blue flights maintain their *V* formations and take headings away from the LZ to increase the separation between flights before letting down to a lower altitude.

When Beyer breaks toward the LZ, I maintain my current heading for a few seconds before following. The air is very turbulent, and I can see Beyer's ship getting jostled about as he makes his final to the LZ. I am less than 100 feet out when Yellow One calls, "Out of LZ." I set up a steeper approach than Davies did in order not to get behind the hill and behind the power curve of the Lycoming engine at the same time. At the last moment, I jerk violently on all the controls at once to keep the Huey on its intended approach path. The skids have not yet touched down when I hear Yellow Three call, "short final." He is rapidly closing in and will have to do a go-around if I cannot get out of the LZ quickly. The skids get close to the hilltop and the troops exit without a landing.

"We are up, sir!" the crew chief yells over the intercom, meaning all troops have exited.

"Yellow Two is out of the LZ! Bandit flights increase your separation—it's rough at the bottom!" I transmit as we are flying again off the windward side of the hilltop.

I continue climbing rapidly for 2000 feet as I watch Beyer climbing for altitude on an easterly heading. "Davies you have it," I say, relinquishing control. Looking all about, and especially below, I worry that an engine failure here would mean certain death. The jungle is about 30 degrees downslope, then 30 degrees up-, with no flat spots whatsoever. It is so dense that I cannot see the earth. Nervously, I look at the gauges for any sign of trouble, then look back at the crew chief and gunner, who stand ready to fire at the first hint of combat. They and I will not relax until we get above 1500 feet and out of the range of small arms.

One by one, each of the 229th Hueys deposits its cargo and climbs for safety. We do three more sorties from LZ Stud to LZ Peanuts, each different from the previous because of gusting winds and the fear of running into a large force of the enemy gunners with large caliber weapons. The first sortie may have been a surprise to them, but the rest would be like shooting quail. It is nightfall when we depart LZ Stud for the silent ride back to Quang Tri.

Although battles are fought and lives are lost, we never see or make contact with the NVA in any sizable force in the entire Pegasus mission. They have apparently chosen not to do battle with the 1st Cavalry.

With all A/229th's Hueys safely in their bunkers, we drag our tired bodies into our tents one step at a time. I drop my flight gear and dig into the handmade footlocker at the end of my cot, finally coming up with my pipe and Cherry Blend tobacco. I get to my feet again and light up, inhale deeply, and lean against the tent pole. As I do, a large candle fly buzzes past my ear. Still puffing large plumes of aromatic smoke, I watch as the unwelcome visitor makes a beeline to the nearest lightbulb and begins to circle it.

I can't help but smile as I remember a time in another place when a warrant officer candidate was "court-martialed" for the "murder" of such a little critter.

■

When it was time to leave Fort Polk, Johnny Kinsey, who lived in Atlanta, and I decided that we would drive to Fort Wolters together. Early in *our 30-day leave, Johnny and his brand-new bride, Judy, drove to Carrollton to visit Pat and me and finalize all the plans. On Friday, August 5, 1966, we loaded up my car with all the necessities and said our good-byes. Pat and Judy would follow us in Johnny's car a few weeks later. The recruiter had said that once we got established in flight school, we could live off-post with our wives.*

Johnny and I drove straight through, stopping only once, for a hamburger and for gas. Fort Wolters is on the outskirts of Mineral Wells, Texas, a friendly small town some 52 miles due west of Dallas–Fort Worth. The drive took 15 hours. We arrived at 0930 hours on the 6th of August.

I rolled up to the entrance of Fort Wolters and pulled off to the side of the road. Our dreams had taken us this far. Here, not 20 feet in front of my 1963 Fastback Ford, was Primary Flight School. Johnny and I were filled with exhilaration. Our bodies, though tired not only from the drive but also from those last loving moments with our families at home, were running wide open with adrenaline.

"Johnny, do you think we should go on in now?" I asked.

"Absolutely not!" was his reply after pondering the question for a few short moments. "We are not required to officially check into class until tomorrow!"

We were well aware of tales about the harassment of candidates at Wolters. Our drill sergeants threatened us regularly with them at Fort Polk. "You're a dumb ass, Johnson!" First Platoon Drill sergeant Worley Henley would say. "Dumb asses like you can't cut it! You'll never make it through flight school! You can't take the pressure! Less than 50 percent of you holier-than-thou smart-asses who get past the gates of Fort Wolters ever graduate! They'll kick your ass out the first week because you're stupid! The Army don't allow dumb-ass people like you flying other Army dumb asses around in Vietnam! That's where they separate the men from the boys, Johnson, and you definitely don't have what it takes to be an Army pilot!"

As we sat quietly beside the road and stared at the huge set of Huey rotor blades that formed an arch over the entrance, Henley's words ricocheted through my brain. Through this archway I would find either my Waterloo or the Yellow Brick Road.

"Let's go on into Mineral Wells, get a motel room, and check into flight school tomorrow!" Johnny said, breaking a long silence. "Hell, those guys play rough! No sense asking for one extra day of it!"

"Not sure, Johnny! They won't likely start up anything until tomorrow.

Why don't we go ahead and check in now? That will give us a chance to get our stuff squared away early. We'll get to know some of the ropes. Maybe we can get a little ahead of their game!"

Kinsey was not really convinced by my reasoning, but after about ten minutes of debate, I won out. It was the first and worst leadership decision made by this warrant officer candidate.

Our class number was 67-5, which meant that if everything went OK, we would graduate as Army helicopter pilots in May 1967. That seemed like a very long way in the future.

Before actual flight school, we would have to get through what was known as "preflight," a four-week course designed specifically to eliminate as many potential Army aviators as possible. The technique used was West Point–style harassment, including the square meal methodology.[3]

From the Army's point of view, the purpose of the first four weeks was to make sure we could withstand the pressures that would be associated with the job.

We drove through the entrance and immediately found the location of preflight. It consisted of several very old World War II–type barracks completely isolated from the rest of the post.

We slowly drove around the company area until we found a sign marked "Candidates of 67-5 Sign in Here!" As we parked the car, I noticed two strangers approaching us. They were dressed in Army green fatigues that were flawless in every aspect. The creases in their shirts and trousers were piercing evidence of much starch. Their military facial expressions betrayed no welcome. As they drew nearer to the car, I could see that, even though their appearances squarely nailed them as officers, they wore no indications of rank except for brass emblems on their collars, which spelled "WOC." Each one also had two funny-looking orange cloth bands with black stripes tucked through his shirt's shoulder epaulets. I soon learned that these people, referred to as senior candidates, were the meanest sons of bitches I had ever run into in my life.

When they actually arrived at the car, Johnny and I had already gotten out and started stretching our tired arms into the Texas air.

Before I could finish my stretch, the tallest senior candidate grabbed

3. When seated at the mess table, you are required to look into the eyes of the candidate who is seated directly across from you, not at your food. Motions made with eating utensils trace a square: out, down into food, up, and laterally into mouth.

both of my arms and shoved them quickly down to my sides. He put his face directly in front of mine with less than 4 inches between our noses. His eyes locked with mine, and he abruptly began spewing out his hatred for me. Instinctively I came to attention. I also got tunnel vision and felt scared.

"Just what is your name, candidate?" the WOC asked.

"Johnson!" I said smartly.

"It's 'Johnson, Sir,' Candidate Johnson!" he roared. "I am Senior Candidate Williams, Candidate Johnson! You will address me as 'Sir!' Do you understand me?" He yelled at the top of his lungs and moved his face even closer to mine. "You are no longer Private Johnson, asshole! You are now Candidate Johnson! You will therefore reply 'Yes, sir' or 'No, sir,' to me, and you will address yourself as Candidate Johnson! Is that understood, Candidate Johnson?"

"Yes, sir!" I replied in a moderate tone of voice.

"'Yes, sir?' 'Yes, sir?'" came the voice of the other candidate, who was standing directly behind the guy who was in my face. "What do you mean 'Yes, sir'? What did Senior Candidate Williams just tell you, Candidate Johnson? Are you that much of a dumb ass, Candidate Johnson? Do you forget that quick, Candidate Johnson? We don't need any more dumb asses like you here! You were just told to address senior candidates as 'sir' and to address yourself as 'Candidate Johnson.' Therefore, the only answer you are allowed to give to Senior Candidate Williams will begin with your name! You will say your name first; then and only then will you be allowed to address any senior candidate!"

Now I had not only the butthole with his face in mine, but another one just like him in my left ear. Neither was talking in a normal tone of voice; both were yelling at the top of their lungs. I guessed they could have won every hog-calling contest ever held in the state of Georgia.

"Candidate Johnson, yes, sir!" I yelled back.

But I had made a serious mistake by looking away from the senior candidate in my face to focus on a movement to my right. This movement, much to my dismay, was two or three more senior candidates walking down the hill from company headquarters to join in the melee already well under way around my immediate position.

"Just what are you beady eyeing, Candidate Johnson?! Who told you you could look at anything else?!"

"Candidate Johnson, didn't know I had to have permission to look away, sir!" I replied, snapping my head straight forward into Williams's face again.

Whereupon all hell broke loose! The growling and yelling of unanswerable questions besieged me not only from the first two buttholes, but now also from one of the morons from the hill above. Johnny was not escaping the intimidation either. He, too, was being set upon by persons of the senior candidate persuasion.

The next thing I knew I was down on the hot Texas pavement in the front-leaning rest position.

"Give me fifty push-ups, Candidate Johnson! You're in civilian clothes, which are not authorized on this post!"

As my nose touched the hot pavement, I could see under the Ford that Johnny was undergoing the same punishment on the other side. Between repetitions, I glanced at him long enough to catch him mouthing something to me about my mother.

For the next 24 hours of our precarious flying careers, a brigade of senior candidates continuously harassed us. They were obviously working in shifts. By dawn the following day, Johnny and I had run nearly 2 miles around the company area with empty wooden footlockers and had cleaned commodes with toothbrushes until they were spotless. In addition to everything else, I had to listen to Johnny's endless nice comments about my mother.

As daylight came, other candidates checked into preflight. This fresh meat delighted the senior candidates, who by now had become bored with harassing Johnny and me. Finally we were able to catch up on a few minutes of sleep, interrupted regularly by the clamor of voices and footsteps entering our barracks. With each candidate's entry, there would be one or more senior candidates loudly barking orders in their ears just as they had done to us. We could not allow a senior candidate to discover us asleep; we had to be at attention at the foot of our bunk whenever any of them entered the barracks. As the senior candidates left the barracks to pick on some other poor soul, we would leap back into the horizontal position and attempt to obliterate with sleep the waking nightmare we had bumbled into.

Senior candidates were candidates like any other warrant officer candidate except that they were in their last month of training at Fort Wolters. These senior candidates who hazed and harassed preflight WOCs were known as "snow birds," but we didn't dare use those words around them. They had completed the primary flight training course and, as a result of various screw-

ups in paperwork, were being held over at Fort Wolters awaiting a class to start at Fort Rucker—much as we had been held over at Fort Polk. They had not only survived preflight but had also actually graduated from it. Soon they would be sent on to Fort Rucker, Alabama, for advanced training and be replaced by other snow birds. Within the preflight company area there were approximately 20 or so of these people.

During the next four weeks, preflight did not get easier. There was no flying at all, only intense classwork and harassment. Our days began before the sun rose and ended with lights out at 9:00 every night. At every meal, we had exactly 15 minutes to enter the mess hall, eat, put away our dirty trays, and exit the building. The hazing was so intense that four candidates, all of whom were "prior service"—they were already in the Army and had applied for flight school—simply quit the flight program. They had had enough bullshit and decided this life wasn't for them. The majority, like myself, had come into the flight program as civilians, and therefore were military virgins. We thought that the Army was going to be this way for the next four years.

We were constantly oppressed not only by senior candidates, who resented our very existence, but also by the real bosses of the flight program, the TAC officers. These guys were all mean as snakes, and their bark was just as bad as their bite. They were far fiercer than any senior candidates ever were. TAC officers were real Army warrant officers and Vietnam combat helicopter pilot veterans, so they had our respect. Each TAC officer was assigned one flight of warrant officer candidates—approximately 45 fledgling helicopter pilots. Their stated goal was to teach self-discipline, stress management, and the proper conduct of an Army officer. Their actual goal, every minute of every day, was to eliminate the weak. Each TAC officer was a force to be reckoned with, and they hung together like the Gestapo. Their personal appearance and conduct were above reproach even by West Point standards. There was never so much as a hair out of place.

About the third week of preflight training, during a Wednesday morning inspection of quarters, a TAC officer found a dead candle fly in a candidate's desk lamp. It also seemed that this same candidate had cut himself while shaving that same morning. What followed was simply unbelievable. The candidate was accused of murdering the candle fly during a scuffle with a knife in which the candidate was wounded. According to one of the TACs, this was definitely an army candle fly, which he himself had sent to the candidate's location the night before to observe the candidate's personal hygiene habits.

Since this was an Army candle fly, there would now be an official board of inquiry comprising other WOCs. All training was now stopped for the entire company. At first we laughed, but soon they had us believing that they were serious about the whole thing. The board of inquiry, under the direct hazing of the TACs, found that there was enough evidence for a court-martial. So, the following day, candidates who were to serve on the court-martial board and those picked to defend the lowly candle fly killer convened. As if this wasn't enough, we each had to pitch in a dollar to hire a civilian hearse so that the candle fly would get a proper burial. We did, therefore, at Fort Wolters, Texas, bury one candle fly with full military honors, including a shoe box casket, a real hearse, a funeral procession containing some 180 candidates, a 21-gun salute, a tombstone, and some twenty-odd WOC keeners who cried out during the ceremony for the candle fly to come back from the dead. With alarming attention to detail, the court-martial proceeded step by step with us now believing they were really going to do it: the United States Army was really going to convict a WOC for the murder of a candle fly. The only question that remained was, were they going to give him a dishonorable discharge or shoot him in front of a firing squad? Late that afternoon, when the officers of the court returned the verdict of guilty and the sentence of death by firing squad, all I could say was, "You gotta be shitting me—somebody call a congressman!"

In the end, it turned out to be a training exercise in becoming an officer, and the WOC was turned loose. The Army figured that somewhere in our careers, we would be picked to serve on a court-martial or funeral detail and that we should be trained in the proper proceeding—even if this involved the death of a candle fly.

19

Near Disaster, Night Insertion at Thor

April 8, 1968

Since the initial assault into the Khe Sanh operational area, all Bandit crews have flown long hours. Our workday begins long before the sun breaks over the horizon and ends with a touchdown between the sandbags using landing lights. Most of us are logging eight hours a day flying time. By the time I wake up, have breakfast, do mission briefings, preflight the helicopter, fly, have dinner, and maybe take a shower, it's time to go back to bed. I have time to write home every other day at most.

The good weather is on again, off again, but mostly off. Sometimes we see blue sky between the broken clouds, but most days we have to fly in very unsafe low-cloud conditions.

The 1st Cavalry Division has committed over 15,000 men to Operation Pegasus/Lamson 207, all of whom depend on helicopters to keep them in ammo, water, and hot food, and to carry out their wounded.

By now the enemy is in flight. He chose to beat up the small Marine base of Khe Sanh, but at the first tip that the 1st Air Cavalry was en route, he hastily packed up and headed north. We arrive in full-division strength, intent on kicking his ass all the way to Hanoi, but find only scattered pockets of enemy in full retreat to Laos and North Vietnam. Instead of doing combat assaults into hot LZs, all of our flying is ash-and-trash missions, keeping the troops already there supplied with food, water, and ammo.

Only one of the engagements in which I take part during Operation Pegasus involves hot lead. It is a night emergency insertion of a platoon-size force to break up a surprise attack on LZ Thor.

LZ Thor, located 4 miles southeast of Khe Sanh, is a hilltop artillery base. It is guarded by B Company 1st of the Eighth, a battle-hardened company of sky troopers. On the night of April 8, 1968, at 0100 hours, an attack begins with volleys of mortars and small arms fire. No one knows how many NVA troops are involved.

The division-level people are still nervous, having failed to find the 40,000 NVA troops that we were expected to engage. Relying only on the preliminary reports of the engagement at Thor, Black Horse quickly raises the red flag. This could be the initial thrust of the long-awaited counterattack by the clandestine enemy.

The company assigned to ready reaction force duty for the 1st Cavalry Division on this night is us—A Company of the 229th Assault Helicopter Battalion.

All the pilots and crews are awakened and put on alert at 0200 hours. It is then that we realize Major Beyer has left for An Khe, which remains the rear-echelon base for the entire division. Beyer will be going home soon and needs to take care of some personal business.

On what promises to be my most dangerous night mission yet, my flight leader, Rick Tomlinson, is newly promoted from lieutenant to captain. He has flown with Major Beyer since he arrived in country to develop his flight leader status, but like any pilot with less than 100 in-country flying hours, he possesses questionable flying skills. It is one thing to fly yourself into the rolling hills and high mountains of the Khe Sanh area at night, but to lead a tight formation of 20 aircraft who are depending on your every move is an altogether more dangerous stunt.

"I'm just too short for this shit!" Bill Lee fumes as he enters the mess tent and reaches for a cup. "I'm fifty-two and counting!"

About ten other pilots, including me, laugh and take another sip of the hot steaming brew, but no one replies. My own thoughts are on the rain pelting the roof of the mess tent.

"God, this is going to be a suicide mission, Eighty-Eight," says Jack Bailey, one of the original "fearless foursome" of LZ English days, addressing me by my proper call sign. Since those days Jack has logged many hours and has grown out of his carefree manner. He has become a very "in-country" conscious aircraft commander.

"You're the safety officer, Johnson; will you tell those know-it-all bastards at division that this mission is too dangerous?"

"Jack, I'd like to do that, but I'm afraid they'll give us back the old cliché."

"What cliché?"

"War is hell!"

Jack slumps his head and shoulders to meet the rising cup of coffee and retreats into deep personal thoughts.

"Hi, y'all!"

I look and see Larry Gore picking up a clean white porcelain coffee cup from the stack. Larry is a Southerner like myself, but in this case he uses an exaggerated drawl to convey sarcasm.

I nod my head while others answer in low, flat tones. Larry gets his coffee and sits beside me on the long wooden bench.

"You do know Tomlinson will lead tonight if we take off."

"Yeah, Larry, I know. That bothers me a lot. How about you?"

Larry looks around to see who is paying attention to our private conversation before replying. "Scares the hell out of me. I flew with him yesterday. He's a great guy but he can't fly."

"What happened yesterday?"

"He damned near killed us on an approach up at LZ Tom. He ran out of luck, rpm, and forward airspeed all at one time. If I hadn't taken the controls, we would have crashed right into the middle of the artillery people."

"Hell, Larry, all of us had to learn at some time. He's no different."

"The hell you say. At less than seventy hours Nam flying time, the rest of us never had to lead the entire company on a combat assault without Major Beyer, much less a company-size emergency night insertion."

"You've made your point." I continue to think about what Larry has just said and take another sip of coffee.

"I flew with him three days ago." James Jackson enters the conversation, leaning over from the bench behind us. Keeping his voice down, he continues. "It was not a good day for either of us."

James's opinion is well respected. He did 12 years in the Marines before getting out and into the Army flight school. He is almost as old as Major Beyer, and he generally keeps his opinion to himself. I have never before heard him complain about anything. Jackson will be the senior aircraft commander after Lee, Gore, Martin, and I DEROS.

"Look, guys. Beyer is not here and Tomlinson is leading the flight. Good or bad, we don't have much to say about the matter." I light my pipe. "Who's he going to fly with?"

"Gebahazy!" Gore advises and grins.

"Gebahazy!" I choke on the tobacco smoke. "How come Gebahazy?"

"Since this thing is going to take all the experienced aircraft commanders to fly the twenty birds, he asked for the most experienced peter pilot in the company." Gore pauses. "Wendell gave him Gebahazy."

"Doesn't he know that Gebahazy has been in the company longer than any other pilot including us? Hell, he's the only helicopter pilot I know who will leave Vietnam without ever making aircraft commander." I take a long drag from the pipe and ponder. "Hell, Gebahazy can kill all of us by himself. He doesn't need Tomlinson's help to do that."

"Maybe you ought to talk to Tomlinson, Johnson." Jackson speaks again.

"Oh, no—not me. You go talk to our newbie leader. I'm just going to hang loose."

Just as I have my last say, the CQ enters the mess tent and gives us the bad news: It's time to be cranking. All pilots meet in the operations tent for a briefing.

The mission will be typical except for one major adjustment that makes my day.

Spooky is the call sign of the antique DC3 aircraft flown by the Air Force. These old 1950 vintage birds are retrofitted with eight miniguns—four to the side—and are the Vietnam-renowned night support aircraft. They have saved many asses from being overrun. Spookies bristle with so much firepower that they could put one 7.62mm round in every square inch of an area the size of a football field in one 360-degree turn. I have seen them "work out" several times, and it is always quite a sight. The tracers come out every fourth round. Their rounds look like red liquid spurting from a water hose. A Spooky will orbit a unit in trouble and level everything for hundreds of meters outside their perimeter. Even small trees will be laid on the earth after one pass.

Spookies carry hundreds of flares to illuminate their targets. Tonight, three of these aircraft will be on station over LZ Sharon waiting for us to depart. Unlike Army helicopters, they have sophisticated navigation systems. Using LORAN (long-range navigation), they can figure out their exact track across the ground; thus they can accurately drop one flare after another, each a half mile apart, in a straight line from LZ Sharon to LZ Thor. All we have to do is fly underneath the line of flares and go directly to LZ Thor in the unnatural daylight. This is going to be an unprecedented airmobile assault.

Captain Tomlinson revels in announcing this to the pilots just as though he thought it up himself. Some pilots seem to go along with that, but the older pilots, like me, know that this is a gift from some Black Horse strategist. I want to give that guy a big kiss. Someone at division has his shit together tonight.

So that we don't have to fly through the dark to some ill-placed PZ in a rice paddy to pick up C Company of the 1/8th, they are trucked in by deuce-and-a-half to the Bandit location. The twist is that, for the first time, we will be required to lift out of the narrow sandbag revetments loaded to the gills. Taking off and landing with less than 3 feet to spare on each side of the aircraft is always a near disaster each time it is done, but doing so at nighttime with full loads will make it even tougher.

The Bandit parking area is alive with dark figures. Red flashlight beams shoot here and there as crew chiefs and pilots scrutinize every nut and bolt of the helicopters they are about to fly.

Considering how dark it is, Tomlinson and the Major of C Company do a good job of organizing who will fly on which helicopter. After inspecting the tail rotor gearbox, I crawl off the tail stinger, only to find six combat-ready sky troopers sitting in my helicopter.

"How you fellows doing?"

"Ready, sir."

"Sir? Damn, son, I'm just a driver. Don't belittle me by calling me a sir. I'm *Mister* Johnson, a low-ass warrant officer." White teeth reflect smiles as I use my flashlight to search their faces. "It's the damn sirs that have our butts flying this stupid mission tonight." My humor is an attempt to ease the tension for these brave men. Maybe it will make the apprehension go away for all of us.

"Can you do it, Mister Johnson?"

The straightforwardness of the question catches me unawares. Releasing my grasp on the Huey's doorway, I step back on the ground again and turn to the dark cargo compartment.

"Son, I'm only worried about one ass on this helicopter, and that's mine. I'm sixty days and counting. If there was ever a driver that will get your butt into the LZ in one piece, it's me. I'll get you there, but it's your job to kick those bastards that caused this wake-up! Agreed?"

"All right, boss! Light the fires and let's get this show on the road!" comes the thunderous battle cry from within, followed by the thumping of 12 feet on the aluminum floor.

My impromptu speech has also elicited a rousing chorus from other sky troopers within the sound of my voice. These killers are not apprehensive; they are ready to kick ass, and the smell of battle is thick. It grows thicker as all 20 of the helicopters come up to flying rpm with their red and green lights blinking a cadence.

Tomlinson's lights go full on and he calls out of the revetments. Newbie warrant officer Donald Chapman and I are assigned the Red Three position. We sit tight as five Yellow birds lift off into the darkness. Red One departs and I pull collective till our Huey is light on its skids. It takes more power than usual.

I turn to the dark cargo compartment and advise the six passengers that takeoff is about to happen. "Hold on, guys, we're out of here."

Red Two lifts off, and now it is our turn. The revetment slopes downhill on the right side, so additional skill is required to bring the two-ton Huey level. I cannot let her drift an inch in the direction of either sandbag wall. Applying hard left cyclic, I pull in enough power to get the right skid off the ground. The left skid remains firmly earthbound. The right skid begins to break free and the controls come alive. Using a little luck and much experience, I have felt out the dead controls just right. Now level, with one skid in the air and one still in the bunker, I pull the collective again.

We break contact with the earth, and the Huey and I are as one. Responding like a perfect lady, she makes no sudden moves in either direction.

The N1 turbine speed gauge holds at a steady 100 percent, meaning I have rapped in almost all the power that Army 17645 can give. There can be no tail wagging here.

I nose her over gingerly and nudge in maximum power to lift out of the revetment. The N1 now is steady at 103 percent. The left pedal at times is tapping the stop. I nurse the takeoff, then nurse it some more as we fly forward through the revetment and into the inky night air. The landing light exposes the tops of the Bandit GP Mediums. Illuminated, the ghostly images of the ground crews wave good-bye. This is unusual, and the thoughts of it spook me for a few seconds after takeoff.

Soon after departure, Donald turns off the landing lights and we are alone in the Vietnam night. Only the tiny white navigation light of Bandit Red Two gives us any sense of direction. We climb at a lazy 600 feet per minute, and Red Two's light seems motionless, showing that both aircraft are climbing in unison. Only the altimeter and the IVSI indicate that we are putting distance between us and the ground.

Far out ahead, I can see the other Bandit helicopters, a long line of red, green, and white navigation lights like something strung on a Christmas tree. Some have reached their cruising altitude while others continue to struggle.

Bandit Yellow One has already reached his cruising altitude of 2500 feet and made his turn from north to west. He heads into the mountainous country by following the river that flows from the valleys southeast of Khe Sanh, through Quang Tri province, and into the South China Sea.

The radios are uncomfortably quiet while our Lycoming L13 engine hums at a noisy high pitch. In the past few weeks, I have found myself checking the engine gauges nervously, especially during idle time. It is a habit of all short timers. At the beginning you see no light at the end of the tunnel. At about 100 days, you have a whole new perspective; you think you might just survive this thing. At 50 days, the bold get a little nervous. Below 25 days, most pilots start to feel that they have done their part and simply want to survive long enough to see their loved ones again. With this attitude, they can no longer remain an integral part of the war effort.

We arrive at 2500 feet and turn west down the river. Off in the distance there come sudden bursts of lights in the clouds—one, then another much further west. It is Spooky throwing out the flares.

The scene is ghoulish. Flares, still high in the translucent clouds, give off a flickering light that changes the low rolling clouds into amber-colored angel hair. In contrast, the silhouettes of the dark mountains under these clouds stand out rigid and forbidding.

The flares, spaced approximately every two miles, light the way. As the formation flies under the first flare, the Huey's fuselages become visible as a succession of silhouettes.

"Mister Johnson, this ain't no good," says Specialist Fourth Class Jackie Hunter, the crew chief.

"What's wrong, Hunter?"

"We'll be in a helluva shape if ol' Spooky runs out of flares, won't we?"

Up to this moment, I had not given this any thought. He is right. It would be impossible to navigate through this mountain range in darkness without striking something right on the nose. The only option would be to get on the gauges and climb to 6000 feet in a tight circle in the hopes of clearing the mountains on all sides. This, too, would be a horror—20 Hueys all bunched up and orbiting in the soup. The odds of our reaching altitude without a midair would be slim to none. Moreover, we will not be refueling any time on this trip. The way I have it figured, if we go straight to the LZ and straight back to Quang Tri, we will be running on fumes when all 20 of us get into the POL. Without any question, anyone who has to climb to an altitude of 6000 feet will not have enough fuel to even attempt a GCA landing at the Quang Tri airport. The possibility Jackie Hunter has raised is chilling. If "Spooky" were to have three dud flares in a row, we would fly into darkness. I choose not to reply to him.

As Yellow One enters the first mountains, he dodges left, then right, in an attempt to straddle the river valley. The A/229th flight begins snaking its way through the clear air with rotor blades nipping the bottoms of the clouds. Twice, Bandit aircraft commanders have to take sudden evasive actions to avoid becoming entangled with a flare descending from the clouds. The 20 Hueys fly deep into the Khe Sanh operational area, but the radios remain conspicuously quiet for the entire ride. We arrive near LZ Thor at about 0300 hours.

The plan is to land these troops on two separate hilltops some 200 meters outside LZ Thor's perimeter. They will then march overland toward LZ Thor and engage the enemy from his rear. The sky troopers inside LZ Thor are already engaging in hand-to-hand combat with their attackers as necessary.

The sight that lies ahead is unsettling. LZ Thor is lit like daylight. Artillery flares are emanating from other 1st Cavalry positions and from Khe Sanh base itself. From our vantage point, we can see dynamite flashes of light originating from various other artillery LZs; each signals that a round of death is on its way. There is no rhythm to the firing. My best guess is that all positions are firing as fast as they can load their tubes and have walked the rounds as close to LZ Thor's perimeter as they dare.

Monumental explosions are occurring around the perimeter of LZ Thor. The enemy is trapped by the artillery to his rear and the LZ Thor defenders in front. His only possible move will be to overrun the 1st Cavalry position, and even this will only delay his ultimate destruction. The 1st Cavalry boys on the LZ are tough troops and know danger firsthand. After tonight, those who survive the onslaught will have Vietnam nightmares of a whole new dimension.

"Bandit flight, they are about to prep the LZ. Pay attention to where the rounds land," Tomlinson transmits.

I envision half the tubes that were a moment ago firing at the perimeter now being hurriedly cranked by emotional sky troopers toward the LZ. I also imagine the amount of radio traffic between the artillery spotters and those who do the shooting.

Less than 30 seconds after Tomlinson's transmission, two new hilltops begin to light up with artillery high explosives.

"Yellow and Red flights will take the LZ to the west. White and Blue flights take the LZ to the southwest. Form up on your own in trail on the south side of the LZs for the ride back home," Tomlinson in Yellow One orders.

"Oh, shit. Helter-skelter formation!"

"What is helter-skelter, Mister Johnson?" Donald Chapman asks politely.

"If something happens to me, take the aircraft south of the LZ and turn east. Look for some other aircraft to tag onto no matter what flight he's in. Just get into a trail formation at his altitude and follow him home. OK?"

"OK," Chapman replies, but he clearly doesn't like it any better than I do.

The artillery stops right on cue, and the Yellow flight starts the night assault. Yellow One touches down first and calls LZ green. He departs less than 15 seconds after landing. Tomlinson has wisely ordered one-minute separations between Hueys, and Yellow Two is on a very short final as One lifts out. The entire Yellow flight safely executes their deposits of personnel and are closely followed by the first two birds of our Red flight.

"Red Two out of LZ."

We touch down less than one minute after he lifts off and make our drop. One by one, all of Red flight follows us in and out.

Adrenaline sharpens a pilot's skills, and on this night the Bandit crews are in harmony with each other.

It is a flock of Bandit birds south of the LZ. All 20 helicopters are intersecting at one point and attempting to find some order. I pull so close to the tail of Red Two, I can distinguish the glowing filament of his clear aft navigation light. The tighter the flight, the lower the probability that some other pilot will misjudge the separation and make some attempt to squeeze between two other aircraft. It is like driving in Atlanta during Friday afternoon rush hour and is only slightly more dangerous. From my vantage point, I cannot see how everyone else is doing. I only know that I'm tacked onto the trail formation. I hope the Huey pilot ahead of me is headed home.

What starts as small droplets on the windscreen escalates rapidly into a full-blown rainstorm. There was no radio transmission from ahead to give the rest of the flight any warning of the danger. Possibly, those flying ahead of me have no better plan than to fly through it.

I back off from the tail of Red Two by at least one Huey length. His already small navigation light is now only a blur on the windscreen.

"Turn on the wipers!" I command to Chapman, who then fumbles to find the switch in the dimly lit overhead console. Using wipers is avoided because of the windscreen's plastic construction. Wipers invariably leave scratches in the windscreen and make flying the Huey into a late-afternoon sun an IFR proposition. This is the first time I have ever turned them on; Jackie Hunter does not complain at my decision to burn his windscreen.

The wipers improve vision enough for me to maintain a rough idea of the separation between Red Two and us. The air becomes rough and the rain more intense.

Unlike any other time in recent history, I now straightforwardly fear for my life. It is out of my hands. The only thing I can do is follow the aircraft ahead of me.

"BANDIT FLIGHT, BREAK LEFT! BREAK LEFT! BREAK NOW!" Tomlinson's voice is high and filled with terror. "BREAK LEFT—TAKE UP A HEADING!" Bad luck and a newbie flight leader have guided the entire flight into a dense rainstorm. All visual contact with others in the flight is lost. At last sight, the birds to my right and left were less than two rotor widths away. Now, we must turn in unison while loosening up the flight to survive.

"Oh, God!" I exclaim over intercom and break hard left, losing all visual contact with Red Two. "KEEP YOUR HEADS ON A SWIVEL!" I yell, forgetting my terror long enough to be annoyed at the sudden turn of events.

"BANDIT FLIGHT, TAKE A HEADING OF 030 DEGREES! REPEAT: HEADING OF 030 DEGREES! EXECUTE NOW," Tomlinson shrieks.

A quick look at the RMI tells me we have already driven through the 030 heading and are steady on 355 degrees. There is no telling what headings the others are on. I hesitate a full ten seconds before contradicting my better judgment and picking up the 030 heading. Unconsciously I have climbed into the clouds and into solid IFR conditions.

The radios come alive as other pilots attempt to determine the altitudes of their wingmen. Before I can transmit, both Red Two and Red Four report they are some 500 feet lower than we are. That information is somewhat comforting.

I am flying totally blind in the clouds, in a driving rainstorm, with mountains all around. I begin talking to my God and myself, and this must be of some concern to the rest of the crew. I fight the panic that urges me to pull pitch and head for the clear air that lies somewhere above these clouds.

If Jackie Hunter hadn't made his comment about Spooky running out of flares, I probably wouldn't have thought about the risk of running out of fuel, and then I might have mistakenly taken my chances on the gauges and climbed.

"Bandit flight, Yellow One is in clear air! Just hold on and keep your heading! You will fly out of it! Turn on your landing lights!"

"OK, guys, keep your heads on a swivel and clear beneath you. We are going down." My only choice is to descend and pray that no other Huey is below us.

I push down on the collective, and the Huey's blade system starts its *flop-flop-flop* noise. All my attention is on the gauges during the descent. I am now completely dependent on my three crewmembers to see another aircraft in time for me to avoid it.

We break into clear air and the intercom explodes with aircraft sightings on both sides. I jerk my head left to right in a frenzy. None are dangerously close and none of the landing lights seem to be bearing down on us.

"Bandit flight, turn to a heading of zero-nine-zero and form up on me!" Yellow One broadcasts.

I ask for a "clear right" and execute the turn to 090 heading without publicly exhibiting my rampant personal apprehension.

Slowly some semblance of a trail formation is achieved, and I cautiously close in on the tail rotor of the bird nearest to me.

Without further incident, all the Bandit helicopters skirt the rainstorm and resume the track that will lead us to Quang Tri and safety.

No sunlight has yet shown when we refuel and high-hover each helicopter into the parking revetment whence it departed some three hours ago.

Almost all the flight crews assemble in the mess hall. Shaking porcelain cups create tiny ripples in the coffee before they can be steadied by anyone's lips.

Tomlinson, either by sheer luck or the grace of God, has led the flight home safely. Certainly it was not his flying skills. Now that it is over, all the old pilots agree that in time he will become a good flight leader. He kept his head in a time of extreme danger; he has the qualities to be a good flight leader if his current lack of flying skills doesn't kill him first.

The insertion of C Company 2/8th has been the deciding factor in the rescue of the defenders of LZ Thor. A major battle takes place over the next two days. Two full-strength NVA regiments are engaged and destroyed at the hands of the 1st Air Cavalry's sky troopers.

No one, including the NVA, would have ever believed a night combat assault into such a mountainous region in such conditions could have been successfully accomplished, but the 1st Cavalry has done it without the loss of a single aircraft.

This mission was silver star material for the crews and pilots involved, but as usual, it is considered just another day at the office.

20

The Circus Act Extraction

March 10, 1968

On March 9, the CQ awakens me at 0500 hours and instructs me to meet Major Beyer in the operations bunker.

Beyer is grinning and chewing on his unlit cigar. "Tom, how would you like to have a few days off?"

I know that smile very well. "No thanks, sir. My last few days off I ended up attached to the Marines in Phu Bai, doing rescue missions inside the Citadel. I don't want any more of that stuff."

Peter Kretzchmar keeps his back to me and pretends to write assignments on the board.

"Sir, if I may ask, did Kretzchmar have anything to do with this assignment?"

Irritated by my question, Peter pivots on his heels and frowns. Beyer knows that he and I have little use for each other.

"Tom, I thought you might want this one. It's volunteer only, but fact is, no one in battalion knows for sure what you'll be doing. If you don't want it, I'll give it to somebody else."

"What's the gig?"

"You will report to a Special Forces Group at Hue Phu Bai."

"Uh-huh. Hue Phu Bai again, sir!"

Beyer cannot help laughing out loud. "As I was saying, you will report to Hue Phu Bai airstrip at ten hundred hours this morning. Contact Checkmate 29 on 53.46 for further instructions."

"Major Beyer, are you sure you don't have any idea what these people expect me to do?"

"None whatsoever. This is a Black Horse assignment right from Division. You'll be attached to this group for at least five days, so you'll need to pack up your clean clothes."

"The other mission was an 'easy' one too, sir," I reply sarcastically. "I get real queasy about missions that are handed down to us from Black Horse. Seems every one of them begins with soft words and ends with double exclamation points."

"I agree with you. My job is to send my most experienced pilots. You, Lee, Martin, and Gore are it. Do you want me to give it to one of them?"

I delay my answer by sipping on the hot coffee and watching both Beyer's and Peter's eyes, searching for something there that will give them away. Major Beyer has never deliberately misled me before, and I am convinced that he knows nothing about the mission. After a moment, I realize that Peter is also in the dark.

"OK, I'll run it. I'd hate to miss it and then have somebody else tell me it turned out to be a walk in the park."

Kretzchmar assigns WO1 Bruce Farris as peter pilot and Harold Kaney as gunner. By the luck of the draw, the three of us will fly Steven Brown's Huey.

Bruce Farris is not a newbie; he has about 500 hours of combat flying. He graduated in Rotary Wing Class 67-12 and ended up in the Cav immediately after we moved north.

Specialist Fourth Class Steven Brown, having great knowledge of how to care for Hueys, was field promoted from gunner to crew chief when Merritt Hawkins DEROS'd two months ago. He also has several hundred hours of Vietnam flying under his belt.

I know very little about Harold Kaney. He transferred into A/229th from a grunt unit only a month ago.

I stuff all my clean jungle fatigues and other personal items into a rubber laundry bag and walk to the flight line to meet the others.

We know that at least the flight will be nice, because it is a beautiful day. There is not a cloud in the sky as we pass the PK-17 checkpoint and skirt the western edge of the city of Hue. Bruce is flying, which gives me a chance to survey the terrain surrounding Hue that was, only days before, the site of major battles.

Off to my right, I can now clearly see the area where I executed the emergency resupply for Striker. The LZ was camouflaged in low clouds and rain. Now, although the visibility is unlimited, I am unable to figure out the exact whereabouts of the LZ, and once again, I experience the fear I felt then.

After about an hour of flying south, I spot the Hue Phu Bai airstrip. I change the FM radio frequency and make contact with Checkmate 29. We are instructed to land on the eastern side of the runway parking area. Four Hueys are there already.

Shortly after landing and before the main rotor blades have slowed to a stop, Checkmate 29, an Army Special Forces captain, arrives in his jeep, accompanied by a lieutenant and a staff sergeant, all of whom are wearing their soft black berets instead of baseball caps.

"Mister Johnson, you and your crew can throw your bags in the jeep. I'll take you to the billeting area."

Obediently all four of us remove our laundry bags and start for the jeep. On the way, I notice the lieutenant and the sergeant briskly walking to the tail boom of our Huey. The NCO, with the help of the officer, proceeds to climb up on the tail stinger.

"Excuse me, Sergeant! What the devil do you think you're doing?"

Instead of a reply I receive a go-to-hell look that prompts me to return my bag to the Huey's cargo compartment and walk to the rear of the aircraft. On the way I meet the officer on his way to the jeep.

"Sergeant, how about jumping your ass off my helicopter!" My voice rises in anger. No one without either permission or wings sewn on his chest is going to climb like some overgrown monkey all over the tail rotor gearbox area of my Huey.

"It's all right, Mister Johnson," Checkmate 29 says.

"No, it's not all right, sir! This is my aircraft, and I say what's right or not right as pertains to my aircraft." I am both cocky and gritty in saying this.

"You're wrong, Mister Johnson, This aircraft and its crew now belong to Checkmate. You work for me."

"What are you going to do with that?" Now I'm addressing the lieutenant, who has just passed me with a pail of paint in one hand and a well-used paintbrush in the other.

"We are going to paint over your 1st Cavalry emblem."

301

"Not meaning any disrespect, sir, but the hell you say. You people are *not* going to paint anything on this aircraft until my people tell me you can." I reach out and relieve the lieutenant of his paint can with a single quick jerk that nearly pulls him off his feet. Farris, Brown, and Kaney place their bags in the dirt and prepare for the fight that is about to result from anyone daring to paint anything over our 1st Cavalry emblem. When our pride is at stake, as it is here, rank has no privileges, as far as I am concerned.

"Mister Johnson, may I have a few words with you in private." Checkmate 29 grabs my shirtsleeve and leads me away from the others for a discreet discussion.

We are barely out of earshot when he wheels around and meets me face-to-face with only 3 inches separating our noses. If this is to be a dressing-down of a warrant officer by a commissioned officer, Checkmate 29 is about to get a big surprise.

First and foremost, he doesn't own me. I am just accompanying this unit and couldn't care less about military courtesy. I could detach myself from this job just as quickly as I got attached to this job without shedding a tear. I mean, what are they going to do to me? Send me to Vietnam? Ground me? The latter would be just great in my opinion.

The captain and I argue the point for a good five minutes before he wises up to the fact that he is not going to touch this A/229th property without permission from my boss, Major Beyer.

In the end, I take my seat in the Huey while Checkmate 29 fetches his boss, a "light" colonel, who drives out to the parking area. As he exits the jeep, I notice his fatigue jacket label says Creswell. He is probably in his early forties and looks about 5 feet 9 inches or so, and he walks with a slight limp.

"Mister Johnson," Colonel Creswell says diplomatically, and I rise from the sitting position to shake his outstretched hand without a salute.

"Yes, sir."

"Now if need be, I'll get Eugene on the land line."

"You know Major Beyer, sir?"

"Mister Johnson, I've known Eugene Beyer since he was a wet-nosed lieutenant back in Benning. What's got you so riled up?"

"Well, you see, sir, after we landed, this fellow commenced to crawl up on the tail stinger without my permission." I am pointing to the sergeant. "And the lieutenant proceeds to hand him a bucket of black paint like they are going to paint a piss tube. Now, I politely asked the captain over there just what the devil is going on and all he would reply was don't worry about it. Well, sir, I do worry about it. I signed for this aircraft this morning and, therefore, it belongs to me until Beyer says different."

Creswell's brashness diminishes a little and he pivots to address Checkmate 29.

"Did you not explain anything to these people, Twenty-Nine?"

"No, sir. At this time, their top secret clearances have not yet been received."

"Captain, I don't think there will be anything wrong in taking a different approach in this case. All pilots have at least a secret clearance or they wouldn't be flying, and most have a top secret clearance. How about it, Mister Johnson? Do you have a top secret?"

"Yes, sir, I have it."

"See there, Captain. Now what the devil is your problem?"

"Sorry, Colonel. I should have handled this a little differently."

"Mister Johnson, let them do their job here, and I will take full responsibility. Eugene won't mind, I assure you."

"If you say so, Colonel."

"Look, when you get settled in, come by and see me for a drink. I'll give you some dirt on Beyer to take back home." The colonel is grinning so broadly that I calculate he and Major Beyer must have been bar-hopping buddies at some time or other.

Creswell returns to his jeep and drives off in a cloud of dust.

We pick up our bags and place them and ourselves into Checkmate 29's jeep. As we depart the area, I look back to see the 1st Cavalry tail boom emblem disappearing under a coat of flat black paint.

"Folks, I don't think I'm going to like this stay worth a flip."

"Mister Johnson, I agree. Why do you suppose we're using all the 'cloak and dagger' talk?"

"Chief, I don't know, but I'm sure our good buddy here knows everything there is to know. Isn't that right, Captain?"

Checkmate 29, who has heard our conversation very clearly, doesn't acknowledge it and continues to drive toward the heavily fenced compound. I guess he's still chapped off that I got his chain pulled.

As we draw nearer, I can tell that this is not an average Vietnam fortification. Multiple-coiled layers of razor-sharp concertina wire form the perimeter. Every 50 feet or so there are in-ground roofed bunkers sporting M60 barrels as decorations. At the entrance two spit-and-polish MPs stand next to their wooden guard shacks.

When we drive past the MPs and into the compound, I see a mininetwork of well-kept streets that connect wooden billets and underground bunkers. The grounds are so clean and neat it looks like an in-country R&R spot.

As the captain zigs and zags his way through the maze, I am amazed to see several people walking around in civilian clothes—stateside lightweight leisure suits and white buck sneakers. I cannot help staring as we drive by them. It is the first time I have seen civilian dress since R&R in Hawaii.

"Spooks?" I ask out loud.

The captain snaps his head in my direction, then forward again.

"Spooks? What spooks, sir?" Bruce Farris asks.

"CIA."

The crew all take a quick look at the civilians who are now behind us.

"Embassy people, Mister Johnson." These are Checkmate's first words since we left the parking area.

"Embassy, CIA—what's the difference?" I counter.

Checkmate does not reply. He makes a sharp left turn in front of a nicely painted billet and brakes to a stop.

"This is your new home for a while. You'll find everything you need inside." Checkmate volunteers no more information nor does he move from his seat in the jeep.

Farris, Brown, Kaney, and I exit the vehicle, bags in tow.

"Johnson, I have a very long memory," Checkmate 29 warns me and then wastes no time in leaving us standing on the roadside.

"I think he's got a real attitude problem," Bruce cackles.

"Yeah, he's going to be a sore spot as long as we're here," I mutter as I turn to walk up the decorous walkway that leads to the door. I have not seen anything like this since leaving Rucker. Rocks painted white outline the walkway. Real grass has been cultivated and is closely cropped all over the immediate area.

Inside we find eight cubicles with upright metal clothes lockers and cots whose mattresses have been rolled to the headboard, military-style. This is reminiscent of the preflight barracks at Fort Wolters. At the rear is a sink and a flushing commode.

This is definitely not 1st Cavalry quarters, and I begin to feel a little better about having volunteered.

In less than 30 minutes, we have our beds rolled out and our gear stowed. I sit on the steps outside the doorway and enjoy the cooling breezes that occasionally sweep through. After so many hectic days of flying without a break, the unexpected idleness simply feels wonderful.

The four billets on this street face the rear of another four one block over. All of them seem to be empty except the one we occupy. Several blocks in either direction, I can see other Army and civilian personnel walking up and down the roads as though they are going to a PX somewhere. They seem relaxed and even laugh aloud occasionally, possibly at one another's jokes.

Another hour passes before we have contact with another person in the compound. A jeep pulls up containing a specialist seventh class. It is a rarity to see this rank.

"Good afternoon, Mister Johnson," he says as he exits the vehicle.

As he draws nearer, he salutes, and instinctively I duck, expecting a sniper's bullet to crease my skull. I halfheartedly return his salute.

"You guys hungry?"

"You bet!" comes Steven Brown's loud reply before I can open my mouth.

"Climb aboard. I'm to give you a tour of the compound and show you where the mess hall is."

We board the jeep, and he departs with a jerk that nearly throws Harold Kaney over the spare tire. As we drive and he talks, I realize that the compound is much smaller than I had first thought. Three lightly guarded underground bunkers catch my attention. Only their entrances are aboveground.

What's in there?" I am scrutinizing the last bunker we passed.

"Operations and Planning, sir."

"Just what do they plan around here?"

"Mister Johnson, I've never been inside one of those bunkers, so I really couldn't tell you what goes on there. It's the head shed for these folks. I've been told they report directly to MACV in Saigon."

"What kind of people go in and out of these holes in the ground?" I continue to probe.

"Last month General Westmoreland himself spent two days here. He had an entourage of more brass and security people than I have ever seen before."

"Westmoreland? Well, I'll be. Wish I could have been here to tell him what a screwed-up war he's running."

Eventually our tour guide drops us off at the mess hall. Unlike anything in the 1st Cavalry, it has real stainless steel cookware and a tile floor. Much to my displeasure, there are many Vietnamese civilians working as cooks and waiters. I do not trust these people even a fraction of an inch, and we all manage to keep one eye on them for the entire time we are eating.

With our driver gone, we have to hoof it back to our hooch, but I enjoy the short walk, which helps to settle the late lunch.

As we turn to enter the walkway that leads to the entrance of our new home, I see a person moving in the shadows at the rear of the billet. Bruce Farris, walking right beside me, sees him too.

"What the—hold it!" I stop dead in my tracks and concentrate my vision on the movement of the person inside the building. As a result of my quick stop, Steve Brown and Harold Kaney, who are walking immediately behind, bump into Bruce Farris and me. The figure inside pauses for a moment, then disappears.

"Vietnamese inside," I say softly as I remove my .38 from its holster. The others do likewise. "Spread Out! Kaney get some help!"

Harold Kaney races up the street to look for the military police or anyone toting a weapon. The rest of us take positions on opposite corners of the building, just in case the intruder decides to jump out a window. I continue to hear noises from inside as the perpetrator moves about, but I cannot see what is going on. Having no desire to rush inside on my own, I choose to wait for help to arrive.

Time passes slowly and I get more nervous that the individual will attempt to escape before the MPs get there. Suddenly three jeeps at near maximum speed slide around the corner, nearly turning over in the process. As they steady up in our direction, I can see that each is bristling with roll bar–mounted M60 machine guns, and one MP is hanging on to the rear of the gun for dear life. As the jeep slides to a stop in front of the billet, the machine gunners point their barrels directly into the doorway. Farris, Brown, and I take this as our signal to get out of there, pronto.

Other heavily armed people promptly flood the area, including the "civilians" with the white shoes, knit suits, and dark sunglasses. The latter are carrying the most exotic small-caliber machine guns I have ever seen. Three more jeeps and fifty more people speed to the area at the rear of the billet and take up firing positions.

"What did you see, Johnson?" It is Checkmate 29, who has hustled through the crowd to locate us.

"Gook inside," I reply as I holster my Smith & Wesson pistol.

"Gook?"

"Yeah. We were returning from chow, and as we neared the doorway, I saw one non-American individual inside going through our things."

"Was it your hooch-maid?"

"Hooch-maid? What the hell is a hooch-maid?"

Sneering with disgust, the captain departs our conversation and races to a point just in front of the billet. He calls out something in Vietnamese. To my surprise, the individual inside replies in Vietnamese using a normal tone of voice. Checkmate 29 waves his hands in the air and shouts, "HOOCH-MAID, HOOCH-MAID! EVERYBODY, HOLD YOUR FIRE!"

After a few more Vietnamese words from the captain, the individual appears in the doorway. It is an old woman carrying a broom.

I am the recipient of many looks that seem to say, "What a dumbass," from the other individuals called up in this emergency. Then the forces disband. Many are shaking their heads and laughing as they walk and drive away.

I have to admit that I am terribly embarrassed at the whole thing, but I still feel that it's better to be foolishly cautious than carelessly dead.

The captain, holding the hand of the old lady like a Boy Scout helping her cross the road, ushers her into the area where we are standing.

"This is Vong-Ti-Lakk, your hooch-maid," the captain says, using perfect Vietnamese dialect in the pronunciation of her name. "She is

81 years old, but she works like a water buffalo. She will keep your billet clean. Vong-Ti-Lakk, meet Mister Johnson." As the captain looks up at me through his dark Ray-Ban sunglasses, it seems to me he is gloating.

The old lady, who is all of 5 feet tall, uses her free hand to raise the brim of her round straw hat, then looks up at the tall American and smiles. I intuitively smile back until I see her teeth. I think all of us jump back a little, fearing plague. Her teeth are as black as coal.

"What the hell is the matter with her teeth?" I inquire excitedly.

"Teeth?" Confused at first, the captain leans down to look for himself. "Oh that! That's betel nut juice."

"Betel nut juice?" Brown and Kaney ask in unison.

"Yeah, they chew betel nuts. It's a pastime here like chewing tobacco back home. The juice is a mild narcotic. It makes these old bones of hers hurt less. Only thing is, it turns the teeth black."

Up until now, when I've thought of hooch-maids, I've thought of young, good-looking Vietnamese women with pearly white teeth, who not only clean one's living area but also are associated with certain pleasurable activities. Now that I'm meeting my first real hooch-maid, I can't help laughing out loud. The old woman is tickled at my laughing and smiles again, displaying those "pearly whites." That sets me off all over again. Soon all of us, including the captain, are beside ourselves. This is perhaps the ugliest woman I have ever seen, and she is our hooch-maid.

The captain, who is labeled Griffin on his fatigue shirt, again speaks Vietnamese to the old woman. I guess he tells her to go back to work. She replies, "Okeydokey," which are probably the only English words she knows, and toddles across the street and into the billet.

"OK, 1st Cavalry, I guess you people aren't used to being around Vietnamese too much," Captain Griffin says.

"Not live ones," I reply and suddenly realize that he is correct. Due to the nature of our jobs, we are rarely in a position to mingle with the populace except when we get haircuts just outside the perimeter of LZ Sharon.

"OK, Johnson, I screwed up and you screwed up. What do you say we call a truce."

"I didn't screw up, Captain. You did. You people should have done a better job briefing us." I say this with a smile, and Griffin knows I'm not serious. It doesn't matter anyway. To the rest of the compound people, all 1st Cavalry people must be a little short of bricks if they can't tell a hooch-maid from an enemy.

"All right, I accept responsibility. Listen, it will be tomorrow before the top secret clearances arrive from MACV for your other three people. How about I show you guys where the beer hall is and we have a few drinks together." Griffin looks at his watch as he speaks. I guess that since it's late afternoon, his workday is over.

Brown and Kaney nearly knock me over in their eagerness to follow this guy anywhere that will end in a cold beer. I am a little more restrained but feel the same way: A cold beer will surely hit the spot.

The afternoon is spent unwinding at the beer hall. I like this place more and more as each hour passes. At about 1900 hours, four other helicopter crews come in. They have been flying all day and look tired and a little ragged.

I repeatedly ask about their missions, only to be told, "You'll find out soon enough." The only thing I am able to learn is that all four are from different divisions. One group is from the III Corps area, which lies some 300 miles to the south. They are surprised at the fact that we still wear our 1st Cav patches on our jungle fatigues. I notice that their shoulder patches have been removed, leaving only the shadowed outlines of the patches that once were there. This should be telling me something, but right now I am enjoying being half-crocked and choose not to question the newcomers any longer.

Darkness has fallen, along with two gallons of Budweiser, when the tired 1st Cavalry helicopter crewmembers stagger back to their billet. We feel splendid, and for the first time in a very long time, we feel that our war in Vietnam is far away. This will change the following morning.

March 11, 1968

At 0700 hours, the four of us, with another Huey crew that has arrived during the night, find ourselves in one of the underground bunkers for an indoctrination briefing. Our dog tags and other personal identification are confiscated. We are issued razor knives to cut free all the patches sewn on our uniforms.

At 0730 hours, Colonel Creswell enters the room. Without hesitation, he begins uncovering the wall maps labeled "TOP SECRET" in large red letters. I do not like at all the fact that the maps show territory in Laos and have little pin flags stuck deep within this no-man's-land. On each pin flag is an unusual name such as Quick Death, Mother's Wacker, and Coffin.

The president of the United States has repeatedly denied that we are doing anything in Laos or Cambodia. Though I do not particularly like what I am hearing, I am now part of something clandestine and important. Creswell's briefing is repeatedly interrupted by the "civilians" handing him notes. Phrases like "interdiction units" and "reconnaissance-in-force" fall frequently from his lips.

I soon learn that our job is to insert and extract Special Forces Long Range Reconnaissance Patrols deep inside Laos.

"Gentlemen," Creswell says near the end of his briefing, "as far as the United States is concerned, you simply do not exist. Should you go down in Laos, you will make all attempts to make your way into friendly hands. Should you not be able to accomplish this, you will simply be listed as missing in action somewhere within Quang Tri province, Republic of South Vietnam. You are strictly forbidden to divulge anything about these missions in any fashion to anyone, either here in the compound or when you return to your parent units. If you fail to adhere to this policy, you will find yourselves in a court-martial for treason.

"You will be allowed to write one letter home to your loved ones explaining the absence of mail for the next ten days. Your letter must not allude to your whereabouts, and you should also refrain from any 'juicy' stuff, because each letter will be censored by military personnel prior to its being mailed.

"You will remain on standby for your entire stay here. There will be no imminent warnings of a mission about to happen. Therefore, your location must be known to the other members of your crew should you stray from the immediate billet area. I suggest you keep your helicopter in perfect running order, as there will be no time for preflighting prior to a mission. You will want to do a normal run-up every morning as a precaution."

Placing his slim metal pointer on the speaker's podium, he changes gears from commander to grandfather.

"Gentlemen, now that you know something of what will be required of you, you can still back out. At this point, you can load your butts up in your Hueys and return to your units." He watches and waits for any response.

"Sir, how much trouble have your people had on these missions?" I feel compelled to ask.

"Mister Johnson, we have inserted teams and never heard from them again." His reply is shockingly cold and honest.

"How many, sir?"

"Three in the last year."

"Did they get out?"

"Not yet."

"Did you hear from them after the crash?"

"No contact was ever established." Creswell pauses, then changes the subject. "You people will remain with us for five to ten days. For much of the time there will be no activity. Truth is, many crews go home having never cranked for a single mission. If we require your services for a mission, you will complete the assigned task and most likely be released to return to your parent units. No crews have flown more than two consecutive missions while assigned to us.

"We do not run missions at night, so your duty day will end at 1800 hours. You are then free to visit the beer hall. There will also be occasional trips to the main Navy commissary, which is located about a mile or so outside the compound."

Having made his best effort to temper the bitter with the sweet, Creswell goes back to being an Army officer. "Anyone want to leave?" he asks.

There is a long pause that indicates all eight of us are here for the duration.

"Good. I need to talk to the aircraft commanders. The rest of you return to your billets and write those letters. Captain Griffin will come by later to pick them up. DO NOT seal the envelopes please. You are dismissed."

Everyone leaves except Colonel Creswell, another warrant officer, and me. In this private meeting, we are given the necessary maps and a small SOI of only two pages.

"Your helicopters are being outfitted with McGuire rigs. On almost all your extractions and some insertions you will be required to use them. Have you men ever used the McGuire rig before?"

We both answer that we have, and he continues the private briefing. Then we are released.

After finishing my letter to Pat, I find the rest of the crew inspecting Steven Brown's Huey more closely than ever before. We will be flying over some very bad country, and if anything is wrong with the aircraft, we want to know about it now. After an hour of looking inside cowlings and pulling on hoses, we return to the billet to take a nap.

This day and the day following are the same. We wake up around 0800 hours. The mess hall remains open all day, so we eat when we feel like it. The compound has a day room with two pool tables. This is where all the crews assemble to pass the time. There are no more inquisitions about who we are or where we come from. We all repeatedly check our watches for the 1800 hours beer call. I am the most relaxed I have been since leaving Hawaii. It is truly like an in-country R&R. Idleness gives me plenty of time to reflect. I think of Pat more than ever before. I write her a letter each day, knowing that at some time in the future I will be allowed to mail them.

On the morning of the third day, March 13th, everything is different.

The CQ is awakening me by shaking the end of my cot. I guess he has already learned to leave room between himself and 1st Cavalry people when waking them.

"Colonel Creswell wants to see you, Mister Johnson, right away. My instructions are to wake up your crew. You guys have a mission."

In a stupor, I ask him to repeat himself.

"Oh crap! The party's over!" Bruce Farris exclaims loud and clear as he unfolds himself from his cot and searches for his clothes.

We all race to get in some kind of shape to reappear in the sunshine; we brush our beer-fouled teeth and make a hurried dash for the "shitter." After three days of drinking and inactivity, I perfectly exemplify the Wolters term *grundy*. Having only five uniforms to wear, most 1st Cavalry people change fatigues every three days or so. Today, just to make myself feel a little better, I break out a clean, neatly folded set of jungle wear.

Fears I shed three days ago reoccupy the empty spaces of my mind as Creswell starts the briefing.

"Mister Johnson, we need you to extract a four-man team located approximately here." He points to a location more than ten clicks across the Laotian border. I mark my map accordingly.

"These people have been out there over two weeks and were discovered last night."

"Discovered?"

"These teams will normally stay in an operational area for three consecutive weeks before we extract them. Their job is to see and never be seen. Last night, during a movement to a different location, they ran headlong into an encampment of North Vietnamese troops who were asleep beside this river." He points to a small blue line on the map.

"Any current SITREPS?"

"As of 0500 hours they had managed to escape and evade to a location about here." His pointer rests in an area of dense jungle. "They lost two team members in the skirmish with the enemy. That's why you will only need to extract the remaining four. This will be a single-ship mission."

"Oh, Jesus, sir, flying in this area is bad enough, but single-shipping is suicide. I mean, if we go down, I'd at least like to have someone who could say where we went in."

"You won't be alone. In fact, you will be in constant view of several other aircraft. One of them is an O-1 Birddog that will escort you into and out of the PZ. He will meet you here. Be at 6000 feet prior to crossing the border."

I find some comfort in this. Whenever I have had contact with O-1 Birddogs, there have been high-performance attack jets nearby. That is the O-1 Birddogs' job: to find targets for the Air Force Phantoms to bomb.

After the briefing, I am driven rapidly to the flight line. There I find Brown's Huey already cranked and at flight idle. The cargo compartment is awash with neatly rolled bundles of McGuire rigs.

I call for clearance out of the Hue Phu Bai airfield and depart westbound toward the tall mountains in the distance.

In less than half an hour, we arrive at an altitude of 6000 feet and cross the border into Laos. If there are other people out here with us, no one on board can see them. I have an idea what shipwreck survivors afloat in the ocean must feel like. In the South Vietnam theater of operations there is the constant buzz of aircraft flying everywhere; here we are totally by ourselves.

I look at the dense, seemingly endless jungle below. I am thinking of what an engine failure would be like over this stuff. Many other crews swallowed up in jungle like this survive only in the Army's records—as MIA, or missing in action. Now, fearing that it might happen to me, I think of Ross Pentecost.

■

At last, we made it to advanced flight training in Fort Rucker, Alabama. We had watched 33 candidates washed out of the program by IFR training, pack up their families and personal belongings. It was painful; even before the good-byes, a black wedge had been driven between the survivors and the washouts. In spite of everything the survivors did to prevent it, the failures became different people. They were no longer part of our group. Many were crushed by their disappointment and became depressed. With their dreams up in smoke, they seemed to feel no reason to associate any longer with those who had made it. Wives terminated relationships with other candidates' spouses. To those who felt they had failed to measure up, it was like death. They were busted and emotionally splintered people who would move on, forever separate from the rest of us.

For the rest of us, this was a glorious day, and the entire flight was on an emotional high like never before. We had taken three days off between the ending of instrument flight training and the beginning of the Huey transition course. Now we had arrived at the big day; this was it! From day one, I had looked forward to finally becoming the master of the UH-1 Huey helicopter that was the image of the Vietnam War. It was twice as large as any helicopter I had flown before, and three times as powerful.

At 0400 hours, the flight boarded the olive drab Army buses for the short trip to Hanchey Army Air Field at Fort Rucker, Alabama. We entered the flight room in typical warrant officer candidate style and stood until they told us to sit. Two students are assigned one instructor pilot. Much to my surprise, the instructor pilot who was sitting across from Eugene Lyle, the other candidate, and me was very old by instructor standards. His glasses were thick as coke bottles. If it hadn't been a definite no-no, Lyle and I would certainly have said something like "holy shit" to each other.

THE CIRCUS ACT EXTRACTION

It was the usual procedure for instructors to be introduced one by one to the flight, and this was done, except that when it came time for our mentor to be announced, the flight commander went by him as though he weren't sitting there. Anything out of the ordinary always makes candidates nervous, and Lyle and I began to sweat profusely. Who was this guy?

When the last instructor was recognized, the flight leader paused a long time. Then he said, "Warrant Officer Candidates, we are very fortunate to have with us a very special instructor. He currently has over 9000 hours total rotorcraft flight time. He is checked out in every helicopter in the military inventory. He was a test pilot for both Bell and Sikorsky for many years before he volunteered his services to the Army. He is also the only living helicopter pilot whose helicopter license was signed by Igor Sikorsky himself! Warrant officer candidates, please show your admiration by standing to attention!"

The flight immediately leaps to its feet, eyes straight forward and backs rigid.

"Gentlemen, meet Ross L. Pentecost!"

The older man with the thick glasses rose slowly from his chair. Lyle and I had drawn the greatest of all helicopter pilots to teach us how to fly the Huey.

Ross Pentecost was the most unusual instructor I ever met. His age—late fifties or early sixties—immediately made him stand out among Army instructor pilots. His hair was brilliant white, and he often ran his fingers through it before putting on his dirty red baseball cap. Being a civilian, he dressed pretty much as he pleased, outside of the mandatory Nomex flight suit. Instead of the standard-issue military jungle boots, he preferred worn-out slippers with holes cut in the sides, to give his little toe more comfort room. His voice was firm yet smooth as oil. When introduced to our flight, he spoke briefly of his desire to teach the young men who would fly in the Vietnam War. No other job could be more important to him than teaching young combat-bound pilots how to stay alive.

On that marvelous day when Lyle and I climbed into our first Huey, we got another shock from Ross. After preflighting the Huey, I was seated in the pilot's seat and Ross was in the other. To our amazement, Ross carefully removed his thick glasses and placed them into the breast pocket of his flight suit. I looked at Lyle, and Lyle looked at me.

With Ross in the left seat, me in the right seat, and Lyle in the "jump seat"—between and to the rear of the Huey's pilot seats—Ross started up the Huey. We followed his every move on our printed checklist. My heart reached full speed—way ahead of the main rotor blades. I was bursting with the excitement of finally getting to fly the helicopter of my dreams.

I was shocked back to reality when Ross said, "It's all yours, Tom. Lift me up to a hover!"

Now exuberance turned to fear as I slowly took hold of the unfamiliar controls. The Huey was a semi trailer compared to the much smaller OH-23s and TH-13s I had previously flown. To add to my consternation, other UH-1s were parked dangerously close on each side. One wrong move sideways and we would entangle main rotor blades.

"OK, Tom, pull in power slowly and feel her out," Ross coached. "The Huey hovers tail-low, so just before breaking ground, apply a little rear cyclic."

I executed Ross's instructions to the best of my ability. As I slowly pulled up on the collective pitch control, the huge flying machine got lighter and lighter on the skids. As she approached neutral buoyancy, she got squirrelier and squirrelier. I stayed right on top of the situation by applying the corrective control pressures as necessary to keep the Huey right where she was on the concrete pad. Finally, following Ross's original instruction, I applied a little rear cyclic pressure simultaneously with a last minuscule amount of upward pull on the collective.

She rose like a Titan ready to do battle, without moving forward or backward 1 inch from our hovering spot. I was elated beyond words and wished Pat could have been with me to share my delight. My heart was pounding from the excitement that had replaced my fear.

As the Huey rose to a hover, I kept trying to "roll in throttle," which was the response necessary to keep the rotor rpm stable on the reciprocating engine helicopters I had flown previously. The UH-1 had a Lycoming turbine engine instead of aviation gas burners; its engine rpm governor was so good that it actually didn't require twisting the throttle to keep a steady engine rpm.

Ross got clearance for us to hover out to the takeoff pad, and with a motion of his finger instructed me to execute that maneuver. I hovered over to the pad, and we began training in earnest. It was a day I would always remember, but it ended all too quickly. Lyle and I swapped seats, and he, too, took his first turn at piloting a Huey.

There was a great celebration on the buses that returned the warrant officer candidates to the company area. That night, I almost wore out Pat's ear telling her all about my first hover in a Huey. She patiently listened and then put an end to my story with a gentle pull on my arm in the direction of our small trailer bedroom. It was way past our normal bedtime.

Phase two of our training was divided into two distinct parts. In the first part, warrant officer candidates were instructed in the basics of how to fly the UH-1 helicopter. The second part was dedicated to flying the Huey with simulated heavy loads like the ones we would find in the real world. Three 55-gallon drums filled with water were installed inside the cargo compartment. With no load the Huey had been quick as a mouse to leap into a hover. When heavily loaded, she required much more collective just to get her light on the skids. If you listened closely, you could hear the Lycoming 1100hp turbine and the transmission begin to strain.

The additional weight also would make the Huey fall out of the sky much faster during autorotations. With all three drums full, the rate of descent soared to over 1500 feet per minute. In my book, that was plummeting, not autorotating.

It was during the recovery from one of these high-speed autorotations that Ross made an inconspicuous comment that, in a few short months, would save my life.

"Tom," he said, "if you ever lose an engine over trees in a Huey and have no where to go, go in 'looking at God!'"

At first the comment caught me off guard. I surveyed my current position relative to the ground below and found I was indeed over a vast expanse of south Alabama pine trees. "He's going to cut the power!" I thought, realizing that I had been so caught up in the simulated autorotation that I had forgotten to worry about an engine failure. Sure enough, Ross rolled the throttle back to flight idle.

I slammed the collective pitch down to the bottom and used whatever airspeed we had above 60 knots to climb higher. The additional altitude would give me a second or two more to determine if there was an open field within autorotation range. As the airspeed indicator bled back to 60 knots, I placed the nose of the Huey down and made a left turn. I could not see a single area free of trees within the UH-1's autorotation range.

"What are you going to do, Tom?" Ross asked firmly.

"Commit to the trees, sir!" This was the proper thing to do. Many pilots panic in such a predicament and attempt to autorotate to some area outside the Huey's range. Trying to stretch out the glide, they will pull off main rotor rpm and arrive in the treetops with little or no main rotor rotation. This will certainly mean a very hard landing and usually results in the death of all on board.

"Good . . . how are you going to enter the trees?" Ross asked.

"At zero forward airspeed and level, sir!" I was comfortable with this reply because I had read over this emergency procedure just a few weeks before.

"WRONG . . . never do that!" Ross replied as he reached for the controls. "I have it!" He ended the simulated engine failure by twisting the throttle to roll in power. The Huey's engine came smoothly back to life; what had been a whisper became a turbine whine.

I was thoroughly confused at Ross's direct contradiction of what I thought I had read. Before I could formulate a question, he explained.

"Now both of you listen carefully." Lyle, who was sitting in the jump seat slightly behind and between Ross and myself, shifted his weight forward. This was a natural tendency, but since all three of us were wearing helmets equipped with intercom radios, it was not going to enable Lyle to hear any more clearly.

"Forget what the Army teaches you on this!" Ross was looking back and forth at Lyle, outside, and at me in the Huey as he spoke. "All UH-1s are very nose heavy. If you go into the trees flat, you'll end up on your back before you hit the ground. This aircraft can take an enormous impact so long as you hit the ground right side up. However, if you let her get on her back, you're a dead man. Typically, if you hit flat, the nose of the Huey will tuck down as she falls through the trees." Ross demonstrated this with his right hand by pointing his fingers down, then continuing in a rolling motion until his palms faced upward.

"Correct procedure is to wait to the last possible minute, then pitch the nose as high up as it will go. Be looking at God when the tail rotor makes its contact with the trees. If you do it this way, you stand a far better chance of hitting the ground upright. Understand?"

Lyle and I both nodded our heads. We knew that Ross knew his stuff; neither one of us would ever have challenged him on anything associated with flying.

After a few short weeks, I said good-bye to the best instructor pilot I ever knew. Ross L. Pentecost had taught me smoothness on the controls and an alertness I had never before known how to attain. Both Lyle and I passed the final checkride with grades in excess of ninety.

Ross Pentecost was my last civilian instructor pilot. As we began the *final phase of rotary wing flight training, we had only Army instructors, men who had just returned from Vietnam.*

∎

"There he is." Bruce's call over the intercom shocks me out of my daydream. He has spotted the O-1 Birddog. It is a small single-motored Cessna aircraft.

"Jericho Four-Two, Bandit Eighty-Eight. How do you copy?"

"Eighty-Eight, copy you loud and clear. Have you in sight. Follow me. Over."

I roger his transmission and fall in behind him as he banks westward. This is the first time any of us have flown formation with a fixed-wing aircraft. I find it amusing, so I have Bruce tighten up the formation to make the Air Force pilot inside a little nervous. He keeps looking over his shoulder to check on the lumbering Huey that is glued at his eight o'clock position. The tips of the main rotor blades are only 8 to 10 feet away from his vertical stabilizer as we fly through the blue sky with the greatest of ease.

This "daredeviling" takes our minds off the task that lies ahead. Occasionally I look below at the never-ending jungle. It doesn't take much Vietnam flying experience to know that if you crash into that stuff, your chances of being found by anyone but the bad guys are remote. At this point we have flown too many thick jungle miles into Laos to walk back to Vietnam in this century.

"Bandit Eighty-Eight. I'm going to step on out now to mark the spot. Keep me in sight at all times. I have the Circus Act people on the other radio."

"Jericho Four-Two. Do you have a SITREP?"

"LZ is red! They are in contact. I'm trying to find out if they can move out to a new PZ. Stand by, this frequency."

I think of Bruce Farris's words of this morning: "the party is over." We are definitely back in the war again.

"Mister Johnson, take a look at our new blades."

Thinking only of rotor blades, I turn to see what Steven Brown is talking about. I am amused to find him and Harold Kaney brandishing three-foot-long, olive drab machetes.

"Where did you get those?" I ask.

"The captain—you know, Checkmate 29—gave them to us this morning before we took off."

"What are they for?"

"He told us that if we get some of these guys hung up in a tree, we should cut the McGuire rig loose."

"Cut 'em loose? I wonder how the guy on the other end of the rope is going to feel about that?"

"He said it's SOP. You know, that if a guy gets hung up, he actually expects to be cut loose to save the others. If we cut him, he's good as dead—and he knew that before we took off."

"Chief, just for clarification, nobody gets cut loose unless I say so. OK?"

"Right, sir. I'm just repeating what he said."

"Bandit Eighty-Eight, Jericho Four-Two. The Circus Act people have broken off contact and are on the move. I will mark a spot with smoke. Come on downstairs and get ready for the pickup."

"Eighty-Eight. Roger. I have it Bruce, but stay near the controls."

We execute our descent from the reasonably safe high altitudes, following the O-1.

I notice that the dense Laotian jungle below occasionally gives way to open grassy fields. I have been briefed by Creswell that we would see such openings and that we are to use them, if possible, as PZs. If enemy activity prevents that, we are to use the McGuire rigs and fly as long as we have to with the team dangling at the ends of their ropes until we can find a safe area for insertion.

"Eighty-Eight. Steer north and approach the PZ on a southerly heading. All the activity is southeast of the pickup point. When you depart, steer north again so you don't overfly the bad guys. Do you copy?"

"Eighty-Eight copies."

"Eighty-Eight, stand by." He has started to transmit something else and is interrupted, probably from the Circus Act people on the other radio. We can't pick up the conversation.

"Eighty-Eight, the Circus Act people will be unable to make it to another cleared area. You will have to extract them in place on the McGuire rigs."

"Can do" is my reply, but I know this is going to be trouble. If my guess is correct, the bad guys are hot on their trail. I worry that we will be pulling these guys through the trees in the middle of a firefight.

"Eighty-Eight, smoke out in thirty seconds. The area I've picked for you will allow the Circus Act people to make a run for it. Drop your rigs into the smoke and await their arrival."

"I copy loud and clear."

Jericho 42 rolls until he is almost inverted; then he heads straight down. He pulls the trigger, and a smoke rocket mounted underneath his left wing takes flight. The rocket disappears into the trees. It takes a few more seconds for the red smoke to clear the thick foliage and start drifting skyward above the treetops.

"Smoke out!"

Now that I have a fixed target, I continue my descent and turn north up a small valley. In less than a minute, I reverse course.

"OK, Chief. You guys get ready to drop the ropes."

The Huey leaves forward flight and enters translational lift as I enter a fast forward hover above the trees. As we ease into the red smoke, the high winds created by the main rotor system in a maximum power configuration swirl it in wide vortexes.

"This is it! Drop the ropes and get your M16s!"

Steven Brown and Harold Kaney struggle to drop one rope at a time. At the end of each rope is a heavy iron device that looks much like a boat anchor and helps the rope get through the tops of the trees. The crewmembers have to work the ropes among the tree limbs by pulling up and letting down again. I keep the Huey motionless in a very high hover.

I know all four ropes are in position when I feel the movements of Brown and Kaney returning to their cubicles to retrieve their M16s.

"Eighty-Eight, Circus people have arrived at your location. Get ready."

"I see them, sir," comes Steven Brown's excited cry over the intercom. "They're right below us now and hooking up."

I hear what I think is the muffled crack of an AK-47. Whatever it is sends a new wave of adrenaline flowing through my body. Nervously, I check the engine gauges for any change. Luckily, Brown's Huey is an H model with an L-13 engine. I will not have to worry about available power even when we take these guys in tow. I wouldn't be able to accomplish this task flying an older "D" model.

"Eighty-Eight, They're ready! Pull them out!" Jericho 42 transmits in a higher than normal tone of voice.

I pull collective and the Huey responds. We have moved about 10 feet higher when something goes wrong. The Huey's ascent slows to a standstill; it is as if we are attached to a rubber band.

"Hold it, Mister Johnson, we got a guy hung up. Down a little!" Brown is yelling into his microphone.

I relax slightly on the collective and the Huey settles.

"OK, Mister Johnson, try it again."

The Huey again starts skyward, only to be stopped at the same point. Before Steven can call it, I again reduce power to let her settle by 3 or 4 feet.

"Again, sir!"

Just as I apply power, I hear a *tic*, then another; two rounds have penetrated the Huey somewhere. Then I hear the chatter of AK-47s very close by.

"Oh, shit!" I say aloud. "Jericho Four-Two, we are taking rounds! I repeat: we are taking rounds, and we have a guy hung in the trees!" As I am transmitting, I am pulling on the collective. As we reach the same point as before, our progress is halted again.

"Cut him loose, Eighty-Eight! Get out of there!" Jericho 42 commands.

"Cut him loose, sir?" Brown's voice is shaky. I can't see him, but I picture him with his machete drawn back, ready to cut.

"NO! DON'T CUT HIM LOOSE YET!"

As I speak, a round enters the chin bubble on my side of the Huey and exits underneath the radios in its nose, sending splinters of Plexiglas under my feet. The angle of the bullet tells me the shooter is very close.

Without asking for permission, Brown and Kaney open up with their M16s. They have seen something to fire at!

My mind is already made up. I make a positive pull on the collective for more power.

The rotor system loads up, and as I watch, the gauge indicating torque on the L13 Lycoming moves from 50 foot-pounds to 52 foot-pounds of twist. Our Huey remains motionless. I pull for more power. The gauge shoots up to 56 pounds, yet still we go nowhere.

The H model is not theoretically limited in power, but at 58 foot-pounds of torque, the airframe and power train components have been overtorqued and certain inspections have to be made. After 60 pounds, main rotor bolts and tail rotor drive parts have to be replaced, and after 64 pounds, the helicopter is literally thrown away—every moving part in the drive train is overtorqued beyond safe design limits.

My attention is fixed on the torque gauge as I pull for more power.

57 . . . 58 . . . 59 . . . 60 pounds, and she finally shows some sign of moving. Whatever is holding him down is breaking loose, or his body is breaking into parts.

61 . . . 62 pounds.

We break free and the Huey soars skyward like a rocket. I choose to leave the power in, and I keep my eyes glued on the gauge rather than look outside. Somewhere during the ascent, I push a hard right pedal and forward cyclic, not taking account of the loads dangling some 30 feet below us. The Huey noses over and into forward flight.

Like a pendulum, the Huey races forward while the people at the end of the rope remain stationary. As the slack is removed, they soar skyward, then fall in behind the flight path of the helicopter.

I keep the 62 pounds of power pulled until we are away from the immediate area and established at a safe altitude.

"Good job, Eighty-Eight, good job!" Jericho 42 transmits, obviously pleased to see us make our escape.

"How are the people on the ropes doing, Chief?"

"One guy doesn't look so good, Mister Johnson. I think he's passed out. I can't tell too good. All four guys are hugged together in a bundle. Best I can tell, sir, he's bleeding pretty bad."

"Jericho 42, I had to strip one of these guys out of the tree and he's not doing so good. I need to get them inside as soon as possible."

"Eighty-Eight, I roger that. Continue on your present heading. I have you in sight. I'll find you a place to set down somewhere."

The O-1 comes screaming out of the heavens and into view a mile ahead of us. He's moving a little faster than we are, and he continues to "walk away" in order to scout for an open area. A minute of radio silence passes.

"Eighty-Eight, I have a clearing. I can't see your position relative to me, so I'll smoke it."

"Roger, Four-Two."

Again the O-1 dives in and out, leaving smoke on the ground.

When I spot the cleared area, I set up the approach mindful that I must come to a full high-hover stop over the area, then descend straight down so as not to drag these people across trees.

I'm not thinking at all about enemy fire as I bring the Huey to a stop, then start down. The air rushing up through the busted chin bubble feels very strange.

During the entire descent, Brown and Kaney call out how high above the ground our passengers are.

"On the ground, sir," Kaney calls out.

"Tell me when they're loose," I command.

"They are loose now, sir. You can set down. Tail rotor clear, sir!" I ease the Huey all the way to the ground. Our passengers are loaded, the McGuire rigs are recovered, and we are out of there in about 30 total seconds.

When we've reached a safe altitude, I give the controls over to Bruce Farris and look around.

Two of the Circus Act people are working feverishly to stop the bleeding of their comrade. The third guy is just sitting, feet out the door, staring into space.

"Jericho 42, Eighty-Eight. One individual is hurt pretty bad, but our fuel is critical. Do you have medical facilities in the compound? Over."

"That's affirmative, Eighty-Eight. I have already alerted Checkmate Six that you are inbound with injuries. They are standing by with medical people."

"Thanks, Jericho. If your radio is that good, please inform Hue Phu Bai tower that we are going to need a straight-in approach across the runway. We are showing less than three hundred pounds of fuel now. Over."

"Roger. Will do."

We make Hue Phu Bai, and Farris makes a hot direct approach into the pedaprime parking area east of the runway. He carries it all the way to the ground like a pro—without any hovering.

I exit as soon as Brown pulls back the armored plate. The medics are pulling the injured guy from the cargo compartment. His body sloshes like water, and exposed bones protrude from his chest. He is bleeding all over the place. His hair is matted with his own blood. The sight of this makes me unsure about what I have just done.

"Damn great job, Johnson!"

I turn to see Captain Griffin offering his hand.

"We've been listening on the radio. Looks like you guys had a few bad moments." Griffin glances at the missing chin bubble that has become the center of attention of several other curiosity seekers.

"Thanks, man." I turn to find that the voice belongs to one of the Circus Act people I have just brought in. Shoulder to shoulder, the other two former passengers push their way through the crowd to shake my hand. One hugs my neck tightly. He is overcome with what has happened in the past two hours. He turns to walk away, only to return for another hug.

"Dammit, sir, you saved my life and I will never forget it!" A tear rushes from the corner of one of his tired eyes, and he finally turns away to see where the ambulance has taken his friend.

"How bad did I hurt him, you suppose?" I feel compelled to ask.

"He's hurt real bad, sir. From what I could tell both collarbones are gone and he has compound fractures of at least two ribs. His back may also be broken."

"Was he ever conscious?"

"No, sir. He's been out of it all the way. I was afraid to give him any morphine."

"Yeah." My thoughts begin to drift again. "I don't blame you for that."

"Well, thanks again, sir, for saving our lives." One last handshake and he is on his way to find his other friends.

I feel hollow inside as I am debriefed by Colonel Creswell and his people. As I tell the blow-by-blow details of the mission, the power-pull to free the man begins to haunt me. At times, I think I hear the bones cracking as I relate the incident.

After I tell my story for an hour, I am released. Captain Griffin is waiting outside with a jeep.

"Need a ride, 1st Cavalry?"

"Yeah, Captain, if you don't mind. I'd like to return to the aircraft to check for damage."

When we arrive, Brown's Huey is surrounded by a crowd of other flight crews and assorted onlookers inspecting the damage.

Harold Kaney rushes out of the crowd to hand me a cold Budweiser that he has procured.

"Have a beer, Mister Johnson."

"Thanks, Harold. Where did this come from?"

"Checkmate Six, sir. You know, Colonel Creswell. He had a whole trash can delivered to us already iced down."

"How bad is the ship?"

"We took three rounds. One you know about for sure. The other two are just below the tail rotor gearbox."

"Are you shitting me?"

"No, sir! Come over here and look for yourself."

I find Brown perched on the tail stinger; he is poking his fingers into the two holes just inches below the gearbox.

"Mister Johnson"—Brown pauses just long enough to catch a cold beer that is thrown up to him by someone in the crowd—"if this guy's aim had been six inches higher, we'd still be over there somewhere. Wouldn't you agree?"

"Yeah. I agree." The thought of having a tail rotor failure while hovering over trees at maximum power causes a genuine shudder to pass through my body. Loss of a tail rotor during a high hover would have resulted in the fuselage making the Huey spin uncontrollably to its right. Due to the high angle of attack of the main rotor blades, they would have stopped completely before the Huey ever hit the trees. It would not have been a survivable crash for the crew, not to mention our passengers on the ends of the ropes.

After two beers, I ask Captain Griffin if he will drive me to the billet. My legs are getting a little shaky as the mission and the two beers catch up to me.

Bruce Farris rides with us, while Brown and Kaney supervise the cleanup of the blood from the cargo compartment. Checkmate Six has sent four people on his shit list to do what would otherwise be the crew chief's responsibility.

When the Huey is finally secured, all four of us get a hot shower and change into clean fatigues. Patiently waiting on each other and occasionally retrieving cold beers from the trash can that has been delivered right to the billet, we talk about the day. This flight has been Harold Kaney's indoctrination in fear. For the first time in his life, he has seen the grim reaper at his front door.

Like all the rest of us, he has always wondered just how he would react when the time came. He didn't do too badly.

At last, Steven Brown is through primping in front of the mirror. We discharge ourselves in the direction of the beer hall—clean shaven, feeling good, and ready for a party.

We are the celebrities of the day among the aircrews assigned to the compound, so we are given a hero's welcome as we enter. But along with the upraised beer steins and cans are the catcalls to remind us that we are no different from those who celebrate us.

Everyone has his moments in life. Tonight is one of our moments.

Someone puts another cold beer in my hand, and we disburse into different sections of the crowd.

I have only been seated a moment when a deep voice booms out, "WARRANT OFFICER TOM JOHNSON! WHERE ARE YOU?"

A very big sergeant is standing in the doorway with a package underneath his left arm. The crowd goes quiet and points to me; he starts in my general direction. Fearing I might have really pissed this guy off for some unknown reason, I choose to stand and prepare to run for my life.

"You Mister Johnson?" he inquires as he moves in for the kill.

"Yeah, I'm Johnson."

Without warning he thrusts the package forward. I accept it nervously. Taking one step back, he issues a hand salute and holds it until I do likewise.

"Mister Johnson! Please accept this token of gratitude from the men and the officers of our group for your heroic efforts in saving the lives of four of our people today."

"You mean the guy is still alive?"

"Yes, sir. Sergeant Vernon is going to make it, thanks to you and your people."

I am ecstatic at this news. Grabbing a beer from the table and standing on a chair, I toast the health of Sergeant Vernon, and add, "God give us the strength to continue to do what we think is right."

"Hear! Hear!" The others rise to their feet and hoist their steins and cans.

A thousand bricks have been removed all at once from my shoulders. I climb down to the floor and open the package as the others look on. Inside I find a very large bottle of Chivas Regal scotch, which is my favorite.

"How did you guys know I like Chivas, Sergeant?"

"Your crew told us, sir."

I look around to find Brown and Bruce Farris raising their beers in my direction.

I thank the sergeant and sit down. Someone shows up with a clean glass, and the scotch flows freely. It is the exception rather than the rule for me to share my Chivas Regal 12-year-old vintage scotch whiskey, but tonight it is OK. I awake the next day with my head pounding so much, I can't open my eyes in sunlight.

When I'm squared away at around 1000 hours, I seek out Captain Griffin and request a ride to the hospital to check on Sergeant Vernon.

Nearly an hour later we enter his room. My first sight of him, as the male nurse pulls the partition back, makes me sick.

He is in a body cast from his neck to his toes. His head is bandaged, with only his eyes, nose, and mouth exposed.

"Sergeant Vernon," the doctor says. "This is Warrant Officer Tom Johnson. He's the pilot who pulled you out yesterday." The doctor's voice sounds patronizing, as if he is addressing an elderly patient.

Vernon's dark eyes shoot away from the doctor and fix on me. He says something I do not hear. The doctor motions me to come closer.

Vernon looks into my eyes coldly.

"How come you didn't cut me loose, sir?" His voice is barely audible and slurred with painkiller.

I am taken aback by his question. I'm a little afraid that he is pissed-off that I've broken him up so badly.

"Vernon, I'm very sorry that I hurt you so bad. I really had no choice. We tried to shake you loose three times. For whatever it's worth to you, Sergeant, the 1st Cavalry doesn't leave people behind to do battle on their own."

Vernon studies me carefully, and this makes me uncomfortable. "Sir, your orders were to cut me loose." It takes him a very long time to say this, but I understand every painful word.

"I don't always follow orders."

"Mister Johnson, I owe my life to you for not following orders." Now Vernon's eyes twinkle, and he manages to crack a grin. "God bless you, sir. I was a dead man."

"Hell, Sergeant Vernon, from your present condition, I would say that you still got one foot in the grave as far as I'm concerned."

It obviously hurts Vernon to laugh, but the ice has been broken. He is not pissed-off at me for breaking up his only body; he is jubilant that I did not follow orders and cut him loose.

The following day, I meet with Checkmate Six and am released to fly our sick Huey home to the A/229th.

"Johnson, what you and your people did deserves a medal. You know that."

"Haven't thought about it at all, sir."

"I have. Under normal conditions the Awards and Decorations people would easily approve any paperwork I sent them. Unfortunately, due to the circumstances surrounding these missions, it's not going to happen."

"Sir, I'm sure that man's family will appreciate our efforts. We save some and, unfortunately, we lose some, but no one has to tell us when we do a good job."

I grin and Six grins back.

I depart Checkmate's operational area, never to hear from him or Sergeant Vernon again.

The flight home, though well ventilated due to the missing chin bubble, is a happy one. We are all proud of our successful mission.

21

A Shau Valley, Lair of Lucifer

April 17, 1968—Operation Delaware

"Well, it's not a rumor anymore," I announce. I have just entered my tent and dumped my flight gear on the air mattress.

"You mean A Shau?"

"Yep. I mean A Shau."

"How do you know for sure?" a young pilot asks in disbelief.

"I've just had a briefing at Battalion." As I turn to face the young pilot, transistor radios fall silent. Someone goes into 2nd Platoon's tent to pass the word along. Fifteen more pilots converge on my cubicle; they are hanging on my every word. Within minutes, my general area is overflowing with crew chiefs, gunners, and pilots. I am bringing the first word of a top level briefing. The air is heavy with consternation as I fumble to find my pipe tobacco. "Bandits will be one of the lead flights into LZs that I am not at liberty to divulge at this time. You will be supporting 1/8th people."

"Did Battalion say what type of weapons?" WO1 James Jackson asks. "I know they got some heavy crap in there."

"They do." I pause, not wanting to tell all I know. I twist my body in one direction, then the other, still trying to locate the tobacco.

"There are heavy cloud layers, so no high-altitude aerial recon, but Division is sure there are nests of 37mm antiaircraft throughout the valley. This is in addition to the .51-caliber stuff like we ran into at Khe Sanh, not to mention several thousand NVA."

"Johnson, your pipe tobacco is on your bed," Bill Lee volunteers, pointing to the mashed-up foil package of Cherry Blend lying on the cot and, for a change, not choosing to make any smart-ass remarks. Even if no one else can tell, Bill can see that I am rattled.

"Thanks, Bill."

"Any SITREPS?"

"The 1/9th boys flew into the valley this morning, but they couldn't get in to the floor because of the cloud layer. According to their reports, they got the shit kicked out of them. Forty-some-odd were hit, and they had already lost eighteen aircraft when I left the briefing about an hour ago." I light the pipe and draw a calming hit of the nicotine, then sit on my handmade footlocker, still perspiring from the flight back from LZ Evans. The tent is deathly quiet.

Again I speak. "Division is trying to recall the 1/9th so they can Arc Light the whole valley."

"Arc Light?" a newbie warrant officer inquires.

"B-52s, you idiot," Bill Lee informs the newcomer. "Where you been, boy?"

Larry Gore, who has pushed his way up front, asks, "When do we go?"

"The way it stands now, depending on weather, day after tomorrow." I again pause for a slow draw on my pipe. "The show starts tonight with Arc Lights and continues around the clock. On the morning of the 19th, the Air Force boys will drop twelve 10,000-pound 'blockbusters.' The idea is to create some LZs on the sides of the mountains. They'll be the largest bombs ever dropped in Vietnam."

"How did you get into this briefing, Johnson? How come they didn't tell us?"

"Well, I tell you, Jackson. I wish it had been you instead of me."

"Why's that, Tom?" Gore asks.

"About twenty crews, and I'm one of them, have been attached to the 11th Aviation Support Group." I pause to relight my pipe. "On the morning of the 19th, I have to report to LZ Evans to pick up four EOD (explosive ordnance disposal) engineers. We'll take off ahead of the main assault and head for the valley on a solo mission."

"What the devil you mean *solo*?"

"I have to find a single LZ and get the engineers into it. Division wants whatever debris is in the bomb craters cleared out before you guys make your final approach."

"*S-h-i-t!* You're not kidding, are you, Johnson?"

"I wish I were. I have to get them into the LZ by whatever means possible, hang around long enough for them to do their job, then extract them."

"Ah, man!" Bill mutters in disgust. "Is Division crazy? That's suicide."

I stand on the top of the footlocker. "Listen up, all of you!

"Some of the LZs you will have to get into will be at the 4000-foot level, and not many of you here have ever been into an LZ that high. The air will be humid and very thin. You will run out of power quickly. Because of this, the ACL [aircraft combat loading] will be cut to four or, at most, five troops. Don't allow a greater number to board your aircraft. From what I can tell from the photographs I've just seen, these LZs will be on ridgelines, provided the Air Force people can hit the targets. They can slope toward the valley floor at thirty degrees or more. I think your chances of actually setting down in the LZs will be zilch. If you get a low rpm warning light in the LZ, you're dead men."

I sit down again and refuse to answer any more questions. The tent is awash in loud conversations. Most of the other men are sharing their personal fears with one another. Lee, Gore, and, eventually, Don Martin sit down with me. "That's a shit mission, Johnson," Don Martin volunteers.

"You're not telling me nothing I don't know, Don."

"How did you get chosen for it?"

"I don't know for sure. Hue Phu Bai, I think. Some pilots I saw at the briefing were involved in the missions I ran out of Hue Phu Bai a few weeks ago. You remember me telling you we had to McGuire-rig some of those folks out in Laos?"

"I remember. You actually think that had something to do with it?"

"Don't know for sure, but that's what it looks like."

The four of us exchange small talk for the rest of the afternoon. The entire Bandit company is on a two-day stand-down so that Lance "Stew" Stewart, the maintenance officer, can ready the tired Hueys once again for a major battle.

At about 0100 hours I can't sleep, so I walk downhill to the maintenance area near the church. When Stew is not shouting orders to his crews, he talks with me over a cup of coffee. His terse conversation is laced with real concern for the well-being of all the Bandit crews. Stew is not a line pilot and will not be participating in the actual assault. His job is to keep as many birds in the air as he can.

When Stew goes to perform a run-up of a Huey, I refill my cup. Floodlights powered by humming Army generators illuminate all the Bandit Hueys that would otherwise be cloaked in the early morning darkness. I take a casual stroll among them, stopping long enough to chat with the crew chief of each. I have flown every Bandit Huey enough hours to know it well. Each has its own unambiguous personality. Some are stronger and some weaker; some proudly sport patches that cover bullet holes—undeniable testimony to past battles. I know every crew chief by first and last name, and each man, like the Huey to which he is assigned, has his own distinct way of doing his essential job.

As I pat the cold skin of the last Huey as a man might stroke his dog or cat, I am thinking that a few of us will not be returning safely from the A Shau. I finish my last sip of coffee and retire for the night.

April 18, 1968

The day is a lazy one filled with quiet talk. Most of us write letters. It takes almost 12 days for a letter to reach home. Whatever happens tomorrow, Pat will not receive this letter until fate has taken its course. I finish the letter to her without mentioning the impending battle and my fears that this could be the last letter I will ever write. I also write to my mom and my sisters.

As I give this batch of letters to the mail clerk, I notice that the tiny mail room is filled with outgoing mail. I have had stomach butterflies before battle many times before, but this one is different and I'm not the only one who knows it.

All I have to do today is crank and fly to LZ Evans for a late afternoon briefing on my job tomorrow. The Air Force will be parachuting a directional beacon, or ADF (automatic directional finder) onto the valley floor during the night. The entire mission will depend on this navigational aid. We should be able to pick it up as we clear the 7000-foot ridge of the eastern mountain chain.

The meteorology people indicate a 90 percent chance that we will have a low cloud layer with tops somewhere near 6000 feet.

The 20 Hueys, each carrying an ACL of four engineers, will meet at the LZ Evans airfield tomorrow at 0600 hours. Just after daylight, we will depart IFR in flights of five and punch through the clouds. Once on top in clear air, we will fly west until we intercept the ADF signal. We will then disband and let down through any holes in the clouds en route to our individual target LZs. The only change from the instructions given in the original briefing is that now two Hueys are assigned to each LZ. We are told that the engineers will need eight-man teams to do their job. I personally feel this to be bullshit. The real reason is that they do not expect half of us ever to make the LZ. This plan will increase the probability that one of the two teams will get there.

Air Force and Navy high performance aircraft will support us if the weather permits. If the weather doesn't permit, we will be on our own except for a few 1/9th Huey Cobra escorts.

We are issued a case of LRRP freeze-dried rations and additional escape and survival gear. Each Huey will also be equipped with McGuire rigs, in case we have to rappel the engineers into the LZ.

My assigned target is LZ Vicki, which is high on a ridgeline in the northeast section of the valley. A major representing the EOD engineers gives me a hand-drawn sign to hold in the window during loading tomorrow. This will attract the four-man team that is assigned to my helicopter.

The insertion of the engineers into LZ Vicki will not be my only mission. I am to refuel, pick up some engineers of the 8th Engineer Battalion, and transport them to another LZ right on top of the highest peak of the easternmost ridgeline. This LZ will have been assaulted at the same time I am going into Vicki. It will become a vital link for transmissions between the valley floor and Division at LZ Evans. After four sorties in and out of this hilltop LZ, dubbed Signal Hill, I will rejoin the A/229th Bandit flight for combat assault duty.

In case I cannot get into LZ Vicki, secondary LZs—Tiger, Pepper, and Sally—are to be located and engineers inserted.

In the end, the brass finally arrives at the salty spot.

"The enemy is thought to have hand-cranked 37mm antiaircraft weapons," a colonel in clean, starched fatigues announces. "This is unconfirmed, but you will be traveling VFR on top and out of view of these gunners, if they exist."

I wonder where he is going to be when the shit hits the fan in the morning. Probably in some safe sandbag radio bunker.

The three-hour-long briefing finally ends, and we are issued detailed maps of the A Shau valley operational area. On the flight back to Quang Tri, I look intently at the whole map while the peter pilot flies. The A Shau valley is more than 4 miles across at the mountain peaks, but the valley floor is less than 1 mile wide. The tallest peak is 6800 feet; the valley floor is just above sea level.

I calculate that the flight from LZ Evans to the first mountain range will be roughly 35 minutes over dense triple-canopy jungle. I can already see that, after we get in and do the job, available fuel will be at a critical level on the flight home.

We land at LZ Sharon just before nightfall, and I, with nose still buried in the map, go directly to my tent.

The briefing generated much important data on coordinates, frequencies, and call signs. There is so much to deal with, I choose to mark with a grease pencil all the LZs and their respective data. This is an Army no-no, as the map might fall into enemy hands. However, tomorrow I will be too busy to fumble with loose papers in the cockpit, and I envision that the map will help me keep my head above water.

The mess hall remains virtually empty of aircrews on this night before the battle. Only a few move around the company area at all. Most read to pass the time; some pray with sincerity for the first time in their young adult lives.

Near lights-out, more word filters down from the radio bunker that the 1/9th has gotten their asses kicked harder today than yesterday.

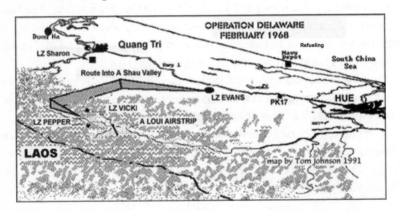

APRIL 1968 AT LZ SHARON, QUANG TRI CITY, VIETNAM. FROM LEFT TO RIGHT: BILL LEE, LARRY GORE (BACK), TOM JOHNSON, DON MARTIN .

Rumor has it that 30 aircraft have been lost, and that some of them have been hit with 37 mm radar-guided stuff. The latter I doubt—hand-cranked likely, but not radar-guided.

April 19, 1968

The CQ wakes me at 0400 hours. I get my usual cup of coffee and go quietly through the company area to the operations bunker. The other crews will not be awakened for another hour or so.

First Lieutenant Peter Kretzchmar is putting the finishing touches on his wall-sized acetate board. He has been up all night attending to the details of crew assignments—matching them to missions and to the Hueys that Lance Stewart has managed to get flyable.

"Johnson, you will be taking Rex Eastman's ship. Roger Whitman will be your peter pilot and Alfred Coleman your gunner. Any trouble with that?"

"Nope." I blow hard across the mug to cool the coffee down to a less than scalding temperature. "Eastman's ship is a good one."

"Ever flown with this new guy, Whitman?"

"Can't say as I have."

"Jackson flew with him yesterday. He said he was OK for a newbie."

"How much in-country time does he have?"

"About twenty hours, I think." Kretzchmar looks me right in the eye and does not smile.

"How did you come to pick him?"

"He's all I had left after crewing up the assault aircraft."

"What you're saying, Kretzchmar, is that you need all the experience you can muster for the assault, and we're the expendable ones."

"Something like that." He turns his back to me and begins writing on his board again.

I call Kretzchmar a very ugly name and depart the operations bunker. I can't help but get steamed up over his attitude, especially since he is not one of us. The only time he flies is to get in his required four hours for flight pay. He has never been exposed to the dangers of combat flying. I have even heard him imply that he actually falsified Army records to ensure his having enough combat time for an Air Medal.

He will be sleeping comfortably when the rest of us are flying into the A Shau valley.

During the flight from LZ Sharon to LZ Evans, I got to know Warrant Officer Roger Whitman a little. I estimate his age at 22. He graduated from Fort Rucker in the class of 68-1. After 30 days leave and some processing time through the rear-echelon Division base at An Khe, he was transported to the 1st Cavalry at LZ Evans. Eventually he found himself the newest Bandit pilot.

In accordance with tradition, a short-timer pilot starts looking for his replacement with each new pilot that arrives. On his first day, Lee gathered Whitman in and walked from tent to tent introducing the newbie as his replacement. As a by-product of this honor, Whitman has become a frequent target of Bill's mockery.

The linkup at LZ Evans's airfield goes without a hitch and we hover out for takeoff with our passengers at 0730 hours. The flight hovers into position at the east end of the hard surface runway.

"Evans tower, this is Crazy Horse Yellow One with a flight of five ready to take the active GCA departure westbound," reports the captain from the 11th Aviation Company.

"Crazy Horse Yellow One, Evans tower clears you for immediate departure runway 24. Contact Red Dog GCA on frequency 241.95 after departure for radar vectors clear of the Evans area."

"Yellow One copies."

"God's speed to all the Crazy Horse aircraft. Evans tower will be awaiting your safe return. Evans out."

The Yellow flight departs loose at first, then tucks in tight for the formation instrument climb through the clouds.

"Whitman, are you any good on the gauges?" I ask as we hover out to the end of the runway.

"I'm afraid I'm not very good, Mister Johnson. I busted my check-ride at Rucker and almost got washed out of the program."

"So did I."

"You did? Really? You're not just saying that?"

"I pink-slipped my first one. Came right back, though. Made a 97 on the next one."

Roger seems a little more relaxed knowing I am as human as he is.

I hover our Huey into the Red One position on the centerline of the runway.

"Red One, Red flight is up," comes the transmission over the FM radio from Red Five, whoever he is.

I request permission for takeoff and receive the same instructions previously issued to the Yellow flight. The Red flight tucks in very tight as we hit the soup.

Fifteen minutes later, on a westerly heading, we break out of the clouds into the clear air. Red Dog GCA maintains separation between the flights during the IFR climb. Yellow flight is slightly off to my right and about 300 yards ahead as we arrive at our cruising altitude of 7000 feet.

Below us is a shiny blanket of white clouds spread from horizon to horizon. Without the military-issue American Optical sunglasses, you can go blind quickly in the brightness. The air at this altitude is cool and crisp, in contrast to the tropical air left behind at Evans.

Ten miles ahead mountain peaks rocket skyward above the clouds. Their lush green jungle colors are breathtakingly beautiful against the snowy whiteness.

I give the controls over to Roger and break out my map.

"Chief, are the other two flights in the clear?"

"Yes, sir, Mister Johnson. They are at your six o'clock at maybe one mile and closing." His reply is distorted by the wind passing through the boom mike as he leans outside the Huey to look behind us.

"Roger, close in on the Yellow flight a little." I motion in the direction I want him to take us.

I quickly find our position using the mountain peaks as a reference and fold the map. I previously turned the ADF radio to the assigned frequency and now I turn up the volume to listen for its Morse-coded call sign. I can hear it faintly, but clearly enough to recognize the taps of the beacon-transmitted identifying letters.

The ADF is a low-frequency homing device that helps us make instrument landings through the clouds. A needle gauge in the instrument panel will point in the direction the signal is coming from. Our needle has been wavering unsteadily, but as we near the tops of the mountain range it jerks into a steady position 25 degrees left of our current route of flight.

Yellow One also picks up the signal and starts a gentle turn of his flight toward the beacon.

"Roger, zigzag a little and fall in behind the Yellow flight. I'll call the separation."

"How's the butterflies, guys?" I twist in my seat to get a visual on Eastman and Coleman.

"I'm scared shitless, sir," Eastman replies.

"Ditto, sir," Coleman offers.

"So am I. My butt has had a grip on the mesh in this seat for so long my cheeks are aching. Well, gentlemen, you are now in the infamous A Shau valley and it's *show time*." I turn my attention back to the map.

I hope my voice has not given away the fact that I really am as scared shitless as Eastman. To me, the A Shau valley is hell on earth just waiting to claim my soul. Two days ago, I made peace with myself and my God. I feel some amount of comfort knowing that whatever is about to happen is out of my control. My hand in this card game was dealt a long time ago. Now it's time to call the bet and lay down the cards. Despite this perfectly sensible attitude, I have never been more afraid in my life.

Far off in the distance, I can see two flights of F4 Phantom jets setting up for a high-speed run down the valley. There is also a heavy-

lift Sikorsky CH54 Flying Crane helicopter with a large crawler trac-
tor slung underneath it.[1] At this moment, there are no other aircraft
to be seen.

After clearing the mountains and entering the A Shau valley itself,
Yellow One descends to an altitude of 6000 feet and takes up a southwesterly heading over the center of the valley floor. We are now skimming the top of the cloud layer that obscures what lies beneath. I have
not seen a single break in the layer.

It's amazing to me that the tops of the clouds in the valley differ
from those outside it. Behind us lie rolling cumulus clouds, while inside
the A Shau the tops are perfectly flat. I've never witnessed such a phenomenon in all the years I've flown.

I look up from my map in time to see Yellow One take a 37mm hit
near the transmission mast. The transmission gears are fouled by the
hit and begin to lock up. The rotor speed slows and the Huey does a
death rollover on her right side. During the rollover a main rotor blade
strikes the tail boom and hurtles outward laterally just before she enters
the cloud layer. The luck of this Huey crew just ran out—if they are not
dead now, they will be in about 40 more seconds.

Yellow Two's cockpit erupts in black powder smoke and emits
brilliant orange phosphorescent balls that shoot some 20 feet out and
disappear rapidly in the wind. After the initial shudder, Yellow Two
enters the clouds nose first, out of control, and disappears.

First Yellow Three and then Yellow Four take violent hits and
disappear right before my eyes, going down in trails of smoke and JP4
fire. Yellow Five, apparently hit by shrapnel from the other aircraft,
enters a violent, uncontrolled left turn and disappears out of view into
the clouds below.

I am stunned. Is this for real? What just happened? Where did
they go? Ten seconds ago, there were five Hueys right there. Did they
have a midair with something? No one else has seen it. Nobody's talk-

---

1. Several days later I saw the first combat loss of a Flying Crane. It was shot in the
    cockpit with 37mm shells while sling-loading a dozer into the A Shau valley. I witnessed
    the black powder explosions and watched as the heavy-lifting helicopter continued
    flying until it crashed into the western mountain range. Twenty years later, I learned
    that the bodies of all except one of the crew were found in the crash site. The wife of
    the missing warrant officer, who was listed as missing in action, lives in Marietta,
    Georgia, less than 50 miles from Carrollton.

ing about it. Are my eyes playing tricks on my mind or did it really happen?

I am totally immobilized—unable to make a rational decision—for seconds after the incident.

"RED FLIGHT BREAK, BREAK! FLY HARD! THIRTY-SEVENS! I SAY AGAIN: THIRTY-SEVENS! YELLOW FLIGHT HIT AND GONE!" I bolt back into reality, grab the controls from Roger, and find myself unconsciously transmitting over the FM radio.

"Roger, put me on 243.00 UHF and hurry," I yell, squeezing the intercom trigger on the cyclic.

He does, as I instinctively dive the Huey at the clouds below for cover.

"ALL AIRCRAFT IN THE A SHAU VALLEY AREA. THIS IS CRAZY HORSE RED ONE TRANSMITTING ON EMERGENCY GUARD FREQUENCY. OUR POSITION IS NORTH. I SAY AGAIN: NORTH OF THE A SHAU RADIO BEACON APPROXIMATELY CEN-TER OF THE VALLEY AREA! WE HAVE BEEN ENGAGED BY HEAVY ANTIAIRCRAFT WEAPONS! FIVE HELICOPTERS LOST. I SAY AGAIN: FIVE HUEYS HIT IN MIDAIR. DOES ANYONE COPY THIS TRANSMISSION?"

The UHF bursts alive with so many acknowledgements that it quickly becomes only a squeal of feedback.

"Mister Johnson, they got the Blue!" Alfred Coleman, the gunner, reports calmly over the intercom just as I plummet headlong into the clouds at red-line speed.

"How many?"

"Sir, I saw two take direct hits and explode just as you hit the clouds. Can't see any of them right now."

"Airspeed, Mister Johnson!" an alert Roger Whitman exclaims.

Coming to my senses, I find the airspeed nearly pegged out and well above the red line. We are hurtling through the clouds out of control. The needle on the IVSI is showing a 6000-foot-per-minute rate of descent. I have never seen a Huey in this posture. I start back pressure on the cyclic to slow down and at the same time put the collective on the bottom. The latter is a mistake. The nose of the Huey begins to tuck under. I pull the cyclic rearward until it hits the travel stop. I am losing it. Eventually I will tear the main rotor blades off if I don't get her into retreating blade stall first, which will roll her upside down.

Now I do the exact opposite of the logical thing. To reduce airspeed, you naturally push down on the collective to reduce power, but I pull the collective up, thus adding power to the overhead rotor blades. It's called "tuck and roll" by some pilots and is an inherent design flaw in the Huey. At and above red-line speeds, the Huey has a tendency for the nose to tuck downward; next, the entire Huey will do a forward rollover. In the beginning of this death roll, the main rotor blades will flex downward, and when one hits the tail boom, it's all over but the impact. We are now very near entering one of these death rolls, and I can imagine the flexing rotor blades coming very near the tail boom with each rotation. To make the main rotor blades flex upward away from the tail boom, I pull up on the collective instead of pushing down. This "loads" them up and the blades' tips come away from the tail boom.

The tuck lessens, and the Huey begins to slow. With cyclic remaining at the rear stop, we finally slow below the red line. The IVSI comes through zero rate of descent into a 1000-foot-per-minute rate of climb. A short roller-coaster ride then follows until I regain control, straight and level.

I have nearly killed us in my rush to evade the enemy.

Now I decide to continue down the valley floor toward the ADF beacon. We are in the clouds, so I have no idea where we are in relation to the mountains on both sides. What I do know is that I am not going to reverse course and I am not going to climb back on top. If necessary, I will put this Huey on the ground and take my chances with the NVA.

Having no idea how low the clouds are over the valley floor, I start a controlled 1000-feet-per-minute descent with the ADF needle pointing right on the nose of the Huey. The beacon is out there somewhere ahead of us.

As the altimeter rolls through 4000 feet, the white clouds give way to dark gray rain clouds, and water droplets in sheets engulf us. We are truly sinking into Satan's backyard.

At 3500 feet above the valley floor, the solid gray clouds begin to break up. Occasionally at first, then rapidly, they split, and we are in clear air again.

There is a sense of relief in the cockpit that we have not hit anything and nothing has hit us. Yet.

The entire valley is cloaked in eerie-looking vapor that rises out of the jungles on each side. It reminds me of home in Georgia when summer rains fall on hot afternoon pavement.

The brilliant brightness of above is gone; here very little light penetrates the thick rain clouds overhead. It is as if we are on the set of some prehistoric monster movie.

Right below us is the road that runs through the length of the valley and is a main artery of the Ho Chi Minh Trail. I expect to see truck convoys, but the road is barren.

"Roger, take it and keep this heading while I try to figure out where we are."

Roger Whitman obeys without hesitation, and I unfold my map.

"We are here," I say to no particular person. "We are further north than I anticipated. LZ Vicki is right over there somewhere." I point 20 degrees east from our present ground track. "The thing should be at the 3000-foot level on the mountainside. Coleman, do you see anything?"

"No, sir."

"Roger, head in that general direction."

I become aware of what I'm doing, and it's unbelievable. We narrowly escaped death only moments ago; I nearly killed everyone aboard in a wild panic to flee for my life; and here I am setting up for an approach into the target LZ, as if it were a milk run.

I have also completely forgotten about our four passengers and the purpose of this whole ride. I glance rearward at the engineers. They catch my movement, and each man turns to meet me eyeball to eyeball. Their distraught faces show their shared concern about what the hell has been going on. They have not been privy to any radio conversations, so it is a good possibility that they did not see the Yellow flight die. For all they know, we are taking some type of evasive action.

"Chief, you and Coleman tell whoever is in charge that we are about two minutes out and that the LZ is most likely hot."

"Roger, sir."

My instructions are to get them into the LZ by whatever means possible, wait on them to do their job, and to extract them. While we are doing this we will be a target like a quail in a South Georgia bird shoot.

"Mister Johnson, they want to know if they will have to rappel."

"Don't know yet. Go ahead and tell them yes."

Promptly there is shuffling behind me. The engineers are busy readying the McGuire equipment and attaching the chain saws and C4 plastic explosives for the drop.

As we approach the ridgeline at an altitude of 3200 feet, we are barely skirting the bottom of the cloud layer overhead. Based on the magnetic bearing of the ADF needle, I'm guessing that we should soon be coming up on a large hole that's been blown open in the triple-canopy jungle.

"Roger, slow it down and head a little more right."

"I think I see it." Roger says sharply. "Right over there. What do you think?" He is pointing to a place where the greenery suddenly seems to recede. We cannot go higher to validate that this is the LZ.

"Drag it. Let's take a look-see. Chief, you and Coleman get ready. This could be some major storage area or something that belongs to the bad guys. May not be what we're looking for."

We drag it as we approach the area, going low and slow, as cautiously as we can and are surprised to find that another Huey of the original Crazy Horse flight is already hovering in our LZ. Either it is our sister ship or someone else has picked the wrong LZ to land in. Right now it doesn't matter. At least someone else has made it into the valley.

Coleman waves at the other crew as we pass by. Unable to land, they are at a high hover as they rappel their passengers.

"Roger, give me a right three-sixty and set up for another drag. Maybe this guy will be out of the LZ when you get back around. Stay in close. The bad guys are out here somewhere." Whitman racks us into a hard right turn. I draw close on the controls and follow each of his moves without impeding them.

We have just reversed our direction and I am estimating our altitude to be 300 feet when a frightening sound fills my ears.

These are not the *tics* of small-caliber rounds passing through the fuselage; this is a sound unlike anything I have heard before. Our Huey is being slammed repeatedly by large-caliber rounds. I hear loud popping noises similar to compressor stalls emanating from our turbine engine, then a belch, after which the high-pitched whine I am so accustomed to fades into a nightmarish silence.

345

"I HAVE IT, ROGER . . . LET GO!" I scream, and Warrant Officer Whitman releases the Huey's controls.

I slam the collective to the bottom to enter autorotation and break hard left in the direction of the valley floor, only to see that my luck has just run out. We are too low and too slow.

If you have an engine failure over trees and there is positively nowhere else to go, first commit to the most survivable spot you can see. Don't panic. You may not be able to prevent hitting the trees but you can still control how hard you hit.

Don't enter the trees level as the Army says to do. All Hueys are nose-heavy. If you go in level, the Huey's nose will tuck under as you fall through. You will most likely end up on your back as you strike the ground. This aircraft will take a lot of pounding on the skid side, but it will fold up like an accordion if you hit top side first. If the latter should happen, you will not survive.

Hit the trees talking to and looking at God.

If this should occur on a mountainside, do not attempt to hit the trees going downhill, or else you will roll up in a ball the minute the tail boom strikes the first obstruction. Fly into the mountain.

Out of the depths of my fear and desperation, these procedures, which Ross L. Pentecost, my first Huey instructor pilot, taught me one day while we practiced autorotations at Hanchey Army Air Field, flash like neon. I listened to these words, as I listened to every word from this man whose knowledge and flying abilities I regarded with so much admiration, but I had no idea how deeply this advice was burned into my mind—or how critical it would be to me at this moment.

A hard left, nose-low, 180-degree autorotative turn uses up what separation there was between us and the jungle canopy below. In an instant, the entire windscreen is filled with the mountain that lies before us.

I pitch the Huey in the vertical with my remaining airspeed—to an upright attitude I have never been in before. I can see only dark gray clouds. Out of airspeed and altitude, Rex Eastman's pride and joy slips earthward, tail first.

As I manipulate the controls to no avail, I realize that I am no longer a helicopter pilot: I have become a passenger like the others.

"KEEP IT UP, MISTER JOHNSON . . . DEAR GOD, KEEP IT UP!" comes the blood-chilling wail of Alfred Coleman.

As the tail boom makes contact with the first earthly object, I squeeze my eyes tightly shut. Then come the sounds of the aircraft being ripped apart.

Violent gyrations sling my head and arms all about the cockpit. I feel like a rag doll in a nightmare, trapped in a metal coffin falling off a cliff toward the jungle floor. My brain can process no more of this and simply shuts itself down.

Consciousness returns, but my mind has yet to catch up with reality. Slowly at first, then in a hailstorm, my body is sending signals of pain.

As my blurred vision clears, I find myself staring at unfamiliar scenery immediately off the nose of the Huey. A falling object lands on the instrument console with a loud thud.

Memory finally locks in, and I realize where I am now and what I was doing a few moments ago.

All is quiet until a leg falls across the radio console. It does not remain stationary but makes jerking motions as it attempts to get a foothold in the instrument panel.

I look and see Roger Whitman slowly removing his helmet and letting it fall to the chin bubble.

The Huey is resting gently on her nose. Roger and I are weightless, suspended in midair by our shoulder and lap harnesses. The pain I feel is from my shoulders being bent backward as my body weight is pulled toward the ground below.

I unbuckle the chin strap on my helmet and painfully remove it. During the struggle, I happen to look through the clear plastic "greenhouse" panels. Normally they provide a vertical view, but in our current position I am looking laterally.

My eyes must be deceiving me. Underneath the darkness of the vegetation is a clothesline full of drying garments. As my eyes adjust to the darkness, I catch movement in the shadows slightly to the right.

I can now see a uniformed individual in the squatting position eating something out of a bowl. As I scan left, there are at least three more individuals, one of whom is standing. A small charcoal campfire is warming the contents of smoke-dulled tin cans and separates the three on the left from the one on the right.

I use my elbow to nudge Whitman to look up. He becomes suddenly still when he catches the sight.

There is a hot rush of blood throughout my body as all my mental turbine wheels ramp up to 103 percent. I hear my heart beating in my ears.

At the same time, survival instincts freeze my every muscle. I pretend that if I do not make a sudden movement, maybe these guys will just go away like a bad dream.

There is a sudden jerking motion behind my seat, and loud groaning follows.

So much for being invisible. Until now the three NVA individuals have remained perfectly frozen as though in a photograph. This begins to change as the one on the right, who is closest to us, smoothly begins the forward motion of his arms to place the bowl on the ground before him.

So far there is no reason for panic. I'm sure these guys are just as surprised at our unannounced arrival into their camp as we are.

My head remains perfectly still as my eyes rapidly scan the encampment. Slightly to the right, at arm's length from the first individual, an AK-47 fully automatic assault rifle leans against a tree, butt on the ground, barrel aimed skyward.

"Out of here, people . . . we have bad guys outside. Carefully, just get the hell out of here now," I say softly but firmly as I release the one buckle that binds both my lap and shoulder harnesses.

My movement is definitely a hostile one as far as the other guys are concerned. With his bowl now firmly on the ground the NVA on the far right bolts toward his AK-47, his body outstretched in midair.

"*OH, JESUS . . . BAIL OUT . . . BAIL OUT!*" I scream at the top of my lungs, as diplomacy is no longer a factor.

It is every man for himself. Now standing erect, using the Huey's pedals as my platform, I pull the emergency door release at the same time as my shoulder hits the door. It falls free and I land on top of it outside the aircraft.

"Rifle! Rifle!" I tell myself and spin backward, pivoting on my stomach. I then reach for my Korean vintage M2 carbine, which is always my flying companion; in my hurry to get out, I have forgotten and left it in the Huey, where it now lies half in and half out of the doorway. I always keep two cloth bandoliers consisting of about 200 rounds each tied to the weapon. Foolishly I stand up and snatch it clear, then do the fastest low crawl of my young life—away from the

Huey and into thick underbrush some 12 feet away, only to be passed by two of the engineers and Alfred Coleman running hunched down.

All four of us attempt to occupy the same spot at the same time. Other places to hide are abundant, and why we four pick the same spot is a mystery we don't have time to dwell on.

Not a single round has yet been fired. The sounds of struggling for cover are replaced by those of heavy breathing and hearts thumping.

"What did you see, Mister Johnson?" the engineer at my right shoulder whispers.

"You didn't see them?"

"See who?"

"Three, maybe four, gooks right there." I point.

The engineer carefully lifts his helmetless head up a few inches and leans to his left to clear the leaf of a large tropical plant behind which we are hiding.

"Damn. Looks like they were drying some laundry." He nudges the other engineer and points.

"What do you think, Mister Johnson? How come they're not shooting?"

WARRANT OFFICER TOM JOHNSON SITTING IN THE COCKPIT OF A HUEY JUST BEFORE TAKEOFF IN 1968. NOTE THE M2 CARBINE, WHICH WAS INSTRUMENTAL IN SAVING HIS LIFE AFTER THE CRASH IN THE A SHAU VALLEY. **FROM THE ARCHIVES OF TOM JOHNSON**

I can only shake my head; I have no idea. Glancing at Coleman, I observe that he does not have a weapon.

"Coleman, where's your M16?"

As he raises his head to look forlornly at the wrecked Huey, it is evident that Coleman has not registered his deficiency until I mentioned it. It doesn't matter where he secured the gun before the crash. Now the flash suppressor on its barrel can be seen sticking out from the tangle of other equipment that has fallen in the cargo compartment behind my seat.

Now that I'm looking up, I can see just how lucky we are to be alive. The Huey has fallen straight down some 300 feet through a triple canopy of tropical tree limbs and vines. It is wrapped in vines, some of which are 4 inches in diameter, like a fly in a spiderweb. I surmise that the vines saved our lives by restricting the velocity of our fall to the jungle floor.

I can now see the Huey's mortal wounds. The engine cowlings were ripped away by the fall, revealing one hole in the Lycoming that is at least 8 inches across. Several feet lower and more to the rear, at a point were the tail boom is attached to the main fuselage, another hole was created when the metal skin imploded. This hole is also about 8 inches in diameter. This is clear evidence of a large-caliber, high-velocity shell hit. This was 37mm stuff, but why did the shells pass clean through rather than explode on impact?

A minute passes and everything remains deathly still—no movements and no sounds except the occasional creaking of the vines. Finally, tired of holding their burden, they begin popping as they stretch earthward under the Huey's weight.

Thick gray smoke floats skyward from the engine compartment, and the air is heavy with the smell of JP4 jet fuel leaking from the ruptured fuel bladder.

I motion for Coleman to draw nearer.

"You need that weapon, son."

A pained look crosses his face, but he surveys his chances without it and nods his head in agreement.

"Cover him," I whisper.

The standard pilot weapons are .38 Smith & Wesson revolvers, not fully automatic weapons like the M16 and the M2. My Korean-era

M2 carbine was a gift I received some months ago. A sniper narrowly missed a company commander as I was landing him at one of his units in the field. While I made an expeditious departure, the sniper's location was identified and 180 M16s were aimed at him all at one time. The sniper did not survive, but his carbine did. The major was black and blue from ricocheting all about the cargo compartment, but he felt that I had saved his life and pronounced the captured weapon mine to keep. I haven't flown without it since.

Maybe the bad guys have fled, but I doubt it very much; this is their backyard, and we are the intruders. But I still can't comprehend why they haven't launched a single round.

Slowly at first, then as rapidly as his body can travel, Coleman approaches the Huey at a low crawl and enters the cargo area. He grasps the M16 and fumbles among the other objects until he finds a metal box containing several cloth bandoliers of M16 ammo. Without incident, he crawls back to our position.

I have no idea where Roger Whitman and Rex Eastman are, or whether they have been injured in the crash. One thing is for sure: they'd better be on this side of the Huey, or we might end up shooting at each other.

I whisper their names several times, and two heads expose themselves from the underbrush on the other side of the aircraft. I motion them to make their way around the underside of the Huey and join us. As they crawl rapidly, the rest of us scan the landscape everywhere, looking for the bad guys.

With all eight of us now in close proximity, the engineers deploy themselves in a tiny perimeter. I notice a thick, moss-covered tree trunk on the ground about 10 feet to my left, and I motion for Coleman to follow me as I crawl behind the log.

I guess the NVA have been watching us all the time and are just as scared to do battle at such close range. I manage to move a couple of feet when the silence is shattered by a burst of AK-47 bullets.

My heart stops, but the rest of my anatomy goes into maximum overdrive. From the prone position, I make the back side of the log . . . a distance of more than 5 feet . . . in one leap. Coleman piles in right on top just as eight or ten bullets tear into the log.

They must have thought we were attempting some outflanking

maneuver when, in fact, we were taking up defensive positions. The irony of this is not something I dwell on. We are engaged with other human beings whose intent is to terminate our lives, and they just made this evident.

Before the bullets whizzed by my head only heartbeats ago, I could not fathom pulling down on another person and squeezing off a round. Before now it has been crew chiefs and gunners who have dispatched projectiles that ripped through flesh.

This firefight will be at very close range, and it will end with death on one side or the other.

None of us dares to raise his head to return fire while 100 AK-47 bullets per second split the air all around us.

The firing tapers off from many AK-47s to only one. All at once, we return fire in their direction.

The engineers, who are behind Coleman and me, fire M16 bullets right over our heads as rapidly as the gooks sent theirs in. The last AK-47 goes silent, and I assume he dove for cover.

Without thinking about it, I hurriedly crawl the length of the fallen log. At the end I take a quick peek, then jerk my head back. I could see nothing. "Try it again," my deranged mind tells my body. As the body is doing this, the other guys let loose with another volley.

This time the peek pays off. I gain a vivid image of one of the bad guys, not 40 feet away, firing from a squatting position. Most of him is behind a very large banana tree leaf; only his head, shoulders, and AK-47 are in the clear.

Now insane with fear, I roll out from behind the log, John Wayne–style, and pull the trigger of the M2 carbine. The carbine has never failed to fire, and it doesn't let me down now.

Everyone else starts shooting at the first sound of the M2.

Everything seems to be happening in slow motion. The other individual and I make eye contact as my first rounds rip through the vegetation slightly to his right. Realizing his failure to take into account all possibilities, he adjusts his body to fire at me. I adjust my trajectory.

The M2's rounds find their target first, and the green banana leaf vomits forth blood and body parts. I dive back to the safety of the log.

Now that I have made the kill, anger surges over my fear. I go out of control. I yell obscenities aloud at my adversaries, growl loudly like a dog, and beat the barrel of the M2 against the log as if it were a battle drum. All this seems to me like the appropriate thing to do.

Coleman, right next to me, is clearly wondering if I have gone off the deep end. It is an obvious concern to him that further crazed actions from me might seriously threaten his safety.

Seconds pass into minutes, and silence fills the air; neither we nor the "bad guys" choose to exchange further lead.

My adrenaline level is ten of a possible ten. My heart is still beating in my eardrums and, for fear of being heard breathing, breaths are few and far between.

Minutes turn into hours. We are afraid to move and afraid not to. I make a hand motion that I saw once in the movies, and everyone seems to know what I mean. The eight of us huddle together at the other end of the log.

"What do you people think?" I say.

One of the engineers, a Sergeant Ramey, replies in a low voice, "Well, Mister Johnson, I don't exactly understand what they are up to. I figure there are ten or more out there. I can't figure out why they haven't hit us hard yet."

"Mister Johnson, they may be taking their time to outflank us or to wait for reinforcements," another of the engineers volunteers.

I mention the M60s still attached to the downed Huey, but we agree that it is too risky to attempt to retrieve them. The guns are some 8 feet in the air and still attached to their bungie cords, so it would take a good minute of exposure, not to mention unbuckling the ammo box from its mount. The NVA are certainly not going to stand still while we try it, and none of us wants to be a dead hero.

"You think we should move?"

"Yes, sir," Ramey and the other engineer reply as one.

I remember from escape and survival training back at Fort Rucker that there is a better chance of being rescued if we remain with the aircraft. I also remember the old Army saying, "Do as the situation dictates."

"OK. Let's kick it around with the rest of the guys."

Ramey and the other engineer crawl down the log to take a survey of opinions. The thought of moving my ass to a safer part of the jungle is appealing to me, but I have no idea which direction would be safer.

"My map."

"Map? Sir, what map?" Coleman replies to my thinking out loud.

I crawl down the log toward the Huey. As I pass the others, I find them in agreement that we cannot stay here any longer. At the end of the log, I motion for Ramey and the other three engineers to follow me. The four of us crawl into our original hiding place in the vegetation that is the cover closest to the Huey.

I poke my head out and examine the aircraft commander's side of the Huey.

"There it is," I whisper. I point to the clear plastic chin bubble.

"There what is, sir?" Ramey asks, raising his head to see.

"Our ticket home. In the chin bubble. My map."

Ramey strains to see and the others do likewise.

"Any of you guys got a compass?"

"Yes, sir, I have one," an engineer named Wilson replies. He reaches deep into the knee pocket of his fatigue pants. "I found it, Mister Johnson." He produces an Army-issue plastic compass and offers it to Ramey to hand to me.

"Keep it, Sergeant Wilson. Hang on to it for dear life." I again direct my attention to the cleared ground that lies between me and the Huey.

"What d'you think, Ramey?"

"I don't know, sir," Ramey replies with a broad grin. "Did your momma raise any heroes?"

"All the heroes I know are dead men, Sergeant Ramey, and that's what we'll be if I don't get that map. We'll never find our way out of here without it."

"What about waiting for night?"

"The way I got it figured, we'll be very lucky not to get lost in broad daylight. Traveling at night will be impossible in this snake-infested jungle. Don't you agree?"

"You're probably right, Mister Johnson." Ramey is not smiling now.

"Don't fire unless they do, but cover me good if the shit hits the fan. OK?"

"Yes, sir. We'll get it done."

Ramey deploys Wilson and the other two using hand signals, and I wait until each finds his spot. Ramey then gives me the hand signal to go.

My heart again races as I build up the fortitude to make the 20-foot dash across the clearing. I take one last look at the others, who are looking back at me. Ramey nods his head.

Low crawling is out as far as I'm concerned. Charlie has a free field of fire from his position, which is on higher ground than the downed Huey. I rise to a squatting position, then put one foot in front of the other, slowly at first until I clear the low vegetation. Once in the clearing, I remain hunched over; I shuffle my feet as fast and as quietly as I can. I am on tiptoes, moving at maximum speed, trying to be invisible.

I reach the Huey and lie flat on the earth. I thought I was scared before.

After a few seconds during which no shots are fired, I ease up and into the open doorway. The upper part of my body is now fully exposed. Aware that you never hear the shot that kills you, I stretch my right arm deep into the chin bubble. I fumble a while among the debris that has ended up on top of the map, until I finally feel its acetate cover, and using a firm grip, I slowly remove it, being careful not to let anything else fall into its space. I again lie flat and listen for any encroaching movements from the bad guys. When I hear none, I rotate on my belly and look around on the ground for anything that might be to our advantage. Just out of arm's reach is a cardboard case of LRRP rations that Rex Eastman has stored on his Huey. I look for the jerry can that contains the water, but it is nowhere in sight. I also think of the C4 plastic explosives on board, but as I look up along the axis of the Huey, I can see no way to get inside and out again safely. I won't be taking the risk of searching for the explosives.

I crawl some 5 or 6 feet to retrieve the case of LRRP rations and tuck it underneath my right arm. Then I turn in the direction of Ramey and the rest, who are waiting nervously for me to make my return trip.

Slowly I rise again to the squatting posture and start to move one step at a time.

Dirt flies up in my face before I hear the sound. The world all around me fills with the noise of AK-47s hammering in unison, followed immediately by M16s returning the fire.

I am caught out in the opening. I run as fast as I can without standing up. As I near the edge of the clearing, I throw the cardboard case into Ramey's position and make a headlong dive for cover. Once inside the bushes, I scramble to find my M2 carbine, which I purposely left behind.

By the time I locate it, the firing has stopped.

Breathless, I lie on my back trying to cope with the situation, telling myself that this is only a nightmare and I will awake from it any time now.

These thoughts are shattered by another burst of AK-47 fire, and this time I hear the bullets traveling just above my head as they cut through the vines.

"TWELVE O'CLOCK! TWELVE O'CLOCK!" Wilson yells as he opens up in an entirely new direction. The VC have managed to quietly maneuver to the downhill slope right underneath the Huey and are within 10 yards of where I had lain not two minutes ago.

I surmise that they did in fact see me as I headed for the Huey and deployed to cut me down at close range. Had I waited another minute before leaving, I would have been history.

I fire in anger. With no concern for conserving precious ammo, I let the M2 rock and roll on full automatic until the 32-round banana clip is spent.

Things again get quiet. I hurriedly break open my first ammo pouch from the bandolier and reload the clip.

"They're trying to get around us, sir," Wilson whispers.

"I know," I reply, though I am too busy reloading to look up.

When the clip is replenished, I unfold the precious map. Glad that I have marked the map with all the LZs, call signs, and frequencies, I digest its information.

"We are about here." I finger an imaginary spot and Ramey looks over. "LZ Vicki is here."

"That's only one click or so uphill, wouldn't you say?"

"Yeah, something like that. But all uphill and through this dense foliage, it will take us a while to get there."

"Do you think our guys have landed there yet?" Wilson inquires over Ramey's shoulder.

"Nope. They should have landed about two hours after we got into the LZ, but I can tell you for sure they didn't."

"Have any idea why?" Ramey asks.

"I'd say they've called off the attack."

"Called it off?"

"Damn, Wilson, as far as I know everyone except us and the bird we saw sitting in the LZ has been shot down. I know for sure there are five down. The entire lead flight got hit at altitude with 37mm. I suspect that Black Horse is reconsidering the whole thing since we've run into this radar-guided stuff."

"You mean they may not come in at all?" Ramey's eyes show a new desperation.

"Possible. One thing for sure, they haven't landed in Vicki yet."

"So what do you think we should do?"

"Vicki is all we have. At least it's a spot on the map that the Cav knows about, and it's a clearing. If we can make it, maybe we can build a fire or something. Damn!"

"What is it?" Wilson jerks his M16 close, first glancing at me and then out into the clearing.

"All the pencil flares are still in the Huey." I raise my head to look in the direction of the downed bird. "I wish I'd thought of that while I was there."

"Sir, it's a good thing you didn't think of them else the bad guys would've been close enough to hand the whole box to you." Ramey smiles as he speaks.

Glancing in the direction of the log, I can see Roger Whitman, Rex Eastman, and Alfred Coleman still huddled up together. They are glancing repeatedly in our direction and obviously wondering what we are talking about.

I motion for Ramey and the rest to join them. One by one, the four of us do a fast low crawl to the log as the others intently survey the underbrush and ready themselves to return fire if necessary.

Safely on the uphill side of the large log, we huddle and tell the rest of my crew what we are considering.

"We have to leave here now," I tell them. "Do you agree?" Every team member agrees. I add, "The bad guys have already moved on the downhill side and may already be on the uphill side. I figure they're waiting for help to arrive so they can get us in a cross fire. What do you think, Ramey?"

"I agree, Mister Johnson. Uphill is our only way out."

"Wilson, where's the compass?"

"Here you go." Wilson passes his prized possession over to me.

"Well, it won't take a compass to tell us that we have to go up this damn mountain, but when we get in striking distance, it will come in very handy," I say. I place the compass, with the folded map, in the side pocket of my jungle trousers.

We recheck our ammo and ourselves for a few brief minutes. When all seems the best we can make it, I receive another simple nod from Ramey to go.

"OK. Trail formation with thirty-second separation. Let's move out." Because my crew and I are still wearing our flak vests, I reluctantly order myself to the lead, followed by them. Ramey, Wilson, and the other two engineers will cover our retreat by falling in line behind us.

I feel that the first 20 yards will be the difference between life and death. As I assume my half crouch and start making my way up the incline I believe that each step will be my last.

Sounds that would otherwise have been meaningless, such as the crunching of dried leaves or the muffled crack of a small twig under my boot, now resonate like artillery going off.

Our route leads us immediately into thicker jungle filled with bushes bearing unnaturally large fernlike leaves. I keep expecting to brush away one of these leaves and expose my adversary standing with an AK-47 pointed in my face.

I look back and realize that the NVA will have no trouble following us. There is no way to prevent blazing a trail. Thick virgin grass that has been pushed aside by our bodies remains spread even after we have passed through it.

The walk is painfully slow. Vines and underbrush tangle our feet, choke our necks, and render our arms useless by handcuffing them to every bush we pass. I become so entangled that I fall on my face again and again, only to rise to my feet each time with the help of Roger Whitman.

The tropical heat magnifies itself as the overhead jungle canopy refuses to allow the 102-degree heat and 95 percent humidity to escape. The last time I saw the sky was when I looked up at the hole created by the Huey on its way down. Although it is semi-daylight with rain clouds above, our area of operation is in twilight.

After about 40 minutes of bushwhacking, I am exhausted and have to sit. I make a hand signal for the rest to close ranks and form a tight perimeter. No one has spoken a single word since our journey began.

My jungle fatigues are wringing wet with perspiration. I am breathing deeply under my cupped hand, which serves not only to hold down the noise but also to keep the millions of mosquitoes and other bugs that have descended on us from entering my mouth. I dare not swat at anything, lest the sharp movement further give our position away.

Now that we are noiseless, I feel cloaked by the jungle and safe for the moment. My thoughts rush back to the jerry can of water. I could sure use a drink of water right now, and I consider how bad my thirst is going to get as time goes on. I also consider that if we had it, one of us would have to be toting the heavy metal can; and there would be the cowbell effect as it banged into vines and branches.

Suddenly there is a snap followed by another loud snap, then a sound like a tarpaulin being dragged over a bush. We dive for the dirt. I find myself lying on my back; I don't dare roll over. I have a clear view downhill of the trail we just created, and I strain my eyes to pick up anything moving. I realize just how stupid I was not to have slithered into the nearby underbrush. At great risk, I roll over, placing my weight upon my elbows and heels. Without raising my chest I ease off the trail without making a sound. Though the trail is now devoid of people, it does end at my doorstep.

I position my M2 for firing. Droplets of sweat run off my nose and onto the wooden stock pressed tightly against my cheek.

I am hoping that the noises emanated from some large animal, when first one, then three more M16s rattle on full automatic. I twitch so hard I nearly pull off a burst of the M2, but manage to release pressure on the trigger just in time. The engineers on the downhill side of the perimeter have definitely found something to shoot at, and it has fewer than four legs.

No AK-47s fire back, and the M16s go silent. I low crawl out of the underbrush and regain my original prone position in the trail. From here I can see Sergeant Ramey some 10 yards down the trail. Once eye contact is established with him, I motion for us to move out and he motions to his people. I feel that we must move quickly now that we have been found.

Again standing erect, I motion for Whitman, Eastman, and Coleman to come out. Turning uphill again, I move through the underbrush ahead as quietly as I can. Maybe my enemy hasn't found a route through the jungle to cut us off, and if that is true, heading up this caravan will not be as dangerous as bringing up the rear.

We push and shove ahead for another two hours, and it feels as if we barely cover the length of three football fields. I am bleeding from so many cuts that I have to use my jungle fatigue jacket to wipe the blood off the stock of the carbine to prevent it from slipping out of my grasp. Thorns have slashed gaping holes in my trousers, leaving bleeding white skin exposed.

I alternate point with Rex Eastman, who has volunteered. Another three hours pass, and the sun sets early behind the mountains on the western side of the A Shau valley. The temperature drops 15 degrees within 15 minutes after sunset. Our wet uniforms feel uncomfortably cold.

The jungle suddenly ends at a clearing full of 8-foot-high elephant grass. Here we can now look up at a clear sky that is barren of clouds. Early afternoon stars are already out, and the last golden rays of the setting sun are shooting across the purple- and magenta-colored sky.

Standing at the edge of the grassy plain, I am mentally and physically exhausted; I feel that I cannot take another step. If we are jumped, I will just have to shoot it out with the bad guys right here.

I motion to close it up for a powwow. We all kneel in a huddle with our faces close together and discuss our situation in whispers.

We come up with a plan.

On first sight, elephant grass seems to be one of God's mistakes. It looks like any grass you might plant back in the States, but it grows to gargantuan heights. It looks lovely from the air, but its overgrown blades are razor sharp and very noisy to walk through. All of this will fit in with our plan, which is good, because it's the only plan we can think of.

With Rex Eastman leading the way, we thrash about 100 yards straight ahead, then make a U-turn to backtrack on a parallel course that is only 10 feet outside our original trail. Satisfied that we are in a favorable ambush position, we lie down to rest. We remain within arm's length of each other so that we can communicate by touch during the night. Sergeant Ramey volunteers for the first guard watch.

One of the engineers has transported the LRRP rations box strapped to his back with a vine. We now quietly open it and survey its contents. I feel we should eat right away, before the bad guys catch up. To my surprise, the box contains C rations, not LRRP rations. Unlike C rations, LRRP rations are primarily pouches of freeze-dried food that require water we don't have.

Using the Army-issued P38 can opener, I open a can of peaches and drink its sweet juice, then devour a can of SPAM and follow it with the wet peaches. "How many VC did you see back there, Sergeant Ramey?"

"Four, sir. But I'm sure there are several more I couldn't see behind them."

"Did you get any of them?"

"We laid two down, I'm sure." Ramey continues to devour his canned pound cake without looking up. Each of us finishes one meal box, and the case is resealed for transport. The empty tin cans are carefully secured so we won't accidentally kick one at the wrong moment.

Cloaked in silence and darkness, I feel safer now than at any time since I departed Evans this morning. Believing that I can only allow myself to doze lightly, I rest my head in the matted wet grass and look into the heavens. Stars are twinkling as though nothing is wrong. Thoughts of Pat turn into a dream, and I fall into deep sleep.

I jerk awake; Ramey has gently touched my arm. Lying perfectly still, I can hear the elephant grass moving under footsteps.

I quietly roll to my left and shake Roger Whitman gently. He also departs the safety of dreamland and reenters the danger of our reality. Roger passes the awakening down the line.

The Charlies, as expected, are tailing us, using darkness as cover. They have fallen into our trap.

I quietly push the M2's safety to the off position just as the first one creeps by, not more than 5 feet from my position.

The engineers have suggested that we let as many as possible go by and take out those at the end of the formation first. This will give us some idea of how many we are dealing with, and it will give us a chance to escape before the others can figure out where the rounds came from. We will open up only after Ramey shoots first.

When I awakened, only seconds ago, this Vietnam night was cold. Now I am having hot flashes and my trigger finger is damp with perspiration.

I count five individuals, separated from each other by 6 or 7 yards, before Ramey springs the trap.

When Ramey's M16 fires the first round, my finger is so tight on the trigger that I jerk from the noise, which causes my M2 to fire a mere fraction of a second later.

Sweeping left, then to the right and back again, we have them in a blistering cross fire. The grass that stood up before me explodes into fine particles.

I hear hard thumps as bullets tear through human clothing and one ringing sound that is most likely a round hitting the metal barrel of an AK-47.

I expend the 32-round clip of the M2 and hastily grab my .38-caliber pistol out of my shoulder holster. By this time, the firing has stopped up and down the line.

Calm replaces chaos, and I strain to hear the sounds of those who got by us racing back to enter the firefight. We lie still for a full 30 seconds, but the only sound I hear is one weak moan from the trail.

Ramey touches my shoulder and gestures toward the rear with his hand. I pass the signal down the line. Sergeant Wilson, who is on the opposite end of our formation, now becomes "point man."

Wilson moves straight across the open trail and into the elephant grass on the other side. One by one, the men follow right behind him. The sounds of movement through the grass are loud enough to draw

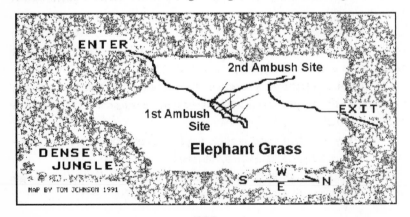

fire, though the enemy might not be able to pinpoint their origin just yet. When it comes my turn to fall in I am totally bewildered as to why they have not counterattacked.

Now last in our column, I hug the ground as closely as possible and snake through the new trail created by Wilson. Wilson's trail ends in another right-hand U-turn, thus setting up a second ambush site 40 or so yards uphill from the original one. Finally things are quiet again, and I hurriedly reload the M2's magazine, one round at a time.

Throughout the rest of the night, we remain vigilant but uneasy. The Viet Cong, for some unknown reason, do not return.

April 20, 1968

Little by little, darkness gives way to daylight. We wait patiently to see if the enemy will come in the daylight.

At about 0800 hours, I speak my first words since early last night.

"Ramey, we have got to get out of here," I whisper.

"Yes, sir, I know that, but there are at least five bad guys with us somewhere in this patch of grass." His eyes are bloodshot from lack of sleep.

"I know that, but some Cobra crew might fly over and mistake *us* for the bad guys."

Ramey thrusts his eyes skyward; he hasn't considered that.

Even from a close study of the contours on the map, I can't figure out even our approximate position. We will have to clear this elephant grass first. I know only that moving northeast will take us closer to LZ Vicki. I check the compass and point northeast. Ramey takes point, followed by me, Roger Whitman, Rex Eastman, and the rest.

We sound like a combine in a Georgia wheat field, as Ramey leads us through the tall grass. I fear that any second AK-47 rounds will cut us down along with the grass, but we have to move on.

After nearly three hours, we clear the grass and reenter the relative darkness of the jungle. Exhausted, we pause to rest some 20 yards into the underbrush.

"Ramey, I've got to get high enough to get a reading on our position." I am looking around for a tall tree.

"Try that one, sir. Right over there." Ramey is pointing to a large vine-covered tree about 20 feet away.

Using all the strength I have left and a boost from several others, I manage to claw my way up the moss-laden tree. Carefully, limb by limb and vine by vine, I arrive at a point some 50 feet above the jungle floor that affords me a reasonably good vantage point.

Unmistakably, the A Shau valley lies downhill to my west. I study the lay of the sharply angled terrain all around me. When I am reasonably sure that the ridgeline I am looking at is the one that contains LZ Vicki, I shimmy down the tree and out of the sunlight.

"How does it look?" Rex Eastman asks, handing me an open can of peaches. Too exhausted to answer him, I choose to drink the sweet juice first.

"We're about one click due south of the LZ." I take out the compass and let the needle steady up.

"It's that way." I point my arm while alternately checking the compass and the direction. "We can make it in a few more hours."

I return the compass to my trouser pocket and continue devouring the peaches.

The others allow me to finish eating and catch my breath before their edginess at sitting in one place too long becomes unbearable.

We move out with Sergeant Wilson on point and me on rear guard. As we make our way through the lush green jungle, I stop just long enough to listen for any noises from behind us. Hearing nothing, I rush to catch up with the column again.

After about three hours, the terrain inclines sharply skyward. We pause to rest.

"This must be the ridgeline," I whisper to whoever is nearby as I extract my map. "I think we must be about here."

"Is that Vicki?" Alfred Coleman asks, pointing to a single grease-pencil dot on the spine of the ridgeline.

"Correct," I reply. "That's LZ Vicki." I motion for Ramey to join us.

"Sergeant Ramey, this is where we are, and this is LZ Vicki."

"We are close, aren't we?" Ramey raises his helmet slightly to let the hot air escape from underneath it.

"I suggest we continue to climb to the ridgeline and travel down the back of it. That way we'll be sure not to miss it."

"I agree, Mister Johnson. Do you think they've assaulted it yet?"

"No. Vicki has not been assaulted yet or we would have heard the heavy stuff when it hit the LZ."

"Sir, do you think our guys will assault it?" Roger Whitman is asking the sixty-four-thousand-dollar question.

"Can't say for sure, Roger."

Whitman's face turns serious at the thought of being permanently MIA.

"Time to go, folks," I order. I stand up shakily.

The terrain leading to the spine of the ridgeline is very steep; at times we must be on all fours to make any forward progress at all. We use scattered low vines to pull ourselves through the loose soil, where it's hard to get a foothold.

At the top, we turn left and follow the ridgeline as it angles uphill to a peak for another two hours.

It is about three in the afternoon when Sergeant Wilson pushes out of the underbrush, and we catch our first sight of LZ Vicki.

About 100 yards dead ahead, on the other side of a dip in the ridgeline, is a vast expanse of exposed dirt. The ten-thousand-pound bomb produced only a shallow crater, but it destroyed all vegetation; we are looking at an LZ some 30 feet across. Trees at ground zero are splintered into toothpicks. Away from the crater, trees have been knocked down and out; their bases point to a common center, like spokes of a wheel.

"Look—no stumps," I say.

"Stumps?" Wilson turns around to see what I'm talking about.

"No stumps. The other team got in OK."

On closer inspection, we can see holes in the LZ where tree stumps must have been. From the blackened earth around each hole, I surmise that the trunks were excavated with C4 plastic explosives.

"Does that mean the good guys will be coming back?" Ramey asks.

"Most likely. The brass probably knows by now that they have at least one good LZ in the valley. They'll be coming back." I hope I'm right to sound so certain.

"Should we go in?" Roger Whitman asks.

"Not on your life!" I am quick to answer. "In fact, we best move downhill. When the shit hits the fan we don't want to get our asses blown away by the good guys."

"Damn, that would be just my luck," Coleman says.

"The Cavalry will definitely prep this place good with high-performance stuff before the choppers arrive. This is out of artillery range. My number one worry is Arc Light." After staying in the game this far, getting blown away by our own people would be a disgusting final card to be dealt.

"Ramey, take your people and backtrack."

"OK, sir."

The retreat downhill is effortless compared to the uphill climb.

Some 200 yards down, Ramey stops and instructs us to hide downhill in the bushes on both sides of the trail. The two teams of four will be separated by the ridgeline itself, so we will again have the bad guys in a cross fire, but it will be impossible for us to shoot each other.

For the rest of the afternoon, we take turns sleeping and enjoying the tropical breezes that glide through our positions. The ridgeline's foliage consists of sparse-limbed trees and scrub brush. The ground is dry and stony. It reminds me of the Great Smoky Mountains back in Georgia.

Darkness falls at about 2000 hours, and the night is colder than ever. I shiver in the dampness.

Throughout the night, I am awakened by strange sounds all around me. I hear night birds suddenly cry in alarm, then fly away. I hear jungle noises that must be made by the movements of something or somebody. Repeatedly I strain my eyes and ears and unlock the safety on the M2, only to have the night go quiet again. As before, we are depending on each other for our security. When the noises dwindle, I make sure that the person on guard is awake before I doze off again into dreamland.

April 21, 1968

I am on guard when dawn breaks the bonds of night. My heart nearly stops at the sight of an individual crouching in the bushes only 15 feet away. I freeze and stare intently at the person, not daring to raise my rifle for fear of giving our position away. More minutes pass, and as the light improves, I realize that the "person" was formed by shadows in a bush. This occurs three times during the early morning hours. I am nearly a basket case when my watch reads 0700 hours on our third day in the A Shau valley.

My body has had a number of hours to rest. For the first time since the crash, I am hungry. My guts are growling, and it amuses me that our ambush position might be given away by a hungry gut-growl. My mouth is parched from lack of water.

Without warning, there is a deafening explosion followed by a concussion that shakes the bushes. Missiles fly through the trees overhead, and dirt and other debris rains down on our heads.

I look at Rex Eastman, Roger Whitman, and one of the engineers, whose faces are asking "What just happened?" when a second explosion occurs even closer than the first.

Covering my ears with both hands, I bury my face in the dirt just as the screaming sound of a jet reaches us.

"Oh shit! Here we go!" I turn my head in the direction of the others and yell, "The Cav is on the way!"

We are too close to the LZ. The Air Force, determined that nothing within 500 yards of LZ Vicki will feel like defending it when they get through, pounds the earth all around us. My body is lifted completely off the ground by some of the concussions. My nose and ears are bleeding. My only hope of survival is those guys' inability to put a round right on the backbone of the ridgeline.

We are on the receiving end of the madness. Bombs make no noise at all while in flight to their targets. I have watched too many World War II movies where all bombs whistle as they fall. Here, the explosions come first; then things fly through the air; then comes the rumble of kerosene-burning engines as the jet goes into afterburner.

I talk to my God and pray to live on.

The bombing continues relentlessly for nearly an hour during which I think that each breath will be my last. Finally, it stops. All the bombs have fallen either in the LZ itself or down the hill from where we lie.

I look over at the nearby guys, who are no worse for the latest wear and tear, and fight the impulse to race to the other side of the ridgeline to check on the rest. My ears are ringing loudly and I have a severe headache.

"Mister Johnson, you guys OK?"

I look uphill to find Ramey. "OK. How about you guys?"

"We're OK. Choppers coming in, sir!"

"What did he say, Whitman?" I ask.

"Choppers coming in."

"Oh yeah?" I suddenly feel good all over. "Let's get uphill."

With that, all eight of us assemble on the top of the ridgeline. From our vantage point, we witness 1st Cavalry helicopters flying in all directions. The sky is blue and cloudless except for them. In trail, with Cobras leading the way, one formation is headed our way.

Air Force high-performance aircraft, with their sophisticated computers and high speeds, rarely see the enemy they blast. The helicopter war is more like the earliest days of aerial combat: You actually see your enemy. Gunship pilots are trained to engage at low speeds and very low quarters. Since there are not supposed to be any friendlies near LZ Vicki, I'm sure that if we're spotted, we will be taken for NVA by the Cobra pilots. I don't want to die by friendly fire after surviving so much. We hide in the underbrush, and this time we hide deeper.

Although we cannot actually see the insertion, we hear the performance loud and clear. The gunships lay continuous fire in and around the LZ while the lead Hueys deposit their cargo of sky troopers.

It is nearly 0900 hours when the aerial activity dies down and the gunships leave the immediate area.

"Well, folks, our ticket home lies out there." I don't bother to whisper.

"How do you want to do this, Mister Johnson?"

"Ramey, your guess is as good as mine. Any of the rest of you got any ideas how to make contact with these guys without getting our heads shot off?"

A long, quiet pause follows before Roger Whitman breaks the silence. "Now this is a hell of a mess. I never really thought about getting killed by our own people."

Whitman's earnest uneasiness breaks the rest of us up, although there is nothing funny about it. I guess we are finally coming down off our natural adrenaline high, and we are very tired and a little giddy.

"No, guys, I mean it." Roger is trying to defend his statement as a serious one. "Those guys are probably as scared as we are. They'll most likely shoot the first thing that moves out here . . . especially if it has two legs and a uniform."

"Roger, we're not laughing at you. You're correct all the way. I just find our current situation somewhat diabolical. We can't go down-hill for fear of running into the Viet Cong; we can't march right in for fear of being killed by our own people; and we can't just stay here." As I say this I do find it quite amusing.

"Mister Johnson, what do you want to do?" Ramey inquires for the second time.

"Well, I tell you, Sergeant, I don't know of anything but to march right in making as much noise as possible. Anyone got a better idea?"

No one has a better idea.

"Now, I'm no hero, but since my people are still wearing these chest protectors, I'll take point and just hope the first guy we run into is not a head-shooter."

No one laughs at this.

We slide out from beneath the underbrush and take up a trail formation on the ridgeline. We walk uphill to where we can see the LZ, which is now alive with many troops running here and there. For all those we can see in the LZ, we know there are just as many, if not more, hidden in the undergrowth on every side.

Considering the distance we have yet to travel, we decide not to make ourselves known until we reach some type of hollering range. If we are too early with our announcement, we might not be heard over the chattering of M16s that is sure to follow.

We walk as quietly as we can until we reach the bottom of the depression that is some 100 yards from the edge of the perimeter of LZ Vicki. We pause there to powwow again and decide that this is as close as we dare to get without yelling something.

"What are we going to say, Mister Johnson?" Rex Eastman asks.

"Hadn't thought much about it."

"Hope these guys haven't seen too many John Wayne movies," Sergeant Wilson replies with a smile.

"How's that?" I ask, a little confused.

"Don't you remember? In World War II, the Germans dressed up in GI uniforms and infiltrated our lines."

"Gee thanks, Wilson, that's just what I needed. How about you taking this chicken plate and walking point for me."

"Oh no, sir. You're doing a fine job so far."

Rising from my squatting powwow position, I take Rex Eastman's question to heart. I am ready to say something, but for the life of me I can't think of anything to say that might make some type of sense.

"HEY, ASSHOLES!"

"Hey, assholes?" The group mutters in nervous unison.

"*HEY! ALL YOU 1ST CAV ASSHOLES OUT THERE!*" My first attempt was squeaky due to my not having spoken over a whisper in three days, but my second effort is loud and penetrating.

"Sounds good to me . . . HEY, YOU ASSHOLES OUT THERE!" Ramey joins in.

I meticulously start walking the final yards toward LZ Vicki, yelling at the top of my voice. The others do likewise. As we near the last 50 yards, the foliage grows dense with wide-leaf plants. I am a lot more nervous about being clearly seen before being shot.

I stumble over a large root and recover only to find myself looking into the barrel of an M16 not more than 8 feet from my nose. Everything goes seriously quiet and I freeze in my tracks, not yet completely erect.

The sky trooper's eyes are dilated in fear, and sweat rains down his face as he and I look intensely at each other. The M16's barrel sways slightly left to the others, then back in my face. He doesn't know which of us to shoot first.

Up to now, I have not been at a loss for words, but now I draw a blank. I am terrified even to blink an eye, much less move an extremity. This guy is at his limit; he has no idea how to handle this situation. We are in a free-fire zone. His instructions are to terminate with vengeance anything that moves.

Fifteen seconds pass as he tries to sort us out as friend or foe. What he is doing has gotten many GIs killed.

Feeling that even the movement of my jaw might send me into eternity, I speak through clenched teeth, "Don't shoot, asshole."

His eyes go intense and his finger clinches harder on the trigger as "fear sweat" drips off his nose. Five seconds pass without change.

"I said don't shoot my ass, asshole." This time I say it a little louder, still not able to move my jaw. This finally registers and locks in. His eyes relax slightly, and he lowers the barrel from my face to a point near my midsection.

"Who are you?" the soldier finally says.

"JESUS CHRIST—who the hell you think we are!" I growl, mad as hell at being terrified of dying for the last 30 seconds.

My knees go weak and can no longer support my body weight. I feel dizzy by the time I sit, and my heart is racing.

"I'm too short for this shit" is the only thing I can think of to say for the moment, and no one seems to hear me over the jubilation created by the others as they step around me to shake the hands of the sky trooper and explain our woes of the past three days.

It does not make me feel any better to see five more GIs stand up not more than 20 feet on either side of us. Any one of them could have opened up without pausing to think.

Our lives on this earth have been only an eye blink from being snuffed out.

With the help of Rex Eastman and Roger Coleman, I finally stand up. As wobbly as a newborn colt, I manage to take a few steps in the direction of LZ Vicki. I accept pats on the back from the sky troopers as I pass.

Inside the LZ, I explain our ordeal to the officer in charge and ask to use his PRIC-25 radio. I change the radio to the Bandit Company's frequency and make the call.

"Any Bandit aircraft, this is Bandit Eighty-Eight. Over."

"Say again. This is Bandit Forty-Six. Over." The voice of Bill Lee is music to my ears. *"Johnson, is that really you?!"*

"That's affirm, Forty-Six. We're inside LZ Vicki. How about a ride home. Over."

"Eighty-Eight. I'm about five out and empty. On the way!"

"Roger, Forty-Six. We will need two aircraft for the recovery."

Other aircraft answer the call immediately, and the FM radio is a useless mess of unintelligible squeals as they all try to talk at once.

Again my knees buckle. This time it is not from fear but from gratitude that so many compassionate people are diving at the chance to rescue us. All this year, I have been the one doing the rescuing—flying hard to save souls. It has been a year of seeing death face-to-face and achieving mastery in cheating the Grim Reaper. I arrived in Vietnam of sound mind, turned twenty-two in February, and have seen more violence in 12 months than any person should experience in a lifetime.

I pull my knees up under my chin and reflect not only on the past three days but on the entire past year in Vietnam. How many more times can I get away with this?

22

No Rest for the Weary

Four hours after being extracted from LZ Vicki and landed in A/229th Company area, I find myself strapped into the seat of another Huey. The following day, April 22, 1968, I am once again flying combat assaults, with the rest of the Bandit aircraft, into the A Shau valley.

During these missions, we are the target of 37mm rounds. The FM radio squeals loudly for three seconds followed by three seconds of silence, then another three seconds of squeal. The first squeal means the gun has acquired you as its next target; the second squeal means your speed and direction are computed by the gun's computer. At the end of the second squeal, a radar-guided 37mm is on its way. To avoid being hit, we immediately dive our helicopters and turn 90 degrees. Many times we can actually see the rounds go by. Every pilot's life depends on his good hearing and reaction time. Loose trail formations are the order of the day. The stress and effort involved in evading the 37mm rounds takes an enormous psychological toll on all the helicopter crews.

Courageous crews, working in impossible weather conditions and treacherous terrain, fly repeatedly into the A Shau valley to resupply the Air Cavalry and extract their wounded and dead.[1] One week after

1. Operation Delaware was conducted under far more arduous circumstances than Pegasus, yet it successfully confirmed that the large cavalry raid was a viable tactical role for employment of an airmobile division. The raid into the A Shau valley achieved its objectives admirably. The raid determined the enemy dispositions and area utilization, disrupted a principal supply area and infiltration route, and ha-

my rescue, LZ Sharon, my home base, comes under attack. Since all the 1st Cavalry's hard-core sky troopers are involved in Operation Delaware, the NVA correctly assumes there will be few troops protecting the home bases of LZ Evans and LZ Sharon.

Very tired gunners, crew chiefs, and warrant officers are on guard duty after flying an average of 14 hours a day when, on April 29, 1968, LZ Sharon is attacked by a major force of NVA. Using "satchel charges" of high explosives, the NVA attempts to destroy the helicopters of the 229th. If these helicopters are disabled, our troops in the A Shau valley will become isolated. Heavily drugged NVA sappers are shot down by high-caliber machine guns only to get up again and run for the Huey's parking areas.

I have already emptied both 32-round clips of my M2 carbine and fired every 12-gauge shotgun shell I have in my possession when to my left comes a sapper in full stride. His route will lead him within 30 feet of the entrance to my bunker. My .38 Smith & Wesson Army-issue pistol is loaded, in violation of the Geneva Convention, with bullets called dumdum rounds. These are blunt-nosed lead projectiles that inflict terrible damage on impact, especially if they strike bone.

I fire four rounds and drop the sapper dead in his footsteps, then go about reloading the M2. Morning light reveals the sapper to be a barber who regularly cut American hair just outside LZ Sharon's perimeter. Only two days ago, he cut Bill Lee's hair and mine, and I took a photo of him and his eight children while he was cutting Bill's hair.

In the end, the enemy are unsuccessful in destroying the 229th, but later, on May 21st, they manage to set off the ammo bunker at LZ Evans, taking a major toll on the lives and almost all the aircraft of the 227th and 228th.

During a stand-up ceremony on May 10, 1968, Larry Gore, Bill Lee, Bill Martin, and I, along with several other aircraft commanders from the 229th, are awarded the Distinguished Flying Cross, the

rassed NVA forces. The tangible success of this division cavalry raid was evidenced by the incredible amounts of enemy equipment captured, including 1 tank, 73 vehicles, 2 dozers, more than a dozen 37mm antiaircraft guns, 2,319 rifles and submachine guns, 31 flame-throwers, and 1,680 hand grenades. The cavalry raid was conducted under adverse weather and in the face of sophisticated antiaircraft defenses, and its casualties reflected these conditions: 86 killed, 47 missing, and 530 wounded troops. Shelby L. Stanton, *Anatomy of a Division*, Novato, CA: Presidio Press, 1987, 147–149.

A/229TH PILOTS ARE AWARDED THE DISTINGUISHED FLYING CROSS FOR ACTIONS IN THE A SHAU VALLEY IN 1968. SHAKING HANDS ARE GEN. JOHN J. TOLSON, COMMANDING GENERAL OF THE 1ST AIR CAV AND WARRANT OFFICER LARRY GORE. NEXT IN LINE, THE MAN WITH THE MUSTACHE, IS TOM JOHNSON. FROM THE ARCHIVES OF LARRY GORE

nation's highest Air Medal. We wear this medal with sadness for those who did not survive Vietnam.

On May 11, 1968, as the A Shau valley battle rages sporadically on, heavy monsoon rains ground all aircraft in the valley. Unable to fly and running low on food and ammo, we aviators are trapped, living in the field just like the sky troopers. With less than 23 days to go in country, I take the subtle precaution of hovering my helicopter near the lip of a water-filled 1000-pound-bomb crater just south of the airstrip. In the event of serious fire, I don't want to have to run a hundred-yard dash to the relative safety of the crater.

Mud from the torrential downpours makes it impossible for Air Force C-130 cargo planes to land at the nearby A Louie airstrip, so on May 13, Division headquarters makes a desperate decision to resupply us by para-drop. The huge C-130s start their runs from the north end of the valley, relying solely on instruments, their God, and guts. They enter the cloud layer at 12,000 feet and descend to 600 feet, doing their best to avoid hitting any mountains. If they time it just right, they will break out right over the A Louie airstrip. After dragging out ammo, food, and medical supplies by parachute, they exit the valley in a steep climb. The mountains on both sides prevent them from taking evasive action during their runs. They are very large airplanes and thus good targets for the NVA antiaircraft radar. The first two C-130s get in, make their drops, and get away without incident.

The rain has given way to a cold drizzle at about the time I figure the next C-130 will be making his drop. I get out of the Huey and close the door behind me. As I look north into the dark valley, I see a brilliant landing light abruptly appear from the clouds. The crew accomplishes the dangerous descent and hits the valley floor dead center—but early. They get into clear air about a mile north when, without warning, a barrage of NVA automatic weapons opens up on them. This is quickly followed by the rhythmic *pom—pom—pom* of 31mm antiaircraft guns.

I watch in horror as the approaching cargo plane takes direct hit after direct hit. When the tail of the aircraft breaks from the fuselage, I run for my life. Yelling to the crew who are still inside the Huey, I slosh past the nose of our Huey and dive headlong into the bomb crater. Although they do not yet know the exact nature of the emergency, they dive headlong from the Huey's cargo floor into the water beside me.

Splash water barely has landed back in the crater when we hear loud crashing and tearing noises. The C-130 is not far away. The pilot, still trying to save his life, is racing the four turboprop engines—high, then low.

Thunderous explosions kick more water out of the bomb crater. Grabbing our ears to protect them from the concussions, we bury our faces in the mud. Shrapnel screams overhead as the ammo on the C-130 begins chain reactions; each ammo crate sets off the next.

Four hours have passed before anyone dares to raise his head for a peek. Luckily for us, none of the A/229th people are hurt, and only one helicopter sustains slight damage.

Three weary days and sleepless nights follow before the weather improves enough for us to get out of the A Shau valley.

On May 16, 1968, A/229th pilots and crews remove the last 1st Cavalry Division unit from the A Shau valley. By late afternoon, the A Shau is totally obscured by low clouds and fog; it remains that way for the next several weeks. In relief of the Cav, the 101st Airborne Division walks into the valley from its southern end. It is supported only by ground-transported supplies coming out of Hue.[2]

Gore, Martin, Lee, and I have a DEROS date of June 6, 1968. It will take at least five days to outprocess and turn in our gear at An Khe before traveling to Cam Ranh Bay airfield for our scheduled flight out of Vietnam. We have already lost two classmates in the A Shau. With our time in country growing so short, it is time for us to start thinking about quitting flying and going home.

Traditionally, helicopter pilots cease flying combat missions on the 25th day prior to their DEROS date. Major Beyer DEROS'd weeks ago. A shortage of pilots and an overload of missions move our new company commander to require Lee, Gore, Martin, and me to fly until May 29, leaving us only six days to get to An Khe, outprocess, and hitch a ride to Cam Ranh.

Certain parts of each Huey are always worn beyond acceptable limits, but this is war, and I have never felt our aircraft to be unsafe, even if they did not meet the tolerances specified in the Army's Dash 10 maintenance manual. We are down to our tenth day before I ground all four spare A/229th helicopters. My actions do not amuse Beyer's replacement nor the 229th maintenance warrant officer, but I stick to my guns by refusing to fly the aircraft. I am the safety officer and I have deemed them unsafe to fly. That's it as far as I'm concerned.

All the radio traffic between myself and operations catches the attention of Colonel Brown, battalion commander for the 229th. He intervenes between my company commander and myself, and after a touchy (near court-martial) situation, he grounds all four short-timers.

Four new pilots arrive from An Khe right on time. Strangely enough one of them is named Tom Johnson. A dawn-to-dusk drunken chorus from us short-timers fills the A/229th Company area: "HOW LONG YOU GOT, BOY? 364 DAYS AND A WAKE-UP! SON, HERE'S MY DAMN PISTOL. JUST SHOOT YOURSELF NOW AND GET IT OVER!"

On June 2, 1968, with personal belongings in tow, Gore, Martin,

---

2. The following year the 101st would return to the A Shau. One of the more famous battles to occur during this return was named "Hamburger Hill." Twenty years later, a movie would depict this engagement, and the accuracy of its portrayal would bring back many haunting night sweats to those who had been there.

Lee, and I make our last Huey flight in the Republic of South Vietnam. As the Huey breaks ground at LZ Sharon for the last time, I wonder how the new pilots will survive without the combat experiences we four might have shared with them. As a "short-timer," I am just beginning to realize that I might actually survive Vietnam. Over the past four weeks, more than at any time before, the fear of dying has been present in my every waking thought. I feel that I no longer have what it takes to be a helicopter pilot in Vietnam. As LZ Sharon disappears, I console myself with the painful thought that A/229th will be better off without me.

We are lucky and catch a Black Horse Huey to fly us to An Khe. The ride is a silent one. Our route takes us down the South China Sea coast until we reach familiar territory at LZ English. We then turn inland and through the Bong Son pass. As we pass west of Dam Tra-O Lake, I grieve over that fateful night and the loss of my friend James Arthur Johansen.

I look at the crash site till the lake disappears from my sight. The pain inside me is intense, but for the first time, I realize how hardened I have become: I am unable to cry.

Appendix 1: What Makes Helicopters Fly

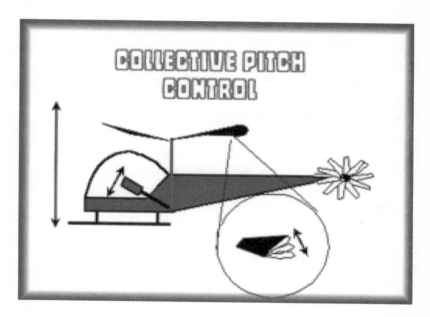

COLLECTIVE PITCH CONTROL Located on pilot's left side. Movement is up and down only. Pulling up on this control will increase the pitch of each blade by the same amount (collectively). As blade angles increase, lift overcomes weight and the helicopter will begin to fly.

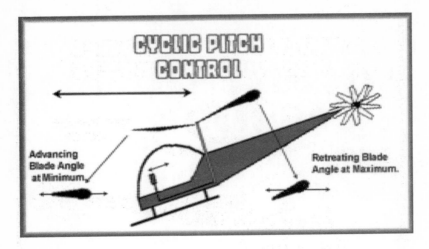

CYCLIC PITCH CONTROL Located between pilot's legs. Movement is 360 degrees in varying distances from center. Tips the plane of the blade's path, thus allowing the helicopter to fly in any direction. If the pilot wants to fly forward, he pushes the cyclic forward, so that the blades overhead no longer maintain an even pitch as they rotate. As each blade rotates from dead ahead to dead aft of the helicopter, the advancing blade will "flatten" to parallel the body of the helicopter as it moves toward the nose; then its pitch angle will increase as it moves aft. This causes the blade to "fly" more in the rear of the helicopter than at the nose, thus achieving forward flight. This same procedure is followed for any direction in which the pilot chooses to fly.

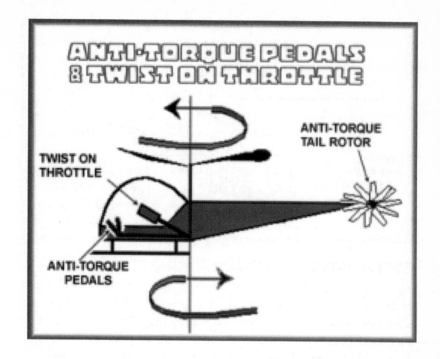

ANTI-TORQUE PEDALS & THROTTLE Pedals are located at pilot's feet. Pedals increase (pushing left pedal) or decrease (pushing right pedal) the pitch angle of the anti-torque tail rotor located on the extreme rear of a helicopter. The engine will attempt to rotate the fuselage of the helicopter in the opposite direction from that in which the overhead main rotor blades are turning. The greater the power that is applied by the engine (torque), the more pronounced this rotation around the vertical axis will become. To offset this engine torque, a pilot must press on the left pedal as power is applied to keep the helicopter pointed in the direction in which he intends to travel. The opposite is also true; any reduction in power will tend to twist the helicopter fuselage in a direction opposite that in which the main rotor blades are turning.

The throttle is a twist-on control located on the collective pitch control. Throttle applies power to the engine. To apply more power, a pilot must twist the device in a clockwise direction. To remove engine power, twist counterclockwise.

A helicopter is much more difficult to learn to fly than any fixed-wing aircraft. The pilot and the machine must be in absolute harmony with each other. Let me describe the coordination required just to take off:

Unlike most airplane engines, helicopter engines—and their associated blades—run at a constant speed from the time they are cranked up until the flight is complete and the engine is shut down. Assuming that our little helicopter is cranked and the engine is at normal operating speed, to attain flight a pilot must first pull up on the collective pitch control to increase the pitch in the blades. As he pulls, this increase in pitch results in an increase in required engine power, and the main rotor system speed will slow down unless more power is applied. To apply more power, the pilot must twist the throttle. As he is doing this, he must constantly watch his tachometer so as not to run the engine too fast. The limits are very close: plus or minus 200 rpm for most piston-driven helicopters. Soon, the lift of the blades will overcome the helicopter's weight and flight will be attained. As the helicopter breaks ground, the pilot must quickly and decisively apply cyclic adjustments to keep the helicopter from drifting; at the same time he must apply anti-torque pedals as necessary to compensate for the power applied and keep the helicopter from spinning on its vertical axis.

If the pilot succeeds in this hover maneuver, he is ready for forward flight. When he moves the cyclic stick toward the nose of the helicopter, his machine will begin to fly forward. This tilt of the overhead main rotor blades will cause a loss of lift. To compensate, the pilot must pull up on the collective for more lift. This additional demand of power on the engine will cause rpm to bleed off. To compensate for the loss of rpm, the pilot must now twist on more power at the throttle. This additional power will tend to rotate the helicopter fuselage so that more anti-torque pedal must be applied to keep the helicopter from rotating in a direction opposite the main rotor blades.

GET THE PICTURE? Every helicopter pilot must learn to coordinate all four controls in a harmony of flight while also looking outside the helicopter so as not to run into anything.

Appendix 2: Confirmed Killed Class 67–5 First Tour

Alvarez, Charles A.	67-5	KIA	02/16/68
Blackmon, Dennis G.	67-3 or 67-5	KIA	10/19/67
Blattel, David L	67-5	KIA	05/05/68
Carlisle, Thomas G.	67-5 or 67-7	KIA	03/29/68
Clark, Terry R	67-5 or 67-7	KIA	11/19/67
Cotton, Charles M.	67-5 or 67-7	KIA	06/19/68
Dechene, Robert N.	67-5 or 67-7	KIA	09/17/67
Eckle, Stephen J.	67-5	KIA	04/12/68
Eisenhart, Guy L.	67-3 or 67-5	KIA	03/08/68
Fitzgerald, John F.	67-3 or 67 -5	KIA	04/12/68
Glider, Lewis C.	67-3 or 67-5	KIA	09/03/67
Hamilton, Dennis C.	67-5	KIA	01/05/68
Hoyt, Ervin J.	67-3 or 67-5	KIA	04/25/68
Koskovich, Michael L.	67-5 or 67-7	KIA	04/25/68
Kretzchmar, Peter	67-3 or 67-5	KIA	02/18/68
Lemaire, Douglas J.	67-3 or 67-5	KIA	01/10/68
Link, Robert C.	67-5	MIA/BNR	04/21/68
Martin, Ronald L.	67-5	KIA	01/01/68
McCoig, Donald B.	67-5	KIA	03/29/68
McKibben, Larry S.	67-5	KIA	05/02/68
Smith, Thomas J.	67-5	KIA	06/25/68
Wallace, Russel L.	67-5 or 67-7	KIA	03/08/68
Yarger, Jeffery W. Jr.	67-5	KIA	03/19/68

Glossary

ACL   Aircraft combat loading: the number of troops being loaded onto an aircraft.

ADF   Automatic directional finding radio. When a pilot tunes in, a preset beacon frequency and a needle shows him the direction of the beacon relative to the aircraft. Each beacon transmits its identifying call letters in Morse code.

AHB   Assault Helicopter Battalion.

aircraft combat loading   The number of troops being loaded onto an aircraft.

ARA   Airborne rocket artillery.

Arc Light   Operation Arc Light: Bombing runs made by B-52s in Vietnam.

ARVNS   South Vietnamese Army Regulars.

ash-and-trash Personnel assigned to these missions transport ammo, food, and water into, and remove refuse out of, given locations.

ASP   Steel planking; solid steel that is not perforated.

Bandit 88   Radio call sign. Bandit refers to A Company 229th AHB. 88 is the official Army designation for a safety officer. Hence, Bandit 88 is the safety officer for A/229th.

break squelch Term applied when a pilot pulls and releases the transmit trigger for his radio in lieu of actually saying anything. This action creates a radio noise that can be heard by others on the same frequency. Breaking squelch twice in rapid succession implies that one has received instructions and will comply or that one understands what was said.

C&C — See *Charlie-Charlie*.

Charlie — Slang for a member of the Viet Cong. Alternatives are *VC* and *Mr. Charles*.

Charlie-Charlie — Command and Control Huey: A Huey outfitted with special radios in the cargo compartment that would be at the disposal of the commander. Normally used by a commander as an airborne TOC to coordinate his troops during a large-scale combat assault. Also called a C&C.

chest protector — A protective vest, in appearance resembling those worn by the gladiators of ancient Rome. Also called a chicken plate.

chicken plate — See *chest protector*.

commanding officer — Generally a captain grade officer or higher. Often referred to as CO for short.

CQ — An orderly who ran the office and woke up pilots in the morning.

C rations — Canned field rations.

CW2 — Chief warrant officer; warrant officer grade 2. The title *chief* applied to all grade 2 through grade 4 warrants.

daisy chaining — One gunship makes its run toward the target, and at a point near the target, it will break off and its wingman will start a gun run on the same target. If executed properly, together the gunships will keep continuous fire on the target.

DEROS — Date estimated return from overseas. Used as slang for "last day in country."

deuce-and-a-half truck — A 2½-ton truck.

DMZ — Demilitarized zone.

EOD — Explosive ordnance disposal; bomb squad: military team that disposes of unexploded ammunition.

GLOSSARY

ETA — Estimated time of arrival.

free fire — Command meaning fire at will. No gunner or crew chief was allowed to fire his weapon without a command to do so from the mission commander, for fear that friendly troops might be in the area.

GCA — Ground-controlled approach tactical radar.

GP Medium — General purpose medium tent. Home for 20 pilots, complete with dirt floor.

greenhouse — Clear green Plexiglas window over the heads of both pilots.

ground effect — An aerodynamic effect caused when a helicopter is hovering near the ground. Air pushed downward by the main rotor blades rebounds from the ground and gives the helicopter extra lifting ability. It takes less power to hover in ground effect than to attempt to hover at a height where the downward push of main rotor blade air no longer makes ground contact. During a vertical ascent, an overloaded Huey will stop climbing at a height of 24 feet (the length of one rotor blade) because of the loss of ground effect.

grunts — An affectionate name given to ground troops in Vietnam because of the sound they made when jumping off helicopters.

IFR — Instrument flight rules: The procedure for flying the aircraft solely by instruments and without any outside visual references.

incoming — Incoming mortar rounds.

IVSI — Instant vertical speed indicator; the gauge that registers feet per minute in climbing or descending.

key — To hold down the transmit button on a microphone for the purpose of transmitting a message over the airways. Keying two or more times in rapid succession without saying anything means your message has been received.

KIA — Killed in action.

logger out — When Army intelligence thought our LZ was about to get hit, all aircraft were moved to a safer LZ.

LORAN	Long-range navigation: very early navigation system, similar to the global positioning system (GPS), that requires a signal from three ground-based transmitter stations. LORAN is accurate to within 50 meters.
LRRP	Long-Range Reconnaissance Patrol. Generally highly skilled Green Berets.
LZ is green	Language meaning the landing zone is clear of enemy fire.
LZ is red	Language meaning the landing zone is currently under hostile fire.
LZ	Landing zone.
M60	.30-caliber machine gun.
MACV	Military Assistance Command, Vietnam, the combined headquarters for all branches of the services in Vietnam.
McGuire rig	A nylon rope that terminates in a butt sling. Soldiers seated in the sling can be lowered into or raised out of the jungle by a hovering helicopter.
medevac	Medical evacuation. The destination of a medevac is the forward field hospital unit, but the term can be used to refer to the hospital itself.
Mermite cans	General-purpose thermally insulated metal devices used to haul food and drink to troops in the field.
minigun	Mounted outside the Huey, this gun has 7 barrels, which fire and rotate at high speed. It is capable of firing 8000 rounds per minute, or 133 rounds per second. Gunships carried two or more of these weapons with the equivalent firepower of 266 rounds per second.
MOS	Military occupation standard: an official military tag that relates to one's job description. For example, 062B is the MOS for a helicopter pilot.
MPs	Military police.
neutral buoyancy	A point where lift provided by the main rotor blades becomes equal to the weight of the helicopter.
NVA	North Vietnamese Army.
num-ba ten	Vietnamese troops' slang for very bad.

O-1 Birddog   Fixed-wing aircraft manufactured by Cessna. Traditionally flown by Air Force pilots to spot targets for high-performance jets and artillery.

pedal turn   While at a hover, a helicopter may rotate on its vertical axis using the anti-torque pedals located at the pilot's feet.

pedaprime   A hard spray-on tar substance used extensively in Vietnam in lieu of pavement.

peter pilots   Slang for copilots. From inside, the aircraft commander sits in the left seat and the copilot sits in the right seat.

POL   Petroleum, oil, and lubrication station.

pop smoke   To pull the pin and throw a smoke grenade, usually in order to assist in finding the physical location of ground units.

PSP   Perforated steel planking: construction material consisting of wide, thin steel planks with round holes in them, used primarily in making runways and parking areas for aircraft.

push   Slang for radio frequency.

PZ   Pickup zone.

RMI   Radio magnetic heading indicator: An electric compass.

RRF   Ready Reaction Force. The 1st Air Cavalry stood at a continuous high alert state, so that one infantry unit and one air assault helicopter company were always ready to react quickly to any unexpected combat situation.

satchel charge   Explosives in a briefcase tied with a rope to a pole. By slinging the satchel in a circle, then letting go, the VC can throw the explosive a greater distance.

stagefield   A landing field in an outlying area. During training, pilots depart main helicopter parking bases and fly to various training heliports where they practice. A stagefield will normally have up to six parallel runways.

sky trooper   Grunt in the 1st Air Cavalry.

SLAR   Side-Looking Area Radar.

Snake Pit   Our name for A/229th's parking area.

SOI   Standard operation instructions: A top secret code

booklet issued only to aircraft commanders and containing all of the 1st Cavalry's unit call signs and frequencies.

TAC officer   Training and command officer. During Vietnam, a veteran helicopter pilot who was in command of forty to fifty warrant officer candidates (WOC) while the WOCs were on the ground. The TAC officer's job was to turn boys into officers and men while the instructor pilots turned them into pilots.

TOC   Tactical operations and control: Command and control center for the company.

trail formation   A flight formation in which one helicopter trails behind the other.

tubes   Artillery.

V formation   A flight formation that, when viewed from below, looks like the letter "V."

VSI   Vertical speed indictor. Dash-mounted aircraft instrument that shows rate of climb or decent in feet per minute.

wake-up   A slang term for awakening on the morning of your last day in Vietnam.

warrant officer   A military rank above the highest enlisted rank and below the lowest officer rank. Warrant officers are addressed as "Mister" rather than as "Lieutenant" or "Captain." Before Vietnam, one had to have gone as far as they could go in the enlisted rank before being considered for warrant officer rank. Warrant officers are specialists in their particular MOS.

WO1   Warrant officer rank 1 of four possible ranks.

WOC   Warrant officer candidate; a flight school rank.

Index

INDEX

INDEX

INDEX

About the Author

From June 1967 through June 1968, **TOM JOHNSON** flew Huey "slicks" for A Company 229th Assault Helicopter Battalion, 1st Cavalry Division. During that time, he accumulated 1150 combat hours and 450 noncombat hours for a total of 1600 hours flying helicopters. Considering that the average civilian pilot will fly about 50 hours a year, he spent a lot of time with his feet off the ground. During his tenure in Vietnam, his unit was involved in major Air Cavalry operations including the battles of Song Re valley, the Tet Offensive of 1968, and operations in Hue, and Khe Sanh.

During the opening attack in the A Shau valley battle in April 1968, he was shot down for the last time; he and his crew are among the few who survived the downing of 22 helicopters during this battle. His awards and decorations include the Air Medal with 5 Silver Leaf Clusters, the Bronze Star Medal, and the Distinguished Flying Cross.

Having learned to fly at the age of 14, Tom became entangled with the Vietnam War because the military needed young helicopter pilots. As he put it, "The government gave me a choice: I could walk or I could fly, but either way I was going to Vietnam."

He lives in Carrollton, Georgia, and is still married to his high school sweetheart, Pat. They were married at 16 and 15 years of age, respectively, and together they have raised three daughters. Tom is president of Johnson Electric Motor Shop, JEMS Computer Systems, and JEMS Equipment Company, a motor shop equipment manufacturing firm. He holds patent #4,753,148 for the first fully computerized light show of its kind, designed specifically for the entertainment industry.

Of the thousands of helicopters that flew in Vietnam, two of them that Tom flew not only survived the war and were returned to the United States, but are now in museums. In 1996, Dr. Peter L. Jakab, curator for the Smithsonian National Air and Space Museum contacted Tom to inform him that UH-1 Army Huey serial number 65-10126, which he flew from June 1967 to September 1968, had been acquired by the museum for rebuilding and display. This helicopter is currently on display at the Smithsonian National Air and Space Museum's Steven F. Udvar-Hazy Center. In 1998, Tom was informed that another Huey he flew can be found in the Pacific Coast Air Museum. This one can be seen on the Internet listed as the Iroquois at http://pacificcoastair museum.org/2002Site/aircraftPCAM/UH1_Huey/UH1_Huey_ home.asp.